Diderot

Lester G. Crocker

DIDEROT

The Embattled Philosopher

The Free Press, New York
Collier-Macmillan Limited, London

To Billie

compañera mia en esta gran aventura

Contents

"A fine genius, to whom Nature had given great wings."
VOLTAIRE

"A transcendent genius which had no equal in his age."
ROUSSEAU

"Diderot is Diderot, a peculiar individuality; whoever holds him or his individuality cheaply is a Philistine."
GOETHE

"To whatever quarter he turned, he caught the rising illumination and was shone upon by the spirit of the coming day."
LORD MORLEY

Escape

1

ON A FALL DAY of 1729, the creaking, dust-covered stage from Langres passed through the gates of Paris. The nose of a sixteen-year-old provincial boy pressed against the thin window pane, while his father more sedately, but no less eagerly, absorbed the animation of the great city. In the confusion of sounds and movement it was difficult at first to single out details. They had a general impression of streets crowded with the open-air stalls of cobblers, jewelers, haberdashers, vendors of chestnuts and apple fritters. Peddlers with colorful aprons and bonnets pushed wheel-barrows and hawked their fish, flowers or hot pies, their hardware and old clothes. Each had a distinctive chant that rose above the din of workshops and the clatter of carriages. Water boys rushed through clear spaces, a pail in each hand, to supply waiting housewives with the quantity they needed for cooking and cleaning—no one drank any and little was used for bathing.

When the first impression had been digested, the travelers took notice of less hurried elements of the scene. Errand boys loafed along as they delivered their urgent messages or packages. Visitors, foreigners, rich idlers strolled in search of diversion or fresh air.

Occasional sedan chairs lumbered through the crowd, although they were outnumbered by rolling chairs and the new and popular hacks. The boy watched his own and other carriages tear through the narrow streets without sidewalks. Pedestrians dashed out of their way, narrowly avoiding being run down—an occurrence which would have aroused no more reaction than a laugh at the unwary victim. They ran not only to escape the horses and wheels, but the flying mud that spattered all who did not crowd against the walls or into the doorways. Hack drivers, probably drunk, were beating their beasts, swearing, insulting women, colliding with private carriages. Here and there a crowd had formed about an accident, or a street singer. In the distance, they caught a glimpse of a religious procession. Finally the coach reached the Seine and crossed over the Pont Neuf.

It is a huge affair, this Pont Neuf. Over its middle roadway rolls an unbroken line of carts and carriages, flanked by two sidewalks crowded with pedestrians. On each pillar of the bridge is a half-tower containing small shops. Near the shops and at both approaches, vendors peddle oranges and lemons; jugglers, charlatans and quacks go through their paces before a gaping crowd. They will cure incurable maladies, restore fallen teeth or pull out aching ones, make glass eyes, sell a miraculous powder that whitens the complexion and makes wrinkles vanish. At one corner an army recruiter challenges the able-bodied youths who pass his way. Here and there on the Pont Neuf, as in any crowded thoroughfare, a street singer croons his ditties to a charmed audience.

Once over the Pont Neuf, father and son made their way through the dark, winding streets of the Latin Quarter, past medieval houses, to the famous Jesuit college of Louis-le-Grand, or perhaps to the rival Jansenist Collège d'Harcourt.[1] There, sentimentalists both, they took leave of each other with tears. But it was only a feigned good-bye. The good Didier Diderot had decided not to return to Langres without being more at ease about his son's happiness in this strange world, among companions many of whom were his social superiors. He had resolved to remain in Paris, saying nothing to the boy. The memoirs of Mme. de Vandeul, his granddaughter, doubtless exaggerating his virtue, tell us of two weeks of boredom during which he never stirred from his inn; but it is difficult to believe that a provincial cutler could resist the temptation of seeing

[1] It is possible that Diderot attended both schools, at different times, but probable that he studied mostly at the Collège d'Harcourt.

the "Big City," or at least of drumming up some trade and exhibiting his pet inventions.

At the end of a fortnight, he surprised the boy with a farewell visit.

"*Mon fils*, I have come to find out whether your health is good, whether you are satisfied with your superiors, with your food, your comrades and yourself. If you are not comfortable, if you are not happy, we shall return together to your mother. If you prefer to stay here, I have come to embrace and bless you."

But the scholar was quite content. Anxious about his progress, Didier had a final word with the principal. The report was not too encouraging.

"Your son is a good student, but his conduct is less praiseworthy. We had to reprimand him severely last week, and if this continues, we may have to send him home."

Of the childhood of Denis Diderot, and of the events that led to his journey, we have no precise information, only some not too trustworthy anecdotes. But we can place the boy in his *milieu*, and grasp the essential character of family and background that played so important a part in the conflicts of his life.

2

Langres is today a quiet and melancholy town of some eight thousand inhabitants; it lies in the hilly, heavily-wooded region of southeastern Champagne, near the source of the Marne. Two centuries ago, its main street (now rue Diderot), rang with the clamor of numerous cutlery forges. Barrelmakers, blacksmiths and tanners —whose fathers had been barrelmakers, blacksmiths and tanners for unremembered generations—added to the cheerful din. None of these trades, however, could match in importance the industry of cutlery, which reached back to the thirteenth century.

Today, there is only one cutlery shop in Langres. The reason for this decline is obscure. One is tempted to speculate—perhaps with more fancy than reason—that the desertion of the Diderot family, cutlers for over two hundred years, marked a turning point for the native industry.

The inhabitants of Langres, well-to-do bourgeois artisans, were of the sturdy and individualistic breed that still dominates the French provinces. They were quite secure in their love of tradition and hard work. Their intellectual horizons were comfortably finite. No unorthodox curiosity intruded on their complacency.

Daily life in Langres was simple; a long hard working day, and then relaxation within a close family circle. On Sunday morning, they went to church, and in the afternoon, took a long stroll circling the town. They followed a quiet but picturesque route, overlooking hills and valleys, with the Vosges and the Alps shadowing the distant horizon.

None represented this tradition better than Didier Diderot. A solid middle-class citizen, he was generous in his charities, regular in attending church, respected by all his neighbors. So wide was the fame of his sound judgment and scrupulous honesty that he was often asked to serve as arbiter in private squabbles; and he was even named executor in the wills of people who scarcely knew him except by reputation. Didier's professional skill was equally esteemed. He specialized in the forging of surgical instruments and is said to have invented special types of lancets. His life was completely uneventful. He spent his days at the forge, where he was a familiar figure with his cap, glasses and tools; his evenings at home, throning in the paternal armchair, distributing advice and charity with serene and Solomon-like demeanor.

As far back as the middle Ages, the Diderot family had been artisans of Langres—conservative, pious and obscure. Their very name is a diminutive of *Didier*, the town's patron saint. By the eighteenth century, it seemed that they were destined to be forever rooted to its soil, and to its spirit.

Didier's son Denis was born on October 5, 1713. That was the year of the papal bull *Unigenitus*, which condemned the Jansenists and started fifty years of bitter strife in France. It was the year, too, of the Treaty of Utrecht, which marked France's first major defeat and signaled the beginning of England's drive for colonial supremacy. It was two years before the death of Louis XIV, the Sun King. All signs pointed to a new era, in whose fashioning Denis Diderot was to play a significant role.

The figure of Denis' father loomed large in his childhood. Even in later years, he never succeeded in completely escaping his ascendancy. So profound was this paternal influence, despite their quarrels, that twice Diderot made him the central character of an important literary work. The attachment was both sentimental and based on genuine respect. For all his conservatism, Diderot *père* was not a fanatic, nor devoid of humor. He could shrug off a philosophical argument with a pithy retort. *"Mon fils, mon fils,* an excellent pillow is that of reason; but I find that my head rests even more softly on that of religion and the laws." He eventually learned to accept his rebellious son with good-natured tolerance. Once, when quite old, he commented drily: "My son, we have both made our little noise in the world, with this difference, that the noise you made with your tools deprived you of peace and rest, whereas the noise I made with my tools deprived others of rest."

Diderot's mother, Angélique Vigneron, sprang from a line as staid and middle class as her husband's. She was the daughter of a tanner and the men of her family had for centuries been tanners or priests. Two of her brothers, two of her cousins, and two of her uncles were canons in the Church. She seems to have been a sweet and gentle woman, self-effacing and completely devoted to her husband and children. She died when Diderot was thirty-five. About her, he was strangely silent; she has left scarcely a trace in his writings.

Into this family, and in this atmosphere, Denis Diderot was born. He was one of nature's mutants. Nothing in his ancestry prepares us for him; nor were his family and fellow townsmen equipped to understand the turbulent spirit and mind that drove him to rebel against the bourgeois traditions which had always bound them. This cleavage brought storm and anguish to himself and to those who tried to restrain him. The story of that struggle is a large part of the story of Diderot's life.

Denis was not the first child. A son, born in November 1712, had lived only a few hours. After Denis, five other children came at brief intervals, but only three of these survived: Denise, born in January 1715, Didier-Pierre, born seven years later, and another girl, who entered a convent. In later years, Diderot found himself united to Denise by a certain affinity of character, but separated from his brother by the latter's relentless hostility to his break with tradition.

Of the few recorded events in Diderot's early life, the very earliest is worth noting briefly for its lasting imprint. With a father's anxiety to perpetuate his own virtue in his offspring, the worthy cutler took his three-year-old son to witness the rare spectacle of a public execution. The lesson had immediate effect. The child became violently ill.

By the time Denis was eight, the family had decided he would be a priest. Doubtless Madame Diderot's brother, the canon Vigneron, influenced their decision by promising to yield his lucrative canonicate to his nephew. To the pious boy was drawn the picture of a comfortable future, of a life of leisure and cozy security. Later events proved that the wrong child had been chosen; it was the younger brother, Didier, still unborn, who was to become the canon and enjoy the position which the Diderots coveted and planned for Denis. Didier junior inherited Uncle Vigneron's personality as well as his post. Diderot later sketched the uncle's character in few and unflattering strokes. "He was a harsh, intractable man; he could not even get along with his colleagues, but satirized them continually in his words and actions."

As a result of this family plan, Denis attended the Jesuit school at Langres until his fifteenth year. The choice was a good one. The Jesuits dominated education in eighteenth-century France. Their course of study emphasized the classics, rhetoric, mathematics and "sound" philosophy. Their teachers were often brilliant and the discipline severe. The Jesuit schools formed the minds of some of France's greatest writers. In the eighteenth century they also produced many of her most notorious anticlericals and freethinkers, including Voltaire.

But the reverend fathers had no reason to suspect Denis of heretical tendencies. He was a brilliant student, excelling in Latin and mathematics. One year he was awarded almost all the prizes, including those for composition, memory and poetry. Unfortunately, his triumph came near being marred. Because of an imprudent fist fight, he was excluded from the academic ceremonies. Fearing this would cause him to lose his justly earned laurels and bring grief to his parents, he joined a crowd and slipped through the entrance. He eluded a pursuing guard who pricked him with a lance, took his seat and triumphantly collected the prizes. His parents, hard at work, had not been able to come. Towards evening, they saw a thin boy trudging along, weighed down with prizes and surrounded by comrades who were helping to celebrate. Quickly they ran to meet him. Joy turned to alarm when they discovered the lance wound which Denis had been too excited to notice. This, at least, is the story as Diderot's daughter tells it in her memoirs, and as her father had related it to her, doubtless with proper embellishments.

Certainly Diderot was no "model boy" at school. Scoldings and punishments were frequent. One day his resentment boiled over into rebellion. "I don't want to go to school any more," he resolutely told his father. "I don't want to be a priest."

Education, far from being compulsory, was a luxury. Didier was a man of few words.

"Then you want to become a cutler?"

"With all my heart," replied the school-weary boy.

He was put to work immediately. But after four or five days in the shop, he had ruined an assortment of knives and proved himself completely inept at manual work. Swallowing his pride, he returned to his father and expressed a desire to go back to school.

"I'd rather be annoyed than bored," he explained.

Once more, then, Diderot prepared to enter the Church. In August 1726, he was tonsured—as was not infrequently done to boys of twelve committed to a Church career. Proudly and piously he paraded the streets of Langres, sporting a black cassock. But here destiny took a hand and rearranged Diderot's life in defiance of his parents' plans. The unsuspected turning point came when Uncle Vigneron died in April 1728. For some mysterious reason, the Chapter of the Langres Cathedral refused—a most extraordinary procedure—to accept the dying man's designation of his nephew as his successor. This decision they must have later regretted bitterly. Safely stowed away in his canonicate, Diderot would never have gone to Paris, never have turned out a renegade and an atheist. Instead of becoming an enemy of priests and religions, he would have lived out his obscure life in the orbit of the Church.

Shut out from the canonicate, Diderot suffered an overwhelming wave of asceticism and decided several months later to take vows as a Jesuit. Doubtless his teachers adroitly led him to his decision, for they saw in their fervent and brilliant disciple a promising colleague. Thinking probably of this experience, Diderot in later life (in his novel, *Jacques the Fatalist*) described the adolescent feeling of religiosity: "There comes a moment when almost all girls and youths fall into melancholy; they are tormented by a vague restlessness that affects everything and finds nothing to calm it. They want to be alone; they weep; they are touched by the silence of cloisters; the image of peace that seems to reign in religious establishments enchants them. They take the first stimuli of a developing sexuality for the voice of God calling to them; and it is precisely when nature is most urgent that they embrace a way of life most contrary to nature." His religious emotion was the expression of his *sensibilité*, that emotional excitability which was to be one of his strongest characteristics. Even when older, he felt his heart beat faster when a religious procession passed, and was often moved to tears.

Perhaps, too, it was one of Diderot's teachers who, a little later, persuaded him to take an adventurous path to the priesthood. This story, like the others, may be open to some doubt. It is hard to imagine why he did not dare to confide the project to his father, who would surely have given his consent. There is some reason to suspect that Diderot had, in fact, broken off with the Jesuits—a more logical motive for going to Paris. But the story, as Diderot related it to his daughter, is at least psychologically true, and reveals his imagination, impetuosity and spirit of insubordination. According to the tale, the boy decided to run away, and for three months plotted his escape. When the decisive moment arrived, lacking courage to set out alone, he made a cousin party to the scheme and persuaded him to go along. This timid creature promptly told the whole story to his own father, who, as was to be expected, informed the cutler. Didier said nothing.

When Denis slipped downstairs in his stocking feet, in the dead of night, trembling with emotion, he was startled to find his father up and waiting for him.

"Where are you going at this hour, my son?"

"To Paris, where I am to become a Jesuit," was the weak reply.

"That is a good idea, but not tonight. Go back to bed now and we'll talk it over tomorrow."

The following day a family council was held. When the fall term came, father and son boarded the stagecoach for Paris.

CHAPTER 2

The
Rebellious
Years

FEW TRACES REMAIN of Diderot's three years at the *lycée*. It appears that he worked hard and well. On occasional holidays he went out with his friends and feasted at a neighborhood restaurant or cabaret. These little excursions taught him the pleasures of good food, good company, and good conversation, and for the rest of his life he never ceased indulging in all three, usually to excess.

Another side of Diderot's character comes to light at school. Always ungrudging with his ideas and talents, he willingly wrote compositions for his less fertile comrades. We know of this because once his generosity brought him to grief. An assignment was given to put into verse the Serpent's seductive discourse to Eve. One of the boys found himself short of wit. Diderot tore up his companion's feeble doggerel and composed in its stead a high-sounding poem. Unfortunately, the professor found it too good to be the work of so poor a student and ferreted out its true author, with disastrous consequences for both culprits.

During one of his brief summer vacations Diderot experienced the first anguish of adolescent love. Probably he was already somewhat dubious of his priestly calling. His words, "the one whom I dared so long to desire," suggest that the maiden was of higher rank, possibly of the provincial nobility. He was deeply shocked when their romance was tragically halted by her sudden death. Always a sentimentalist, Diderot never forgot his first, and only platonic love. Thirty years later he still remembered the grief he had felt when shortly after the girl's death a mutual friend pointed out her grave.

On the second of September 1732, Diderot was granted the degree of master of arts. Here another enigma presents itself. Did Diderot, reluctant still to give up his destined career, attend the Sorbonne, then the great theological seminary of Paris? There is not a shred of direct evidence in favor of this supposition, yet many circumstances, such as his familiarity with theology and scholastic reasoning, and even a possible acquaintance with Hebrew, are difficult to explain otherwise. If it were a definitely proven fact, this period at the Sorbonne, however brief, would be quite intriguing. Diderot would stand out as the only important writer of his large group of deists and atheists who had received theological training and who knew thoroughly both sides of "the great question." We could see the renouncement of his calling, the definite rupture with the Church, the abandonment of his studies, as the first steps in his revolt and his march toward scepticism and anticlericalism.

Whether or not Diderot was enrolled in the Sorbonne, the time did come when his studies ended and he was pressed by his father to select a career. But he had been doing some thinking for himself about the kind of life he wanted. We can imagine Didier's amazement and incomprehension when his son informed him that he intended to follow no career at all. He had no ambition, other than to remain in Paris and study by himself, pursuing the whims of his intellectual curiosity.

"Study what?" queried the uncomprehending father.

"Latin, Greek, English, Italian, mathematics, the natural sciences —everything I can."

To the bourgeois of Langres this was not only foolishness; it was disgraceful and bohemian. His order was clear. "You will prepare yourself for a useful career in society and not bring shame upon your family."

Diderot pleaded. "But there is no career that interests me."

The situation was commonplace, the dialogue stale. Didier was adamant. The would-be philosopher, defeated in his first revolt against his heritage, yielded. Joining the fraternity of great writers who either resisted the pressure to study law, like Voltaire, or who studied it against their will, only to abandon it at the first opportunity, he entered the office of Clément de Ris, himself a native of Langres. This event took place during the winter of 1733-34. Thus there remains unaccounted for the period of a year or more after the conferring of his degree—another fact which seems to favor the hypothesis that Diderot may have studied at the Sorbonne.

For two years the frustrated philosopher suffered as the mutinous clerk of Maître Clément. Deeds, mortgages, wills and the other formalities of the law grew unbearably stupid and boring. Whenever Clément was away, he would run to his beloved Latin, Greek and mathematics. And at night—as an apprentice, he received board, lodging and a little pocket money—only constant nagging could make him keep his nose in law books. Finally, even patient Maître Clément could endure it no longer. He wrote a long letter to Langres, expounding on his clerk's uncooperative attitude and especially on his waste of time in useless reading. Thoroughly aroused by this stubborn resistance, Diderot senior replied with a stern warning.

"Your father gives you the choice of medicine or law, unless you want to go back to Langres and become a cutler," said Maître Clément. "What are you going to do?"

Forced to a showdown, Diderot pleaded for time. He was given one month, then a second, and finally had to announce his decision. It was a grave moment. During those two months, he had doubtless fought within himself, torn between devotion to his family and the irresistible longing to cut his moorings. He felt, just out of his reach, a world of truth and beauty to explore, and the whirligig of Parisian life that pulsed all around him. To gain his freedom, he would have to repudiate all ties, overthrow the weight of traditions and childhood environment. At the end of two months, when Maître Clément repeated his question, Diderot announced rather impudently his declaration of independence.

"I'm happy just as I am now—very happy, so I don't see why I should change."

The exasperated father took the final punitive step, cut off Denis' allowance and warned him that he would pay for no debts incurred. Of course, he gave him his "last chance," urged him anew to choose any career he wanted or else learn the cutlery trade—anything useful and honorable, instead of this outrageous vagabond existence he spoke of.

The young rebel was no longer to be intimidated. With unbounded confidence in his ability to create a great future for himself, he was already savoring the pleasures of his new freedom.

We have sketchy information about Diderot's life in the months that followed, but enough to assure us that it fits into the time-honored tradition. While his money lasted, he studied. And when his pockets were empty, he starved. His lodgings were a garret in the Latin Quarter. At night, he would tighten his belt and go to bed early in order not to feel the urgent pangs of hunger. To a woeful description of his misery, calculated to melt a father's heart, the only response was the repeated order to do something useful to society or come home. Diderot would do neither; there was no going back to the cage. It was here, in this turbulent city of Paris, that lay the high adventure of living, he told himself over and over again. Even with a nagging stomach, he shrugged off the dread image of the sleepy town of Langres. Paris was the hub of the universe, and to feel its throb was to be its prisoner forever.

Still, one must live. In the first weeks of independence, he had managed to extract some money from a fellow Langrois, one Monsieur Foucou. Foucou was a cutler who had turned artist; Diderot had occasion to seek his help again, years later, when writing his article on steel for the *Encyclopedia*. His father repaid these loans through the intermediary of another compatriot, a monk called Brother Angel, of whom more anon; but he warned Foucou not to advance any further funds nor to take Denis into his house. "He is supposed to be at the law office," wrote the irate cutler.

His loans exhausted, it became desperately necessary to seek means of subsistence, and to subsist by expedients. Now the *vie de bohême* began in earnest. Diderot was following in François Villon's footsteps, associating with other penniless would-be authors, artists and philosophers, hungry one day, feasting the next, making the rounds of the cafés and taverns when his pockets jingled with a few coins. Seated with his cronies around a café table, he would perorate over a glass of wine, and an hour later he might seek pleasure in a *maison de tolérance*. One lesson Diderot learned during those hard but happy-go-lucky years, the lesson of generosity. If any of the good companions had money, all ate. They starved together or feasted together.

On Mardigras, not having a sou in his pocket, he was overcome with melancholy and nostalgic memories of the old dinners at home on that holiday, when he sat at the festive and well-provided board.

Unable to work, he decided upon a walk to dissipate his sadness. Sorrow may be calmed, but there is no beguiling hunger. He went back to his inn, sank down on a chair, faint from starvation. Seeing his pallor, the good-hearted landlady gave him some toast soaked in wine. In gratitude he swore that if ever he had anything, he would never turn away the needy from his door.

Maman, of course, was more easily touched. It was hard for her to think of her eldest, even if erring son, suffering from hunger. Saving what she could from her house-money, she three times sent a welcome subsidy to Paris, sent it with their faithful and heroic servant, Hélène Brûlé, who negotiated afoot, according to legend, the three hundred sixty mile journey to Paris and back.

But this succor from home was not enough to live on. So Diderot borrowed when and where he could, and conveniently forgot to repay. When rent was due, he found it easier to slip away and take another garret in the next street. Circumstances were already stamping on him that nervous instability and changeable disposition that were to characterize him so profoundly. The passing days saw him now up, now down, given over to work, to sorrow, to pleasure, to boredom, to want, drunk with gaiety, or drowned in bitter reflections. More than once, when he was penniless and hungry and depressed, he was tempted to renounce his dreams for a place at the fireside and the solid fare of the family table. But then a line of Homer, a mathematical problem to be solved, a passage in Newton, would put this desperate thought from his mind. Never did his pride·and his ambitions allow him to throw in the sponge, to write the word that would have ended all his misery and the story of his greatness.

Diderot managed to survive. He succeeded in getting some pupils for private lessons and lived from hand to mouth by teaching mathematics. Years later he boasted about this as a feat. "I learned by showing others, and I formed several good students." He was a poor businessman, however. If he encountered an apt pupil, he stayed with him the entire day. If he found a stupid one, he left at the end of an hour and never returned. For these lessons he was paid indifferently with books, furniture, clothing or money; visits to the pawnbroker's must have been part of his regular schedule.

One day Diderot knocked at the door of the Chartreux monastery and said he had an urgent message for the prior. Having been led in, he fell at prior's feet and begged to be admitted as a novice. Was it merely a ruse? One can only guess at the crises of mysticism and scepticism through which Diderot was then passing. It was a painful process, this molting the shell of his childhood and adolescence. At any rate, the wise and kindly prior, after a shrewd glance at the emaciated youth, decided not to take him seriously, but fed him and sent him away.

Another time a friend who knew of Diderot's religious interests rushed excitedly into his room and told him of a missionary, about to leave for Brazil, who needed six sermons. Diderot ran over to the Mission House, got the job, wrote the sermons, and received the enormous sum of three hundred écus.[1]

Then he stumbled on a piece of good luck and for a while it really seemed the lean days were to be left behind. Somehow or other, he succeeded in getting an appointment as tutor to the children of a wealthy financier, Eli Randon. The salary, in addition to room and board, was no less than fifteen hundred livres a year. But Diderot could not stand prosperity, at least not at the price of a deadly routine. Rising early, he had to watch the children dress, teach them all morning, lunch and dine with them, take them for walks, supervise their studies. Adieu all the liberty he had fought for! He was not allowed to receive visitors, nor did he have time any longer for walks along the crowded streets of the Latin Quarter, for browsing among the bookstalls, or for gay parties with his friends. He was tied down with the responsibilities and drudgery of a job. Most discouraging of all, his two pupils were lazy and mediocre.

He endured it for three months. Then, at the end of his patience, perhaps recalling La Fontaine's fable of the wolf and the dog, he decided that after all security was not worth the sacrifice of freedom. He asked M. Randon for a conference.

"I have come, sir, to request you to get some one else in my place; I cannot remain in your house any longer."

"Why, monsieur Diderot, what cause for dissatisfaction do you have? Is your salary insufficient? I will double it. Are you poorly lodged? Choose another apartment. Is your table poorly served? Then order your own dinner. Anything you wish, because I want to keep you."

"Sir, look at me. A lemon is less yellow than my face. I am making men of your children, but each day I am becoming more of a child myself. I am a thousand times too rich and too comfortable

[1] The écu was worth three livres, and the livre was equivalent to a franc, about twenty cents.

in your house, but I must go away; the object of my desires is not
to live better, but to live."

Back went Diderot to his freedom and his philosophy. Once
more he tenanted a dingy flat, strewn with second-hand books and
overrun with friends so like himself—friends who thought nothing
of sharing his meager dinner, borrowing his sous, or seeking shelter
with him on a spare mattress. Diderot expected the same of them,
for such was the rule of good fellowship in the Latin Quarter.

One of the few authentic references we have to Diderot at this
period is found in the journal of an engraver, Wille, with whom he
shared an attic for some time. Wille relates how they met:

> Curious to meet my neighbors, I went downstairs where, among
> my hosts, I found a very affable young man who in the course of
> conversation told me he was trying to become a good *littérateur,*
> and a better philosopher, if possible. He added that he would be
> glad to be friendly with me, especially as he esteemed artists and
> loved the arts, and as he thought we were of the same age, and we
> were neighbors. We shook hands and immediately became friends.
> This young man was M. Diderot, who has since become famous ;
> he occupied the apartment beneath me, and had a very nice library,
> and gladly lent me books.

The funds saved during the stay at M. Randon's were soon dissipated. At wits end, Diderot had recourse to another expedient, the
strangest of all. He recalled that Brother Angel was living at the
nearby Carmelite monastery. This monk, a clever man and a
popular confessor, later appears in Diderot's novel, *Jacques the
Fatalist.* He was obsessed by the single ambition of improving the
financial status of his House. To succeed in this, he had practically
made a banking establishment of it, lending to a select clientele of
sporting young men who could look forward to a considerable
inheritance. Frequently he even suggested that the best way for
them to get back into the good grace of their families would be to
take vows in the Carmelite order. Diderot thought it worth while
to pay Brother Angel a visit, pretexting a desire to visit the House
and the library.

The first interview was punctuated with numerous sighs on his
part and one or two allusions to the calm and peace of a secluded
life. Not many days passed before the monastery again received
the visit of the sighing philosopher, and a third and fourth visit
followed. Gradually Diderot opened his heart to the sympathetic

ears of Brother Angel, confessed his sins and his unruly life, the grief he had caused his father and his desire to be reconciled with him. When Brother Angel offered to mediate personally, Diderot, overcome by such kindness, confessed at length the great secret in his heart: he wanted to become a monk. This desire met with instant approval and encouragement.

"Alas!" sighed Diderot, "there is one small obstacle that forces me to postpone the fulfillment of my heart's innermost wish."

"What is that?"

"First I must work a long time to get together twelve hundred livres. You see, I seduced an innocent girl and now the poor creature has no other recourse except to live by vice. It is hard enough to leave her, for we love each other, but at least I must provide her with some money, or else remorse will haunt me all my life. After all, I am young, and another year or two will only strengthen my vocation."

This delay did not appeal to the monk. More openly now, he exalted the advantages of his Order. Diderot appeared interested.

"I'll think of it seriously when I've settled my financial affairs," he promised, turning towards the door.

But Brother Angel could not see his prey escape.

"It would be foolish of you to lead a life of sin any longer. Here are twelve hundred livres, break off with your mistress. Your father will be so happy when you are one of us, that he will be glad to reimburse me and pay the other expenses of your admission."

Diderot rushed away, dancing with joy, and paid off his real debts instead of the imaginary mistress. He had promised to come back next day to occupy the cell in which he was to pass the remainder of his life. But when he returned, he wore a worried and downcast expression.

"I'm not free yet," he said dejectedly. "I don't want to defraud anybody. If only you could get from my father a small sum to pay my back rent, board, and tailor's bill. After all, a monk's habit doesn't free an honest man from settling his debts."

"All right," acquiesced Brother Angel, ready to go the whole hog. "Give me an itemized account. Your father will be more disposed to reimburse me later, when he sees you are leading a decent life. At the present moment he might not trust your plans. When a thing is done, it carries more weight. Just become a Carmelite and all will be well!"

Diderot handed him a bill that would do credit to a Beau

Brummell, pocketed another eight or nine hundred livres, and promised to return the next day. This he did.

"I'm all ready to come in, Brother Angel, all ready. There's just one trifle I've forgotten. I must have a suitable trousseau of clothes, furniture and books. The son of a decent family can't enter orders like a beggar. Draw up a list of the things you think I'll need, I'll buy them and . . ."

"There's no point to that," interrupted Diderot's good angel. "As soon as you are admitted, I'll get you everything you need."

"Brother Angel, won't you give me any more money?"

"No, indeed, I shall not."

"Then I don't want to be a monk any more. Good-bye and many thanks."

The monk, bursting with rage, wrote a furious letter to Diderot's father. The latter called him a fool, and paid.

There was a brighter side to this bohemian life. There were the quiet, reflective afternoons he spent in one or another of the city's many parks. Most attractive of all to Diderot was the Palais-Royal, a carriageless sanctuary, with beautiful gardens and shaded lanes. Intriguers and businessmen alike found it a convenient place for their affairs, philosophers gathered beneath its trees for weighty discussions, and idlers enjoyed the fresh air and the bold looks of charming courtesans. The Palais-Royal was more entertaining than the Jardin des Tuileries. There one could find only honest bourgeois and ladies of quality who wished to stroll without rubbing elbows, as at the Palais-Royal, with workmen, wenches, soldiers, and servants.

At night Paris had a different personality, mysterious and romantic. Its narrow cobblestoned streets, without sidewalks, were dimly lighted and cluttered with refuse—civic sanitation was scarcely dreamed of at a time when fashionable ladies wore long combs in order to scratch daintily their lice-infested scalps. With each gust of wind, the iron signs, picturing boots, spurs, gloves, or whatnot, grated and groaned on rusty hinges. Boisterous parties of men swept down the street, touching the houses with fastened shutters on each side. Diderot was most likely among them. Before the Comédie Française or the Opéra, long lines of cabs and carriages provided a glamorous spectacle as they deposited, and later called for the gay theatergoers—commoners and brilliantly attired aristocrats. There, too, one could surely find Diderot—when he had the money for a ticket. He had a great love for the theatre, which may have been kindled at the Lycée Louis-le-Grand, where the famous professor of rhetoric, Father Porée, is known to have written plays for the students. Diderot himself tells us, "When I was young, I hesitated between the Sorbonne and the stage." And he describes how he would walk in the Luxembourg, reciting aloud long passages from Molière and Corneille. He speaks, too, of interrupting his love of social pleasures "to weep over the misfortune of Andromache, or to laugh at the sallies of the Misanthrope." But if we are to believe what he confesses on another occasion, this love for the theatre was not a pure esthetic flame. Never did he really intend to be an actor, but only "to live familiarly with actresses, whom I found infinitely lovable and whom I knew to be easy to get."

Then there were friends and brilliant conversation, always the greatest of French arts. These he could find at will in the famous cafés, the Procope, Régence, and Gradot, frequented by renowned and budding authors, jammed full at night, resounding with the clamor of drinking, chatter, and laughter. Here Diderot could read the newspapers without charge, keep informed of the latest literary events, or look on at a quiet and tense game of chess. Here he could enjoy the sweet pleasures of society without which few Frenchmen can be happy, and at the same time sharpen his wits and tongue in keen repartees and critical discussions. This was the kind of life his loquacious, expansive personality required.

And then there were the feasts and wild parties *chez Landès,* where Diderot tasted to excess all the pleasures, sensual and spiritual. He never forgot those loud and lively conversations punctuated by the popping of corks and the laughter of pretty women of questionable virtue—or less euphemistically, of unquestionable vice. He would return home, at least half drunk, and then stay up all night writing, for never did he feel more verve and inspiration than after a good orgy.

He could not resist a woman's charms, this young man who had come so near to taking a vow of chastity. One of the incidents he has preserved for us was of a conquest made through the window. Each morning he stood "with his long hair falling over his white shoulders," his shirt open, while his neighbor's wife became intoxicated at this spectacle. "I perceived it clearly. And so I seduced her from one side of the street to the other." No wonder he once admitted to his fiancée that he richly deserved the name of libertine! Years later, in reply to a flattering letter from a woman, he modestly wrote: "Sterility of the chin is the only quality that I have in common with Phoebus. I swear to you that if I had lived like him with nine virgins, and if they had the same good will for me, a feeble mortal, I should have used my time much better than that god."

All his life Diderot remained extremely susceptible to feminine beauty. Even at sixty-two, he gave this piece of practical advice to his English friend Wilkes: "In the midst of the public excitement, keep well; be gay; drink good wine; and when you get a fancy for love, look for women who won't make you sigh too long. They amuse as much as the others; they take less time; you possess them without worries and leave them without regrets."

A discreet silence veils most of Diderot's youthful affairs. He has told us, however, how he met the baby-faced Mademoiselle Babuti, whose retroussé nose, heart-shaped mouth, and coquettish disposition brought many a customer to her father's bookstore. Diderot had set his cap for her. One bright morning he entered the shop, looking as usual, wild and ardent.

"Mademoiselle, Boccaccio's *Decameron* and a Petronius if you please."

"Here they are, sir. Don't you need anything else?"

"Yes . . . but . . ."

"Tell me."

"The Nun in a Nightgown."

"For shame, Sir: Do you think we keep filthy trash like that?"

The next time he went there, she smiled, and so did he. And a week or two after their meeting, Mlle. Babuti was his mistress. Later in life, she was to become the wife of his favorite painter, Greuze. It was said that every time the poor artist turned the corner, he could glimpse the urchins of his neighborhood making horns behind his back. By that time, Mlle. Babuti had lost her youthful freshness. Diderot, commenting on her portrait in the Salon of 1765, praised the face, but "as for the bosom, I just can't look at it; and nevertheless, even at fifty, I don't hate bosoms."

For a while, he had sighed for a certain danseuse at the Opéra, but she herself cured him without realizing it. Admitted to her dressing room, he watched with horror as she covered over with chalk the spots on her white stockings. "Each spot she chalked," he later told his daughter, "diminished my passion, and at the end of her toilette, my heart was as clean as her stockings."

On two of his escapades, he had a close brush with disaster. One evening he was invited to dinner at a home of shady character, and was seated next to its mistress. The party grew gay. Diderot was young and witty; the lady indicated by looks and other less equivocal signs that she enjoyed his company. As the evening grew later, he suddenly found himself alone with her. Having to all appearances to spend the night in a room with only one bed, Diderot politely expressed the hope that she would offer him half of it. A moment later, as he was helping her to undress, someone knocked violently at the door. It was his young friend Le Roy, who had come back at full speed to warn him of the condition of the gallant lady, and the peril of her favors. Diderot did not bother to be polite. He ran away.

The other encounter was with a young woman kept by an army officer. She happened to live in the apartment directly above his in the Rue de la Parcheminerie. One day when her lover had left to joint his regiment, Diderot "mistook the floor" and stumbled into her room. He found her lolling in an easy chair, clad in a transparent dressing gown. She smiled and stared at him insolently. Passionately, he threw himself at her feet and covered her with burning looks of desire which the pretty wench did not seem to resent. But let Diderot finish the story:

> I took the edges of the gauze that covered her and threw them apart ; she let me do as I pleased. I told her she was beautiful, and indeed, in my position and at my age, it was rather difficult not to think so. I got ready to back up my praise, but, placing her hand between her charms and my desire, she stopped me with these strange words: 'My friend, you are very sweet ; but I'm not sure of myself, and, though I don't know why, I should be sorry to see you suffer from my satisfying your desires. Behind that door is an old fool who has been bothering me. First I'll indulge him and later we'll know whether you can safely accept what I am only too glad to grant you!'

The experiment was duly tried, with disastrous consequences to the guinea pig. Whenever Diderot recalled these incidents in later life, he shuddered and thanked his protecting gods.

Diderot prided himself on being a connoisseur of feminine beauty and psychology. Nothing in the world is more ridiculous, he declared, than a woman who attaches any importance to her favors after the first time. The most eloquent thing in the world is a lovely woman with a beautiful voice. Her face, her look, her accent, form an irresistible harmony with what she has to say. On the other hand, nothing is uglier than a woman in a fit of temper; Diderot was destined to know all about that from his wife. Women, according to his theory, all die at the age of fifteen. After that, they become what the men they love want them to be. The character of women who give themselves to many men is, consequently, a composite jumble. In 1772, Diderot composed an *Essay on Women*, an analysis of their virtues and weaknesses, some lines of which would do credit to Schopenhauer.

If Diderot's life seems unbridled and dissolute, it was only a faithful reflection of the times. The debauchery of the regency of Philip of Orléans (1715–1723) had turned to sheer recklessness after the collapse of Law's Mississippi Bubble, that fantastic "get-rich-quick" scheme. Anyone who reads Prévost's immortal *Manon Lescaut* will get a graphic picture of the period. Now Louis XV was continuing in the same spirit. In 1733, his minister, Fleury, began the first of a series of ruinous wars, the War of the Polish Succession. In 1742, the monarch conferred on the beauteous Mme. de Châteauroux the honor of royal mistress; she was the third of three sisters to occupy that envied post. Under her sway, the government passed into the hands of the "favorites," never again to leave them, while the Treasury was ruined by the unending lavishness of their festivals and revelry. From that moment, the monarchy was lost and the embryo of an undreamed of revolution started to germinate.

CHAPTER 3

Love

Finds

a

Way

1

WHILE DIDEROT WAS LIVING the life of freedom and shady adventure, he was constantly nourishing his mind and equipping himself for his future work.

If the twentieth century is the age of specialization, then the eighteenth was the age of versatility. It was the period when men took all knowledge for their province; when a Voltaire was to write comic and tragic plays, lyric, satirical and epic poetry, novels, philosophy, history, science; when a statesman like Turgot wrote not only on economics but on philosophy and history, and considered himself competent in other subjects as well. Diderot shared this universal spirit of his age. His curiosity embraced the entire field of human knowledge, and he prided himself on it: "It is this ambitious curiosity that leads us in spite of ourselves to examine things and thus in the long run dissipates all sorts of falsehoods." Curiosity, in the eighteenth century, usually led to scepticism via rational examination of church doctrines previously unquestioned; this is the path Diderot was to tread.

To satisfy his passion for knowledge, he attended as many public courses as possible, on chemistry, biology, physiology. He continued his mathematical studies; as he says himself, "always coming back to mathematics, as an unfaithful husband, tired of his mistress, returns to his wife from time to time." He had devoured almost all of the Latin, Greek and French classics. Never did he go out without a copy of Homer or Vergil in his pocket. Horace he knew by heart. "For several years," he tells us, "I was as religious about reading a canto from Homer before going to bed as a good priest about reciting his breviary. Quite young I sucked the milk of Homer, Vergil, Horace, Terence, Anacreon, Plato, Euripides, varied with that of Moses and the prophets." To this list, add Lucretius, whose materialism and naturalism left a deep mark. Turning next to the study of English and Italian, he acquired a fluent if not always exact reading knowledge of these languages, and steeped himself in their literatures. He enjoyed Tasso and Ariosto; but it was the literature of England that aroused his keenest enthusiasm. What French poetry could compare with Pope and Dryden, and especially with Thomson's *Seasons,* in which he discovered a feeling for nature absent from his own literature? Shakespeare, though a Gothic barbarian lacking in good taste, had many unsurpassable flights of genius. Milton was magnificent, Swift incomparable in his satire, while Defoe and Fielding put the English novel far above the French. A little later came the discovery of Richardson, of Gray, Young, and "Ossian." They enraptured him still more, for he found in them fresh sources of emotion. A new current of feeling was rising up alongside the rationalism and controlled emotion of French classicism, although the two may not have been consciously opposed, at first. Diderot, who was in many ways a *homo duplex,* represents both. This new current was to become a source of romanticism. Diderot, as always, sought not to prolong the past but to anticipate the future.

His reading was not passive, but a goad to his own thinking. He would begin a scene of one of Corneille's plays, then close his eyes and try to fill in the rest. His imagination carried him beyond the printed page, and his own thoughts, easily provoked, led him down a long trail of associations to new and bold conclusions. "What a fine text for philosophizing! " he cries again and again. The book is only an excuse; in it he finds his own ideas, his own personality. "You read men," he later wrote to Mme. Necker, "as they tell me I read books: it is yourself that you see in them."

When he is held by the magic spell of a good book, he forgets his own existence, fuses it with those of the characters, and all their emotions become his. In a fit of enthusiasm he cries, "Oh Richardson, I cannot help playing a role in your novels. How many times have I surprised myself, like children who go to the theatre for the first time, shouting: *Don't believe him, he is deceiving you!* Or, *If you go there, you are lost!* My whole being was kept in constant agitation." He is stirred to tears by any work that teaches charity, virtue, or justice and is naturally inclined to believe any fact that ennobles human nature. More than once his friends, on bursting into his study, would find him reading and weeping. The opposite effect was produced when a book or a character cast an unfavorable light on human nature. The reading of history always filled him with pessimism and bitterness. "I am not violent, but on going through certain reigns, my heart was swollen with rage and I found myself using a dagger with marvelous facility."

The impact of English literature on Diderot's sensitive and enthusiastic personality was deep and permanent. Even more important than the literature was the discovery of English civilization and philosophy. Voltaire's *Letters on the English*, written in 1723 after his two years of exile in that country, stirred the young philosopher's imagination profoundly. A country did exist then, where men were virtuous and tolerant, instead of persecuting each other like cruel beasts; where every man had the liberty to think as he pleased and to express his opinions publicly, in speech or in writing, without facing incarceration in a dungeon like the Bastille; a country that governed itself, instead of squirming under the heel of a licentious and incapable despot; where every peasant was proud of his freedom instead of having to humble himself before the insolence and cruelty of a privileged and corrupt nobility. What a contrast with France!

That the picture was not entirely true matters little. It was the picture that Diderot kept in his mind, as he embarked upon the task that was to engage him all his life. It was not a reformer's dream that moved him; although Diderot hated every abuse that lay upon his country, he felt no missionary call. It was the urge to get back to fundamentals, to create for himself a satisfactory and livable philosophy; to examine all over again the essential questions—God, the universe, and man's place in it; to discover, through a study of human nature, morality, and the social structure, how man can best live in that universe; to explore all the fields of knowledge and determine what hope lay in them for man's future; finally, to know all forms of beauty, for if life was an evil thing, there always shone three bright stars that could never be extinguished: Truth, Beauty, and Good.

He set out from the new naturalism that was emerging from a complex of revolutionary intellectual factors. English philosophy was one starting point. Bacon and Newton had destroyed the opium of scholasticism. Science was free and was rapidly tearing away the veil of nature. Newton revealed a universe ruled by law. Locke had opened the door to a new understanding of the human mind, by his denial of innate ideas and instincts, and his theory that all knowledge comes, directly or indirectly, through the senses. His empirical psychology ended the Cartesian dualism of a spiritual mind and a mechanical body. Only three things exist, according to Locke: the mind, ready at birth to be molded like wax; the external world; and the ideas which are produced in the mind by the external world. If the mind could be molded like wax, thought Diderot, could not a wise education and a well-organized society make man virtuous and happy? The hope lay in rediscovering "natural law" and in reconstructing society on its basis. No one stopped to think of the contradiction between a "natural law" that assumed universal needs and responses in men, and a psychological theory that justifies only relativism.

Then there was Hobbes, who reduced all phenomena—including the mind—to mechanical motion, and explained society as a sort of contract between people and a sovereign ruler; without this renunciation of our unlimited natural liberty, life would be "a state of war of every man against every man." There were the deists, such as Toland and Tindal, who gradually detached Diderot from Catholic orthodoxy. Most influential of all was Shaftesbury, whose ethical theories, involving sympathy and enthusiasm, appealed strongly to his temperament. The stimulus of English literature on Diderot's mind seems never to have diminished, though its form changed. His first publications were translations. Of his original writings, *On the Sufficiency of Natural Religion* was in part inspired by Wollaston's *The Religion of Nature Delineated;* the *Thoughts on the Interpretation of Nature* by Bacon; the novel, *The Nun,* by Richardson's *Pamela; Jacques the Fatalist* by Sterne's *Tristram Shandy; The Paradox on Acting* by Garrick. No wonder the French critic, Brunetière, exclaimed with hostile exaggeration, "If you said he was all English, you would be quite close to the truth."

From sources outside of England, he took much less. He was most attracted by Leibnitz' law of continuity, which ruled out

sudden jumps in nature and held everything to consist of impercep-
tible gradations in the "great chain of beings" leading from the
most insignificant to God. Spinoza's pantheism and determinism
left some deep marks on his thought, though it is not certain how
well he understood him. Lucretius and the ancient atomists were
also a starting point, soon to be surpassed.

England and its philosophy were already working as a ferment
in French minds, in men such as Voltaire and Condillac, even before
Diderot "discovered" them. The English thinkers were a powerful
catalyst. But France had been well prepared for them by her own
intellectual, social, and economic evolution; by the rise of the bourgeoisie; by the degeneration of the monarchy, the Church, and the
nobility; by the development of critical rationalism and social preoccupations. If all this had not taken place, the English would have
found the soil as barren as in the seventeenth century, when the
French had turned their backs in smug complacency.

Among the French writers, Descartes was the greatest of the
philosophers. Although the eighteenth century rejected his philosophic and scientific systems (which ruled almost unchallenged until
the 1730's) and his belief in innate ideas, his influence on the French
mind remained, and still remains strong. The rejection was part of
a mounting distaste for the abstract reason of seventeenth-century
metaphysical systems, including those of Leibnitz and Malebranche.
If most philosophical thought in France will remain on an amateur-
ish level, we can attribute it to this turning away from the great
philosophical tradition toward the bright dawn of a new scientific
age, that as yet was far from developed and understood.

While eighteenth-century French thinkers followed Locke almost
unanimously, they were divided between upholders of Newton and
the mathematical method, and partisans of a radical naturalism.
The second group had Descartes as their spiritual father. Descartes,
true enough, was a mathematician, and evolved an abstract metaphysics. But it was he who also had insisted on the exclusion of
metaphysics, final causes, theology, and providence from physical
inquiry. He had given matter a status independent of mind, and his
physics had showed there was no need of mind to explain the
universe. Everything had evolved necessarily from the original chaos
of matter and motion, according to laws that belonged inherently to
matter and motion. True, Descartes held that motion had been
imparted to matter by God, but once given, all proceeded according
to law, giving us *necessarily* the universe as it is today. It was an

easy step, for John Toland, Fontenelle, and others, to place the motion inherently in matter itself, along with its other laws. The Cartesian universe was dynamic, a continuing process of change, of building and destroying. Again it was an easy but momentous step to apply the idea of transformism to life itself. Impulse to this step was given by studies in biology and geology in the 1740's, culminating in Buffon's *Theory of the Earth*. It was this naturalistic materialism that Diderot was destined to bring to its complete fruition, after he finally abandoned Newtonian deism in the last years of that decade.

In more general terms, Descartes furnished a method to eighteenth-century thinkers. He made universal doubt the basis of philosophy and insisted on clear and cogent reasoning. When Diderot praises Condillac, it is in Cartesian terms, for "descending from clear perceptions to clear perceptions (for that is the author's method of reasoning, and the good method)." Critical rationalism and scepticism had reached their heights, about this time, in the *Persian Letters* of Montesquieu and the writings of Voltaire, which owed much, in spirit and argumentation, to the great work of Bayle, whose *Dictionary* was the eighteenth-century Bible of scepticism, secular morality, and materialism. Still more effective were pamphlets and broadsides that were clandestinely printed and surreptitiously circulated; in these deism and atheism were expressed with an audacity and a defiance of censorship that could not yet be found in the "regular" literature. There is no doubt that these *petits papiers,* and the more "radical" elements among the unrecognized would-be writers and philosophers of the Latin Quarter played a major role in Diderot's loss of faith.

2

In 1741 France was in the midst of the disastrous and humiliating War of the Austrian Succession, Fleury's greatest error. Frederick the Great's star was rising, and Voltaire was incurring public wrath for having congratulated him on his victories over the French. "Do not speak to me of greatness of soul," said the Prussian monarch, "a prince should only consult his interest. If there is something to be gained by being honest, we shall be honest; if we must deceive, let us be rogues."

To Diderot's personal life and emotional development, the years 1741–42 brought two important events: friendship and love. Among his many cronies, during this footloose period, one was destined to play an important role, first as his bosom friend, later as his bitterest enemy.

He was an unknown young Swiss who had just arrived in Paris. His name was Jean-Jacques Rousseau. He had come to Paris to win fame and fortune as a composer. When that bid failed, he was to play a trick of irony and conquer world renown by attacking the society that had refused to recognize him. There is nothing in the early environment and upbringing of these two indigent bohemians that augured an affinity between them. Compared with Diderot's careful upbringing and calm life in a staid, middle-class family, Rousseau grew up isolated and neglected, with a shy and introverted personality. His mother having died in childbirth—a not inappropriate beginning for a tragic life—his father "took care" of him, intoxicating the boy's imagination with fantastic novels far beyond his years. Flight from Geneva after a singular and unbalanced childhood was followed by wanderings across France and innumerable adventures, best recounted in his own remarkable *Confessions*.

Despite their different beginnings in life, the two men immediately felt impelled towards each other. They were of the same age, both penniless, both striving for a place in the sun. The same fire burned in their breasts. Their personalities were in certain ways alike, enthusiastic, and explosive, "prompt to ecstasy or revolt, inclined to paradox." Both possessed more than a normal share of *sensibilité*. They were individualists and enjoyed a keen sense of personal independence. Finally, Diderot had emancipated himself, with struggle and pain, from his own conventional childhood, and joined, albeit later than Rousseau, the ranks of the free corps which admitted no bond of prejudice, authority, or convention.

Putting formalities aside, they fell to talking enthusiastically about their hopes and ambitions and the many things that interested them in common. Music was first of these, for Diderot loved music, though he had no technical knowledge of it, while Rousseau had a comic opera, *The Gallant Muses*, in his baggage. As keys to the door of fortune, Jean-Jacques had also brought with him to Paris a new system of musical notation, and in case that failed, a comedy, *Narcissus*. And so, we may imagine, they talked for many hours, and when finally they said *bonsoir* in the deserted streets of Paris, each felt the exhilaration of having discovered a true friend.

From then on they had almost daily rendezvous. They took long walks on the Left Bank or in the gardens of the Palais Royal, discussing books, music, ideas. When they could walk no more, they stopped for dinner at the *Panier fleuri* or for a cup of coffee at the Café de la Régence. At the Régence, they would remain to watch the chess players and sometimes had a little game themselves. It was then that Diderot's natural generosity of character and Jean-Jacques' pettiness were revealed. Diderot was a good loser, Rosseau a poor winner. When Diderot suggested that Jean-Jacques give him an advantage at the beginning to make the play more equal and more interesting, he refused.

"Do you mind losing?" Jean-Jacques demanded.

"No, but I could defend myself better and you would get more fun out of it."

"That may be, but let's leave things as they are."

Towards the end of the year Rousseau left for Venice, as secretary of the embassy staff, and did not return to Paris until 1744. Absence did not weaken their comradeship. Rousseau returned after a violent quarrel with his chief, Count de Montaigu, and brought back with him a new enthusiasm for Italian music and one or two tales of adventures with women. In this respect, they had different temperaments. Jean-Jacques did not, like his friend, pursue every woman who showed him the least sign of encouragement. Violently passionate when in love, he was timid and uncertain of himself. He amazed Diderot by telling him that he had approached women only twice in eighteen months.

Their close friendship was to last fifteen years. Then these two men, who had once felt a magnetic attraction, were to be driven apart by the accumulated poisons of rancor and misunderstanding.

Perhaps Diderot and Rousseau were in a measure drawn together by a weakness they shared. Both were ill at ease among strangers, awkward in formal society to the point of being at times ludicrous. They were keenly sensitive to this defect, and it was to figure largely in both their lives, in entirely different ways. Rousseau idealized his fault and built an antisocial philosophy around it. He became a singular figure, a tragic phenomenon, and derived tremendous publicity from his partly self-created martyrdom. Diderot, on the other hand, simply "played possum," avoiding social success. To the best of his ability, he shunned notoriety, and obtained relative tranquillity at the cost of much fame.

"I was not made for society," he later admitted, "where people listen so little to each other. I have too delicate a soul. . . . I do not like occasions for stammering, and I always stammer the first time I meet somebody, and then everything is reduced to banal phrases reciprocally exchanged. And I don't have a cent of that kind of money . . . Grimm has told me several times that I was made for another world . . . What is certain, is that it will soon be fifty years that I have been a stranger in this one, that I have been living an imitative life that is not mine, that I constantly bend myself to the gait of others, and that I am like a dog who has been taught to walk on two legs."

It was not merely that both men were quite unpolished, never at home amidst the ultra-refined sophistication of the eighteenth-century salons. Rousseau, at least, and perhaps Diderot, too, suffered from a deeply rooted inferiority complex, which in society oppressed and paralyzed his personality, while Diderot was often brash, tactless, and overtly overconfident. Both lacked poise, to such a degree that the approach of a stranger startled them and sent them scurrying into their little shell. When spoken to, their embarrassment and gauche replies frequently brought a smile or a snicker. With their self-conscious independence, they found it difficult and disagreeable to lend themselves to the empty conventionalities and meaningless formulas of politeness. Diderot reconciled himself more and more easily to this necessity, but Rousseau was to become embittered at the artificiality and "hypocrisy" of civilization.

Curiously enough, it was Rousseau who dragged him into a larger social group. Throughout his life Diderot would never venture into strange milieux unless practically forced to. But Jean-Jacques was something of an intriguer and had important connections. Indeed, until his revolutionary break with society, he curried acceptance by the aristocracy. Diderot got to know Sartine, later to be chief of police; Bernis, the future cardinal and minister; the young Condillac, who was soon to pursue Locke's theories to their ultimate implications and become the outstanding French metaphysician of the eighteenth century. Among other contacts and acquaintances of this period were the dramatist Baculard d'Arnaud; old Lesage, author of *Gil Blas;* Le Guay de Prémontval, a mathematics professor whose interest in religion was to involve him in persecution; and Toussaint, also to be persecuted for his notorious philosophical work, *On Manners.* He met the abbé Desfontaines, Voltaire's dogged enemy. When Diderot brought him a poem, Desfontaines tartly advised him to write for the theatre.

One friend, an eccentric by the name of Gousse, was an unbalanced bohemian who alternated between acts of heroism and roguery. "I need a valuable book," relates Diderot, "he brings it to me. Some time later, I need another valuable book; again he brings it to me. I offer to pay him, he refuses. I need a third valuable book. This one, he says, you will not have. You should have spoken up sooner, my Sorbonne professor is dead.—And what does your professor's death have to do with the book I want? Did you take the other two from his library?—Of course! —Without his permission?—Why should I need his permission to perform an act of distributive justice? I have only moved his books to a better place, transferring them from where they were useless to where they would be used."

Gousse will figure in *Jacques the Fatalist;* the idea implicit in his reasoning, that morality is an arbitrary set of conventions and that the "superior man" can create his own, will have a place in Diderot's ethics, especially in his masterpiece, *Rameau's Nephew.*

Of all his new friends, Diderot had greatest admiration for Condillac, a man of profound intelligence. Condillac, Rousseau, and Diderot soon had regular meetings at the *Panier fleuri;* delightful rendezvous, where good fellowship, good food, and wine were mingled with intense discussions of the newest, as well as the oldest, philosophical theories. When the reasoning became too profound, Rousseau listened silently, while Diderot excitedly and Condillac coolly matched wits. These conversations stirred the smoldering fires of Diderot's own meditations. His ideas crystallized to a point where he was tempted to express them in writing. But at that very moment, an even more fateful event was about to alter the course of his life.

3

In 1713, the year of Diderot's birth, a young widow and her two daughters, aged three and one, came to Paris from the provinces. This widow, *née* Marie de Malville, was the only child of an impoverished country nobleman. She had married a wealthy manufacturer, Ambroise Champion, and thought it a good match. Poor management and unlucky speculations soon ruined Champion and brought about his early death. The unfortunate widow was forced to accept shelter in Paris at the home of a wealthy childhood friend. The older girl, Antoinette, was put into the Miramionnes convent on the Quai de la Tournelle, where she could learn to work for her own livelihood. When her benefactor died, in 1726, Mme.

Champion withdrew her sixteen-year-old daughter from the convent and together they set up a small lace and lingerie shop. Here they lived peacefully for sixteen years. Their business prospered. They bought new furniture and even saved a tidy sum against a rainy day. Antoinette, a shapely and dark-eyed lass, attracted more than one well-to-do merchant; some, on encountering her inexpugnable virtue, even asked her in marriage. She would have none of them, however; a strong-willed girl, she knew her own mind, and preferred her independence to a husband she did not love. In 1741, Antoinette was thirty-one and the idea of marriage no longer disturbed this tranquil existence to which she was completely resigned. But toward the end of that very September, a young man almost four years her junior had other thoughts.

Diderot was still slipping from garret to garret. According to the *Memoirs* of his daughter, Mme. de Vandeul, he was at the moment living in the same house as the Champion ménage. This account is a deliberate falsification. The exchange of letters between him and Antoinette, as well as the address on the envelopes, proves that they were living in different streets. The real story was quite simple. Somehow, Denis had chanced to see Antoinette. Quickly appreciating her possibilities, he decided that he wanted to see her again. This was not easy; the one or two more obvious pretexts he could think of were soon exhausted and he had made no progress towards winning her love.

By now Diderot had become a master of desperate expedients and skillfully played hoaxes. One day in August he entered the Champion establishment, and taking the two women into his confidence, explained to them, with evident embarrassment and shyness, his extraordinary plight. In January, he was to enter the Seminary of Saint-Sulpice, but his linen was in a most pitiful state. If his mother sent him the cloth, would they cut him some shirts? A most unusual request, to be sure. The two women consulted each other for a moment and finally decided that they could not turn away a future priest, especially such an upright and evidently intelligent young man.

Diderot went away, happy and excited. He still had to get the linen, but that could be arranged. If the same hoax worked once, why not try it a second time? A close friend of his father, Pierre la Sallette, happened to be in Paris. Diderot lost no time in going to him and putting on the same act. The good contryman was easily convinced of his sincere repentance, and wrote home to that effect.

Hoping this was not just another trick, Diderot's family sent him the cloth, or more probably, sent it to la Sallette. Doubtless a letter expressing their fond hope came with it. Denis threw aside the letter and ran with the cloth to the shop of his pretty neighbor.

This whole episode is surrounded by considerable uncertainty and confusion. Some biographers have thought that Diderot really intended becoming a priest, even at this date. For he later wrote, in the *Salon of 1767,* "I arrive in Paris. I was going to take the fur and install myself among the doctors of the Sorbonne. I meet a woman as beautiful as an angel. I want to sleep with her. I do so. I have four children by her, and there I am, forced to give up Homer and Vergil, whom I always used to carry in my pocket; the theater, for which I had a fondness; very lucky to undertake the *Encyclopedia,* for which I shall have sacrificed twenty-five years of my life." However, the first lines of Diderot's statement clearly indicate a syncopation of time on his part which is sheer poetic license.

Two letters from la Salette to Diderot's father confirm the episode. "He has let me come to the conclusion that it would be better to send him the cloth for making shirts and collars instead of sending him the shirts and collars ready-made. I have examined his linen. He simply must have some: he was obliged to have the shirts that his dear mother sent him remade . . . For the rest, he is very well and perseveres in his promises. Saint-Sulpice will be his residence on 1 January next. May God grant him the grace to carry it out for the satisfaction of his family, since it is the profession that he chooses and which no one has urged him to take in preference to all others." However, far from proving that Diderot intended really to become a priest, these lines may only confirm the hoax he was playing.

At all events, Diderot was able to pay several visits to the Champion establishment, which he utilized properly to further his suit. Antoinette began to find herself peculiarly attached to this facile-tongued young man. She probably told herself it was nothing serious; after all, he was about to become a priest.

The day arrived, nevertheless, when the shirts were completed. And still Denis came to visit them almost every evening, until finally Mme. Champion began to object on the score of propriety. According to the story in Mme. de Vandeul's *Memoirs,* when the Champion family moved soon after this, they found the ardent philosopher installed by accident in the same house. This is another fabrication; the Champion removal actually took place a month or more later.

What actually happened is that Diderot was forced to admit his ruse. This admission he covered with words of passion and assurance of honorable intentions. He would never again be happy, until Antoinette was his wife. Mme. Champion forgave the ruse, perhaps secretly admired its romantic character; but as for marriage, that was another matter. The man had no money and no job; besides, his character was too flighty and undependable. She did not trust that gift for smooth talk with which he had turned her daughter's head—nor the wild ideas that seemed to fill his own head.

Later, Mme. Champion changed her mind. She decided to give her consent to the marriage, with the sole proviso that Diderot obtain his family's consent. What had happened in the interval? Had Antoinette, as Mme. de Vandeul records it, worn down her mother's resistance by declaring that she could never love any one else, that her entire happiness was at stake? It is certain that Diderot took his turn in pleading with the obdurate mother and, his eloquence failing, shed copious tears—another of his facile gifts. Or did Nanette, as can be deduced from the intimate expressions of Diderot's letters, suddenly burst into tears and confess that she was "Ninot's" mistress? For the one reason or the other, in the early part of November 1742 the marriage was agreed upon, with the single aforesaid condition, that Diderot obtain his father's consent. About this, however, he was worried, and not without reason. How would his father react to this sudden marriage, after all the deceits he had practiced on him? A worthless and jobless son asking permission to be married! The paternal anger at his previous escapades was trifling indeed compared to the outburst he was preparing for himself now. This was no mere prank. Marriage was not as lightly considered in the eighteenth century as it is in the twentieth. It was a matter of family even more than individual concern; financial and social considerations were often paramount.

The month of November was a troubled one for the young lovers. Diderot was writing home and trying to sound out his father's disposition toward him, trying to re-establish amicable relations after years of silence. He met with little encouragement. The good cutler had not changed his stand. One of his replies was "a sermon two yards longer than usual," containing permission for his son to take any job he wanted, as long as he did something. This slow progress was not to the liking of the impatient Antoinette. She tormented Diderot with her worries and began to sulk. He would plead with her and try hard to rouse her from her moodiness.

"What is the matter, my darling Nanette? Is there some worry that is agitating you? . . . Open your heart to me. Am I not destined to share all your pleasures and all your pains? . . . I have no secrets from you; you should hide nothing from me."

It was no use. Nanette was obdurate in her silence. Diderot knew well what was bothering her. When were they going to be married?

"You are the most unjust of all women if you suspect the sincerity of my promises. I swear that I love no one in this world except you!"

To make matters worse, Nanette suddenly began to show herself unreasonably jealous. She sent him a petulant note, accusing him of writing love letters to another woman, or of thinking of somebody else while he wrote to her. The first time this happened, Diderot skirted the question adroitly. "You could not give me a better proof of your tenderness than by refusing to share mine. That feeling is very delicate." Delicacy, however, was wasted on Antoinette, and when she renewed her charges, he felt compelled to dispel energetically such foolish notions. With his remarkable gift for self-delusion, he imagined that a man as passionately in love as himself could never be unfaithful. He replied with the eloquence that never failed him.

> You possess me entirely. Your Ninot loves and always will love no one but you. How could he do otherwise? . . . The tears I shed when I was on the point of losing you, my oaths, your love, your beauty, your character and intelligence, everything should assure you of my eternal love. Ah, you wicked girl! What malice in your pesky letter! I want you to be sure of this, Tonton: the flame of a young libertine, for I have richly deserved that name, for his neighbor's wife, is a fire of straw that dies out soon and forever; but the flame of an honest man, for I merit that name since you have made me one, never dies. These are my feelings towards you: rather to die a thousand times than not to marry you as soon as you say the word; rather to die a thousand times than to think for a moment of any other than my Nanette as soon as she has crowned my love. It is to you that my last love letters were addressed, and may Heaven punish me as the most wicked of all men, the most traitorous of all men, if ever in my life I write one to anybody else. Ninot suffices to his Tonton; Tonton alone

will suffice all her life to her Ninot. They will increase the small number of happy marriages. It cannot be otherwise ; they love each other too much ; they have no faults ; therefore they will always love each other.

Rarely have such unprophetic words been written! A few days later matters reached an impasse, and Diderot made a heroic decision. There was only one way out. That was for him to return to Langres and use his utmost diplomacy to win his father over.

On the seventh of December 1742, Diderot said his good-byes to the Champions. He set out with trepidation in his heart, hoping to gain his father's consent, but determined to do without it if necessary. It was ten or eleven years since his last visit home. As the stagecoach jogged along the one-hundred eighty miles of pitted roads, Diderot's thoughts must have turned to the past, to the happiness of his childhood, the angelic presence of his mother, the loving protection of his father, then to the last ten years of disorderly living, in open defiance of his family's wishes. And now this sudden, madcap love affair. How would they receive him? Would they rush to embrace him as the errant son returning to the fold, or would they treat him as perhaps he deserved? How would he get out of the mess in which he was now inextricably involved? Would life put him again in the role of the disobedient son?

Diderot was not to learn until years later the strength of paternal love. The reception was more than he had hoped for. His mother and sister greeted him tenderly, and even his father, after a pre-liminary show of coolness, joined in the general celebration. Only the younger brother, Didier Jr., was missing; he had accepted the career against which Denis had rebelled ten years earlier and was now at the seminary. It is apparent that little sympathy existed between these two brothers. A rebel and a traditionalist were scarcely made to understand each other. Besides, Diderot hardly knew "the abbé," as he liked to call him; there were seven years between them, and because of his early departure for Paris, they had not lived much together. It is not surprising that Diderot expressed satisfaction to Antoinette that the abbé was "out of the way," and his own position strengthened thereby. "As I think that career suits him, considering the most eminent devotion he loves to display, I am not at all sorry at this event . . . *Ma foi*, it is a good thing to be almost alone in the family."

The first days were happy ones. There was a round of visits and visitors; the curious provincials could scarcely wait to see "the local boy" about whom they had heard such amazing and horrifying tales. Three times a week, Diderot received from Paris the proofs of his forthcoming translation of Temple Stanyan's *History of Greece*. This made a wonderful impression on his father and mother. "They realize that I am doing something useful," he informed Nanette. He might have added, "much to their surprise," or "it was about time." As yet, not a word concerning Nanette had left his mouth. With peasant-like trickiness, he was trying to get his father to assign him a modest income of two-hundred livres a month; the confession could be made later. Meanwhile, Nanette addressed her letters to cousin Humblot, with a cross on the envelope to indicate their true destination.

Weeks passed, and Antoinette again began to chafe. Once at home, under his family's influence, "Ninot" might be persuaded to change his mind. After all, the strongest resolve could be shaken, and she was none too sure of her lover's resolve! In this she was mistaken, but it made her no happier to learn that Diderot's father had offered to keep him at home with complete liberty to do nothing. Fortunately, he was too prudent to tell her that a more profitable match was also being urged upon him. Her letters rapidly grew more bitter and stinging. She questioned his sincerity and scoffed at his too readily shed tears. The harassed philosopher answered in a different vein this time.

Dear Nanette, I hope that you began this year more happily than I. You have written a letter full of harshness and injustice. You know how sensitive I am. You can imagine in what a state you have put me. . . . Why don't you tell me the truth about your feelings? You don't have to fear any more those tears which have so often moved you. You will not witness them. Do not spare my weakness. Have you stopped loving me? Must I die? Then kill me with one blow, that is the only favor I have to ask of you.

Diderot was playing for time, in order to regain his father's confidence. He felt that he was about to succeed in getting what he wanted. "I shall soon have all the papers necessary for our union," he hastened to inform the restless sweetheart, "for they seem even more anxious than I to see me set up." About the pension: "If I can draw a reasonable conjecture from people in whom they confide, they at least expect that I shall ask for it, and if they had resolved to refuse it to me, I would not remark that good humor they display and all the attentions they shower on me."

But Denis had chosen a woman hard to cajole. The nagging letters continued to arrive. There was nothing to do with such a woman but give in. And in the middle of January, before the time was ripe, he was forced to bring matters to a head. Adieu all the well-laid plans! Nervous, prodded from behind, he hurried his moment and blurted out the fatal words. "Father, I am in love, and I want to get married."

Diderot felt the house crashing down about his ears. Questions and exclamations were followed by pleas and by threats. Scene followed upon scene for several nerve-racking days. But pleading and tears and harsh words were equally without effect. The disobedient son was not to be shaken from his determination. "I am resolved to do anything," he wrote back. "I am made terrible menaces, so terrible they don't frighten me . . . Do not worry, dear Nanette, and rest assured that nothing can stop us." He displays a trait that he was to show again and again in time of crisis: an unbreakable will to accomplish what he set his mind on. Obstacles seemed only to irritate him and intensify his determination to triumph at all costs.

Finally the outraged father was moved to a radical expedient. In the eighteenth century, there was a recognized manner of dealing with wayward sons. He secured a *lettre de cachet* and had Denis carted away by force and imprisoned in a monastery. Then the unhappy father wrote the following letter to Antoinette's mother. This was on the first of February 1743.

> Dear Madame. If I have put off writing to you until the present moment, it is because I thought that the advice of your daughter and my opposition would put a halt to the actions of my son.
>
> But, to judge from their excess, I do not doubt that she approves them. He passed so brusquely from requests to menaces and from menaces to actions, that I thought it my duty to take precautions against a passion so fatal to your daughter and to him. What will she do with a man who has no profession and perhaps will never have any? Is he rich enough for both? If I may believe what he says, nature has been more prodigal to him with her favors than with fortune. No, madame, I will not allow him to make an unhappy creature of her, nor to make himself unhappy.
>
> This inclination, which I must disapprove, has already done him considerable harm by making him lose a suitable match which

had been planned for him. If you don't take a hand, it will ruin him completely, for you are not unaware that disinheritance is the usual result of engagements such as the one that he is dictating to me.

If your daughter is as well born and loves him as much as he thinks, she will urge him to give her up. It is only at this price that he will recover his liberty, for with the aid of my friends who are indignant at his boldness, I have had him put under lock and key, and we have more power than is necessary to keep him there until his sentiments have changed.

A son for whom I have done so much, threatens to send a sheriff after me! And you have permitted it!

I dare not, madame, express myself as a less moderate father would in such circumstances. But put yourself in my place! Suppose that it was your daughter who acted like that with you, what would you think? what would you say, what would you do?

If you write to my scatterbrained son in the proper way, I will see to it that he gets your letter, where he is, with all the consideration that I owe to a wise mother and a virtuous daughter.

Your very humble and obedient servant, DIDEROT

This letter conveys some intimation of what went on under the Diderot roof. The cutler was mistaken, however, about his ability to keep his son imprisoned. Diderot was burning with rage and frustration, and his recalcitrant attitude did not induce his jailers to treat him more gently. To prevent his running away, they cut off his hair. How long he remained a prisoner is a mystery. But one night, desperate and resolved to escape, he tied his sheets together and slipped out of the window. Taking back roads, weak from fatigue and hunger, in constant fear of pursuit, he tramped to Troyes, ninety miles away. Fortunately, he had hidden enough money in the tail of his shirt to buy a trip to Paris on the stage.

More than anything else, perhaps, he feared Nanette's irascibility. How would *she* receive him now? A letter informed her of his mishaps. He has suffered so much for her, that he will kill himself if she does not receive him well. "My father is in such a great fury, that I do not doubt that he will disinherit me." This news was scarcely calculated to put Nanette in a receptive frame of mind! "If I lose you as well, what will remain that can keep me in this world?" continues the desperate lover. He has lost some of his cockiness about the future. "Perhaps everything can still be remedied. Everything that is put off is not lost. I am yours as much and more than ever." Most urgent of all, she must locate a furnished room where he will be near her, yet hard to find. For Brother Angel, whom his father had already charged with observing him and reporting on his conduct, would be only too glad to send him back to prison if he could.

The next few months witnessed more recrimination and scenes. Diderot exhausted his two resources, eloquence and tears. Mme. Champion was firm. She would have no disinherited son-in-law, bearing the paternal malediction. To avoid this dire eventuality, she persuaded him to write home and promise to renounce forever his project of marriage. In spite of all this tension, the two "lovers" continued to maintain some sort of relations throughout the spring and summer of 1743.

Diderot had moved to a different neighborhood. The static condition of their relations eventually led to quarrels that fall, lasting about a month, but there was no definite break. "To judge your ideas by the harshness of your ways," wrote the unhappy suitor, "what can I think except that for a month you have been affecting to desire something that you really are afraid to obtain?" When he fell sick in October, Nanette did not bother to come to see him. Instead, she sent a mutual friend, a Monsieur Duval. The latter brought back an alarming report to the effect that Denis was quite ill, living in a filthy room, uncared for and depressed, so penniless that he lacked even broth. Overcome by a sudden moment of sympathy, Antoinette persuaded her mother to let her pay him a visit. One morning Diderot received a letter addressed in the handwriting he knew so well; they had given in and were coming to see him. He immediately dispatched an answer, not devoid of bitterness.

> In truth, Mademoiselle Champion, you did love me. Then devote to reflection the quarter hour that will precede your visit. Examine yourself, examine me, and remember that if I have lost your heart, the greatest danger you can run is to give me your hand. What makes a husband and wife happy is their mutual tenderness. I have more than ever for you, but I have reason to think that you no longer have any for me. . . . I am the man who desires most what you desire least, to be your husband.

Either Nanette had not taken back her heart, or else she decided to run the risk. The visit took place, and the lovebirds flew into each other's arms. For an hour they kissed and caressed each other with tenderness and passion. How foolish they had been! How happy

they were now! They would always be sweethearts. Nothing could
ever part them again. They would be wed secretly.

The ceremony took place on the sixth of November 1743, at
midnight, in a small church on the Ile de la Cité that specialized in
clandestine marriages. Immediately after, the young couple moved
to their new apartment on the Rue Saint-Victor. And so, about two
years after Diderot had met Antoinette, ten months after he had
sworn to get her by hook or by crook, his wishes were consummated
and he began to taste the joys of wedded bliss. Not many weeks
went by before both husband and wife regretted bitterly an ill-
assorted match.

As a wooer, Diderot seems weak-kneed. In his letters to Nanette,
he is constantly pleading with her, using in turn reproaches, flattery,
coaxing, oaths, menaces of self-destruction, and especially tears. At
one point, the pathetic failing of effect, he replies sharply, but then,
after a few harsh words, softens again pitifully. The idyllic tone
expected of sweethearts occurs once only, when he writes from
Langres that he has set aside an hour each night to think of her
and kiss her and talk sweetly with her of their love.

Why was Diderot so tenacious about marrying Antoinette? His
own daughter's explanation, "that he never could get her in any
other way," is of dubious worth; she was scarcely in a position to
know the secrets of her parents' youth. The reasons are deeper. For
one thing, he was growing older; at thirty the passionate desire for
personal liberty was perhaps dulling and the romance of bohemian
life losing its savor. Ten years of this had yielded little fruit. He was
still without a vocation, even without orientation. From the depths
of the past, memories of a warm fireside and the tender happiness
of family life came upon him in more and more nostalgic waves.
True, his letters from Langres show a somewhat ironical and bored
reaction to his old home. But at thirty a man is detached from his
childhood family and longs for a hearth of his own, for the care
and companionship of a wife. At thirty, there is a new need, for
stability and security. What then? The bourgeois, whom Diderot
thought he had buried, is not dead?

There were other reasons. Diderot considered it a test of his
mettle, as a man, not to bow to the challenge of opposition. And
then, another simple thing. Although the letters to Antoinette, compared with those to a later inamorata, Sophie Volland, do not ring
true, still Diderot loved "Tonton"—or at least he imagined he did.
This love he based on Antoinette's beauty, evidently, but also—

amazingly enough—on what he considered her intelligence and fine character. Truly, no man ever found self-deception easier than Diderot!

When one considers the long years of misunderstanding, the unhappiness and bitter quarrels that lay before them, little dreamed of the day they were secretly united, it seems remarkable that Diderot could have been so deluded, that two people so utterly dissimilar and so poorly mated could have come together.

Nanette, even before her marriage, had revealed herself as jealous, suspicious, quarrelsome, and harsh. Her education, tastes, and friends were mediocre and plebeian, her intelligence and interests limited. Rousseau, who was already living with Thérèse Levasseur, the woman who was to bear him five children, came to see the newly weds and was at a loss to understand his friend's infatuation. He called Nanette "a shrew and a fishwife." He himself did not feel the necessity for marrying Thérèse. Mme. de Vandeul, in revenge for this insult to her mother, later called Thérèse "that wench of a dishwasher."

People of such opposing natures were destined to quarrel on every little point; and they did, from the first weeks of their marriage, and even before their marriage. Antoinette's piety and passion for neatness about the house were minor causes for bickering. But the great storms were not to come until Diderot started on a long string of infidelities. Then he would come home and complain, with charming naïveté, of her unreasonable temper and lack of understanding. Their quarrels were so bitter and furious that often husband and wife spoke not a word to each other for weeks on end. Diderot had fought for a year to get married, and now he was to fight for the rest of his life to escape the consequences of marriage!

The first infidelities probably took place a few months after their union. These were mere *passades*, inconsequential affairs of a night's duration. Diderot could not understand why anyone should create a terrific fuss for so little. He soon forgot that he had made Nanette leave her business because it forced her to receive too many strange men.

Possessing only Diderot's account, his biographers have heaped scorn upon Antoinette, whose version of their married life remains unspoken. The only word in her favor comes from her daughter. "She was a noble and proud soul, with a frankness that never knew the dissimulation of polite formalities"—a neat way of describing her lack of social refinement. "Solitude, the domestic cares to which she was condemned by a meager income, the chagrin of my father's love affairs, her ignorance of worldly manners, had all embittered her temper, and scolding had become a habit."

Antoinette's limitations are clear enough. Diderot's blame—too often lost sight of—lay in making little effort to understand her and to conciliate their opposing dispositions. He was never a patient person, and lacked completely the instinct of delicacy without which intimacy begins to grate. Nor did he have, at least in the beginning, proper appreciation for the real qualities she possessed as an efficient and devoted wife. There were no complaints from Antoinette because of their poverty. Frequently she remained hungry, or supped on bread so that he could have more the next day. They could not afford coffee at home, but she did not want to deprive him of a pleasure to which he was accustomed; every day he had six sous so that he could drink his coffee, discuss politics and philosophy, and watch the chess players at the Café de la Régence.

The truth is that no matter whom Diderot would have married, he was too inconstant by nature, too libertine by temperament ever to have been a faithful husband. Perhaps a Parisienne, of higher social rank, would have resigned herself and taken the usual revenge. Antoinette, raised in a more modest and less cosmopolitan milieu, and perhaps truly in love with her husband, could not suffer his estrangement without developing a profound bitterness.

During the first three years of his marriage, Diderot's income came largely from hackwork (he mentions some kind of a *mémoire* written for one Gabriel Poulain, "businessman") and from three translations. Thanks to his knowledge of English, he translated and published in 1743 Temple Stanyan's mediocre *History of Greece;* in 1745, Shaftesbury's *Inquiry Concerning Merit and Virtue;* and in 1746, in collaboration with Toussaint and Eidous, the *Dictionary of Medicine* of Dr. Robert James. The latter was done for the publishing firm of Briasson, David, and Durand, which was soon to assume an important role in his life. There is also some possibility that for a time Diderot again entered a solicitor's office (an idea he had assured his father he was contemplating); but this is quite uncertain.

These precarious contributions were scarcely sufficient to meet the additional expenses caused by two events in the Diderot family. The first was the birth of a daughter, Angélique, in August 1744, just nine months after their marriage. She survived only six weeks.

Diderot

The second, a year later, was the intrusion of another woman into Diderot's life. She was Mme. de Puisieux, the wife of a fellow-translator. Frivolous, coquettish, and a writer of trashy, sophisticated novels, she became Diderot's mistress and an additional source of torment.

CHAPTER 4

Call

to

Arms

1

THE YEAR 1745 was destined to be a fateful one. It was on the twenty-fifth of February of that year that the roving eye of Louis XV was caught by the sensuous face and supple figure of one of the younger court ladies. Born in the Third Estate, Antoinette Poisson had captivated and married an aristocrat, Lenormant d'Etiolles. But she was not to stop there. In eighteenth-century France, women ruled all, and significant matters were often determined (as Diderot wrote, with customary *esprit gaulois,* in one of his letters), "by a woman's lifting her skirts." Within a short time, by favor of the king, Mademoiselle Poisson was to become the marquise de Pompadour, for twenty ill-starred years ruler of France in all but name. And it was in this same auspicious year that occurred the most important event in Diderot's life. To state it is anticlimactic: he was asked to assist in an advisory capacity in the translation of Chambers' *Cyclopædia.* But from this trivial incident, an unsuspected climax was to develop, a climax to the whole struggle between the decaying aristocratic world of Louis XV, and the rising middle-class world of his humble subject, Denis Diderot.

In 1728 and 1729, an Englishman, Ephraim Chambers, had published in five volumes his *Cyclopædia,* or *Universal Dictionary of the Arts and Sciences.* This was far from the first effort of its kind. Learned compilations had been numerous in the middle ages, and nowhere more so than in France; in the seventeenth century, Moréri and Bayle had written two great "Dictionaries." Chambers' work, however, although based on preceding ones, was more thorough, clearer, and better composed, having such new features as cross-references. As a result, it had gone through several editions. In January of 1745 another Englishman, John Mills, and a German from Danzig, Gottfried Sellius, went to Le Breton, a leading publisher, and proposed making a translation of it into French. The work was to consist of four volumes of text and one of plates. Le Breton welcomed the suggestion and a prospectus was issued in the spring of that year. Suddenly Mills, who was completely ignorant of French formalities relating to printing licenses, or "privileges," became suspicious of the fact that theirs bore only the name of Le Breton. In August, he dared to ask for some money, as a sort of guarantee, but the none too scrupulous publisher turned down his request. Hot words were exchanged and when Mills started to draw his sword, Le Breton fell to with his cane. The maltreated Englishman demanded prosecution for attempted murder, but Le Breton had powerful connections who quashed the indictment. They even did him the service of having the contract canceled by Chancellor d'Aguesseau and the old privilege annulled by the king's Council of State, so that a new work could be undertaken.

In October, Le Breton's planning became more ambitious. The revised work was now projected in ten volumes; to cover the investment, he associated three other publishers in the undertaking, Briasson, Durand, and David, keeping a half interest for himself. A new license was granted Le Breton in January 1746.

Although Sellius continued to furnish some translations, a new editor had to be found. The actual work of editing the translation of Chambers was confided to an economist, the abbé Gua de Malves, who held a chair at the Collège de France. In December 1745, Jean Le Rond d'Alembert, and then Diderot, who had been translating for Briasson, were engaged as advisors. Diderot and d'Alembert were to criticize the translations carried out under his direction, as well as those that Sellius was entrusted with making from Harris' *Lexicum.* For this work, each was to receive one hundred livres a month.

In August 1747, the abbé Gua de Malves was forced to resign, following a series of disagreements with his collaborators. With his obfuscated metaphysical mind, he had succeeded only in amassing a pile of hopelessly confused notes.

At that point Briasson suggested Diderot as the man for the job. Le Breton, who had come to respect his clear thinking powers and his knowledge of English, agreed to offer him the editorship.

"We want you to continue where the work was left off and complete the translation and revision. Do you feel capable of such a large job and are you willing to undertake it?"

Diderot accepted at once, and inquired about the remuneration. The impecunious philosopher needed no further persuasion. The contract meant security for his little family. The days were over when he could indulge in happy-go-lucky living. He was a *pater familias*, a man of responsibilities, a bourgeois returning to the fold, and the innermost aspiration of every bourgeois is security. A contract was worked out. Diderot would receive 7,200 livres: 1,200 on publication of the first volume, the rest at the rate of 144 livres a month. Thus the anticipated duration of the job was three and a half years. On October 16, 1747, he was officially appointed editor-in-chief, with d'Alembert as assistant in charge of mathematics.

To Diderot, the entire accumulation of material, as he reviewed it in his mind, seemed to lack shape and unity. That terrifying enthusiasm of his was aroused. For hours he paced his room and walked the streets, bursting with a great idea. Then he went to Le Breton and proposed that the whole translation be sacked. He argued persuasively.

"The French are great enough to write their own encyclopedia! My plan is to do something never before attempted. No one man, in a brief lifetime, can possibly embrace all knowledge, much less set it down in writing. We will have each subject treated by the most eminent specialist in that field. Our encyclopedia will be not only the best work of its kind, but the greatest collaborative intellectual enterprise in the history of mankind, a synthesis of French genius, the monument of our century!"

We do not have Diderot's exact words, but we can safely assume he reasoned along these lines. And so was conceived the model of all encyclopedias, and the cooperative undertaking that was to produce the first, the greatest, and the most important of all such works.

Wily publisher that he was, Le Breton immediately realized the financial possibilities of the novel idea wrapped in the enthusiastic philosopher's verbose eloquence.

After much calculation, it was agreed that the work would be in eight volumes and have at least six hundred plates—another feature Diderot insisted upon as increasing a thousand-fold its practical value. The plates were to be largely in connection with technical information on the trades, a subject never before included in encyclopedias, but one dear to his heart. Furthermore, he decided, we shall not be satisfied with a mere compilation of scientific and historical facts. They must be digested, related by cross references, coordinated into a system of human knowledge, exposed according to general principles that will guide all our work. Thus we will gr ther together and unify all of man's scattered knowledge, and leave a priceless heritage for which posterity will always be grateful to us.

Diderot's appointment, and the new privilege, had to be approved by the aged and pious chancellor d'Aguesseau. He interviewed the aspiring editor, was won over by his fervor and eloquence, even though it was in June of that year that Diderot had been secretly denounced to the police by his parish priest as a dangerous free-thinker and "a monster of impiety." In April 1748 a privilege for the new work was issued.

For the tremendous task ahead, no man was better fitted, by his energy and enthusiasm, by his versatile talents and encyclopedic interests, than Diderot. Realizing the proportions of the work, he set about securing collaborators of the quality he wanted. He already had d'Alembert, famous as one of the greatest mathematicians of the eighteenth century; famous, too, for his liaison with the passionate and faithless Julie de Lespinasse, who has breathed her ardent soul into her love letters. D'Alembert was the illegitimate child of the witty and licentious *salonnière*, the marquise de Tencin, who abandoned him on the steps of a church and shunned him all her life. He and Diderot were good friends, very good friends, con- sidering the character of the mathematician; although witty, generous, and a man of honor, d'Alembert was cold, reserved, and independent, irritable and sharp-tongued.

To d'Alembert was entrusted the essential preliminary of develop- ing a system of classification of knowledge on whose lines the *Encyclopedia* would be built. The result was the separately pub- lished *Discours préliminaire*, one of the significant works of the century. Equally important in the early development of the enter- prise was d'Alembert's prestige which enabled Diderot to induce recognized figures to collaborate. Theology was handled in the early stages by Mallet, Yvon, de Prades and Rastré, later by Diderot himself. Daubenton was entrusted with natural history, La Condamine with physical sciences. Still in search of famous names, Diderot later secured articles on literature, among the best in the *Encyclopedia*, from Marmontel, the author of two rather insipid novels, famous because of their condemnation by the Sorbonne. To Rousseau were given the articles on music. Another on Nature was extracted from the great scientist and popularizer, Buffon. Montesquieu could be persuaded to contribute only one mediocre piece, on taste, but the spirit of his works dominates the political side of the *Encyclopedia*, just as that of Buffon pervades the scientific aspect. Turgot, a good friend of d'Alembert, wrote five articles, all excellent, on philosophy and economics. What about Voltaire? The "leader" of the philosophic movement was, as usual, away from Paris, out of contact with the vanguard of new developments. He was, at the moment, at Cirey, and later went to spend several years at the court of Frederick the Great. Through the efforts of d'Alembert, he was persuaded to add his weight to the enterprise. In fact, prompted by his great "party spirit" and his desire to "crush the infamous" *(écrasez l'infâme)*, he soon came to see in the *Encyclopedia* the great rallying point of all who were opposed to fanaticism, superstition, and current abuses. Besides, secure in his world-wide fame, Voltaire felt that it would scarcely injure him if he lent a helping hand to such an obscure and "right-thinking" man as Diderot. Voltaire's enthusiasm grew, lasted from 1755 to 1758, and then suddenly collapsed, when he found himself disappointed with the results. His concrete contributions were forty-three typically Voltairean articles on subjects such as "wit" and "grace."

Diderot still had the lion's share of the job. This included, first of all, direction of the work, the obtaining and correcting of contributors' articles, the task of cross references, the unification into an organized whole. But he was more than editor; he was, next to Jaucourt, the most fertile contributor. He wrote articles on almost every subject, his major concern being philosophy and the trades.

In the salons of Paris, the *Encyclopedia* was the favorite topic of conversation. Diderot, only recently an obscure translator, suddenly found himself a leading literary figure. He had started out on this project with the purely practical intention of earning some money by hackwork. Now he was inflamed by a grandiose scheme for a gigantic production that would spread truth and knowledge and destroy the superstitions and errors that chain a suffering humanity. The more Diderot thought of it, the more the *Encyclopedia* appeared to him the great, perhaps the only affair of his life.

2

It was Diderot's yearning to live and think independently that had brought about his revolt against the ties of tradition, family, and upbringing. A dozen years had passed, restless, fallow years. At the age of twenty-two, Voltaire had written a successful tragedy. Diderot, at thirty-two, had as yet produced nothing. Late in attaining maturity and lacking self-confidence, he now put one rather timid foot forward. The initial impulse came, as may be expected, from his English readings. In 1745, he published a translation of one of his favorite works, Shaftesbury's *Inquiry Concerning Merit and Virtue*, under the title, *An Essay on Merit and Virtue*. Because of the addition of Diderot's comments, and the affinity of many of their ideas, at this time, it may be regarded as the earliest expression of his own thought. It was, incidentally, the first of four works written to obtain money to satisfy the demands of his mistress, Mme. de Puisieux. The translation is preceded by an ironical dedication to his brother. The opposition that existed in his own mind between his family and his ideas is only too clear in this foreword. His marriage and the *Essay on Merit and Virtue* are the two events that signal a final breaking off of home ties.

In Diderot's thinking, from the outset throughout its final phases, man never ceases to hold the center of the stage. He has been justly called the greatest French humanist since Rabelais and Montaigne. It is quite natural then that this first publication should deal with the subject nearest his heart—morals.

The development of moral thinking in France, during the early eighteenth century, can best be explained as a multiple reaction against the intellectual and social atmosphere that prevailed during the long reign of Louis XIV. Revulsion against the religious absolutism and moral severity of the Court led to the dissoluteness and corruption that prevailed during the regency of the duke of Orléans (1715–1723). The Church itself, and the prestige of religion along with it, dipped low in public esteem, as a result of the bitter wrangling between Jesuits and Jansenists, the hysterical public "miracles" of a mystical Jansenist group, and the excessive flagellations of fanatical penitents. Religious dogma was no longer sacred, or even respectable. One basis for the new orientation was found in "libertinism," a persistent current of free thought in the seventeenth century that maintained a link with the naturalistic humanism of such Renaissance sceptics as Montaigne and, beyond him, with the school of Epicurus. Most called for was the separation of morality from religion, and the establishment of ethics on a rational, secular basis. The great Protestant scholar and sceptic, Bayle, gave clear expression to this demand. Descartes, before him, had urged an approach to morals through the scientific study of man, and La Mettrie was to take up his suggestion.

In a word, the demand was for common sense, for an understanding of man as he really is, with his frank egoism, unconquerable passions and thirst for happiness in this the only life he is sure of. The love of luxury and indulgence in sensual pleasures that characterized the society of the regency could stomach no absolute sanctions of a transcendental revelation. Part and parcel of all this was a trend toward sentimentality. It was less evident among the aristocracy than among the rising bourgeoisie; but it was destined to flourish—passing through such moralists as Vauvenargues and Lemaître de Claville, through the sentimental novel and comedy, the art of Chardin and Greuze, reaching its explosive climax in Rousseau. The eighteenth century was already taking its characteristic form: a scorn for systematic rationalism tied to a worship of science, with a current of sentimentalism that was strong in some writers and left others untouched. The chief product of this mixture was, ironically, rationalistic speculation on science, religion, morals, cosmology—and sentiment. Utilitarian "common sense" yielded a strange harvest of sour pessimism or gossamer-thin optimism—often a combination of both in the same man, as in d'Holbach or Rousseau. Rational naturalism and sentimental moralism flourished in rivalry and in alliance. If the end result was an undigested mass of inspirations and brilliant ideas, there is little matter for surprise. A new age of man was being forged. There was, in fact, much more consistent direction than in the similar revolutionary upheavals of the twentieth century. For if the men of the Enlightenment, like ourselves, knew not where they were going, at least they knew what they wanted to leave behind.

In Shaftesbury, the only one of the English deists who emphasized morals, Diderot found his first master. Shaftesbury's ethical theory was rational, built solely on human nature—although, we must add, on an optimistic, not an empirical view of human nature. For he refused to believe in natural evil or moral wickedness. He held that virtue is part of universal harmony, a relationship of part to whole, of that within to that without. Beauty, truth, and good are identical, and absolute. Diderot agreed that they were related, but most often denied they were absolute, or that we have a special "sense" for perceiving them. Since "natural affections" are good, man is naturally good; and although corrupted by "self-affections" (which in moderation are biologically necessary), he is perfectible. Man is also possessed of an innate sympathy for his fellow creatures, and is able thereby to overcome his egoism. Born to be a social being, his happiness is in consequence a function of his "benevolence" toward others.

Diderot's own reactions are developed in his introduction to the translation, and in his notes. Religion and virtue, he insists, are separable, and virtue is more important. There is in man an innate feeling of right (conscience), and of justice. Evidently Locke has not yet started to work on Diderot; conscience is regarded as an ultimate, not a derivative faculty, and this ethical formalism will persist as one current in his thought. Passions and self-interest are useful, even necessary to self-preservation. Pleasures are good, for man's essential need is happiness; but the individual's sacrifice for the general good is the best assurance of his own happiness. Virtue—what is good for all—is always good for the individual, too. This morality of "enlightened self-interest" was being accepted by the majority of French thinkers. Optimism, utilitarianism, and theism were the ingredients of the desired formula. It allowed ample liberty for individual satisfactions that were not socially harmful.

Virtue inevitably produces happiness, and vice, misery. This absolutism is again characteristic of ethical formalism. Doubtless Diderot is a humanist, far more than a rigorous moralist. It is not virtue that interests him solely, but also happiness. He is a hedonist and utilitarian, in ethics, more than a pre-Kantian formalist. But the two opposing positions are, and will always be confused in his thinking. If it were proved that virtue could lead to unhappiness, and vice to happiness, then he would, in theory, renounce his morality of virtue. But that was a possibility he refused to entertain realistically. Here is where rationalism dominates observation, and feeling overrides reason. Diderot was enamored of virtue, to the point of breaking into tears at the thought of a virtuous deed. His position, then, is determined not by logic, but by the needs of his own inner being. He must have virtue, and can allow no other possibility. He rejoices at finding proof of this theory in Tacitus' statement that none of the cruel emperors of Rome was happy, and concludes: "No compromise. Either we accept the way of life of this prince, if he was happy, or agree with his historian, that on plumbing the hearts of tyrants, we find incurable wounds and . . . the continual remorse of crime."

For the time being, then, Diderot has embraced an aristocratic, optimistic and social morality. Evil is denied, except in local terms. When a tiger destroys its prey, there is no good nor evil except for the individuals involved; the act is part of the total harmony of things. Moral ideas have then no reality in nature; they exist only by virtue of human mind and human physiology. Here Diderot is already headed towards an empirical ethic and his eventual immoralism, which he as yet avoids by his theory of virtue and enlightened self-interest. He rejects final causes, and declares: "I must have causes particular to man." If good and evil do not have an absolute existence, they exist in relation to us, and therefore we must have a morality equally in relation to ourselves. Ethical systems, such as the Christian, which are based on an abstract, metaphysical theory, will be powerless to control men; we must have a realistic morality, built to man's own measure, bound to his special instincts and requirements. A human morality will respond to man's needs—as an individual, and as a social being. But Diderot rejects atheism as incompatible with his view of harmony and virtue, and even more, as a dogmatism that assumes an understanding of the universe that we do not have. Here is a stand that Diderot will always hold to, even when violating it himself: our ignorance is neither judge nor limit of the things that be.

How can such an ethic be put into effect, so that man may start living according to its utopian tenets? Diderot shared an illusion common to his century (and still not entirely dispelled), that we can control morals by legislation. To eliminate evil-doers, it is up to our lawmakers to legislate so that they will find no profit in their actions. In a well-ordered society, the criminal cannot hurt others without hurting himself.

Diderot's moral theory rests on a base of optimism. It assumes that human nature, though egoistic, is not evil, and that men need only to be shown where their best course lies; that they will let themselves be swayed in action by objective judgment rather than by passion or egoism. In spite of frequent waverings, he held to this opinion throughout his life. "No, dear friend, nature has not made us vicious; it is bad education, bad examples, bad legislation that have corrupted us. If that is an error, at least I am glad to find it at the bottom of my heart, and I should be very sorry if experience or reflection ever disillusioned me. What would I become? Either I should have to live alone, or believe myself constantly surrounded by wicked men; neither prospect suits me." It is evident at what school Jean-Jacques Rousseau learned the ideas which he was to develop into the most powerful philosophy of the century.

Christian morality with its conception of sin appeared to frustrate in so many ways what seemed essential human needs. Diderot did not realize that it is made far closer to the average man's measure than his own abstractions, and controls him in a more effective manner—through his emotions. Diderot came to feel that virtue was entirely unrelated to religion, and it was virtue that he loved. "When he spoke of virtue," wrote the *littérateur* Marmontel in his famous memoirs, "I cannot convey what charm was imparted to him by the eloquence of his feelings. His soul was in his eyes, on his lips. Never did a face better paint goodness of heart."

Diderot scoffs at cynics who point to the sufferings of upright men and to the prosperity of wicked ones. The recompense of virtue lies in itself, in the happiness it unfailingly gives. The punishment of vice, too, is in itself, and is inevitable. It comes sometimes in the physical and moral degeneration inflicted by an outraged nature, always in the castigation of the conscience. The cry of conscience and the idea of virtue are present in all men, no matter how vicious.

This passionate love of virtue again betrays a persistence of fundamental bourgeois traits in Diderot. It is intimately associated with the exaggerated sentimentalism and emotionalism in vogue with the French middle class. Diderot's reactions were characterized by a sudden flood of emotional energy, as when one presses an electric button. "If the spectacle of injustice sometimes transports me with such indignation that I lose my judgment and that in my delirium I would kill, I would annihilate, the spectacle of equity fills me with gentle emotion, inflames me with such an ardor and enthusiasm that it would cost me little to lose my life: then it seems to me that my heart expands within me, that it swims; an indefinable sensation, sudden and delightful, traverses me; I can scarcely breathe; over the entire surface of my body arises a kind of shudder, especially at the summit of my forehead; and then the symptoms of admiration and pleasure mingle on my face with those of joy, and my eyes are filled with tears."

In spite of this lachrymose facility, Diderot's *sensibilité* was not of the sickly variety. It generally leads to a fine enthusiasm. "Do you think," he cries, referring to the use of stenography in English Parliamentary debate, "that a man would dare to propose a harmful project or oppose a useful measure in front of a whole nation?" More than once he exclaims that he would rather die than retract his writings. How could he brand himself a coward before the world? How could he refuse a sacrifice for truth that a hundred fanatics have made for a lie?

Diderot's intellectual attitude may be resumed as a tendency toward violent reactions to ideas and to beauty. "Everything that bears the mark of truth, grandeur or virtue moves me and carries me away." It is natural, then, that he should defend human passions in the *Essay on Merit and Virtue* and in many later writings. He is really defending his own temperament. "I can take nothing with moderation, neither pain nor pleasure, and if I let myself be called a philosopher without blushing, it is a nickname that they have given me . . . It seems that my mind is wild when the wind blows strong. Whatever the weather, that is always the state of my heart." Like Dante, he hates lukewarm souls, prefers even extremes in evil to a namby-pamby moderation that can result only in mediocre living and in mediocre art.

Anything that passion inspires, I can forgive: only the consequences shock me. And then, you know, I have always been the apologist of strong passions; they alone move me. The arts of genius are born and extinguished with them; it is they who make the criminal and the enthusiast who paints him in his true colors. If the atrocious actions which dishonor human nature are committed because of them, it is by them too that we are carried away on the marvelous flights that elevate human nature. The mediocre man lives and dies like a brute. He has done nothing to distinguish himself while he lived; there remains nothing of him to talk about when he is dead; his name is pronounced no more, the place of his burial is unknown, lost among the grass. If I had to choose between Racine, a bad husband, bad father, false friend and sublime poet, and Racine, a good father, good husband, good friend and ordinary man, I prefer the former. Of Racine, the wicked man, what remains? Nothing. Of Racine, the genius? His work is immortal.

Here is a first glimpse of Diderot as a forerunner of the romantic generation.

3

Despite the requirements of his tremendous undertaking, Diderot found time to continue his own thinking and writing. From 1745 to 1750, his thought was dominated by the religious question. Morals were his greatest interest, from first to last; but after freeing himself from the transcendental ethic of Christianity, he had to explore the nature of the universe and the meaning of man's position in it.

Diderot was not that fortunate type of sceptic whose religion drops away effortlessly and overnight; nor was he one of those who emerge after an intense but brief crisis. Rarely has a sceptic experienced a more painful liberation than his; for years he wrestled with the problem of God.

In the *Essay on Merit and Virtue*, Diderot had declared himself a Christian, but he evidently takes that term to signify belief in the moral philosophy of Jesus Christ and not allegiance to the dogma and hierarchy of any Church. True, he defends Christianity warmly; only it is a weak defense that relies not on the truth of that religion but its usefulness: religion still seems to him a help to virtuous living. In reality, Diderot has retained only belief in God, the immortality of the soul, the idea of future punishment and reward. By founding morality on man's natural and social requirements, he definitely renounces the Christian doctrine of virtue and vice based on absolute revelation and transcendental evaluation.

Mme. de Puisieux, Diderot's mistress, was a source of anguish to his wife, but posterity—and this would be Diderot's own opinion—should be grateful to her. Capricious and frivolous, she kept plaguing him for money as the price of her favors. Since his income was barely enough to keep his family going, writing would have to supplement it. The first result of this pressure had been the *Essay on Merit and Virtue*. But so paltry a sum as fifty louis did not last long in the fingers of a coquette. Diderot was forced to set to work again. The result this time was his first original piece, the *Philosophic Thoughts*, written—or collected from accumulated notations—between Good Friday and Easter Sunday of 1746. This work netted Diderot—or rather Mme. de Puisieux—another fifty louis.

The *Philosophic Thoughts*, a vigorous, yet withal a cautious work, reveals that within the preceding months Diderot has taken a decisive step along the road of disbelief. Now he has definitely renounced the religion he was clinging to in the earlier work. Now Christianity is indicted before the tribunal of Reason, and found wanting. The very purpose of Diderot's new book is to point out the "contradictions" and "absurdities" of Christianity, to cast doubt upon the historical integrity of the Scriptures, and to demonstrate the trifling value of miracles where rational proof would serve the purpose much better. The "thoughts," as a casual selection will indicate, reflect the spirit of the times, the tone and approach of the anti-religious brochures which were decidedly *à la mode*.

How ridiculous are they who castigate their flesh, to appease a God of love. . . . There are no true Christians. . . . What has never been questioned has never been proven. . . . Who is impious? The Christian in Asia, the Moslem in Europe. . . . If the religion you preach to me is true, its truth can be put in evidence and proved by invincible reasons ; find reasons, instead of annoying me with miracles. . . . Faith is a chimerical principle that does not exist in nature. . . . If there are a hundred thousand damned for one saved, the devil still has the advantage, without having sacrificed his son. . . . A true religion should be eternal, universal and self-evident. . . . How to reconcile eternal punishment with God's infinite mercy? . . .

The tone of the *Philosophic Thoughts* is rigidly rationalistic. "Leave your miracles, and let us reason. I am more sure of my judgment than of my eyes. . . . The criterion of truth belongs not to the senses but the mind." He wants faith to be based entirely on reason, not realizing they cannot be the same, anxious above all to reject authority as a basis of belief. He attacks Christianity, here and elsewhere, on social grounds (the horrors of fanaticism and obscurantism, the parasitism of hermits and celibates), and on humanistic grounds (the unnaturalism of asceticism and humility). Anticipating Rousseau, he ridicules teaching small children the concept of God. Reflecting the rebellious, inquiring spirit of the age, he writes defiantly: "Scepticism is the first step towards truth." Throughout, he seems to feel that religion is a vestigial structure that no longer touches meaningfully on modern life. In "thoughts" like these there was little originality except in the particular turn of phrase. The English deists, and numerous French writers and pamphleteers, including Voltaire, had preceded Diderot along this line. Their criticism is narrowly rationalistic and bears witness to scant understanding of the religious impulse, which is essential in man, whether or not we approve of religions. They consider religion a fabrication springing from superstition, ignorance and guileful dupery, imposed by force and fraud.

Diderot had to reject Christianity. Its spirit was opposed to his own naturalism in all fields, its transcendentalism and authoritarianism were contrary to the deepest tendencies of his mind. He was hostile even to religious art. "Christian art has depreciated nature! " he cries. Yet even here there is a curious complexity in Diderot. He had certainly experienced the religious emotions, and later in life admits that the experience still occurred to him. He understands the power of ritual over men. The most effective enemies of religion are not the philosophers, he later argued, in the *Salon of 1765*, but those who would destroy images, processions, and the whole apparatus of cult. "Cut out these sensual symbols, and the rest will boil down to a metaphysical gibberish that will take as many strange forms as there are minds." He describes the effect of ritual:

> I have never seen that long line of priests in sacerdotal robes, those young acolytes dressed in their white stoles . . . ; that crowd that precedes and follows them in religious silence ; so many men, their brows prostrated against the earth ; I have never heard that grave and pathetic chant of the priests, and the affectionate reply of an infinity of voices, of men, women, girls, and children, without being moved and shaken deep down inside. me, without tears coming to my eyes. There is in all that something great, sombre, solemn, melancholy. . . . My friend, if we love truth better than beauty, let us pray to God for the iconoclasts.

Diderot agreed with the sceptics of his age that religion was a great error of the human mind, born of the credulousness of dupes and the cleverness of impostors. But in the *Encyclopedia* he was to go beyond this narrow view. There he sees primitive, superstitious religious feeling as an inevitable product of society at a certain level. It was commonly held that the origin of all human activity had to be accounted for on psychological grounds, that social influences only guided their later evolution. The psychological explanation, to Diderot, seemed a matter of primitive imagination working on natural phenomena. But the source could not have been fear primarily, as many claimed, else religion would have existed before society, and there would have been no feeling of love for the gods. It was rather a combination of hope, fear, love, and hate, toward what helped or hindered the food production and safety of the group. The objects of cult were mostly useful objects, although Diderot supplements this utilitarian view by taking some account of animism and hero worship. At first a general pantheism, primitive religion degenerated into polytheism and priest-led cults. The priest's sole purpose was to further his ambition for power. He deformed the religious feeling by foisting ceremonies, sacrifices, and superstitions upon it. Religion is then, for Diderot, in his later and more mature work, a normal function of the human mind, a social fact that he attempts to account for, on psychological, social, and utilitarian grounds.

Far more delicate is the task of interpreting Diderot's stand in relation to the deity, in the *Philosophic Thoughts*. Some critics would have him a deist, others make him out to be a thorough-going atheist. Diderot declares himself a Christian, but that was an only too obvious sop to the censors. To call him an atheist at this stage, as some recent critics have been inclined to do, is equally rash, since the real conflict in Diderot's mind is the very marrow of this little book. If his purpose in not expressing outright atheism was only to deceive the censors, he not only bungled that job, but also succeeded in concealing his true thought from his readers. There is, however, no doubt that Diderot now views the atheist's logic with a more sympathetic eye. Using Bayle's method of "impartial" presentation of both sides of controversial questions, he lists a series of atheistic arguments. It is just as easy, according to the atheist, to believe in the eternity of the universe as it is to believe in the eternity of an extra-natural spirit. True, it is difficult to see how motion by itself could engender the universe. But the solution offered by the idea of an inconceivable being is no solution at all. Furthermore, argues the atheist, if God's providence is responsible for physical order, it is also responsible for moral disorder. Diderot does not take into account the Christian point of view: a perfect moral order could exist only if God deprived man of his free will, of the very human status Diderot is anxious to emphasize. Perhaps he already holds that man has no free will, and that God, if he exists, is responsible for a necessarily determined order.

The deist's view is expounded with as much vigor as the atheist's. He accepts the world as a machine, finding in its order the best proof of a Maker. Experimental science, he insists, not metaphysics, has given the lie to atheism. Most significantly, Diderot puts Malpighi and Nieuwentit, two great biologists, next to Newton. The problem of life, he implies, holds the key to the great riddle. "The discovery of germ cells has dissipated one of the most powerful arguments of atheism." Life is a phenomenon that matter and motion cannot produce. It must come from what is already living, and in the last analysis, from God. Diderot gives a new direction to the teleological proof of God. Borrowing an analogy from Pascal, he uses it to develop further the conclusions of Réaumur, Bonnet, and other students of insectology, which had become popular in the 1740's. In organic life, there is not only a complexity, but a purpose, or finalism, that is far more convincing than the purely physical proofs of order in nature.

"You believe firmly that man thinks, do you not?" asks the deist. "And yet you would have a difficult time proving that he thinks any more than an ant does."

"What does that have to do with the question?"

"It follows that if the universe—what am I saying, the universe! —if the wing of a butterfly presents traces of an Intelligence which are a thousand times clearer than your proofs that man thinks, it would be a thousand times more stupid to deny that God exists than to deny that your fellow-men think. I appeal to your conscience. Have you ever noticed in the reasoning or actions of any man more intelligence, order, sagacity, consistency than in the mechanism of an insect? Is not the Divinity as clearly imprinted in the eye of a mite as the faculty of thought is in the works of the great Newton? What! Is the world, formed, less proof of intelligence than the world, explained? . . .

"Just think that I objected to you only the wing of the butterfly and the eye of a mite, when I could have crushed you with the weight of the universe!"

But the atheist has not spoken his last word. With some enthusiasm, Diderot has him explain the godless creation of the universe as a simple mathematical necessity. Given space, matter, and motion as eternal entities, and an infinity of time, the proper combination to form our universe becomes a mere matter of patience. It is like throwing dice. In the course of an infinite number of throws, every combination must come up. Then the universe becomes a necessary result of chance and time. It is likely that Diderot took this idea from Epicurus or some later disciple, such as Gassendi or Cyrano de Bergerac. Voltaire, in one of his marginal notes, reacted strongly against it. After challenging—incorrectly—Diderot's mathematics, he goes on to note that dice will be only dice. Sand in any combination will be only sand, and never be parrots, monkeys, or men. Here Voltaire has put his finger on the heart of the problem, the same problem that Diderot has realized fully in the analogy with the butterfly's wing. While Diderot seems convinced by the atheist's argument, he realizes that it leaves too much unexplained, beyond mere creation. It still leaves the universe mechanical, not evolutionary; quantitative, not qualitative. It offers no solution to the problem of change and diversity, to the *dynamics* of the universe.

The brusque intrusion of the idea of virtue reveals the inseparable link in Diderot's mind between metaphysics and morality, and the continuing influence of Shaftesbury. The *Philosophic Thoughts* are, in fact, a prolongation of Diderot's notes to the *Essay on Merit and Virtue*. The deist accepts, the sceptic doubts and the atheist denies God. Consequently, comments the Philosopher, "the sceptic has one motive more than the atheist to be virtuous, and one less than the deist."

To explore both sides to the very end, therein lies the joy in the game of thinking. Throughout his life, Diderot's characteristic mode of expression was in loose-jointed thoughts, or tightly knit, brilliant dialogues. Always, his mind worked in *reaction*. This book, like most of his early writings, takes the first and less artistic form; but the section where the atheist and the deist take turns in exposing their arguments already begins to approach the dialogue. In one form or the other, by this multiplication of his personality, Diderot was able to explore without necessarily committing himself to a dogmatic stand. He possessed a magnificent breadth of vision, well expressed in his pregnant phrase, "Every mind has its telescope." Truth, for him, was always too complex ever to be found entirely on one side. In the present case, he is unable to take a stand, seeing elements of truth in both positions, and a clear victory for neither. Atheism and deism stand side by side in his mind.

From Newton's thought stemmed a school of mechanism, and also a school of deism that saw in the mechanism—in a clock-universe—proof of the clockmaker, God. Diderot is not overly impressed by this cosmological, or clock argument, since the atheist can get around it by his chance theory of creation. But in organic life he sees a biological finalism that is not accounted for by atheistic mechanism. Another important deterrent from atheism was the ethical question. As yet scarcely explored by him, it will always remain at the core of his thought. Rousseau, too, held on to religion partly because of morality. This common preoccupation explains much of their affinity and the bitterness of their separation. The two men will evolve in separate directions, as the logic of Diderot's thinking will force him to give up theism and explore new possibilities for ethics. His metaphysical evolution will result from a solution of these three phases: the mechanical, the biological, the ethical.

Always seeing complexity where more dogmatic minds were able to crystallize fixed theories, Diderot gives us occasional hints of a deep tendency toward pantheism. "Enlarge God! " he cries. "See him wherever he is, or say where he is not. The walls of a temple limit his view." This feeling that God *is* Nature could have roots in the tutelage to Shaftesbury, or in a superficial reading of Spinoza. More fundamentally, it springs from Diderot's emotion of awe before the Cosmos, from the enthusiasm that always rides in the same saddle with his rationalism.

Still another path is indicated in Diderot's division of atheists into three categories: true atheists, sceptical atheists, and hypocritical atheists. At various points in the *Philosophic Thoughts,* Diderot's preference leads him strongly into the camp of the "sceptical atheist," who is none other than the agnostic. "I shall never feel any chagrin at not knowing what it is impossible for me to know. . . . I might as well weep over not having four eyes, four legs and two wings. . . . There is neither more nor less danger in being a polytheist than in being an atheist; alone scepticism can guarantee us, in all times and places, from these two opposing excesses." To Diderot, it would seem, reason and senses no longer permitted belief in God; but at the same time, by virtue of their own insufficiency, they indicated that the possibility of a God could not justifiably be denied.

Another aspect of the *Philosophic Thoughts* is Diderot's continued defense of the passions, as a source of virtue, of inspiration in the arts, and as the fountainhead of energy and greatness in all activities. This was a common note at the time, part of the defense of human nature, although rarely have the passions received the *passionate* support Diderot gives them. Actually, it was the much maligned Descartes who had reinvigorated this attitude. Although Descartes submits passions to the will, he recognizes in them, like Diderot, the source of pleasure and an important element of strength in thought. Diderot, not unlike Descartes, would avoid the dangers inherent in excess of passions by organizing them into a kind of harmony (although here his idea is but an abstraction and a banality). Voltaire notes at this point, in the margin of his own copy of the *Philosophic Thoughts,* that the equilibrium Diderot seeks is wisdom, and that it actually excludes enthusiasm.

Diderot's originality lies in exalting the passions as a great natural force, as the principle of creativity. It is, however, much exaggerated to claim that he saw in them a principle of knowledge, opposed to Cartesian rationalism. Rather than opposition between the two, he finds in the passions the life-giving element without which reason is arid and fruitless.

The *Philosophic Thoughts* was highly successful, partly because of what Diderot had to say, partly because of the enthusiastic and highly personal way he said it. Throughout his writings we are impressed by the same union of feeling and thought that characterizes Rousseau's works—the great difference being that Diderot evolves in the sphere of science and philosophy, while Rousseau fired the world with a revolutionary social and political program. The title of the work was itself well chosen. The word "philosophic" had already acquired a combative, sectarian connotation. Tacitly, it seemed to purport a reflection of Voltaire's famous *Philosophic Letters* and a rebuttal of Pascal's *Thoughts.* The work immediately ranged Diderot among the most radical thinkers of his day. Although the *Philosophic Thoughts* was published anonymously, under the imprint of "The Hague," and attributed by some to Voltaire or La Mettrie, the word was spread among the knowing and Diderot's fame increased by a tremendous bound. In fact he was to remain always, in the mind of the uninitiated public, the editor of the *Encyclopedia* and the author of the daring *Philosophic Thoughts* and the *Letter on the Blind.* There were a dozen editions, some pirated, and a number of refutations. On the seventh of July, the Parlement of Paris condemned the work and ordered it burned in effigy, an honor it shared with many other famous books of the century. They accused it of "presenting to restless and bold minds the most absurd and most criminal thoughts of which the depravation of human nature is capable, and of placing all religions, by an affected uncertainty, nearly on the same level, in order to end up by not recognizing any."

4

Giddy with the unexpected success of his book and the toasts of his comrades at the Café Procope and the *Panier fleuri,* the happy philosopher scarcely heard the rumblings of coming disasters.

Shortly after finishing the *Philosophic Thoughts,* he expounded, in a series of apothegms, the deistic view that only "natural religion" is needed or is true. A brief, eleven-page piece, *On the Sufficiency of Natural Religion,* remained unpublished until 1770—by which time it was too conservative to attract notice.

The police were watching him. In June 1747, an agent was put on his trail. His investigations revealed that for some time Diderot had been working on a new book in the same vein as his *Philosophic Thoughts,* that he was a dangerous man who spoke with scorn of "the holy mysteries of our religion," a man who corrupted morals. Worse yet, all these charges were completely confirmed by Diderot's parish priest.

> M. Diderot is a young man who passed his early life in debauchery. At length he attached himself to a girl without money, but of social position, it seems, equal to his, and he married her without the knowledge of his father. The better to hide his so-called marriage, he has rented lodgings in my parish at the house of M. Guillotte ; his wife goes by her maiden name. . . . The remarks that Diderot sometimes makes in this household amply prove that he is at least a deist. He utters blasphemies against Jesus Christ and the Holy Virgin that I would not venture to put in writing. . . . It is true that I have never spoken to this young man, that I do not know him personally, but I am told that he has a great deal of wit and that his conversation is most amusing. In one of his conversations he confessed to being the author of one of the two works condemned by the Parlement and burned about two years ago. I have been assured that for more than a year he has been working on another work still more dangerous to religion.

The book mentioned in the police report was *The Sceptic's Walk.* If one anti-religious work had succeeded, why not try another? This time, he was perhaps a little indiscreet. As he sipped his *café noir* and displayed his eloquence for the benefit of his admiring friends, seated at the round tables of the Procope, he had talked a little too excitedly about his new opus.

"Open in the name of the king! "

The terrifying words, accompanying a forceful knock on his study door, startled Diderot from his meditations. When he opened the door, he was confronted by Monsieur d'Hémery, of the criminal police, and two of his henchmen. D'Hémery wasted few words in demanding the manuscript and Diderot wasted no time in giving it to him. As a reward for this cooperative attitude, d'Hémery's parting shot was an admonition to be careful about the wrath of his parish priest, who was offended by his lack of attentions.

Such is the traditional story, as reported in the frequently unreliable memoirs of Diderot's daughter. There is another possibility: that d'Hémery merely warned him and made him promise never to publish the book, after which Diderot entrusted it for safekeeping to a friend. The actual seizure, according to this version, took place at a later date, in February 1752, after he had again gotten into trouble with the authorities.

Whether or not his manuscript was confiscated at the moment, Diderot was frightened. His work wasted, Mme. de Puisieux kept waiting, the police on his trail—it was too much for his excitable nature. When calm returned, he took an energetic step. He would move to the Rue de l'Estrapade, to a different parish. Perhaps what irked him especially was the precaution he had taken to hide his identity and pass the book off as the work of a convalescent soldier wounded at the battle of Fontenoy! The manuscript eventually passed through the hands of several police officers and administrators but Diderot never saw it again, although he several times requested its return; it was not published until 1830. It had no influence on contemporary thought, since there is no reason to assume it was circulated in manuscript.

The Sceptic's Walk is an allegory, weighty for the most part, but illuminated by a number of brilliant passages. The first section, called "The Lane of Thorns," is a heavy-footed attack on the "irrational absurdities" of religion, and on the obscurities, quarrels, and contradictions of its priests; the latter are branded proud, avaricious, hypocritical, unscrupulous, cruel, and quarrelsome. The travelers on this path of life are pictured as walking with a band around their eyes.

The second part, titled "Chestnut Lane," portrays the philosophical way. Its first section, containing a spirited description of various philosophical viewpoints and an amusing debate between an atheist and a member of The Lane of Thorns, is followed by a stimulating round-table discussion. Curiously, the deist's speech contains the complete program for a civic religion that Rousseau later set forth in his *Social Contract*.

Diderot is still sensitive to the strength of reasoning on many sides, and he clearly does not give his allegiance to any viewpoint. The atheist still argues for the eternity of matter and its mechanical arrangements, the deist for design and order. But Diderot feels that if we are too ignorant to conclude there is a plan, we are also too ignorant to conclude there is none. If he does not lean to the atheist's side, it is again because of the biological and moral problems already raised in the *Philosophic Thoughts*. The structure and purposiveness evident in organisms is simply not explained by the atheist's theory of fortuitous creation.

The pantheist argues that intelligence cannot be derived from brute matter, nor vice versa. Therefore, "the intelligent being and the material being are eternal, these two substances compose the universe, and the universe is God." This is not, as a scoffer had said earlier in the discussion, making insects and molecules divine. On the contrary, "I am working to banish from the world presumptuousness, lies, and gods."

If we may conclude anything from the fact that the Spinozist has the last word, then Diderot is inclining to a peculiar view of the universe that combines the Cartesian dualism with pantheism. At this stage, he has found no other way to explain matter and mind without an act of God. He puts himself in the almost untenable position of doubting teleology and upholding the possibility of mechanism in the physical world, and proclaiming exactly the opposite in the organic world. But if the universe, as a consequence of organic rather than Newtonian teleology, is more than "a machine that has its wheels, its cords, its pulleys, its springs, and its weights" (as he had said in *Philosophic Thoughts*), then the Spinozist, on purely metaphysical grounds, finds himself in a strong position. There is as yet in Diderot's mind no theory of a process of continuous creation, or of gradual development or evolution. Highly organized forms of life do exist, with characteristics different from those of inorganic matter—different in complexity, and much more significantly in the evidence of purpose, of the part designed for a function in the whole, and the whole designed for the ability to carry on life. Their existence can be explained only by a creative power. Either there has been an act of creation on the part of God— a theory Diderot does not definitely reject, but that is weakened by the atheist's arguments—or the divine force of creation must be identified with Nature.

There is only a tentative entertaining of this view, nothing more. Diderot has already held up to ridicule the "absurdities" he thought Spinozism can lead to. He is aware that he is still exploring, still groping.

The atheist's philosophy is also found imperfect on practical grounds. It is here that the moral deterrent recurs as the conclusive and final argument in Diderot's consideration. The atheist returns home, finds his house pillaged and burnt down by the "blind man" (believer) whom he has taught to despise conscience and law when he can get away with it. Diderot still considers deism a necessary support to good morals. Yet his pitiless and inexorable reason is gradually weakening his logical opposition to atheism.

In this section of *The Sceptic's Walk* we also encounter one of his first excursions into psychology. The atheist points out—and Diderot does not disagree with him—that the "soul" is only the result of corporal organization, a position now termed epiphenomenalism. Although possessing functions of thought and imagination beyond those of the ordinary material sphere, it can exist only as long as the body does, and is affected by what happens to the body. This is essentially a materialistic view, since matter is the only ultimate reality. It is not clear to what extent Diderot is wavering between such a position and that of the pantheist.

Worthy of brief mention is his acceptance of a theory that was an unquestioned assumption of most eighteenth-century minds; natural law and the universality of human nature. The differences in morality between peoples have only accidental causes. Basically human reason is everywhere the same, a law peculiar to the species, indicating a single line of conduct. Without the pathological deviations of circumstance, man would everywhere follow an identical moral law.

The last division of *The Sceptic's Walk* is "The Lane of Flowers." It is a satire of those who give themselves up to a life of sensual pleasure. Most have escaped from the Lane of Thorns, but frightened by its "guides" (priests) eventually return to it. Diderot mocks at the perfidy of love, friendship, and society in a misanthropic tone that crops up only at rare intervals in his works, usually under the stimulus of discouragement.

5

Diderot decided to try again. The next production was to be in a different genre. "Philosophic" writing was too dangerous. He had been teasing Mme. de Puisieux about how easy it was to write the lascivious novels so in vogue, some of which she herself had penned. It was merely a question of finding a clever theme and then abandoning oneself to the natural current of licentious thoughts. Somewhat piqued, Mme. de Puisieux defied her lover to produce a work of the kind, and he accepted the challenge.

Digging into the old *fabliaux* of the middle ages, he found a story to his liking. Then he developed it in the style of Boccaccio, Marguerite de Navarre, and his notorious contemporary, Crébillon *fils,* author of *The Sopha. The Indiscreet Jewels,* as this bawdy tale is called, tells of a prince whose magic ring, when properly pointed, could make a woman's "jewel" talk truthfully and reveal all its love affairs! Carlyle, an "eminent Victorian," called it "the beastliest of all past, present, and future dull novels," and Lord Morley could not defile himself by naming its title.

But *The Indiscreet Jewels* is more than a light and licentious novel. Diderot could not resist introducing serious subjects, always in an amusing vein. He ridicules women, the soul, priests, kings, magistrates, fops, the Court, academicians, authors, critics, pedants, bawdy tales, and the sentimental novels devoured by the bourgeoisie. But Mme. de Pompadour is defended as the beautiful and ever wise friend of enlightenment. His satire of love reduces it to the physiological, foreshadowing his later moral radicalism and his positivistic treatment of sexuality. His criticism of the French theater is noteworthy. He dares to attack the great classical tragedies worshipped by all of France, indeed by all of Europe. Exalting realism and deriding convention, he charges that instead of imitating nature, Corneille and Racine imitate the ancients; that the rule of the three unities destroys all probability; that the dialogue and the traditional declamation of the actors are pompous and unnatural. All thoughts that will continue to ferment in his mind for years and lead eventually to a revolution in dramatic theory.

The Indiscreet Jewels was published in 1748. It was a success, went through three editions, and is still reprinted today—in fact, it has had more editions than any other of Diderot's works. Diderot followed it immediately with another spicy story, *The White Bird, a fairy tale.* Heavier than the earlier novel, it recounts in allegorical fashion the adventures of a young prince with Truth, Falsehood, Bizarre, and an assortment of other personages. *The White Bird* was not published until 1798, after Diderot's death. As a matter of fact, he always denied authorship of it, and it is possible that he did nothing more than rewrite it for his mistress.

When Diderot decided to keep *The White Bird* in his desk, he was prompted not so much by the spectre of the Bastille, evoked by its allusions to the court, as by the unflattering criticism which had greeted his first novel. It had sold quite well, to be sure; but it cast the shadow of the pornographic on his philosophical reputation and the umbrage of scandal over the *Encyclopedia*. The abbé Raynal, for instance, soon to become a companion in arms, called it "obscure, badly written in a cheap, vulgar tone, by a man who does not know the social sphere he is attempting to paint. The author is M. Diderot, a man of wit and extensive knowledge, but who is not made for this kind of writing."

The objections of d'Alembert and of Mme. de Prémontval, the shocked wife of his friend, the mathematics professor, determined him to publish something serious to counteract this scandal. Perhaps it was they, too, who persuaded him to do some work in the field of mathematics, which had been his first love and means of subsistence. "I am giving up the cap and bells forever," he promised. "I want the scandal to stop, and I return to Socrates." The forecast was not entirely accurate. A "healthy licentiousness" was part of his personality, and it enlivens even his most serious writings. Much of his intellectual life was a form of play, just as in "playing" he sometimes found his most brilliant ideas and turned to serious considerations.

The five *Mémoires* he published that year were sound pieces that proved he had kept in contact with the latest mathematical problems and techniques. Two of them deal with acoustics, two with physical questions (the tension of cords and the resistance of air to the movement of pendula) and one with geometrical theory. Always imbued with the spirit of experimentation and the desire to improve the experimenter's tools, he proposes a new geometrical instrument to draw involutes as a compass draws circles; then he demonstrates its possible uses by a series of original theorems and problems. He also projects an organ which even those who knew no music could play, and which would increase the acoustical range of current hand-organs—a piece which testifies to his curiosity and inventiveness.

These interests persisted. He was later to propose the first version of a cryptography machine and of the typewriter. In 1761 he published two additional mathematical memoirs; one of these, on the theory of probability, is a rectification of d'Alembert's work. Not long after this, he became tremendously excited over a solution he thought he had found to the age-old problem of squaring the circle. This was never published—probably his excitement and confidence

79

were suddenly pricked—and the manuscript has only recently been found.

Satisfied with his mathematical articles, and resolute in his intention to devote himself to the most serious writing, Diderot next turned to the psychological and philosophical problems raised by a modification in the human sensual apparatus. Since all our knowledge, as he believed, came to us through the senses, would a man born without sight have the same scale of values that we do? The work that resulted from this investigation, the *Letter on the Blind, for the Use of Those Who See,* turned out to be even more serious than he had intended.

CHAPTER 5

A
Guest
of
the
King

ON THE 24TH OF JULY 1749, at nine o'clock, Diderot had just settled down at his desk for a morning's work on the *Encyclopedia*.

A violent knocking at the door startled him from his reflections. Instantly his heart began to pound, as he heard the words he was instinctively prepared for: "Open in the name of the king!" Trembling, he hastened to comply, expecting fearfully to see his old friend, M. d'Hémery. And d'Hémery it was, with Maître Rochebrune, the king's attorney, and several guards.

"We have orders to search your house and seize whatever books and papers we see fit, including the *Letter on the Blind*, the *White Bird*, and the *Philosophic Thoughts*."

"Go ahead, messieurs," assented the philosopher weakly.

An exhaustive search followed, during which we may be sure Diderot cursed himself for his rashness in publishing the *Letter on the Blind* and cursed his persecutors each time they scattered his carefully arranged papers. The search over, and nothing having been found except two copies of the *Letter on the Blind*, he had a moment of relief. Then Rochebrune drew a paper from his coat.

"You are under arrest, by order of the king! You will get dressed immediately and come with us."

Panic overcame him. He tried nervously to dress. Bitter recriminations for his foolhardiness and a sickening fear of what was to come agitated him. How long would they keep him in prison? Perhaps ten years. What would happen to the *Encyclopedia?* What would his wife say and what would become of his little family? At the thought of his wife, Diderot asked permission to say good-bye to her, and it was granted. Taking firm hold of himself he decided to put on a show of calm and unconcerned innocence. After all, what could they prove?

Antoinette was fondly dressing her son, their second child. "I have to go out," he told her. "It's some annoying business concerning the *Encyclopedia*. I don't think I'll be able to get back for dinner, but I'd like you to meet me this evening at Le Breton's."

He kissed her and left. Some instinct, perhaps the noise of the horses, perhaps the unaccustomed kiss, led her to the window. In the street, beside a stout coach, she saw her husband surrounded by several men. Then a printer's boy came up and tried to give him a package of proofs. She saw one of the guards step between them, push aside roughly Diderot's outstretched arm and send the lad scampering away. She screamed and fainted.

An hour later, Antoinette was at the knees of police lieutenant Berryer, pleading for her husband's release. It was Le Breton who had directed her there; and while she pleaded he waited outside and fumed, worried about the fate, not of his editor, but of his *Encyclopedia.*

"Well, madame, we have your husband, and he will have to talk. You could save him a lot of trouble and hasten his release, if you would indicate to us where his books are, what he is working on now, and where the *White Pigeon* is."

"I have never seen or read any of my husband's works," sobbed Antoinette. This was the truth; she had no share in Diderot's intellectual life. "I spend all my time taking care of the house; I know nothing about any white pigeon or any black pigeon. All I know is that his writings must resemble his conduct. He esteems honor a thousand times dearer than life, and his works reflect the virtues he practices."

This was better than Diderot deserved from his wife. Berryer, who had within arm's reach a report on his liaison with Mme. de Puisieux, was not to be persuaded by this defense of his prisoner's character. Instead, he proffered some consoling words to the weeping woman, and promised to let her see her husband within a few days—a promise he did not keep.

Diderot was not the only one arrested that morning. The government had suddenly become alive to the attacks of the *philosophes*. Louis XV, annoyed by their sniping, had commanded his ministers to wipe out these persistent guerrillas. The absolute monarch's patience was being taxed by criticism from all sides, and he was easily convinced that the *philosophes* could be the object of a spectacular and not unpopular reprisal. The treaty of Aix-la-Chapelle, ending the War of the Austrian Succession, had been signed on October 30, 1748 and published on February 12, 1749. For the blood spilt and the money wasted, France's reward was to lose her Flemish provinces. "As stupid as the peace" became a by-word among the populace. The emergency taxes imposed during the war had not been lifted, and royal expenditures continued unabated. Backed by the Parlement, the people were beginning to refuse to pay them. Ministers, king, court, and Church were lampooned in a hundred satirical songs. "Louis," wrote one pamphleteer, "if you were once the object of our love, it was because all your vices were still unknown to us; in this kingdom, depopulated because of you, and given over as a prey to the mountebanks who rule with you, if there are Frenchmen left, it is to hate you." Posters menacing the king's life were found on the walls of the Louvre. More hated even than the king was his mistress, Mme. de Pompadour, the effective ruler of France. There were complaints, too, from the Church, which wished to escape taxation, and from the jurists, whose prerogatives had been weakened. And this was the time when Montesquieu's great and popular work, *The Spirit of the Laws*, published in 1748, exposed the laws and limits of monarchy and spread the idea that a good government is one that corresponds to the needs of a nation. In the spring of 1750, the police had to put down a number of riots, and the king was forced to avoid Paris in his journey from Versailles to Compiègne.

But the government had been swift and firm in its reaction to the troublemakers. A flood of *lettres de cachet* was released. By July of 1749, the Bastille was filled to capacity with writers and scientists; prisoners were now being taken outside of Paris, to Vincennes. Even a man of Buffon's stature was forced to make a public retraction. "I have had no intention of contradicting the text of the Scriptures; I believe firmly everything related there about the creation . . . and I renounce whatever in my book treats of the formation of the earth and everything in general that might contradict the narration of Moses." This was the time when those who peddled forbidden books were pilloried, whipped, and sentenced to ten years in the galleys. And this was also the time Diderot had chosen to publish his *Letter on the Blind*. Had he known what we have learned from the archives of the police, that he had been under continuous surveillance ever since his parish priest's denunciation, he would have hidden or burned his manuscript.

The minister of war, Count d'Argenson, had a brother, the marquis d'Argenson, formerly minister of Foreign Affairs. That month the marquis made the following entry in his famous journal:

> Within the last few days they have arrested a flock of *abbés,* scientists, and *littérateurs,* and put them in the Bastille, such as Monsieur Diderot, some professors from the University, revered doctors from the Sorbonne, etc. They are accused of having written verses against the king, of having recited and spread them, of having criticized the Cabinet, written and printed in favor of deism and against good morals; to all of which they are trying to place a stop, this licentiousness having become too great.

Thus the law had whisked Diderot away, not to the Bastille, but to the dungeon of Vincennes, then in the suburbs of Paris. The sight of the thick grey walls and the nine forbidding towers made his heart sink. As he was marched down the passage lined with heavy doors sealed with ancient locks, he was filled with wild panic. Without any formalities, he was thrust into an octagonally shaped cell, about nine feet across and illuminated only by a narrow slit, high in the wall. There he spent the next anguished days thinking dejectedly of his family and his work. The horrors of solitary confinement depressed him; he was filled with nostalgic thoughts of the lively dinners and conversations with his friends. Never had liberty appeared so dear. Never had the world appeared so attractive.

The summer of 1749 was unusually hot and humid. The heat and lack of exercise impelled him, five days after his incarceration, to request permission to walk a little in the garden or in the Great Hall; this was summarily denied. He suffered from the abundance of vermin—and from the absence of his nightcap; charitably, the warden had it fetched from his home. Moreover, having a gourmet's taste, he did not relish the food: for dinner, according to accounts, he had boiled beef, usually from the neck, and some beef liver with onions, or tripe; for supper, an entrée and a roast; one pound of bread and one bottle of wine a day. On Thursday and Sunday fruit was served at one of the meals; on Friday, vegetables and fish, usually herring.

For one long week, Diderot had all day to reproach himself bitterly, to oscillate from optimistic hope for a quick release to a pessimistic vision of long imprisonment and a broken life. After all, the *Encyclopedia* was an approved work, he reassured himself bravely. As for the *Letter on the Blind,* it could have been found on anyone's desk, why not on the work table of the editor of the *Encyclopedia?* But an hour of equanimity was followed by an hour of despair and weeping. Was it wiser to confess and throw himself on the mercy of d'Argenson, or was it braver and more worthy of a philosopher to put up a stony resistance?

Meanwhile, on July 28th, the publishers had written a pleading letter to Count d'Argenson.

> This work which will cost us at least two hundred and fifty thousand livres, and for which we have already advanced more than ten thousand livres, was about to be announced to the public. The arrest of M. Diderot, the only man of letters whom we know that is capable of such a vast undertaking and who alone possesses the key to the whole work, may cause our ruin. We dare to hope that Your Grace will let himself be touched by our plight and grant M. Diderot his liberty. In the minute search of his papers that was made, nothing was found to aggravate the fault by which he has had the misfortune of displeasing Your Grace and we believe we can assure you that, whatever that crime may be, it will never be repeated.

This letter was not even answered. Another to police inspector Berryer produced no immediate results. But a few days later Berryer decided that a week of solitary confinement had probably softened his prisoner's resistance. He summoned him for an official interrogatory. In a drab room draped with guards, before the solemn police lieutenant clad in his official wig and gown, the pale philosopher declared in an unfaltering voice that his name was Denis Diderot, that he was thirty-five years old, and that he belonged to the Roman Catholic faith. A clerk copied down carefully all his statements.

"Are you not the author of the *Letter on the Blind, for the Use of Those Who See?*"

"Non, monsieur."

"Who printed that book for you?"

"I did not write it."

"So you know who did?"

"Non, monsieur."

"Have you ever had its manuscript in your possession?"

"Non, monsieur."

"At least, you sent some copies to different people, did you not?"

"Non, monsieur."

"And you are not the author of the *Philosophic Thoughts*, condemned and burnt by order of Parlement?"

"Non, monsieur."

"Are you not the author of a novel called *The Indiscreet Jewels?"*

"Non, monsieur, I am the author of none of the books you mention."

"Are you the author of *The Sceptic's Walk?"*

Diderot knew better than to disavow a book with which he had been caught at his home; perhaps this admission, he thought quickly, would give weight to his denials.

"Oui, monsieur, but I have burned it."

"And you are also the author of *The White Bird?"*

"Non, monsieur, I am not."

Berryer leaned back in his chair, looked thoughtfully for a moment at the recalcitrant prisoner and then declared coldly: "I am afraid that you are going to be here for a while, Monsieur Diderot, for a long while."

In his Journal, the marquis d'Argenson, who made it his business to know everything that went on in Paris, set down the following note: "The aforementioned Diderot, author of *The Indiscreet Jewels* and of the *Clairvoyant Blind Man,* has been interrogated in his prison at Vincennes. He received the magistrates with the haughtiness of a fanatic. The examiner told him: 'You are an insolent person, you will remain here a long time.' This Diderot had just composed, when he was arrested, a remarkable book against religion, called *The Tomb of Prejudices."*

The long dreary days began again. To keep from going mad, he improvised a makeshift pen from a toothpick. For ink, he broke some slate from the wall outside his window, crushed it and dissolved it in wine. A glass was his inkwell. Having a volume of Milton's *Paradise Lost,* he reread it and scribbled notes as he went along.

Each day the jailer brought Diderot two candles, but since he went to bed early and awoke with the sun, he did not use them. After a while he offered to return his supply.

"You had better keep them, sir," replied the jailer. "You don't need them now, but they'll come in handy in the winter."

Panic flowed through him. He asked the jailer to bring him pen and paper. Humble, yet proud, threatening vaguely to commit suicide, he sent one letter to count d'Argenson and one to Berryer. To d'Argenson he protested the "exaggerated punishment" dealt out for a few *intempérances d'esprit*. At the least, he pleads, permission should be granted to continue his labors on the *Encyclopedia*, "a work dedicated to the glory of France and the shame of England." With Berryer he used a more bombastic tone, protesting the poverty and ruin brought down upon the family of a respectable writer of serious mathematical works—a man respected for his talents, generosity, and impeccable morals. As character references, he cites Voltaire, Mme. du Deffand, Buffon, and a string of well-known names. Until his justly demanded release, he requests that books and visitors be allowed to reach him freely.

Berryer was a man of considerable finesse and intelligence, writes Arthur M. Wilson. Knowing that his prisoner was no scoundrel, but a frightened young radical, he used Diderot's request as bait, replied that he would grant it in return for a confession and a vow never to offend again. As a token of his good intentions, he will at once allow Diderot freedom to read and write in the comfortable Great Hall adjoining his cell.

On the 13th of August, Diderot sent Berryer the following letter, an unusual psychological document:

Monsieur, my suffering has gone as far as it can ; my body is exhausted, my spirit broken, and my soul weighted with sorrow. I shall admit to you, however, that I would rather a thousand times die here than leave dishonored in your mind, in mine and in that of all honest men. Therefore I am far from thinking that you despise me so much as to make such an attempt. Nevertheless, you wish to be satisfied, and you shall be . . .

I yield, therefore, to the high opinion that I, like all other enlightened people, have of you, to the ascendency that you have over intelligent men by your superior talents and your unusual qualities of heart and mind ; . . . finally, to the complete confidence that I have in the word of honor which you have given me that you will have consideration for my repentance and the sincere promise that I make to you never again to write anything without submitting it to your judgment ; and to your promise that my confession will never be used either against myself or any one else, except in case of a second offense . . .

I admit to you then as to my worthy protector, what a lengthy imprisonment and all imaginable punishments would never have made me say to a judge ; that the *Thoughts,* the *Jewels,* and the *Letter on the Blind* are debaucheries of the mind that escaped from me ; but I can in turn promise you on my honor (and I do have honor) that they will be the last, and that they are the only ones. I have had no part, either direct or indirect, in the work entitled *On Manners,* and I have known this book only with the public. That, Monsieur, is what belongs to me. . . .

As for those who have taken part in the publicity of these works, nothing will be hidden from you. I shall depose verbally, in the depths of your heart, the names both of the publishers and the printers. I even undertake to tell them, if you require it, that they are known to you, so that they may be in the future as well-behaved as I have resolved to be.

I have the honor of being, with most profound respect and complete confidence, monsieur, your very humble and obedient servant   DIDEROT

As for *The White Bird,* it is not mine. It is the work of a lady whom I could name, since she does not conceal the fact. If I have had some share in that work, it was perhaps to correct the spelling, in which the cleverest women always make the most mistakes. It is not printed, and I do not think it ever will be.

Diderot has sunk very low, indeed. Never in his life does he appear more abject and less admirable than in this letter. Clearly, it was not written by a man in his normal state of mind.

Meanwhile, he took advantage of his new privileges, and sent for his Plato and for Buffon's sensational new *Natural History of Man.* With intense interest, he absorbed Buffon's theories and covered the margins with closely written notes.

On August 20th, after four weeks of confinement, Diderot desperately took out his pocket copy of Plato and decided to use it as an oracle and seek an augury. He opened it at random, he relates, and the first passage his eye hit upon read: *This affair is of a nature to end promptly.* The oracle was a true one. A quarter of an hour later, the warden of Vincennes, M. du Châtelet, came to his cell. He would be released from the dungeon the following day. From now on he would be allowed to stay in that part of the fortress known as the Château, where he would have a comfortable room, full liberty to walk in the gardens, and permission to receive visitors.

The next day all his books and notes were confiscated—despite his protests that they were purely scientific—and he was told to sign the following paper:

I, the undersigned, declare that M. Berryer, police lieutenant, has notified me of the orders and intentions of his Majesty which I am to observe in the château of Vincennes, where I am prisoner by virtue of the order of the King; and consequently, to show my deep respect and my complete submission to the said orders which I shall never transgress, I promise the Lieutenant-general of police that I will not leave the said château, nor its grounds, nor the enclosure of the royal garden, nor cross the bridges, during the entire time that it pleases His Majesty to keep me a prisoner there, agreeing, in case of disobedience to the above, to be imprisoned for life in the dungeon from which I have been taken by the clemency of the King.

> Done at the château of Vincennes,
> the 21st of August, 1749.

Just as soon as he was installed in his new and less oppressive quarters, the first visitors began to arrive. For once, he greeted his wife with genuine pleasure. He flew into d'Alembert's arms. Together they all wept. Le Breton shook his hand warmly, relieved to feel his investment safe. The very next day, the boxes containing the notes and articles for the *Encyclopedia* were transported to Diderot's spacious room. Since his arrest, work had come to a halt; without its general, the little army was disorganized. From Vincennes went out the new rallying-call, and the collaborators, engravers, printers, all went back to their jobs. The prison of Vincennes had become the field headquarters of the encyclopedic army!

On the following days, other visitors came to congratulate the philosopher. Among the first was Mme. de Puisieux, coquettish and provocative as ever. Fortunately for him, she did not know that he had denounced her as the real author of *The White Bird!* But more than anyone else, Diderot was anxiously awaiting his dear Jean-Jacques. Rousseau had been away, and did not know at once of his friend's release to the château. As soon as the good news reached him, he left immediately for Vincennes, and lacking the money to travel by coach, made the trip afoot. One day Diderot spied him trudging weary and dust-covered up the long road. The tenderest embraces were followed by excited conversation.

"I found him greatly affected by his imprisonment," Rousseau tells us in his *Confessions*. "The dungeon had made a terrible impression on him, and although he was comfortable in the château and allowed to walk where he pleased in a park that was not even surrounded by walls, he needed the society of his friends to avoid giving way to melancholy."

Jean-Jacques made him describe once again what it had been like.

"I really thought they were going to keep you there for life," he commented. He did not mention the letter he had written to Mme. de Pompadour, pleading passionately either to have Diderot released or to be incarcerated with him.

Then they went out and walked in the garden, while Rousseau in turn told his story—about his delightful stay at Fontenay-sous-Bois, as guest of the prince of Saxe-Gotha. He had met many interesting people, especially the Prince's private secretary, a certain Melchior Grimm, a young German expatriate who was a great music lover.

Among the first things Diderot did, once he was out of the dungeon, was to write to his father. He correctly suspected that Brother Angel, who nourished a grievance against him, had hastened to inform Diderot *père* of his son's disgrace. He did not know that Brother Angel had also informed him of the clandestine marriage which he had kept secret these six years. Diderot described to his father the unfortunate situation he was in, attributing it all to the vengeance of a woman—he, of course, was innocent—and, finally, asked for some money. Towards the beginning of September, Antoinette brought him the paternal reply. The good father, who was aging, had begun to long for his favorite child, after so many years of estrangement. He had sent the following letter; unfortunately its quaint style and spelling are untranslatable.

Langres, September 3, 1749

My son,

I have received the two letters which you wrote to me recently, informing me of your detention and its cause.

But I cannot help saying that there absolutely must have been other reasons aside from the ones given in one of your letters, for your being put between four walls.

Everything coming from the Sovereign is respectable and must be obeyed . . .

But since nothing happens without God's consent, I do not know which is better for your moral well-being: that the imprisonment which you have had in that pebble-box should be ended, or that it should be prolonged for several months during which you could reflect seriously on yourself.

Remember, that if the Lord has given you talents, it was not for you to work to weaken the doctrines of our Holy Religion, which you must certainly have attacked for such a large number of ecclesiastical persons to protest against one of your works, or, at least, against those that are imputed to you.

Until then, I have given you sufficient proof of my love. In giving you an education, it was in the hope that you would make good use of it and not that its results should throw me, as they have done, into the most bitter sorrow and chagrin, on learning of your disgrace . . .

Forgive, and I shall forgive you.

I know, my son, that no one is exempt from calumny, and that they may impute to you works in which you have had no share.

But to give proofs of the contrary to the influential people whom you know, give to the public some Christian production of yours which will free your pen of all contrary thoughts they may have concerning it, I mean about your way of thinking.

This work will bring you the blessings of Heaven, and will keep you in my good graces.

However I warn you that you will never receive any consideration from me until you have informed me, truly and unequivocally, whether you are married, as they have written to me from Paris, and whether you have two children. If this marriage is legitimate and the thing is done, I am satisfied. I hope you will not refuse your sister the pleasure of bringing them up, and me the pleasure of seeing them under my eyes.

You ask for money.

What!

A man like you who is working on immense projects, as you are, can need money?

And you have just spent a month in a place where it cost you nothing to live!

Besides I know that his Majesty, out of his kindness, gives an honorable sustenance to those who, as a result of his orders, are placed where you are.

You have asked me to send you paper, pens and ink. I invite you to make better use of them than in the past.

Remember the memory of your poor mother. In the reproaches

that she made to you, she told you several times that you were blind. Give me proofs to the contrary. Once again, and above all, be faithful in the execution of your promises.

You will find enclosed a draft for one hundred and fifty livres on the account of Maître Foucou which you will spend as you see fit.

I await impatiently the happy day which will calm my worries by informing me that you are free.

As soon as I find out I shall go and render thanks to the Lord.

Meanwhile, my son, with all the love that I owe to you,

Your affectionate father,

DIDEROT

Diderot's answer to this little masterpiece has been lost.

October brought an incident that has caused a stir in literary history ever since. In imitation of the great French Academy, provincial academies had sprung up all over France. These bodies played an important role in the intellectual life of the eighteenth century, both by their discussion meetings and by the prizes they offered for essays on topics of current interest. That year, the Academy of Dijon had proposed this question: "Whether the renaissance of arts and letters has contributed to purify morals."

According to Rousseau's story, he chanced upon it in the current number of the *Mercure de France*, while he was resting under a tree, on his way to pay Diderot another visit at Vincennes. Immediately he was seized with an inspiration that made his whole being dizzy. He had conceived the idea that was to be the theme of all his writings and the misfortune of his life! Man is naturally good, but civilization and all its trappings have corrupted him and enslaved him.

Rouuseau remained there in a trance, and composed an eloquent discourse on the subject. Then he arose, exhausted and bathed in tears.

Diderot's friends, Marmontel and Morellet, present a somewhat different account of what happened that day. In reality, they say, Rousseau came to Diderot and asked him which side to take in answer to the proposed topic. Diderot laughed at Rousseau's intention to take the affirmative, called it, after the famous theorem, the *pons asinorum*. "Everyone will take that side. Only the other side will give you the chance to write something new and eloquent." And Rousseau was convinced.

Since then, a dozen contradictory arguments have been brought to bear by the partisans of each philosopher. Diderot's own recollections are equivocal and difficult to interpret. Yet, if they are read carefully and dispassionately, it becomes evident that Diderot admits Rousseau's original conception of the paradox, and claims only to have encouraged him in his uncertainty. "Rousseau *had to* disagree with everyone else," he wrote in later years, after the bitterness of their quarrels. On the other hand, it is undeniable that Diderot's influence on his friend was considerable, and that it stemmed largely from his more paradoxical and wilder ideas. It was when this influence was strongest and most direct that Rousseau produced his most radical work, the *Discourse on Inequality.*

Another incident of dubious veracity is related by Mme. de Vandeul. When Mme. de Puisieux came to visit Diderot, he noticed that she was dressed with more than everyday pretention.

"Where are you going?" he inquired with an unmistakable nuance of distrust. Recently, he had suspected her of becoming friendly with a certain lawyer.

"Oh, to a little party, at Champigny."

"Are you going with a friend?"

"Mais non, chéri!"

"On your honor?"

"I swear! "

But Diderot placed little confidence in a woman's honor. That night, he slipped out of the Château, ran to Champigny and saw his mistress in fond *tête-à-tête* with her friend. Then he rushed back, the next day admitted his escapade to the warden, and was forgiven.

The adventure is possible, considering Diderot's jealous and impetuous disposition. But in view of his pledge not to leave his enclosure, under penalty of being sent back to the dungeon for life, it seems scarcely probable that he would have risked such a catastrophe.

Diderot's daughter also relates that as a result of what he saw, her father's passion for Mme. de Puisieux cooled off. "This little adventure hastened his rupture with her." From these words, it has been assumed that he broke off with her very soon thereafter. On the other hand, Mme. de Vandeul herself says that their relations lasted ten years, which would bring them down to 1755. She also declares that he wrote for her his *Thoughts on the Interpretation of Nature,* composed in 1753.

A third version holds that the break actually came in 1750, but as a result of domestic strife. An apocryphal anecdote of the time relates that after Diderot's wife forced him to break with Mme. de Puisieux, the irate mistress stood in front of Mme. Diderot's house and shouted insults at her. Antoinette threw open her window and replied in kind, and a few minutes later ran down into the street to express her feelings at closer quarters. An old fashioned barroom brawl is supposed to have ensued, during which the philosopher hid in the corner of his study, not daring to show his face. The hair-pulling contest was finally ended by a dousing with two pails of cold water. It is somewhat difficult to believe that Antoinette's scoldings finally took effect, after so many years, but the story is perhaps supported by some frigid references to Diderot at this date in Mme. de Puisieux' writings.

Meanwhile, the *Encyclopedia,* despite Diderot's best efforts, had been advancing slowly. He was unable to consult the books and see the people he needed while away from Paris. Twice the publishers had written to d'Argenson, begging that their editor be released, out of consideration for "the finest and most useful enterprise" ever undertaken by a publisher. These pleas, and another written by Diderot in his official capacity as editor, fell on deaf ears. Not until the 22nd of October did d'Argenson sign the order for his release, and it was not executed until two weeks later, November 3rd, 1749.

That was a day of feasting for Diderot, first in his little apartment in the Rue de la Vieille-Estrapade, and later, with his rejoicing companions, at the cherished Café Procope. Nothing could be compared with the sensation of freedom after three and a half months of imprisonment. We can imagine his new zest for life as he again freely walked the streets of Paris.

But he was never to forget Vincennes. Each time some anonymous work was attributed to him, he trembled and ran to police headquarters to disclaim it officially. When a friend, Landois, sent him a manuscript to revise, he wrote back furiously: "That is a book capable of ruining me. . . . You were perfectly aware that I am under surveillance, and you put.me in the position of a second offender."

The government's campaign to crush the *philosophes* was to fail. They kept under cover during the height of the barrage, and returned to the attack immediately after. Besides, the government was now having its hands full with the clergy, which privileged body was resisting to its utmost the attempt to tax its wealth—about two fifths that of the entire country. Another event was to help. In 1751, Lamoignon de Malesherbes, a young nobleman in sympathy with the new ideas (and who was to meet his death on the guillotine because of his defense of Louis XVI's life in the Convention) was named supervisor of publishing *(Directeur de la librairie)*. This was a most important post because of its control of all printing licenses. Without Malesherbes, the *Encyclopedia* might never have been completed.

CHAPTER 6

The
Two
Letters

1

WHAT WAS THIS EXPLOSIVE *Letter on the Blind,* that had provoked so violent a reaction, sending its author under special escort to the royal dungeons of Vincennes?

Early in 1749, the famous scientist Réaumur was experimenting on a young woman who had been born blind because of cataracts on both eyes. An operation was performed by a Prussian surgeon. It was announced that the bandages would be removed before a select audience of scientists and writers, curious to observe the first reactions. According to the conventional account, Diderot managed to get himself invited. When the bandages were lifted, the patient's words revealed in spite of herself that she had already seen, that Réaumur was putting on the show for a second time. The spectators started to grumble; some one admitted that the genuine experiment had been performed in private for Mme. Dupré de Saint-Maur. Thoroughly disappointed, Diderot left in a huff, muttering, "M. de Réaumur has preferred to have a pair of pretty eyes for witness rather than people worthy of judging his work." Later Diderot attributed his arrest to the vengefulness of the offended lady, who prided herself not only on her anatomical knowledge, but on her influence as mistress of count d'Argenson.

While this story may well be true, all that Diderot actually says, in addressing his *Letter on the Blind* to Mme. de Puisieux, is that Réaumur had refused to include him among the invited few. For this snub, there was an obvious reason. Réaumur was afraid the *Encyclopedia* would overshadow the description of the arts and trades that he was editing by authorization of the Academy of Sciences.

But Réaumur's demonstration turned out to be of value after all. Diderot's curiosity was aroused. Together with some friends, he journeyed to Puiseaux, to make personal observations on a blind winegrower who lived there. Still not content, he consulted a memoir about an Englishman also born blind, one Nicholas Saunderson, professor of mathematics. It was disappointingly uninteresting. Ever resourceful, he decided to invent along his own line of inquiry a probable death-bed conversation for Saunderson, pretending he had taken it from a book written by one of the Englishman's disciples, a mythical William Inchcliff. The Royal Society never forgave Diderot for this stratagem, and never nominated him for membership.

The result of Diderot's observations and thinking was his first major work. *The Letter on the Blind, for the Use of Those Who See* consists then of a combination of notes on his real interview with the winegrower, his imaginary conversation with the English professor, and his own speculations. Although the letter is more philosophical than scientific in the questions it raises, it is permeated with a true scientific spirit. It is keenly analytical, but analysis is attempted in the light of positive fact. Its chief concern is the origin and validity of our moral ideas and of our idea of God. The precise subject of Diderot's investigation is "how far the modification of the five senses, such as the congenital absence of one of them, would involve a corresponding modification of notions acquired by normal men."

In the beginning, the winegrower explains how he thinks of sight as a sort of touch in the distance. He has no conception of what is meant by the word *see*, just as a deaf-mute cannot conceive of sound. A ray of light is a thin thread. A mirror is "a machine that puts things in relief at a distance, if they are properly placed in relation to it." To Diderot this seems brilliant reasoning. Touch gives only the idea of relief. Therefore a mirror is a machine that puts us in relief outside of ourselves. But what the blind man cannot understand is how that "image" of ourselves cannot itself be touched. On learning of the winegrower's remarkable memory for sounds, Diderot comments, "the help our senses give each other prevents them from perfecting themselves"—an idea he will develop later into an explanation of human superiority over animals.

Despite certain errors resulting from his own reasoning and from the excesses of Condillac's sensualist philosophy, which limited reason to a recombination of sensations, Diderot has been justly hailed as the first to understand the psychology of the blind and the mechanism by which one sense is substituted for another. He was the first to propose the education of the blind, and of blind deaf-mutes by a system of touch symbols.

Diderot next goes on to show how many of our ideas and those of the blind appear reciprocally absurd. "If a man who has seen for just one or two days fell in with a people of blind men, he would either have to keep silent or else pass for a lunatic. Every day he would announce to them some new mystery, which would be one only for them and which their freethinkers would refuse to believe." This reminds Diderot of how those who had the misfortune of finding truth in centuries of darkness and the imprudence to reveal it to their blind contemporaries were cruelly persecuted.

Because it is hard to find things, order becomes a paramount virtue for the blind. They are not affected, as we are, by exterior signs of power (such as the garb of magistrate or priest). Although they can learn the idea of symmetry which makes us consider things beautiful, they are unable to comprehend the idea of beauty; there is only utility. While this is a loss, comments Diderot with some irony, at least their ideas on beauty are clearer than those of the esthetic philosophers. From the winegrower, Diderot learned that the blind do not understand our idea of modesty. As for women, in a society of the blind they would probably be held in common. On the other hand, the blind can conceive of no greater crime than stealing, for they are helpless to protect themselves against it. Their feeling of pity is less than ours, for they are affected only by vocal complaints.

Here Diderot has come to a turning point in his ethical thinking, although he claims never to have doubted "that the state of our organs and senses influences greatly our metaphysics and our morals, and that our most purely intellectual ideas . . . result from the structure of our bodies. . . ." Distance and size change our feelings and our ideas. It is comparatively easy to kill from a great distance, or to crush an ant. Where then is this absolute moral sense, the knowledge of right as right, the innate love of virtue? "Ah, madame! how different from ours is the morality of the blind! how a deaf man's would be different from a blind man's, and how a being who had one more sense than we would find our morality imperfect, not to say worse! "

This empirical morality implies a view of the self that is more scientific than that which obtained in much of eighteenth-century thought. The self depends on our physical equipment and the environment in which it functions. It consists of processes, experiences and relations. We can see Diderot's materialism in the making. Yet this does not mean that he has given up the idea of a universal human nature, basic to eighteenth-century rationalism. Human nature does not give us ideas, it is only the limit to ideas, inasmuch as it defines the character of our reaction to the external world. However, the value of Diderot's inquiry into moral ideas is limited. It refers only to their content. It omits—if it does not implicitly deny—the basic forms of ethical intuition: right and wrong, duty and obligation, an order of values.

Our metaphysical ideas are similarly relative. In Saunderson's imaginary deathbed conversation (or rather, monologue) with the minister Holmes, Diderot abandons the proof of God's existence which he had found in the structure of nature. Visual proofs have absolutely no effect on Saunderson; he demands arguments he can "touch." Where is this perfection in nature that proves the existence of God? Saunderson perceives plenty of evils and imperfections, including his own blindness.

> Is a certain phenomenon, according to us, above man? We say at once, *It is the work of God ;* our vanity is not content with less. Might we not put a little less pride in our talk, and a little more philosophy? If nature offers us some hard knot to untie, let us leave it for what it is ; and let us not, in order to cut it, resort to the hand of a Being, who afterwards turns out to be another knot even more difficult to untie than the first.

Biological finalism was the thread that had bound Diderot most strongly to theism. In the *Letter on the Blind* he breaks that thread, too. Since the wonders of the universe have no effect on Saunderson, Holmes tells him to feel his body. Saunderson, however, finds no valid proof of God in its organization or order. Holmes' error, he counters, lies in assuming that this order has always obtained. That is not so. Once there was chaos, and because of movement, things came to be.

Here he has a beautiful Lucretian vision of matter moving and chaos disentangling itself. Among the products of this natural creation were "a host of ill-shaped beings for every few well-organized ones." Saunderson sketches a crude theory of natural production through trial and error and survival of the fit. Among the first animals were some without head or feet or stomach. But "the monsters were successively annihilated; all the imperfect combinations of matter have disappeared; only those remain in whose mechanism there was no important contradiction and which could exist by themselves and perpetuate themselves." (The entire thought may be based on Epicurus' idea, that "at first monsters were produced, shapes not adapted to their surroundings.") If the first man had been unfit for survival, there would be no human species. "I therefore conjecture that, in the beginning, when matter in fermentation produced the universe, my fellow men were quite common." Finally, Saunderson extends this concept of trial-error and fitness. It is a continuous and a cosmic process.

> But why should I not apply to worlds what I believe of animals? How many misshapen worlds have dissolved, are reformed and dissolved again, perhaps at this very moment, in the immensity of space, where I cannot touch, and you cannot see, but where movement continues and will continue to combine accumulations of matter, until they have found an arrangement in which they can persist? Oh philosophers! transport yourselves with me to the ends of this universe, beyond the point where I can touch and where you see organized beings ; walk over this new ocean, and seek through its irregular agitation for vestiges of that intelligent Being whose wisdom you admire here! . . . What is this world, Mr. Holmes? a composite subject to revolutions that all indicate a continual tendency to destruction ; a rapid succession of beings that follow each other, push each other and disappear ; a passing symmetry, a momentary order.

These ideas have generally been taken as a proto-theory of organic evolution. Closer analysis makes it clear that Diderot has as yet no theory of the evolution of species. There is only trial and error in the production of a variety of forms. No transformism is involved. In some manner, matter spewed forth these beings as formed species that stand or fall on the fitness of the combination they embody. Nor is fitness specifically related to environment, or to changing environment. Instead it is considered only in regard to the inherent structure and its viability according to some abstract or intrinsic requirement. On the other hand, Diderot is, without yet realizing it, on the road to a true theory of evolution. The general idea of growth and decline and the succession of worlds and beings is based on the Heraclitian idea of change. Time and "becoming" are hereafter inherent parts of the concept of being, for Diderot. The process of trial and error, the selection of the fit from the multiplicity of new forms will become important parts of evolutionary theory.

But Diderot's mind is focused elsewhere. His purpose is partly to prove that there is no divine order, and that nature's variety can be explained without recourse to divine creation. Whereas the atheist in the *Philosophic Thoughts* admitted that he could not conceive how motion could engender the universe, especially organic life, Diderot is now able to offer such an explanation.

He had found the germ of it in La Mettrie's *Man a Machine* and *Man a Plant*, published the year before. In the universe, Diderot sees a continuous creation from forces inherent in matter, all force being a principle of change. Counteracting the force that produces new combinations is a seeking for temporary stability. It is this self-creativity in matter that makes the idea of God unnecessary and disposes of the argument of biological finalism and design. It explains variety in the universe. It explains order as what can survive and disorder as what fails. It accounts for the monsters and misfits, like Saunderson, that a system devised by an intelligent God could not provide for. No longer does the structure of the butterfly's wing prove God by its intricacy and its designed part in the organic whole. It is because of trial and error and elimination of the unfit that we are able to wonder at the intelligent adaptation of life. The infinite number of nature's untiring efforts suffices to account for such seeming marvels.

Diderot's theory of the self-creativity of nature sprang partly from the biological developments of the 1740's. Trembley had discovered the regenerative powers of the polyp, while La Mettrie had suggested a theory of muscular irritability that gave "vital powers" to elementary organic matter. In 1747, the work of Needham on spontaneous generation was made known in France.

It is generally held that Diderot surpasses the materialism of

Epicurus and Lucretius, who envisioned only simple combinations of atoms according to mechanical laws. He approaches closer, in a sense, to Bergson, who considered the universe almost as a living being that has within itself the principle of its development; or to the stoics who held there is no matter without force, that the universe is a unity, evolving in endless cycles. But at this point Diderot has not reached a clear and cogent concept of a truly creative force leading to qualitative differences, to emergence of new levels of law, over and beyond new permutations of basic building blocks. He indicates no principle of action other than the mechanical forces of matter, though he will soon add a new property of "sensitivity."

Diderot must be put back in the climate of preconceptions of his own time. God, it was held, could create only perfect and fit beings. The haphazard type of "creation" of temporary worlds and beings more or less fit for survival; the very need for such a constant effort at creation; and possibly even the effort towards ever higher forms— these were not marks of the working of a perfect intelligence. As Diderot put the matter in his later *Elements of Physiology*, adaptation in man does not prove finalism, for the adaptation is always imperfect. Saunderson, and other mistakes in nature, prove that there is no intelligent purposiveness. It may seem surprising that Diderot could write, in the *Physiology*, "From the molecule to man, there is a chain of beings that passes from the state of living stupidity to that of extreme intelligence," and see in this process nothing but a blind and chance development. But Diderot could admit no direction without abandoning materialism. For direction implies choice, the rejection of some causes in favor of others; and this would be replacing determinism with intelligence, efficient causes with final causes.

We must give Diderot credit for not putting implicit faith in his own theory. At the very end of the *Letter*, he seems to shrug his shoulders at it all. "Alas, madame," he confides to his mistress, "when we have put human knowledge in the scales of Montaigne, we are not far from adopting his motto. For, what do we know? What matter is? Not at all. What mind and thought are? Still less. What motion, space and time are? Absolutely not . . . Therefore we know almost nothing; and yet, in how many writings have authors pretended to know something!"

Two conclusions of deeper historical import lie at the base of Diderot's cosmological speculations. The first, the refusal to separate the organic and the inorganic, underlies the rise of modern mechanistic biology. The second, the rejection of a psychophysical dualism, is similarly the foundation of modern psychology.

The epistemological question is approached through the famous Molyneux problem, which had also attracted Voltaire, Berkeley, and other writers of the time. If a man born blind is enabled to see, will he identify his visual perceptions with the same objects he formerly knew only by touch? Will he be able to distinguish a cube from a sphere? The philosopher, in Diderot's discussion, answers negatively, thereby casting doubt on the equivalence of sense impressions and reality. The mathematician replies affirmatively; the abstract knowledge derived from one sense will match that derived from another. His view would make mathematics, the highest of abstractions, closest to reality. But it is the ignorant, unreasoning man who will cast the truest light on the relation between sensation and knowledge. Diderot holds that such a blind person would not recognize the objects, and twentieth-century experimentation has proved him right beyond question. Such a person would lack the experience to translate sensation into knowledge. He would have to learn to see meaningfully, as a child does, by comparing a sensation with what causes it. Since sensations "have no essential resemblance to objects, it is for experience to teach us analogies that are purely conventional."

However, Diderot is not yielding to subjective idealism. He holds that the result of this process is a representation of reality, though of doubtful and unascertainable accuracy. Things do exist, even if our picture of them is deformed by our own apparatus for acquiring knowledge. Especially, he trusts the sense of touch as the most faithful, and believes it corresponds closely to reality—a Lockean view, denied by modern physics. This is explicit here, and implicit in the article "Encyclopedia." In that essay he affirms that our minds are unable to distinguish redness, which belongs to our sensation, from roundness, which belongs to the object (and which our touch, as well as our vision confirms). Since our sensations are passive, they must have a cause, therefore objects exist. As for the solipsists, "they have lost their common sense, reject a fundamental truth dictated by natural intuition and justified by the common consent of all men." Their arguments show only the limits of the human mind, but do not disprove our intuition. "The idea I have of a circle is not this circle, since this circle is not a form of being of my mind." Redness comes from some quality or movement in the circle that causes a sensation we experience as red. The redness belongs to my mind, but only inasmuch as it perceives the circle. Since the sensation is ours, we have at the same time the idea and the sensation of the object. In our clear idea of the object, we know it to be extended and round, and we distinguish the circle from the perception we have of it. But the visual perception is itself confused with the object, and so we attach color to it, regarding color not as a property of sensation but of the object.

What is most interesting in this development is that it is not Lockean at all, but Cartesian. Knowledge of objects as an "intuition of the mind" is separated from our sensual awareness, and placed above it. Diderot has followed, quite closely, Descartes' reasoning in the *Meditations,* especially the Third.

Throughout the *Letter on the Blind,* Diderot gives evidence of maturity of thought, and of awareness of the interrelations of problems. He reveals a methodology, which he was often to follow, of studying the normal through the abnormal. This work, which was above the reach of most of his contemporaries, is a large step forward in his progress. It develops a scientific view of the universe, a materialism, as yet incomplete, and the elements of a theory of knowledge. The *Letter on the Blind* is truly a source book for nineteenth-century materialism and naturalism. It is particularly important, in Diderot's development, because it lays to rest the religious problem and opens the way for constructive thought along a number of lines. The idea of God is held to be sterile—to conceive of anything outside the material universe is useless and solves no difficulties. The *Letter* disposes of the two arguments that had previously kept him from embracing atheism: the ethical difficulty, and biological finalism. As Diderot's scientific preoccupations now come to the fore, his humanistic morality weakens in favor of positivistic naturalism. Morality and ethics have their roots in the organic reaction to nature, not in anything specifically human or psychic. Biological finalism is only an interpretation that our order-loving minds thrust upon the blind and necessary drive to creation embodied in matter in motion.

These are the conclusions apparent in the *Letter on the Blind.* Yet how sure can we be that Diderot accepted them wholeheartedly? One important part of Diderot's findings is that all knowledge is relative to our experience, so that the truth of a proposition does not depend on whether the mind can or cannot conceive it. "Our experience is neither limit nor judge of the possibility of things." Has a profounder epigram ever been conceived? Our judgments are distorted by our peculiar physical structure and by our brief span in time. "Beware of the sophistry of the ephemeral," he warns, bringing to mind Pope's line, "His time a moment, and a point his space." The order of things we see was once different, and will be different. Diderot's scepticism seems to anticipate Eddington's view that any true law of nature is likely to seem irrational to man, indicating a complete dichotomy between ultimate reality and human experience.

What gives point to these considerations is the exchange of letters between Voltaire and Diderot that followed publication of the *Letter on the Blind*. For the work was widely read and commented on, and Voltaire ever had an open eye for the noteworthy productions of his contemporaries. A superficial metaphysician himself, Voltaire was especially fascinated by Diderot's bolder ideas. He wrote to him, mingling praise and dissent. It was their first contact.

I have read with extreme pleasure your book which says much and suggests more. For a long time I have esteemed you as much as I despise the stupid barbarians who condemn what they do not understand, and the evil-doers who join with the imbeciles to outlaw what would enlighten them.

But I confess that I am not at all of the opinion of Saunderson, who denies a God because he was born blind. Perhaps I am mistaken, but in his place I should have recognized a very intelligent Being, who had given me so many supplements to sight, and, perceiving by my thought the infinite relations between all things, I should have suspected an infinitely clever Workman. It is very impertinent to try to guess what He is like, and why He has made everything that exists ; but it seems to me quite bold to deny that He is.

I desire passionately to converse with you, no matter whether you think you are one of His works or whether you think you are a necessarily organized portion of an eternal and necessary matter. Before my departure for Lunéville, I should like you to give me the honor of taking a philosophical dinner with me, at my house, together with several sages.

Diderot's reply is dated June 11, 1749.

The moment when I received your letter, *monsieur et cher maître*, was one of the happiest of my life.

Saunderson's opinion is no more mine than yours ; but that may be so because I see. These relationships which strike us so keenly are not so evident to a blind man . . . You should not imagine that Saunderson must have perceived what you would have in his place: you cannot substitute yourself for anyone without completely changing the status of the question.

I would have made him say: if (at some time) there were no beings, there never would have been any at all; because to give oneself existence, one must act, and to act, one must be. If there had been only material beings, there would never have been any spiritual ones . . . together they compose the universe, and the universe is *God*. What force would be added to this reasoning by the opinion which you share with Locke: thought may be only a modification of matter. *I believe in God,* although I get along very well with atheists . . . They say that all is necessity. According to them, a man who offends them offends them no more freely than a tile that works loose and falls upon their heads: but they do not confuse these two causes, and never do they get indignant at the tile . . . It is very important not to mistake hemlock for parsley, but not at all important whether or not you believe in God. The world, said Montaigne, is a ball that he has abandoned to the philosophers to bat around; and I say the same for God Himself.

There is obviously a good portion of diplomatic exaggeration in Diderot's answer. When he says, "I believe in God," it is impossible to take him at his word, for as he later admitted, he was anxious to win the good opinion of the respected patriarch of the *philosophes*. His materialism is quite frankly avowed. Nevertheless, analysis of the last paragraph reveals that Diderot has not irrevocably excluded the type of pantheistic attitude we encountered in *The Sceptic's Walk*. Most significant of all, we observe that the moral problem still torments him—as indeed it always will. Materialism involves necessity, and necessity eliminates moral responsibility, therefore morality. Why, then, are atheists inconsistent, living according to an ethical doctrine they have disproved?

Whether or not Diderot has embraced atheism is actually a matter of secondary import. The essential point is that from here on, his philosophy will be a *godless* one. His religious evolution had been a painful process. In him an enthusiastic, perhaps even religious temperament was at war with a sceptical mind. Unable to satisfy his yearning for God, he will always keep a deep reverence for the beauty and mystery of Nature. This, too, is a form of religion. A nostalgic, though fleeting longing for faith clung to him. It can be glimpsed from time to time, in his writings, as in the prayer that concludes his *Thoughts on the Interpretation of Nature.*

Diderot's first writings were not essentially an attempt at propaganda. Their innermost purpose was the painful need to understand; the need to investigate the greatest of all problems, since he could no longer accept the explanation that had been forced upon him in his childhood; and having investigated it, to arrive, if he could, at the truth. He had found what he considered to be the truth only in small fragments. But he was satisfied. The question had been explored, and laid aside; for a long while, at least, it will cease to torment him.

2

In 1751, two years after the *Letter on the Blind,* Diderot took time out from his overwhelming encyclopedic labors to pursue his investigations on the modification of our sensual apparatus. Again he produced a work of profound thought and unusual interest, the *Letter on the Deaf and Dumb, for the Use of Those Who Hear and Speak.* In spite of its resemblance in title to the lamented *Letter on the Blind,* he made sure that it contained no dangerous implications. It takes an entirely different direction, and the modification of our senses ends up by having only a minor role in the discussion.

As was so frequently the case, Diderot was prompted not by a spontaneous inspiration but by his reaction to another book. His mind operated in sudden bursts. It was an anvil. Each time it was struck by the hammer of some outside stimulus, ideas flew off like sparks. But when no external impulse fired him, it lay cold.

In this instance, he was stirred up by the famous work of the abbé Batteux, *The Fine Arts Reduced to One Principle,* which he had doubtless been consulting for his great encyclopedic article, "On Beauty." Reading in his characteristic manner, he found himself boiling over with objections and original ideas. He replied, too, in characteristic style. The *Letter on the Deaf and Dumb* is somewhat disconcerting by its lack of method or orderly progression of thought; occasionally obscure, it abounds in bold reflections on little known subjects that had excited his curiosity by the very reason of their difficulty and obscurity.

Diderot's initial intention, in the *Letter,* is to study the order in which words came into language. The origin of languages was a matter of considerable speculation in an age that had just abandoned the Biblical explanation, and Diderot gives us a theory that combines his experimental and rational methods. He is not essentially interested in linguistics, however, but in problems of psychology, in the origin of our ideas and their relation to language. Language is the instrument by which the mind "decomposes its own sensations and perceptions." In accord with contemporary rationalism, he believed that all tongues sprang from one common ancestor, and that there exist universal principles of language, even a universal grammar—a theory being revived today. "The human mind, being everywhere the same, should use the same logic of expression."

In studying the growth of languages, Diderot conceives his famous imaginary deaf-mute, an idea ultimately inspired by La Mettrie, as a means of determining the natural order of words. He proposes submitting questions to the "deaf-mute," to which the latter would have to reply by his natural gestures. This would be one way of studying the growth of language. Ever since his early days in Paris, Diderot had been much fetched with the range and impact of effective gesture. Like Cahuzac, a contributor to the *Encyclopedia*, he holds that gestures precede language, and are inseparably linked to it. He takes the opportunity here, *en passant*, to express his conviction—later to be embodied in his dramatic work—that "there are sublime gestures that the greatest oratorical eloquence can never express."

Returning to his theme, he now suggests that the imaginary deaf-mute be "decomposed" into his five senses, and a study be made of the exact contribution of each. We might find "that of all the senses, the eye is the most superficial; the ear, the proudest; the smell, the most voluptuous; taste, the most superstitious and fickle; touch, the profoundest and most philosophical. It would, in my opinion, be an amusing society, that of five persons, each of whom would have only one sense; without doubt each one would treat the other as insane . . . but they could all be geometricians and understand each other perfectly." This idea caused quite a sensation; one young lady, Mlle. de la Chaux, impertinently inquired how we could learn geometry with only a sense of smell. Condillac borrowed Diderot's idea and made it the basis of his *Treatise on Sensations,* one of the major works of the century. Diderot is more scientific and concrete in his approach, but less of a systematic metaphysician. As always, he could inspire others, by the written or spoken word, in his flashes of inspiration, but he was himself too impulsive and inconstant to pursue a patient investigation, too easily seduced by the uncertainty and many-sidedness of truth to construct a system of thought.

Using his imaginary deaf-mute, Diderot tries to determine "experimentally" the natural history of language. The mind, he points out, grasps a whole idea instantaneously, and there is no question of order. But language must function in time, decomposing a single sensation or idea, or a complex of sensations or ideas, into a sequence of analytic expressions.

> Our state of mind in an indivisible instant was represented by an enormous crowd of terms which the precision of language required, and which distributed a total impression into parts ; and because these terms were pronounced in succession and were heard only as they were pronounced, we were led to believe that the mental states they represented had the same sequence. But it is not so at all. Our mental state is one thing ; the account we give of it, either to ourselves or to others, is another. The total and instantaneous sensation of that state is one thing ; the successive and detailed attention we are forced to give to it in order to analyze it, express it and make ourselves understood is another. Our mind is a moving picture, according to which we are ceaselessly painting ; we take much time to render it faithfully, but it exists in us as a whole and all at once ; . . . the brush executes gradually what the painter's eye takes in at a glance.

In this brilliant passage, comments Georges Poulet, we have an anticipation of Bergson's history of the total life of the mind spilling over the limitations of successive and detailed attention, and of his distinction between intuition and intelligence.

Expression must then follow order. Current theory held that logical order and linguistic order in sentences were naturally identical. Diderot declares that this is not so. All orders, inverted or logical, are equally "natural." But historically, the primitive order was not the logical, or "social" order, but was based on cries, reactions to sensations, and gestures. The imaginary deaf-mute offers "experimental" proof of this thesis.

Of surpassing value, in this brief work, are Diderot's ideas on word values, foreshadowing theories of the nineteenth and twentieth centuries. Words do not merely convey ideas, he observes; they have intangible picturesque and sonorous effects. They have the power of creating specific physiological reactions that go beyond the mere sum of rational and visual content. This is their "emblematic" value, involving what we would call a process of association. The total effect of a word far surpasses its literal meaning.

Through this power of words, language is enabled to overcome the limits of its analytical function. The poetic emblem is our only means of synthetical expression, corresponding to our true experience. Our imagination, Diderot explains in the later *Salon of 1767*, is incapable of "keeping up" with the succession of images of poetry, of analyzing the pictures and values each conveys. Instead, the words and images act directly on our minds and sensations. Or, as he puts it in the *Letter*, poetry bypasses the conceptual imagination, evoking the whole concept of an experience in its simultaneity. Necessarily, great poetry is often obscure. Indeed, all art is this kind of synthetic intuition. Poetry is then far more than conveyance of thought, more even than harmony and rhythm. That is why it cannot be translated. There passes into the words of the poet "a spirit that animates and gives life to every syllable. What is this spirit? I have sometimes felt its presence; but all I know of it, is that because of it, things are said and portrayed at the same time; the mind grasps them, and at the same time, the soul is moved by them, the imagination sees them and the ear hears them; the discourse is no longer merely a chain of energetic terms that express the thought with force and grandeur, but also a tissue of hieroglyphics piled up one on the other that paint it. In that sense, I could say that all poetry is emblematic."

Again Diderot flirts with idealism for a brief moment. Many of the abstract words we use, such as essence, substance, matter, actually convey no knowledge of the external world. In using them, we never leave ourselves; "it is our own thought we are perceiving." But Diderot's intention is probably not to support Berkeleyan idealism. It is rather to affirm, as in the *Letter on the Blind,* the active part of the mind in the knowledge process; he is on the road to Kant's rejoinder to the idealists. Language, like the sensations it represents, is not a mere imprint of the external world on a passive mind. It represents truly external reality, in that form which our mind is equipped to grasp, as the two meet.

But we must not go too far in this direction. Diderot does not abandon Lockeian sensualism. The mind, he still holds, is passive in its reception of sensations, if not in its reaction and interpretation. Again he uses an analogy, borrowed directly from La Mettrie.

Consider man as a walking clock ; let the heart represent the mainspring, and the other organs in the chest the principle parts of the movement. Imagine in the head a bell equipped with small hammers, from which radiate an infinite multitude of threads that end at every point of the box. Put over the bell a little figure such as we use to ornament the top of our clocks ; let it have its ear cocked, like a musician who is listening to see whether his instrument is well tuned : this little figure will be the soul [consciousness]. If several of the threads are pulled simultaneously, the bell will be struck several blows, and the little figure will hear several sounds at once. Suppose that some of the threads are always drawn ; as we realize the daytime noise of Paris only by the silence of the night, some sensations will often escape us by their continuity. Such is the sensation of our own existence. We are conscious of it, especially in the state of health, only when we concentrate on thinking of ourselves. When we are healthy, no part of the body informs us of its existence.

The healthy body functions in silence—this principle has been emphasized by scientists of our own day. The sounds produced by the "bell" do not die out immediately. They resound—this was another idea inspired by La Mettrie—and their resounding ties in with the following signals. These the "little figure" compares and judges. Memory is the resonance of the bell; judgment is the formation of harmonies *(accords)*.

In the *Letter on the Deaf and Dumb,* Diderot, Herbert Dieckmann has pointed out, links esthetic ideas with "the analysis of the genesis of our knowledge and more exactly the analysis of the relation between thought and language." Another scholar, Paul H. Meyer, has emphasized the importance of this work in the development of Diderot, the literary critic. He has found himself in conflict with the traditional academic critics, who were dogmatic and more interested in finding faults than positive values. Diderot, on the other hand, is already searching for a "sympathetic and perceptive individual, in an exchange of ideas with whom he will find a perfect medium for the dialectic progress of his mind."

Starting with the problem of inversions, raised by the abbé Batteux, Diderot has been led to a profound and provocative discussion of the nature of language, of its psychological, esthetic, and epistemological significance. Language is a social phenomenon, and he treats it as such. In this sense it has evolved toward the requirements of logical reasoning. But it is also a psychological phenomenon, involving the mechanism of man's reaction to the world around him, and his mode of thought. In this second sense, it has not evolved. Through poetry, finally, the primitive effort to express at once the total content and emotional context of an experience can be attained. Poetry is, then, the highest use of language.

CHAPTER 7

The
Battle
Begins

AT THE HOME of the prince of Saxe-Gotha, Rousseau had met a certain Melchior Grimm, the son of a Lutheran minister from Ratisbonn-on-the-Danube. In February 1749, possessing solid linguistic and literary equipment, Grimm had come to France as companion to the younger son of count von Schoenberg. He was then twenty-six, ten years Diderot's junior. Not long after his arrival in Paris, he was appointed reader to the prince of Saxe-Gotha. Rousseau soon introduced Grimm to the young radical group that included Helvétius, d'Holbach, and Raynal. Diderot, detained at Vincennes, could not as yet make his acquaintance.

A year after his arrival in Paris, Grimm became private secretary to count von Friesen, a well educated and pleasure-loving young blood. Aside from his bacchic parties, the count was accustomed to setting aside one day each week for a strictly philosophical dinner. At these epicurean feasts gathered a strange assortment of men. Among them, in addition to Grimm and Rousseau, were the pastor Klüppfel, Marmontel, and Helvétius. The latter was a wealthy young tax collector and philosopher who was soon to become notorious for his radical books on psychology and ethics. Soon

Grimm began to hold his own weekly gatherings. "At these bachelor dinners," Marmontel notes in his memoirs, "complete freedom of expression was the rule; but that was a dish Rousseau tasted soberly of." Klüppfel was known to be keeping a very pretty and very young girl, but because of his modest appointments, he was forced to share her with others. Rousseau tells us in his *Confessions* that one evening, when he and Grimm were feeling gay, they accompanied him to her apartment and the three of them took turns in making love to her. The poor girl did not know whether to laugh or cry. "Grimm has always maintained that he did not touch her. It must have been to amuse himself by keeping us waiting impatiently that he stayed so long with her." And Rousseau adds maliciously, "If he did abstain, it was scarcely because of scruples."

After Diderot met Grimm, the three became inseparable friends. They talked fondly of a trip to Italy they would make together. It would be a voyage of discovery. First they would explore the ancient world on whose culture they had been nursed; then the Italian Renaissance, the fountainhead of modern culture; and finally the new music, which had aroused their enthusiasm. None of them, unhappily, was in a position to leave.

This idyllic period lasted several months. Then Rousseau began to inject a discordant note into the triangular friendship; he was a little jealous because Diderot and Grimm were growing more and more attached to each other. It was not very long, in fact, before the young German took even more complete possession of Diderot's heart than he ever had; and it was not long before Diderot realized that this was to be the great friendship of his life.

His affinity with Rousseau is understandable; both had an emotional temperament, remarkably similar in many respects. With Grimm, it appears on the surface to have been a case of the attraction of opposites. Unemotional and self-possessed, Grimm never gave himself completely, whereas Diderot, without any reserve, "a volcano in permanent eruption," put his whole enthusiastic soul into his friendship. He envied Grimm because his heart was always in agreement with his head, while he himself could rarely make them agree. Actually there was much common ground. Both men were intensely interested in music, opera, the theatre, and above all, in moral analysis and literary criticism. Both were steeped in classical and English literatures. "Grimm," writes Sainte-Beuve, "becoming the most French of the Germans, was attracted, by a sort of natural affinity, to Diderot, the most German of Frenchmen."

Through the long years of friendship, Diderot and Grimm were to grow ever closer, sharing joys and triumphs, trials and problems. They found endless pleasure in talking together about anything and everything. "We dined, Grimm and I, near one of the statues in the Tuileries. A long walk before dinner; we ate gaily and with good appetite; a long walk after dinner. In this interval, we spoke of morals and of love, of love and of morals; the conclusion, to make ourselves better, to forgive the wicked, sufficiently punished by their own wickedness; to make everyone happy, and above all our friend and our mistress." It is apparent who did most of the talking!

As time went on, Diderot fell more and more under the domination of his friend, despite the fact that Grimm was ten years his junior. No matter what his thoughtlessness, Diderot always found an excuse for him, never allowed anyone to criticize him. He took delight in boasting of Grimm's superior character and intelligence. "There is a man as superior to me as I dare think myself superior to d'Alembert, with all my good qualities and many others I lack, wiser and more prudent than I, having more experience with men and the world than I shall ever have. He has the same ascendancy over me that I sometimes have over others. What most men are for me, children, I am for him!" And that was exactly how Grimm treated him, as a precocious child.

The passage is curious and revealing. Diderot appears over-anxious to compensate for his submissiveness to Grimm by an exaggerated belief in his own superiority and domination over others.

In a letter to Grimm, Diderot compared their two natures. "I need only a little vexation to make me lose a day. Your soul is like a clock supplied with a good pendulum that measures the oscillations without anything disturbing it either in its movement or its rest; mine is like a hair that flutters at the least breath." Grimm's coldness has perhaps been exaggerated. He was not demonstrative. But Mme. d'Epinay's memoirs reveal the depth of feeling he had for his friends, despite the contrast between his self-possession, or reserve, and the quickly aroused emotions of his French comrades.

Grimm's ascendancy over Diderot seems to have filled a need in both. Each had found that greatest of rarities, a friend with whom he could experience a complete communion of mind and of heart.

The year 1750 was one of relentless labor on "the great undertaking." Happy and tragic events interrupted the intensity of Diderot's preparations. On the 30th of June, his four-year-old son, François-Jacques-Denis, died of a fever. He had already lost his first child, Angélique, when she was still an infant. The blow was a heavy one, but the worst was yet to come. A second son was born to the grieving mother in September; he was taken for baptism to the beautiful little church of Saint-Etienne-du-Mont, which still crowns the hill of Sainte-Geneviève, in the heart of the Latin Quarter. The infant, it is said, slipped out of the arms of his godmother and fell on the steps of the church. He died before the end of the year.

The happy event was the announcement, on July 18th, of the triumph of Rousseau's *Discourse on the Arts and Sciences* in the Academy of Dijon's essay contest. Jean-Jacques, Diderot, and their friends toasted the proud victor and the triumph of Truth. Diderot, always ready to contribute his time and talent, had already promised to help Jean-Jacques revise the text, and to have it printed for him. Quite different was this enthusiasm from the opinion expressed of the *Discourse* in later years, after he had quarreled with Rousseau: "many eloquent sophistries whose ultimate conclusion would be to break up the musical instruments, burn the paintings, smash the statues, perhaps to desert the cities and disperse into the forests."

Despite the distracting effects of these moving events, Diderot gave up his life, that year, to the *Encyclopedia*. It had been decided —although this plan eventually had to be abandoned—that nothing was to be printed until all the contributions were in. Diderot made great and unending efforts to get his collaborators to do their work and turn in their articles on time; frequently this meant coaxing or flattery, or satisfying their unreasonable and selfish demands. D'Alembert had delivered the mathematical sections on schedule, but others were far behind. Rousseau was practically forced to complete all the musical articles within the space of three months. The publishers' petition (September 7, 1749), requesting Diderot's release from Vincennes, indicates that at the time most of the scientific articles had already been turned in. Long hours were spent in securing collaborators, in editing and revising the contributions, in reading proofs, in consulting with printers and engravers. Most of all, Diderot devoted his days and nights to his own share of the work. It is true that he wrote fewer articles than are sometimes attributed to him, but there were still very many—how many, we shall never know certainly. At first, he had undertaken only the arts and crafts. For these, he utilized existing plates and writings, and sent technically competent subordinates to shops and factories— though he occasionally made such visits himself. Later, when persecution brought about the loss of those to whom he had entrusted the philosophical articles (the abbés Yvon, de Prades, Pestré), he took them upon himself. For his philosophical articles, he sometimes went through dozens of tomes in order to digest the best authorities and write something really worthwhile. His chief source was Jacob Brücker's *History of Philosophy*. Often, all too often, he satisfied himself with copying and compilation. But even then, he made the dry and austere Brücker readable.

About the trades, which he had taken almost entirely on himself to cover, Diderot actually knew little; but his ignorance was compensated by the will to learn and the interest derived from his childhood environment. What made his task more difficult was the absence of technical books; a trade was passed down from father to son, and nobody bothered to write about it. This lack he supplied by direct observation. Here there lay another difficulty. Methods of manufacture were often trade secrets, jealously guarded from business rivals and tax spies. Some uneducated artisans, who worked by habit, were unable to offer a clear exposition of their processes. Diderot was puzzled—and fascinated—by the chaos of technical vocabularies.

Yet he succeeded in overcoming these obstacles. Whereas Chambers had found a stocking loom too complicated for description, Diderot went to see one, "had it explained to him, learned to work it, then had its very numerous parts designed and engraved, and wrote a full article and an explanatory text for the plates. In substituting this thorough and painstaking method of work for that of mere compilation, he was the initiator of all succeeding encyclopedias worthy of the name." When no satisfactory information could be had in Paris, he did not hesitate to write to manufacturers and artisans in the provinces. "I am very satisfied with your *mémoire* on glovemaking," reads one of his thank-you notes, "so satisfied that I shall not spare you the one on furriery you promised me. Please write as much as you can on this subject." The fact that Diderot did not himself become acquainted with each process, as he had hoped to do, but leaned heavily on those who possessed technical competence, does not detract from his accomplishment. He did all that time would allow.

In his encyclopedic labors, Diderot was aided by his remarkable capacity for work. "Tomorrow will be eight days since I have left my study. . . . I am 'encyclopedizing' like a galleyslave." "Oh let me work as much as I wish," he cries to his mistress, who had scolded him for neglecting his health. "It is my life, my rest, my happiness, my health."

In November appeared the *Prospectus*, written by Diderot. It describes the importance and usefulness of an encyclopedia as a means of spreading knowledge. Equal attention is to be paid to the sciences, the liberal arts, and the mechanical arts; their inter-dependence is stressed as a guiding principle of the work. Alpha-betical order is considered insufficient. Rational order, the place of a subject in the whole of knowledge, will be indicated as well. Classi-fication is, then, necessary. Diderot borrows and develops, with a few modifications, Bacon's genealogical table of knowledge, according to which sciences are classified not by subject matter but by the mental faculty on which they depend. Memory, Reason, and Imagination are the three faculties around which all the arts and sciences are grouped, and history, philosophy, and poetry are their three spheres. This is the same classification that was used by Thomas Jefferson for his personal library. Reason, for example, gives us philosophy, which divides into the science of God, the science of man, and the science of nature; then there are further subdivisions. "From bracket to bracket," comments André Billy, "from division to division, we reach hosiery, for example, which is connected with the science of nature as wool industry, a trade, and more generally, a use of nature; we reach gymnastics which, through hygiene, is connected with medicine, medicine with zoology, zoology with physics, physics with the science of nature, and the latter with philosophy . . . Strange classification which puts the locksmith's trade under Memory and falconry under Reason!"

Fortunately, this introduction does not reflect the spirit of the *Encyclopedia;* although its classification is subjective and rational-istic, its contents will attempt to be scientifically progressive and forward-looking. The purpose of the *Encyclopedia* was set forth even more precisely in the article "Encyclopedia" which Diderot had already written: "To assemble knowledge scattered over the earth's surface . . . ; to assure that the works of past centuries will not have been useless work in the centuries to come; that our descendants, better educated, may at the same time be happier; that we should not die without having deserved well of the human race."

The work is to consist of eight volumes of text, announces the *Prospectus*, each of two hundred and forty sheets, and two of plates. The total subscription price is two hundred eighty livres, to be met in nine payments, while separate purchase of the volumes will cost a total of three hundred seventy-two livres. It is expected that the work will be completed within two years. Should there, by chance, be an addition volume, subscribers will be entitled to a special discount.

The response to the *Prospectus* was highly satisfactory, both the general critical reaction—which delighted Diderot and d'Alembert —and the more practical reaction of the reading public who hastened within the next few weeks to put in their subscriptions. No subscriptions were supposed to be accepted after May 1st, but the demands were so numerous that the lists had to be reopened. As the initial payments of sixty francs kept pouring in, Le Breton, Briasson, and David complimented each other gleefully on their foresight and business acumen.

Still more favorable was the reaction to the *Preliminary Discourse,* which appeared in 1751. D'Alembert had been selected to write it, since he enjoyed a more dignified and less suspicious reputation than the editor-in-chief. The *Preliminary Discourse* is a short history of human accomplishment, based on the avowed belief that empirical knowledge, gained through observation and experiment, and not rationalistic thought, is responsible for man's progress. At the same time, it is itself a masterpiece of rationalism, following the analytical tradition of Locke and Condillac. To trace the origin of the sciences, d'Alembert goes all the way back to the beginning, when the first man had a first sensation. He then sketches the transformations of this sensation in the mind: the first ideas ("I exist, other things exist outside of me"), the development of language and communal living. Society established, men seek to live more securely and more comfortably—and thus the first sciences and arts are born. D'Alembert concludes the work with a superlative account of the progress of knowledge since the Renaissance.

Meanwhile, interest in the *Encyclopedia* had become so widespread that Diderot was elected to the Academy of Berlin (though this was partly the result of the purchase of some manuscripts from its secretary, Formey). Under the sponsorship of Frederick the

Great the Academy had become a Mecca for persecuted French authors. Voltaire himself was at the moment an honored guest of that philosophical monarch.

Finally, on July 1, 1751, the first volume made its long-heralded appearance. It was a beautiful in-folio volume, bound in calf, and dedicated to Diderot's old "friend," the powerful count d'Argenson, who was one of the protectors of the enterprise. Immediately, several thousand impatient and curious readers plunged into its enormous pages.

Not all these readers examined its contents with friendly eyes. The *Encyclopedia* had already aroused the hostility of the reactionaries. For one thing, the array of contributors, including the best writers of the day, was too imposing, and not "reliable" enough, for their taste. Then, they looked with fear and horror upon these philosophers "who dared to assert that there was no mystery which Reason could not make plain." The Church saw itself directly menaced, and many high in the government were uneasy.

Most fearful of all, and most determined to crush the enterprise, were the Jesuits. This powerful order enjoyed tremendous influence in France and throughout Europe. In spite of the opposition of the Jansenists, who controlled the Parlements and the University, they dominated the king, the queen, the dauphin, and other important figures, through their confessors. Through their schools, they reached thousands more. The Jesuits were annoyed by the personalities and the purpose of the work, by the prospective competition with a publication of their own (the *Universal Dictionary*, published in 1704), and by their failure to have the theological articles put in their charge.

The *Journal de Trévoux*, the famous Jesuit periodical, was one of the most influential and widely read in Europe. Like their school system, it was undeniably good; each issue contained some excellent literary criticism and much information from all over the world, easily gathered by their far-flung and unique organization. Among the more important writers for the *Journal de Trévoux*, and later its editor, was the keen and learned Jesuit professor, Father Berthier. As soon as the *Prospectus* appeared, he examined it with a hostile eye, suspicious of the purpose of this *Encyclopedia* and of the men who were writing it. He became rather worried when he read of its desire to emphasize the spirit of enquiry, to spread "truth" and destroy "errors." He found nothing more specific to object to, however, than the plagiarism of Bacon. Although this borrowing was already acknowledged by Diderot, he made it the basis of a somewhat spiteful attack in his periodical. An exchange of letters followed, in which the philosopher, by his frankness and wit, easily won the decision. But that was only the first skirmish.

Father Berthier returned to the attack as soon as the first volume appeared. He hastened to scan its pages and came out with a sternly disapproving review. He pointed out that many of the articles were plagiarized compilations of earlier writings. But that was the least. In a sly, underhanded manner, religion had been mocked. The work was full of Lockean sensualism, the denial that man has any innate ideas, even that of God. The article "Political Authority" was positively scandalous. Its author (Diderot) had borrowed from Hobbes an idea which Rousseau was later to transform into the Gospel of democracy. "The government, although hereditary in one family and put into the hands of one person, is not a private but a public property, which can never be taken away from the people, to whom, alone, it belongs essentially and entirely." Berthier did not mention that this "radical" idea was followed by the Hobbesian sequel, that the ruler has absolute power, by terms of the contract, and that the people can only intervene when the ruling family is extinct. The authority comes from the people, but they are helpless to do anything about its use or abuse. Rousseau was to remedy this absurdity, though his system is akin to the totalitarian democracies.

But Diderot's article expressed another radical sentiment, that was his own. "No man has received from ·nature the right to command others. Liberty is a gift of heaven, and every individual of the human species has the right to enjoy it as soon as he enjoys reason." This was truly dangerous. Can we not hear already in Diderot's lines the passionate words of a great disciple of the French Enlightenment, that "All men are created free and equal"?

Shortly after the Jesuit attacks, Diderot received an anonymous note. "If M. Diderot wishes to avenge himself against the Jesuits, we are able to put money and pamphlets at his disposal; we await his reply." Too proud not to disdain any such assistance, possibly suspecting a trap, the philosopher replied: "I am perfectly able to fight out my quarrel with Father Berthier without anyone's help. I have no money, but I do not need any. As for the pamphlets, I could use them only after having examined them carefully, and I do not have the time for that."

Diderot did have a good friend among the Jesuits, and corresponded with him frequently. This was Father Castel, one of the strange figures of the century. An initiator of esthetic criticism and also a physicist of some standing, Father Castel had invented a machine to transmute sounds into their "corresponding colors," in order to enable deaf-mutes to "hear" with their eyes—thus suggesting a theory of the correspondence of colors and sounds which has attracted modern artists and estheticians. Father Castel was withal a practical man. He had very sensibly advised Rousseau that the best means to get ahead in Paris was through the influence of women. Doubtless he would have been more sympathetic to Diderot's ways of thinking, but unfortunately he had no voice in the *Journal de Trévoux*.

While the philosophers, including Voltaire, were rejoicing at the success of the first volume, the Jesuits were busy exerting their influence on the rulers of France in an effort to crush the enterprise. More crude than the Jesuits in his immediate and open opposition was the former bishop of Mirepoix, Jean-François Boyer. He complained to the king himself that the censors had been made fools of; while the theological articles had been very properly censored, the encyclopedists had slipped their vicious anti-religious propaganda into articles on history and law and physics! Even an article with the innocuous title "Love of Literature" *(Amour des lettres)* contained their insidious venom. Did it not say that "most men honor letters as they do religion and virtue, that is, as something it is not possible to know, practice or love"?

The king sent the outraged Boyer to chancellor Malesherbes, who in turn directed him to his son, the new director of publications. A man of noble character and fine intelligence, the younger Malesherbes was keenly aware of the abuses that were crippling France and sympathized strongly with the new ideas. Charged with the censorship of books, with their suppression when decreed by king or council, Malesherbes believed firmly in the freedom of the press. He fulfilled the obligations of his office scrupulously, but at the same time did his best to assist and to guide the reformers. He pretended to be duly horrified at Boyer's recital. He promised that each and every article would henceforth be censored, and allowed the mollified bishop to name on the spot three censors of his choice. In this way, Malesherbes felt that he was appeasing the enemies of the *Encyclopedia* and protecting its editors from their own rashness.

It was about this time that Diderot met his third great friend. Curiously enough, he too was ten years Diderot's junior and a German by birth, although French in spirit, having been brought up in Paris. Paul Thiry, baron d'Holbach, was wealthy, an atheist, and a partisan of the *philosophes*. His hobbies were subsidizing starving men of letters and giving vent to his fanatical hatred of priests. D'Holbach rapidly became attached to the little group of encyclopedists. Each Thursday he invited the entire clan, together with sympathetic foreigners who chanced to be in Paris, to his home for a magnificent dinner. At these renowned feasts the female sex was excluded and restraint of expression was unknown.

The baron soon became famous throughout Europe as "the maître d'hôtel of philosophy," and his home, among its privileged guests, was referred to as "the synagogue of the Rue Royale." Dinner began at two and frequently lasted till six or eight in the evening. The regular company included Diderot, Rousseau, Grimm, d'Alembert, Turgot, Buffon, Helvétius, Condillac, Marmontel, the freethinking abbé Raynal, and the poet Saint-Lambert—a group of the most brilliant and most daring thinkers in France. Only Rousseau was ill at ease at the baron's house, as he felt his conscience—and his characteristic spirit of disagreement—rebel against the irreverent talk. His appearances grew more infrequent, and stopped entirely in 1754.

What a treat for posterity if the conversations and repartee of this group could have been preserved! They talked eagerly of scientific problems; examined and condemned religion, priests, and fanaticism; debated abstract questions of morality, politics or metaphysics. Of all the *salons*, none was as brilliant as the synagogue, none so important in intellectual history. "For this group was devoted to a cause, to the Enlightenment, and from the clash of ideas was born many an inspiration for Diderot and others. Nowhere did Diderot have a better forum for his forensic art. Fiery, rhetorical, unquenchable, talking with his entire face and body, he magnetized his audience with his keen thought and startling paradoxes. Nowhere were the hosts more gracious, generous, and urbane." So writes Sainte-Beuve.

There was a lighter side to their gatherings. Once, as a rather cruel practical joke, Diderot brought some misguided priest from the provinces to dinner. Thinking he had written a great tragedy, he had come to Diderot for an expert opinion. The philosopher could not resist the temptation to display the rustic genius to all his friends. As the curé read his atrocious verses, the company heckled him constantly with silly questions and grave objections. The curé's definition of comedy and tragedy is worth quoting. "In a comedy, it's all about a marriage, and in a tragedy, about a murder. The whole plot turns on this point: will they get married, or won't they? Will there be a murder, or won't there? They will get married, there will be a murder, there's your first act. They won't get married, there will not be a murder, there's the second act. A new way of getting married and of killing presents itself and that's the third act. A sudden difficulty arises to the marriage and the killing, there's the fourth act. Finally, worn out with the struggle, they get married and kill, and that's the last act." The philosophers exploded with laughter—all except Rousseau, who had suffered throughout at the cruelty of the proceedings. At this point he jumped up impulsively and shouted to the harassed curé: "Your play is worthless, your talk extravagant, all these gentlemen are making fun of you. Go back and preach in your village!" This scene was the first outward sign of the growing coolness between Rousseau and the others.

Of all his friends, d'Holbach by far preferred Diderot. He in turn appealed to Diderot for a variety of reasons—his generosity, his simplicity, his love of good food, and his encyclopedic knowledge. He was an omnivorous reader of philosophy, history, politics and natural science. "Whatever system my imagination forges," Diderot wrote, "I am sure that my friend d'Holbach will find the facts and authorities to justify it." Yet he never inspired in Diderot the same intense feeling of friendship that Grimm and Rousseau did. As a friend, Diderot always felt the need of unreservedly opening his heart, of giving himself freely and completely, and of proving his friendship by a constant ardor for performing services. With d'Holbach, he could do none of these. "It is impossible that his soul and mine can ever touch each other with a certain intimacy. I can't explain that to you. It means nothing to others; it means everything to us. There are tiny things that grate on me more than atrocious actions." The baron was not only egotistic but extremely moody and ill-tempered. "I suspect that man of being bored in the midst of all the wealth and happiness that surround him," Diderot commented when d'Holbach went to England. "All that means nothing without a sensitive soul and a healthy mind. Run, run, my friend; run as far as you want, you will never escape yourself."

Once when d'Holbach had returned to Paris, Diderot avoided seeing him for several weeks. Then he wrote to his mistress, "I see that he doesn't forgive me the solitude in which I left him. I pay absolutely no attention to his sulking, he'll get tired of it." Quite a contrast with his attitude toward Grimm!

But again, one naturally hears more of the stormy side. There was a sincere feeling of friendship between these two philosophers. "His reproaches about my absence moved me. That man has in his heart chords that affect me strongly." In the years to come, they will see each other more and more, and spend many happy days together.

4

The second volume of the *Encyclopedia* came off the presses in January 1752. Once again, trouble was already brewing for its ever imprudent authors. Among the collaborators was a certain abbé de Prades who had written a thesis for the doctorate in theology, entitled *To Celestial Jerusalem*. In this supposed work of orthodoxy, he had the impudence to include his decidedly heterodox opinions, and even to cast doubt on the authenticity of prophecies and miracles. Certitude, he argued, must be based on the principle of empirical knowledge, not on revelation. On the 18th of November 1751, he defended his thesis and easily obtained his degree. The committee in charge of his examination simply had not bothered to wade through the boring ramifications of his masterpiece—an oversight that has happened many times since! Strangely enough, some Jansenist did take the trouble to scan its weighty pages. What he found startled him. Immediately the scandal broke out. While all of France laughed at the hoax, to the great discomfiture of the Sorbonne, the archbishop of Paris, a leading enemy of the *Encyclopedia*, condemned the thesis. Soon the pope added his condemnation. The abashed professors reversed themselves. Next, the Parlement of Paris ordered it burned. The abbé de Prades was stripped of his degrees and position, and a warrant was issued for his arrest.

The enemies of the *Encyclopedia* lost no time in using this incident to exert pressure against that hated publication. Just as in 1749, when Diderot had been thrown into prison, persecution of the *philosophes* was again a retaliatory measure against general unrest among the people. The spark this time was not a lost war, but a trivial incident. A parish priest had refused the last sacraments to a dying Jansenist priest because of his refusal to submit to the bull, *Unigenitus,* which outlawed the Jansenist doctrines. Throughout Paris and the provinces, a wave of protest spread, with the Parlements, which were Jansenist and Gallican, leading the opposition, while the king remained firm in support of the Jesuits and Ultramontanists. Then came the de Prades affair. His thesis was immediately linked with the *Encyclopedia.* The article "Certitude," which had also been written by de Prades for the *Encyclopedia,* was found to be similar in content and critical method to his thesis. The magistrates pointed out that the bitter controversy between the Jesuits and the Jansenists only favored their common enemies, the encyclopedists. "The haughty *philosophe,* who, insanely jealous of the Divinity itself, rejects the homage that is paid Him, has judged this the suitable time to publish a monstrous system of incredulity. It was reserved to us to see a public thesis upheld without protest in the leading university of the Christian world, a thesis that establishes all the false principles of incredulity." Diderot was charged with having helped the abbé write his thesis—probably a true accusation. Furthermore, when the abbé published his *Apology,* it was immediately evident that Diderot alone had written the third —and best—part of it. When it became known that still another collaborator, the supposedly "safe" abbé Yvon, had also taken a hand in helping his colleagues, a warrant was issued for his arrest too.

Diderot's part of the *Apology* is a good example of his theological and polemical talents. With delightful finesse, he removes the suspicion of heresy from de Prades and proves that it is he precisely who is the authentic Christian. Here and there Diderot inserts one of his favorite theories. We must not believe blindly, but judge religion by reason. There are no innate ideas, we know only through our senses. Self-interest and self-preservation are man's primary instincts, and precede any ideas of good or evil, or of God; all our moral concepts come through our senses and through physical experiences. Finally, why persecute the abbé de Prades? Internal quarrels, Diderot remarks truthfully, have done religion more harm than all the freethinkers in the world.

With his usual tact, he had only made matters worse for his collaborator. The abbé fled to Holland, then to the court of Frederick II, where he was welcomed among the ever increasing group of philosophical fugitives. A few years later, he recanted publicly—to Diderot's great disgust—and was restored to grace.

Meanwhile a thousand hostile eyes examined every line of every article in the second volume of the *Encyclopedia*. Yes, they had done it again, eluded the vigilance of the censors and slipped in their dangerous ideas. How had they managed this time? Innumerable Parisians were asking. The censors had examined every article in manuscript and found them perfectly ·innocent. So they were; but before they went to press, numerous insertions had been made—it was all quite simple!

The authorities, civil and religious, were aroused. Malesherbes had attempted at the last moment to prevent the outburst by substituting innocent articles for the objectionable ones; but it was too late. Although he suspended the sale, a large portion of the subscribers had already obtained the volume. The "devout party" (as the enemies of the "philosophic party" were termed) had all their guns trained, and on February 7th the king's privy council issued an order suppressing both volumes of the *Encyclopedia*, forbidding further printing and ordering seizure of the manuscripts.

"His majesty has recognized that in these two volumes, [they] have presumed to insert several maxims tending to destroy royal authority, to establish the spirit of independence and revolt, and, beneath the obscure and equivocal terms, to raise the foundations of error, moral corruption, irreligion and incredulity."

It seemed beyond doubt that the enemies of progress had won a decisive victory. According to Grimm and the marquis d'Argenson, the Jesuits acquired Diderot's confiscated papers. D'Argenson, in his journal, accuses them of systematic persecution, and also notes: "Nobody doubts that they will continue the work in order to recompense the subscribers." Grimm reports that the Jesuits tried to utilize the papers but that they were unable to make head or tail of most of the notes they had seized, for Diderot alone possessed the key to them.[1]

The Philosopher was urged by his friends to follow the example of the abbé de Prades. This indeed was his initial impulse, in the terror of the first alarm. But instead of fleeing, he declared firmly to his friends that he would never abandon the enterprise. As long as a warrant was not actually issued for his arrest, he would run

---

[1] It is incorrectly reported by most historians that Malesherbes, at this time, saved the manuscripts by having them transported to his own house.

the risk of sudden seizure. Voltaire advised him to take the whole thing to Berlin, but Diderot felt that he could not appropriate the property of Le Breton. Besides, he knew that powerful anti-Jesuit influences were starting to work for his side. Among them were d'Argenson, and also Mme. de Pompadour, who hated the Jesuits and was friendly towards Voltaire, Montesquieu, and d'Alembert. Doubtless a struggle for power at the French Court was involved, as well as the deep respect for the property rights of the publishers and the subscribers.

Malesherbes had already gone into action in an effort to salvage the *Encyclopedia*. By spring he had succeeded. The order of the privy council was to apply only to the first two volumes. Although a legal printing license could no longer be issued, because of ecclesiastical opposition, a "tacit license" was extended. This was an evasion commonly employed when the government had to permit a book but could not openly admit tolerating it. They merely told the publisher to carry on secretly, while the police would close an eye. In case scandal made a search necessary, the publisher would have ample advance notice.

There was general rejoicing among the little band when the good news reached them. The Jesuits were foiled! Le Breton mopped his brow in relief, as he thought of his two thousand subscribers. Diderot, too, was relieved, as he had felt mighty close to that dungeon at Vincennes. There was one little obstacle: this time the censors would not only read every article in manuscript; they would examine them in proof! Oh well, other means of evasion would be found.

Once again Diderot sounded the call to action, and his men resumed their positions. That is, all except Rousseau and d'Alembert. The cautious d'Alembert would never do anything to compromise his cherished independence; he was smarting under the attacks that had been directed against him and did not wish to be in the center of a dangerous controversy. It took six months of persuasion to convince him that it was his duty and to his advantage to continue his collaboration. As for Rousseau, he had completely lost interest.

Only Diderot's enthusiasm, only Diderot's faith in the job to be done was not impaired. Under his inspired leadership, the little army returned to their patient work of sapping falsehood and spreading truth.

But throughout France, trouble was not at an end. The Parlements issued order after order against the Jesuits, and each was broken immediately by the king's council. Their remonstrances to the king fell on deaf ears. D'Argènson, in his journal, predicted anarchy or revolution. On the night of the eighth of May, the exasperated monarch issued *lettres de cachet*, exiling the judges and attorneys of the Parlements to their provincial residences. The Parlements countered on May 23rd by publishing their "Great Remonstrances," attacking the temporal power of the Church, and reminding the king that "if subjects owe obedience to kings, kings, for their part, owe obedience to laws." People were heard whispering that it was high time the Estates-General were once more convoked and the basic law of the land re-established. The nation, after all, was above the monarch. The bishop of Montauban went so far as to recall that Charles I of England had met an untimely end, and that the Parlement of Paris might also condemn a king to the scaffold. Military patrols appeared on the streets of Paris.

But the Parlements were recalled by the harried king, and the agitation quieted down. Persecution of the encyclopedists was halted and even the Protestants were allowed to build new churches. The time was not yet ripe for Frenchmen to achieve their liberties. But the *Encyclopedia* was saved. It could continue its work of forming a new spirit, a spirit of reason and freedom.

CHAPTER 8

Round
Two

THE STORM OVER THE *Encyclopedia* was not the only one to clear up that year. The long rift with Langres was finally healed when the wayward son confessed his marriage and was forgiven by his father. Then, to seal the new peace, Diderot decided to pack Antoinette off to Langres for a missionary visit.

The prospect of a sojourn with her husband's family was not an attractive one to the unwanted daughter-in-law. But Diderot impressed on her the very practical importance of a complete reconciliation. Doubtless he filled her ears with endless instructions on what to say and how to act. Doubtless, too, he rejoiced at the prospect of a holiday from domestic squabbles.

"She left yesterday," he announced to his father. "She will arrive in three days. Tell her whatever you want, and send her back whenever you are tired of her."

The visit was more successful than he had dared to expect. The first hour or two were rather uncomfortable, the first evening a little less so. But by treating the good cutler as if he might have been her own father, and by helping willingly in the household, Nanette won him over completely. She remained at Langres for about three months; when she left, she carried with her quantities of gifts and the friendly wishes of the family and all their friends.

While Antoinette was away, Diderot plunged into a different sort of controversy. In August and September of 1752, an Italian troupe threw all Paris into a furor with a series of comic operas, chief among them, Pergolesi's *Serva Padrona*. Pergolesi's opera had been presented once before, in October 1746, but little comment had been aroused at that time. In the interval, Rousseau had written his *Letter on the Musical Drama in France and in Italy* (1751), stimulating public interest in the question of Italian versus French music. Rousseau himself defended the French music, as represented by Lulli and Rameau, as more emotional. Grimm, in February 1752, replied to Rousseau with his *Letter on Omphalus*. When the Italian troupe returned, the encyclopedists threw themselves into the quarrel. They favored the Italians because they were instinctively opposed to the stilted, traditional style, and were open to innovations and cosmopolitan influences. Early in 1753, they organized the "Queen's corner" at the Opéra. Fréron and Rameau countered by organizing the "King's corner." For the monarch had to have his say in the dispute, and it was in favor of national tradition, while his Polish queen, Maria Lesczynska, led the innovators. Opera-goers were careful to ask not merely for tickets, but to specify in which "corner" they wanted their seats. Pamphlets flew thickly. Both sides agreed on principles; they disagreed as to which music carried out these principles. The *philosophes* derided the shepherds and shepherdesses and mythical gods of the French libretti. Grimm's brochure, *The Little Prophet of Boemischbroda*, mocked the French opera for its inane ballets and absurd pomp, and incidentally contained a number of sly digs at religion. Voltaire was so delighted with Grimm's piece that he wrote, "What is this Bohemian thinking about, to have more wit than we?" Grimm's success prompted another batch of pamphlets, in support or attack. Diderot published three; while favoring the Italians, he tried to reduce tempers on both sides. Toward the end of the year, Rousseau contributed his *Letter on French Music,* in which he went over to the Italians. The fickle public had forgotten about the *Encyclopedia;* the "Querelle des Bouffons" monopolized polite talk in the salons and the debates that took place after the theatre and at the crowded cafés.

Rousseau, although a superficial student of music, was himself a composer of light operas. Grimm was also a clavecinist of parts. Diderot, in spite of numerous conversations with Rameau and

Philidor, which he liked to call "lessons," had only a limited technical knowledge of music. This did not bother him in the least, for he thought himself qualified to judge and theorize in all fields. Enthusiasm and intelligence, he felt, were adequate titles.

Romain Rolland, in his *Musicians of Other Times*, has defended both the competence and the aims of the encyclopedists. French music was bogged down in artificial conventionalities, infantile plots, and boring recitatives. Diderot and his group were fighting for simplicity, naturalness, and intelligence. It was Diderot's belief that human speech, or declamation, should be the operatic composer's model. Declamation should be considered one "line" and the singing another line twining around it. In other words, good music, like good declamation, conforms to the natural, living passions that inspire the text. Meaningless conventions and stereotyped phrases should be discarded. In the *Letter on the Deaf and Dumb,* Diderot had already declared that music must express and communicate ideas or emotions, as well as merely please. Like poetry and painting, it should be, in its own way, an imitation of nature. In the *Conversations on the "Natural Son"* (1757), he calls for a closer accord between music and libretto. He distinguishes two kinds of imitation: the human voice imitating the cry of passion, and instruments imitating natural sounds. The dance is a different type of imitation, a kind of poetic pantomime, and should be separated from the opera. This idea he later enlarges, in *Rameau's Nephew,* to allow both voice and instrument to imitate either natural sounds or human passions. The violin is the mimic of the singer.

"With his fire, his eloquence, his verve, the physical action of his whole body, the sudden leaps of his imagination," one biographer has commented, Diderot must have been an incomparable propagandist for the new music—even though his side did not win. In February 1754, the Royal Academy banned Italian opera, and the "Querelle des Bouffons" was over. But the "bouffons" had conquered French taste.

Nothing the encyclopedists did remained isolated, in the public eye, from their great enterprise. Though their gallant sallies in the jousts between French and Italian music served to draw them closer, Rameau, the greatest and most influential of French composers and theorists, was alienated—despite their care to exempt him alone from their criticisms. A surly and egoistic person, he responded later, after the Quarrel had already died down. In 1755 and the two following years, he put out a series of three pamphlets pointing out the errors in Rousseau's hastily written articles on music which had appeared in the *Encyclopedia*. These attacks created a sensation among the public, and cast umbrage on the "great enterprise." Diderot fumed helplessly. Later he got his revenge—in a way—by painting a most unflattering portrait of Rameau in *Rameau's Nephew*, a book he never dared to publish.

Work on the *Encyclopedia*, meanwhile, because of interruptions and delays, was advancing slowly. The season of 1752-1753 went by and Diderot's preoccupations had been largely musical. It was not until November 1753 that the third volume, with a preface by d'Alembert, finally appeared. D'Alembert, who was still vexed by the charges that had been hurled at him, set forth anew the purposes of the work and defended its methods. He announced also the addition of a new collaborator, who was destined to be second in importance only to Diderot. The chevalier Louis de Jaucourt was a man intensely interested in all fields of human knowledge, but completely lacking in creative imagination. Jaucourt brought to the enterprise the prestige of an irreproachable reputation and a well-known piety. Up till now he had spent his life studying philosophy, science, history, literature, and archeology, in France, England, Switzerland, and Holland. A doctor, he had confined himself to research and never practiced except for the benefit of the poor. Jaucourt's devotion to the enterprise was such that he sold one of his houses in order to maintain his secretarial staff. Ironically, he sold it to Le Breton, the very publisher of the *Encyclopedia*, who was to reap a fabulous profit from the work. Without Jaucourt, without the years of unremitting labor he contributed, the *Encyclopedia* might not have been completed. He wrote articles on every subject, on medicine, literature, the arts, the trades, politics. The latter were his best efforts, most of the others, unfortunately, being indiscriminate complications.

The third volume turned out all the better for the delay. The prestige of the work was steadily rising. Notoriety being no hindrance to popularity, the number of subscribers now topped the original two-thousand mark.

When the third volume suffered no open attack on the part of the Church or the civil authorities, Diderot felt greatly relieved. Fundamentally gay and lighthearted, under the least contrary stimulus he became excited and melancholy. Frequent indigestion was one cause of temporary moodiness and pessimism. The ups and downs of the *Encyclopedia,* most of all, and the difficulties, struggles and persecutions involved, made Diderot's life a perpetual seesaw between the extremes of his natural optimism and his easily excited pessimism.

This changeable temperament is constantly reflected in his thought; when Diderot speaks ill of civilization or of human nature, a too sumptuous repast, or a recalcitrant collaborator is usually at the bottom of it. In such circumstances, he is likely to complain bitterly about his troubles. His fate is to be tormented until death, he cries. He envies obscure writers who have neither worries nor fame. Besides, what is the use of all his efforts? "Be useful to men! Is it at all certain that we do anything else except amuse them, and that there is much difference between a philosopher and a flute player? They listen to one or the other with pleasure or disdain, and remain what they are."

Sometimes, too, Diderot is sad without apparent cause and then he awaits "the peace that sleep will bring." This vague *Weltschmerz,* strangely pre-romantic in nature, is the symptom of a general weariness that sometimes overcame his more usual zest for living. Pleasure is but an illusion. "We run to embrace it, but we embrace only pain in the garb of pleasure." Men learn too late that life is a gigantic lie, a chain of deceitful hopes. One day, feeling particularly depressed, he summarized life in a bitter sentence: "To be born in imbecility, in the midst of pain and cries; to be the plaything of ignorance, error, need, sickness, wickedness, and passions; to return step by step to imbecility, from the time of lisping to that of doting; to live among knaves and charlatans of all kinds; to die between one man who takes your pulse and another who troubles your head; never to know where you come from, why you came, and where you are going! that is what is called the most important gift of our parents and of nature, Life."

Despite these brief fits of depression, optimism was really a profound need of Diderot's nature; without optimism his love for humanity and his entire philosophy of virtue and beneficence would founder. If he could no longer believe in men, he wrote, he could no longer be happy. Unfortunately, his optimism was a shaky one; any annoyance or difficulty immediately upset him. Under such conditions, he finally came to the system of two principles, good and evil, and accepted the latter as necessary; without suffering, after all, there would be no virtue; "men would be only a vile herd of happy beings."

After the publication of the third volume, Diderot had been spared an attack *en masse*. He was relatively unconcerned about the flock of petty guerrillas who tried continually to harass him. Chief among these was Elie Fréron, famous mostly for his polemics with Voltaire and their exchange of coarse diatribes. Fréron was editor of a critical journal, *The Literary Year;* he was a man of narrow but judicious taste, a lover of classical purity and an enemy of innovation. Although the *philosophes* were his pet abomination, he too had been a guest of the king at Vincennes, and was later to reside at the Bastille. About this time, Fréron was urged by his former Jesuit teachers at Louis-le-Grand, and also by the dauphin and his group of reactionary nobles, to take up the cudgels against the *philosophes*. He needed little persuasion, and soon set to work with a will, in his journal and in pamphlets. Although a good polemicist, Fréron was a poor philosopher and no match for the best minds in France. His fulminations were annoying, but not dangerous. He wrote to Malesherbes, criticizing the *philosophes* for their obscurity and the harm they were doing to literature. "Diderot and his group are dangerous innovators in matters of literature and taste, to mention only these subjects, the only ones in which I am competent." In the spring of 1754 he mocked them with his *Reflections of a Frenchman on the Three Volumes of the Encyclopedia*. These prickings continued, with no answer from Diderot and his friends.

They were too busy working on the fourth volume of their *magnum opus*. It appeared in October of that year; like the third, it aroused no special hostility. Only d'Alembert was enraged at the reaction to his attack on Jesuit control of education. His critic not only urged the government to wipe out the encyclopedic nest, but took pains to insult d'Alembert on his illegitimate birth. Malesherbes pacified him, and when he was elected to the French Academy, in December of that year, there was great rejoicing among the faithful. With the success of each volume, new men were attracted to the great collaboration. The preface to Volume IV heralded the names of Voltaire, Turgot, Boulanger, and Bordeu.

The situation on the battlefront being relatively quiet, Diderot decided to satisfy at last a longing that had grown keener since his wife's return from Langres. He had not seen his father and sister for more than eleven years, not since the memorable struggle over Nanette. When the fourth volume appeared, he could resist that yearning no more. Bidding his wife a cheerful *au revoir*, he boarded the stagecoach for the three-day trip to Langres.

Little is known about this visit, except that it was a happy one. The two causes of friction with his father—the selection of a career and his marriage—had disappeared. The cutler now was proud of his famous son, in spite of misgivings about the sources of his fame; the son, moreover, did all he could to conceal his unorthodox opinions. With his brother, the abbé Didier, it was different. They had already had an open skirmish, when Diderot prefixed his translation of Shaftesbury with a "Letter to my Brother" that was a fine plea for tolerance. Now he found the abbé cold and estranged, highly resentful of his anti-religious writings. Soon their father discovered himself preferring the gaiety and tender affection of the elder son to the "right thinking" and cold piety of the younger one. "Alas," he is reported to have said with good-humored resignation, "I have two sons; one will surely be a saint, and I fear that the other will be damned, but I cannot live with the saint and I am happy with the sinner."

This visit marks the beginning of a new period in Diderot's relations with his family. When he returned to Paris he felt refreshed and quite satisfied with life.

2

Diderot was thoroughly familiar with the work of the scientific thinkers of his age. In biology these included Boerhaave, Bonnet, Buffon, Linnaeus, Malpighi, and Bordeu. He had taken courses in chemistry, physiology, and medicine, supplementing them with extensive readings and conversations; and he had translated James' *Medicinal Dictionary*. More and more, his own thought veered toward the sciences of life. In this he drew apart from his distinguished colleague, d'Alembert, whose conception of science was mathematical and logical. Even in his earlier writings, the problem of life, rather than physics, seemed to him to hold the key to the whole cosmological riddle. It is not surprising, then, that his next work, *Thoughts on the Interpretation of Nature* (written and published in 1753 as a reaction to Maupertuis' *System of Nature*), was composed under the aegis of Bacon, who was much concerned with physiology and medicine, rather than of Newton. "I never tire of praising that philosopher, because I have never tired of reading him." While there is little immediate influence, Bacon's inquiring, experimental spirit is the guiding light. Diderot continues to prepare the way for nineteenth-century materialism. Although the current of thought he represents has left him vulnerable to the findings of twentieth-century physics, it still represents one main aspect of contemporary biological science.

The biological work of the 1740's had led to a fusion of several ideas: beneath the "kingdoms" and forms, nature is a unit; it has its own dynamic force; it is spread out in a "chain of beings." Speculation on the origin of life and of heterogeneous forms was the order of the day. Theories of transformism were being generated. The consequences of this new theory of materialism, which had its first impact on his *Letter on the Blind*, grew in his *Thoughts on the Interpretation of Nature* and will reach their fullness only in his masterpiece, *D'Alembert's Dream* (1769).

Diderot's first concern is to assess the present position and future possibilities of science. "We are on the threshold of a great revolution in the sciences," he proclaims. In the brilliant future that lies ahead, there will be little room for abstract metaphysical systems or for mathematics. Here again he does not follow Galilean-Newtonian currents, which proclaimed that all of nature, including man, would be explained in mathematical terms. Had not La Mettrie proposed a calculus of the human mind, Quesnay equations of economics and social life? "All nature," wrote Voltaire, "is nothing but mathematics," and Buffon, Condorcet, and others agreed. So positive is Diderot in his prediction, that he even assures his readers there will be no more progress in mathematics, that the next hundred years will not see three great mathematicians. Diderot's new contempt for mathematics follows his shift of interest to biological materialism. He now holds mathematics to belong to the abstract, conventional world of metaphysics, having no real truth until checked by experiment. The most beautiful mathematical reasoning can be upset by a single fact. But why use experiment to correct mathematics? Why not begin with it? The only road to scientific progress is the hard road of experimentation, indefatigable observation, and patient collection of facts. This stage must of course be followed by bold theorizing, the results of which are again to be checked by exhaustive observation.

Diderot misjudges the role of mathematics and physics, although we agree with him today that mathematical truth and objective truth are not necessarily coincidental. For the twentieth century, in the words of Sir Edmund Whittaker, "mathematics is the key to the interpretation of the universe. . . . The whole creative work has to be done in the region of mathematical thought." Science has now gone beyond purely empirical knowledge, beyond explanations conceivable in mechanical terms, and mathematics is our chief means of transcending these limits, of getting closer to ultimate reality. Much of our scientific thinking today reverts to the classic types of Cartesian abstract reasoning. Descartes, in contrast to Kepler and Galileo, held that reality is ultimately reducible to one set of principles, that knowledge could be obtained by "all-embracing theories of the universe, without waiting to study its processes in detail." "All my physics," wrote Descartes, "is only geometry," and geometry has again become the basis of our pattern of the universe. Science must use purely abstract concepts, such as infinity, irrational, and imaginary numbers. Diderot returns to the tradition of Aristotle, we go back to that of Pythagoras. But this is only in his theorizing about methodology. In his own approach to problems, he is Cartesian (but not mathematical) in his fondness for vast hypotheses, in his seeking for unitary principles. We see this in the second part of the *Thoughts on the Interpretation of Nature*, where he sets down various rules for the conduct of scientific investigations, and illustrates them with examples and suggestions for experiments. While the Baconian method tends to random experimentation, and has the defect of confusion arising from too many phenomena and too many possible explanations, Diderot is modern in seeing the immediate need for hypotheses. "At an early stage," writes Dampier of the methodology of our own day, "insight and imagination must come into play." Hypothesis comes early, if not at the beginning of the process, and deduction often precedes experimentation. As a modern biologist, Hans Zinsser, has put it, "Scientific thought continually sets sail from ports of hypothesis and fiction . . . The history of science is full of examples of what, in art, would be spoken of as inspiration, but for which Whitehead's definition 'speculative reason,' seems much more appropriate." Diderot praises hypothesis and imaginative intuition as a fruitful part of scientific method. An hypothesis is a hunch, an inspiration, often extravagant, "a facility for supposing or perceiving opposi-tions or analogies." But he failed to foresee the combination of mathematics and experimentation that the twentieth century has achieved.

While Diderot's enthusiasm is as great as ever in the *Thoughts on the Interpretation of Nature,* his optimism is not unlimited. Nature is so complex, so far beyond our understanding, that at best we shall never have more than pieces of it. The new age in science will produce much that is *useful* to men (this is Bacon's utilitarian view of science), but the fundamental questions will always remain unanswered. In fact, the more complete our knowledge becomes, the more difficult it will be to integrate and understand our data. While our understanding is limited, our senses uncertain and our instruments imperfect, phenomena are infinite and their causes hidden. "What is our purpose then? The execution of a work which can never be accomplished and which would be far above human intelligence if it were achieved." When we try to understand nature's secrets, we are building a tower of Babel to touch the sky. Diderot gives science a few centuries, before it exhausts its useful potentialities and, like mathematics, is abandoned. There is one weak point in Diderot's reasoning, even if he has correctly gauged the limits of human understanding. In his emphasis on the utilitarian, he greatly underestimates the powerful impulsion of curiosity in man, and his unending drive to surpass himself.

It is in the second part of the work that we get Diderot's own theorizing about nature, and witness the development of his materialism. He now takes a long step forward in the construction of his concept of nature as a living whole, acting under the dynamic impulse of internal forces.

Setting out from the current notion of the fundamental unity of all forms of life, he goes on to inquire whether there is not one basic law governing *all* of nature's manifesations, whether all phenomena are not interdependent. The absolute independence of any single fact would break the existence of the whole and destroy the concept of order in nature. Nature "has perhaps never produced more than a single act." He predicts that the progress of physics will reveal an essential unity beneath phenomena such as matter, weight, electricity, gravity, magnetism, elasticity. In chemistry, he conceives a diversity of irreducible elements as the explanation for the variety of compounds, wonders how many there are, and speculates on an even greater mystery: whether, some day, the unit form (atom) of each element will not be broken down, "by some artificial operation, further than it has been, is, or will be in any operation of nature working by herself." This is a remarkable intuition of the atomic theory, and Diderot explores it further. It is probable that molecules, because of their shape and the law of attraction, always have definite relationships to each other. "This system is what I call an elastic body. In this general and abstract sense, the planetary system, the entire universe is only an elastic body; chaos is an impossibility; for there is an order inherently consistent with the primary qualities of matter." Thus the universe forms an indestructible, eternal system. If dispersed into space, it will form again at some point in time. In the formed universe, we have a complicated interaction between many such systems. He predicts that some of these may eventually be changed by man, by the extraction or the introduction of particles that will change the pattern and characteristics of the whole.

If all is in constant flux, there is no reason to suppose that animals and plants have ever stopped or will stop transforming themselves. A fantastic theory of transformism had been adumbrated by Maillet (1748) and Maupertuis (1751) had come remarkably close to the modern genetic theory—an idea which Diderot unfortunately ignored. But he was aware of the evidence of comparative anatomy (through Buffon's work) and of embryology (possibly through courses he had followed). In addition, we must remember that already in 1749, while not clearly expressing an evolutionist theory, he had shown himself aware of a principle of organic viability.

Observing that nature has varied the same mechanism an infinity of times, he reasons that there is a basic force at work beneath nature's ceaseless variety.

> When we consider that among the quadrupeds, there is not one who does not have an anatomy and physiology quite like that of another quadruped, should we not conclude that there has never really been but one first animal, prototype of all the others, which nature has only transformed, obliterating a few organs? . . . When we see the metamorphoses of the embryo bringing closer the different animal kingdoms, we are led to believe that there was only one first being which was the prototype of all others. It is an hypothesis that must be considered . . . Is not nature still at work, natural history still being made, the universe still being transformed?

And later:

> If beings change successively, passing through the most imperceptible nuances, time, which does not stop, must eventually put the greatest difference between forms that existed in ancient times, those which exist today and those that will exist in far-off centuries ; and the *nil sub sole novum* is only a prejudice based

on the weakness of our organs, the imperfection of our instruments and the shortness of our life.

And finally:

> Just as in the animal and vegetable kingdoms, an individual begins, so to speak, grows, exists, declines and dies, is it not the same with entire species? . . . Would not a philosopher without religious faith suspect that the necessary elements for animal life have existed from the beginning of eternity; that it chanced that these elements united, because such a thing was possible; that the embryo formed by these elements has passed through an infinity of forms and developments; that it had, successively, motion, sensation, ideas; . . . that millions of years passed between each one of these developments; that there are others yet to come, unknown to us; that there has been or will be a stationary period . . . and finally decay, existence in another form? Religion spares us these errors.

At this stage, Diderot has no glimmer of what Julian Huxley called the quintessence of Darwinism—the selective action of external conditions. Nor does he take up Maupertuis' suggestion of mutations. His ideas, purely speculative, were of no particular value to scientists. They are interesting chiefly as characteristic of his insight and imagination and as part of his general philosophy of nature.

No problem is more compelling, or more baffling than the origin of life. Are there not (as Buffon had said) inorganic molecules, and organic molecules? Comparing insects and "the matter that produces them" (a reference to spontaneous generation), it seems evident "that matter in general is divided into inert and living matter." Yet this idea is repugnant to his concept of unity. "But how is it possible that matter is not one, either all inert or all living? Is inert matter really inert? Doesn't living matter die? Doesn't inert matter ever begin to live?

The question was engaging the best minds of the time. Through modifications of Leibniz' monad and Descartes' mechanical view of life, vitalism and Cartesianism were joined in a concept of a material nature that evolved through its inherent forces and laws. Buffon speculated that "dead matter" might become "living matter" through mechanical development, creating "organic molecules" which combined, again on mechanical principles, to form living beings. Diderot, seeing also only a difference in organization, is particularly fetched by Maupertuis' materialization of Leibniz' monad.

Maupertuis had theorized that matter, in addition to mass and motion, also has "sensitivity," down to its smallest atom. This "sensitivity" includes desire, aversion, memory (especially in the mechanism of heredity), and even intelligence. In organic combinations, each element loses the memory of itself and partakes in forming the consciousness of the whole.

How can we explain, asks Diderot, the transition from the non-living to the living organizations of these molecules? It seems to him that as a result of "sensitivity," every molecule has only one most "comfortable" location, which it tends to assume through a kind of "automatic restlessness." An animal, then, is "a system of different organic molecules which, by the impulsion of a sensation . . . have combined until each one has found the place most proper to its shape and to its rest." This thread of pan-vitalism continues through his writings, and even in the late *Elements of Physiology*, he defines sensitivity as a form of, or a result of, motion.

Diderot's concept grows out of his idea, in the *Letter on the Blind*, that matter is constantly seeking stability of form. However naïvely expressed, it is pregnant with the scientific laws and hypotheses that were to be developed by nineteenth-century materialism. Certainly it is open to criticism. The effort to break down the wall between the non-living and the living, in order to arrive at a materialistic monism, involved not only a misunderstanding of the nature of "matter" (for which we cannot blame the *philosophes* or their nineteenth-century disciples), but a metaphysical acrobatics that attempted in some way to spiritualize matter without giving the impression of so doing. Matter and its attributes were joined together as ultimate substance, whereas matter is now no longer considered to be the elementary, irreducible reality; the forces that are attributed to it seem to be more elementary and to obey laws that are different from those of matter. Diderot does not go so far as some others, especially Maupertuis, in attributing psychic properties to matter. He stops at sensitivity, perception, and aversion. Life, memory, intelligence, he considered to be properties that somehow emerge from complexities of organization. The eighteenth-century theory was also nonchalant in overlooking what is distinctive in life—design, persistence, and purposiveness (related to the possession of needs, a *unique* characteristic), consequently, behavior. It seems that Diderot was vaguely working towards a theory of "emergent evolution." But even emergent evolution cannot explain the purposive force that drives things on to an ever higher stage, nor have such qualitative differences been satisfactorily accounted for by the quantitative laws and processes of the material world.

Diderot has, by and large, accepted the materialism developed by the advanced philosophers of his time. Better than they, he sees the total consequences and the shortcomings of their theories. An open-minded reading of Diderot's lines reveals that he has not accepted the new materialism implicitly and totally. It is only the Marxist interpreters of Diderot who would see in him no ambiguity or hesitation, no pan-vitalism. Descartes' philosophy and La Mettrie's creative view of matter led to a mechanical theory in which the fortuitous element of Lucretian "atoms plus chance" was discarded in favor of an inevitable determinism. The universe is an evolving machine and man is part of it. Diderot felt the uniqueness of man too strongly to embrace this philosophy wholeheartedly. He always expressed aversion for La Mettrie's notorious masterpiece, *Man the Machine*. In his discussion of evolution, we have seen that the element of chance is explicitly conserved. "Chance," he will say in his *Refutation of Helvétius*, "and even more the needs of life, dispose of us at their will." Life becomes inevitable as a result of his theory of "automatic restlessness" only when a "possible situation" for life happens to arise (else there would be life everywhere). He seems to want to keep the Lucretian hypothesis and to enlarge it with the new concept of the self-creativity of matter, rather than cancel it out.

Nor is there any serious reason for doubting his sincerity in the words that open the *Thoughts on the Interpretation of Nature,* even if we discount his reference to God as highly ambiguous: "Always keep in mind that nature is not God; that man is not a machine; that a hypothesis is not a fact; and rest assured that you have not understood me whenever you think you see something contrary to these principles." If the universe is a great organism, then perhaps it has a soul. "That soul of the world I do not say is, but may be God." Were these words written only for the censor?

And the work closes with a "Prayer to God"—a strange prayer that is obviously agnostic, but suffused with his feeling of ignorance and humility before the still-locked door. The riddle is expressed in the final enigma of the prayer. Everything is necessarily determined: "Here I am, what I am, a necessarily organized portion of an eternal and necessary matter." But his last words are: "Since God has permitted, or the universal mechanism we term Destiny has willed that we should be exposed, during life, to all kinds of events; if you are a wise man, and a better father than I, you will persuade your son early that he is the master of his existence, so that he will not complain about you who have given it to him." Determinism is not mechanical, machine-like. There are many possibilities, that for us at least are as unpredictable as chance. In the grinding of the wheels, we are aware of where we are necessarily going, and awareness is what separates man from the machine of which he is a part. Perhaps Diderot even feels that it allows him to change necessity. It would almost seem that while admitting determinism as a theory, he denies it as a fact, for us who are men. It would seem that while declaring man to be governed by the same laws that regulate the universe, he feels that man has reached a new level of law distinct from that which governs all other things.

There is one more corollary. In finding an explanation of life, Diderot has also discovered for himself, at least, the meaning of man. He has answered the question of our destiny. Man's status, although superior, is apparently without cosmic significance. We are merely one of nature's accidents, one of her recurrent patterns, perhaps a step to something else yet to come with the unfolding of time, but not the result of an intelligent, meaningful process. Ethically, the consequence is overwhelming. Men as a species must live for their own happiness.

The *Thoughts on the Interpretation of Nature* had a rather narrow appeal, despite the enthusiastic response among the *philosophes*. Many objected to the tone of the book, which was pompous and even somewhat arrogant. Commenting on the opening line, "Young man, take this and read it," Frederick the Great snorted, "There is a book I shall not read. It is not made for an old fellow like me." Réaumur, Nollet, Trembley were more modest, had a better technique and exerted greater influence on their contemporaries. Daniel Mornet summarizes Diderot's scientific accomplishments in these words: "His originality is less that of a great thinker than of a temperament that can assimilate, diversify, and animate with intense life, ideas that were common, or at least, not revelations." But Diderot went far beyond all the others, in his relating of science to man, in his insight into human nature and destiny. There lies his great achievement. In the nineteenth century, Auguste Comte gave the *Thoughts on the Interpretation of Nature* a place of honor in his Positivist Library.

3

The next two years were relatively uneventful. They saw no original work from Diderot's pen. The *Encyclopedia* was appearing at the rate of a volume each year. In January 1755, he signed a new contract with the publishers, after considerable haggling. "My wife, who is sometimes of good counsel, persuaded me to affect the greatest indifference; they thought that they should play the same role, and so we remained for two weeks, on one side and the other, without making a move. I don't know why, during this interval, impatience did not overcome me and why I didn't send the whole business to the devil—them, the *Encyclopedia*, their papers, and their contract." Squabbles with the publishers were not the only reason for this fit of discouragement; the criticisms of his friends, who were already advising a second edition of the *Encyclopedia* to perfect the first, were also disheartening. And then, Diderot's health was cracking under all this hard work and sedentary living, despite his strong constitution.

He finally came to terms with Le Breton and Briasson. For each volume, they would pay him twenty-five hundred francs, and the day the text of the last volume was delivered, he would receive a bonus of twenty thousand francs. The financial situation, at least, had improved!

Volume V came off the press in September 1755. It was prefaced by a eulogy of the great Montesquieu, who had died the preceding winter. Of all the thinkers of his century, Montesquieu was most highly respected, by men of all opinions; he had been a great source of inspiration to the *Encyclopedia* and to its writers individually. He was considered a patron saint of the "party." D'Alembert wrote the eulogy. It was warmly praised, together with Diderot's own article, "Encyclopedia." Voltaire, enthusiastic about both, wrote his good friend d'Alembert that as long as he had a breath of life, he would be at the service of the *Encyclopedia*, which he considered the greatest and finest monument in literature. The number of subscribers passed the three-thousand mark.

Winter witnessed the renewal of Fréron's attacks on the *Encyclopedia* ("a scandalous work") and on d'Alembert in particular. The *philosophes*, who were not loath to use against their enemies the same suppression they complained about so bitterly when it was applied to themselves, had d'Alembert protest to Malesherbes. Always anxious to avoid trouble, Malesherbes warned Fréron's censor against permitting any more such diatribes in the future.

That summer Antoinette made her second and last visit to Langres. She went not alone but with their fourth and only surviving child, whom she had borne at the age of forty-three, the three-year-old Angélique, so named after their first-born and Diderot's mother. This time it was his father who had requested their visit; feeling that his advanced age and poor health would not spare him much longer, he was anxious to see his only grandchild before his death.

Relations with his brother were not so happy. The abbé was having a bitter dispute and lawsuit with a certain chevalier de Piolenc. Diderot, always ready to render service, tried to settle the matter amicably, but was frustrated by his brother's violent and uncompromising attitude. He finally washed his hands of the whole affair. The snappy exchange of letters between them reveals that a deep antagonism and not a mere incident lies at the bottom of their friction. "Your letter," Diderot wrote, "is that of a lover of lawsuits and a fanatic. If those are the two qualities your religion imparts, I am very glad of mine, and I hope not to change it. You feel that religion is necessary to be an honest man; if you feel that need, so much the worse for you." As for the abbé's adversary, "I believe the chevalier to be an honest man, even though he is a good Christian."

Eleven years earlier, Diderot's letter to his brother on tolerance had been prompted by an uneasy feeling of the abbé's hostility. Now they were openly embroiled. The abbé was proud, uncompromising in his ideas, cold and satirical, resentful and slow to forgive—the opposite, point by point, of the philosopher. He had come to regard his elder brother as a disgrace to the family, an enemy and a traitor to the religion of which he was a priest. His attitude was always that Diderot had offended him, sinned unforgivably, and must therefore come to Canossa.

4

The year 1755—the year of the great Lisbon earthquake—was one of the most important in Diderot's life. His affair with the flirtatious Mme. de Puisieux had ended somewhere in the neighborhood of 1754. He probably wasted little time on tears. Soon after he found not merely a mistress, but a woman he could truly love.

As early as January or February 1753, in connection with a complicated and annoying financial transaction, Diderot had met a certain Mme. le Gendre. She was the daughter of a pitiless collector of the *gabelle*, the infamous salt tax, and the wife of an insufferable government official, whose death, shortly afterwards, was a relief to all who had to deal with him. Diderot became friendly with her younger sister, Mme. de Salignac, later Mme. de Blacy. This unfortunate woman was afflicted with a worthless husband, a good-for-nothing son, and a blind daughter. It was at her home, seated at a little green table, that Diderot met the third and unmarried sister, Louise-Henriette Volland, known forevermore as Sophie, the nickname he gave her to represent her wisdom. This was on October 4th, 1755. With what fond reminiscence he referred to that table in later years! Around it was begun the great love of his life.

Born on November 27, 1717, Sophie was then about thirty-eight years old. Diderot was past forty-two. This was no adolescent love affair. Even more, it would seem from Diderot's own descriptions that Sophie was not a beauty. She wore glasses on a rather "dried-up" face, and her legs were far from slender. Yet she must have had great charm, for it is impossible to conceive of Diderot, as one biographer has put it, "falling in love with an ugly creature and squeezing in his arms a bony and withered prey." He was too sensitive to beauty and ugliness, and, after all, he did throw kisses at her picture! Sophie was also rather sickly. Several times, in his letters, Diderot scolds her for lack of caution. "So you too are going in for overeating! That's just the thing to do. And who allowed you to act like healthy people?" The famous Dr. Tronchin described her as having "the soul of an eagle in a house of gauze."

From the outset, the strong feeling of attraction that brought them together was based on intellectual at least as much as physical communion. Sophie possessed a fine intelligence and a wide familiarity with books. She read everything—novels, politics, philosophy. She was frank, clever, spontaneous, and a good conversationalist, but disliked gossip and chitchat. Diderot felt drawn to her by their mutual *sensibilité* and love of virtue, by their common fondness for discussion of abstract questions. "Is wickedness always punished? Is a man's infidelity to his mistress always unforgivable?" Sophie was more typically feminine in her fondness for knickknacks—scarves, fans, and such—and for shopping expeditions. She loved social life, especially when surrounded by witty men and women. "Sophie Volland is the lovable personification of the French woman in the second half of the eighteenth century," writes Hélène Celarié. Well, not quite, we hope. We like to think of the typical Frenchwoman as a little prettier, a little less masculine, and a little more ardent!

But there is no doubt that she was the object of Diderot's deepest love and admiration. "Ah, Grimm, what a woman! How tender she is, how sweet, honest, delicate, sensible! She reflects, she loves to reflect. We don't know any more than she in customs, morals, feelings, in an infinity of important things. She has her judgment, her views, her ideas, her own way of thinking, formed according to reason, truth and common sense; neither public opinion, nor authorities nor anything else can subjugate them."

Even more than Grimm, Sophie was made to be Diderot's intellectual and emotional partner. "I had great joy," he writes to her apropos of Voltaire's tragedy, "at thinking that you were reading *Tancrède* while I was seeing it. I said to myself: What pleasure she will have in this spot! She will not hear that *Well! my father!* without bursting into tears." To Grimm he wrote, with all the joy of having two great friends, "Don't you know that we are three? Don't be offended if I count her with us. In truth, her soul is the most beautiful of any woman's, as yours is the finest of any man's under the sky." Most important of all, Sophie understood him. With her he could satisfy a primary need—as he could with no one else except Grimm and Rousseau—the need for an outlet for all his ideas and emotions.

Rather curious is Diderot's emphasis on Sophie's virility of character. It was useless to ask her for gossip. "That is true woman's game. But you are scarcely a woman." He used to warn her not to let Mme. le Gendre read the risqué parts of his letters; "Uranie," as they called her, was a modest creature, while the unmarried Sophie was never embarrassed, "because my Sophie is both man and woman when it pleases her." When she became excited over a little trinket, he made fun of her. "Oh woman! Will you always be a woman in some way or another? *Jamais la fêlure que nature fit en vous ne reprendra-t-elle entièrement?*" He is constantly worried about her health. She is so fragile, he warns her. Her tiny voice tires so quickly, her legs swell if she walks too much, her eyes are weak, and she catches cold so easily. When her digestion is bad, Diderot, an enthusiastic amateur physician, prescribes a diet for her. One would almost say husband and wife, instead of lover and mistress.

Diderot was on friendly terms with the entire family—Mother Volland considered herself flattered by the attentions of so famous a man. He saw them formally on Thursdays and Sundays at their home on the Rue des Vieux-Augustins. For the rest, precautions were necessary. His private visits to Sophie were effected by means of a back stairway. Sometimes he would wait in vain for his circumspect mistress, feeling a gentle and poetic despair. On one such sad occasion, he wrote her a long letter in the dark, until he could no longer see. Then he concludes, "Adieu. Wherever you cannot see the words, read, 'I love you'." Sophie, for her part, in order to avoid the prying eyes of Mme. Diderot, usually wrote to him at the home of one of his friends, Damilaville. Almost daily the philosopher would rush to the Quai des Miramionnes, impatient for her mail.

Another curious aspect of Diderot's love for Sophie is his complaints about her lack of complaisance for him. Some have gone so far as to suppose a platonic friendship, but these passages indicate no more than a lover's unsatiated appetite. Undoubtedly there are one or two references that remain puzzling. In one of them Diderot speaks to her of the happiness a woman has in being loved by a tender and devoted man. "His lips are pressed on yours, you feel your soul rush forward to unite with his, everything announces an infinite happiness to you, everything invites you to it: and you do not wish to die and make him die of pleasure! If you leave this world without having known this happiness, can you flatter yourself that you have been happy, that you have seen and made another happy?" And how is one to interpret this passage, written in answer to Sophie's equally puzzling statement: "I could not bear the thought that a man has had that advantage over me"? "That man," was the reply, "is an honest man. He is devoted to you, body and soul, he lives only for you. He would circle the globe to fetch you a straw that pleased you, and when you grant him the only recompense he promises himself, you call that 'giving him an advantage over you'? In any other circumstance, you would call it an equitable return. Coquettes give men 'an advantage' over them, women who put no price upon their favors, women you can possess without having earned them. But it is not so with others . . ." (Diderot then interpolates the story of a friend who conquered the virtue of the woman he loved.) ". . . He was happy. He saw the moment that awaits me, doesn't it, my Sophie? And when that moment comes, will I be taking an advantage over you? No, no, no."

These passages, written in 1760 and 1765, are not easy to explain. Yet in spite of them, one who has read Diderot's love letters, even in the truncated form in which they have come to us, cannot accept the hypothesis of a platonic love. There is in them an evident tone of intimacy that can be felt but not expressed, and which is the strongest of proofs. Why, moreover, should Diderot's family have destroyed so many of his letters, especially those of the first years, and expurgated the rest with such care? Both in writing to Sophie and in writing of her to his friends, Diderot calls her his mistress, calls himself her lover. In assuring her frequently that he has never betrayed her, that he will always be constant, can he be referring to a platonic infidelity?

There are other passages in Diderot's letters that cast a heavy shadow over Mlle. Volland's virtue. During a long separation, Diderot bids her be patient till their reunion. "They will come back, those moments when you will see my passion, when I shall force you to admit in your heart that the favors of an honest woman are always precious. I kiss you all over. You are and you always will be entirely beautiful for me." He tells of his friends' trying to belittle the voluptuous intoxication of love, while at the very moment, "I was burning to find it in the arms of my sweet one, because there it is renewed whenever she wishes, and because her heart is pure and her caresses true." When Mme. Volland annoyed him with her interference, he wrote to a friend: "I am making myself more and more agreeable to the daughter and avenging myself properly for the mother's harshness." To what vengeance could he refer?

Only to his mistress could a man write a paragraph like the following: "Remember what Thomas replied to the apostles who assured him of the resurrection of Christ. You are in a tomb like him, and for far longer than three days and three nights. And if I don't have of your return the same proof that the incredulous apostle demanded: *nisi immittam digitum. . . .*"

Or this one: "But isn't it a very strange thing that in my dreams my imagination shows me only the narrow space necessary for volptuousness, a sheath of flesh, and nothing more?"

When Sophie was in the country, he would think back with

nostalgia and longing to their secret rendezvous, and the dangers they ran. "How often hasn't a sky that broke into torrents of water been favorable to me? The noise of a bed, creaking under the weight of pleasure, gets lost, or is ascribed by a mother to the wind . . . Ah if I were at Isle and if you were willing!" Evidently Sophie was not always "willing," evidently she was at times loath to accept the solicitations of the ardent philosopher. But there is no doubt that on many an occasion she succumbed to an assault that can scarcely be described as philosophic.

Sophie's relations with her sister, Mme. le Gendre, are another odd feature of this affair. At first one is puzzled by Diderot's references, in his early letters, to Mme. Volland's "jealousy" of her two daughters, to her keeping them apart. But shortly after that, he himself began to develop an abnormal jealousy of "Uranie." "I have become so wild, so unjust, so jealous; you say so many nice things about her that . . . I don't dare to finish! I am ashamed of what is going on within me, but I can't help it. Your mother claims that your sister likes attractive women, and it is certain that she loves you very much; and then there's that nun for whom she had quite a liking, and that tender and voluptuous way she sometimes bends over you, and those fingers so singularly pressed between yours! *Adieu*, I am going crazy!"

This jealousy creeps into many of Diderot's letters to Sophie. Once he inquires whether their beds still touch each other. Another time, he sends her a half-playful, half-serious warning. "Sophie, be careful, do not look at her more tenderly than at me; do not kiss her more often. If you do, I shall find it out." He closes one letter in this strange fashion: "Meanwhile, I permit your mouth only to your sister. I do not suffer; I should almost say that I enjoy following her. It seems to me then that I am pressing her soul between yours and mine. It is a snowflake that melts between two burning coals." Another letter has this ending: "*Adieu*, my dear, I approach my lips to yours; I kiss them, even if I were to find there the trace of your sister's kisses; but no, there is nothing. Hers are so light, so superficial."

These passages require no comment, except perhaps to recall Diderot's recurrent allusions to Sophie's shrinking from his amorous advances: "Ah, if I were at Isle and if you were willing!"

Time soothed this source of pain, too. Diderot learned to overlook any pecularities in Mme. le Gendre's conduct. "Uranie" became "our dear sister." He admired her more and more, and developed a genuine affection for her. "She is beauty, virtue, honesty, sensitivity, delicacy itself." With Mme. le Gendre, Diderot was able to enjoy a particular kind of conversation he relished: a bold, flirtatious sparring on questions of love and sex. To be sure, he practiced it with Mme. le Breton, Mme. d'Holbach, and other women, but best of all he obtained from "Uranie" that delightful provocation he sought. With the frankness that characterized the conversation of the century, he even told her that if Sophie were not his mistress, she would have had to be. Her death in 1770 was a great blow both to him and to Sophie.

5

The first frontal attack against free will, in a letter to Landois dated June 29th, 1756, is the only event in Diderot's intellectual life that year. Free will is an illusion, he insists, born of the variety of our actions and our habit of confusing willing with freedom. All we do is determined by our organization, our education, and by the chain of events. He is fully aware of the moral consequences of this position.

> It is no more possible to conceive that a being can act without a motive than one of the arms of a scale without a weight, and the motive is always outside of us, foreign, related by some nature or cause which is not ourselves . . . But if there is no freedom, there is no action that merits praise or blame; there is neither vice nor virtue, nothing to reward or to punish. How then can we distinguish between men? By their good or evil actions (*la bienfaisance et la malfaisance*). A wicked man is one we must destroy, not punish; doing good is a matter of luck, not virtue.

How then can we justify society's punishing inevitable acts? "Although the good or wicked man is not free, he is nonetheless a being subject to modification . . . Punishments are a way of correcting the modifiable being called the wicked man and of encouraging the good one." Susceptibility to modification is proven by the effects of sermons, examples, education, pleasure, pain. Punishments are justified by their practical results.

Logically, Diderot has succeeded no better than any other determinist in his "justification," since it is not a person's fault, on this theory, if he is *not* sufficiently modified. Equally interesting, in this letter, is the first glimpse it affords us of his future moral radicalism, with its denial of a special status in nature for man.

> There is only one kind of necessity ; it is the same for all beings, regardless of the distinction we may like to place between them . . . Reproach no one with anything ; and never repent—those are the first steps to wisdom. Anything else is prejudice, false philosophy.

Such was the year 1756. It saw the publication of Volume VI of the *Encyclopedia*, enhanced by contributions of the highly respectable Président de Brosses, of Saint-Lambert and Morellet, of Necker, and the physiocrat Quesnay. It also witnessed the renewal of resistance by the Parlements, the renewal of religious strife between Jesuits and Jansenists, and most important of all, the renewal of war against England. This time, by her determined aggression in America and the reversal of alliances in Europe, England had prepared a trap in which France was to meet her greatest disaster. The Seven Years' War, which was to decide the destiny of North America and assure the glory of England and Prussia, this critical war of modern history, was lost by the frivolity, irresponsibility, and corruption of the French Court. Mme. de Pompadour, it is said, marked out campaigns on a map with beauty spots. Disaster was not long in coming. Soon Voltaire was again congratulating Frederick the Great on his victory over French arms at Rossbach and over the French allies at Leuthen. Diderot, too, evinces little interest in the misfortunes of his country.

The year 1757 began inauspiciously. On January fifth, an assassin, Robert-François Damiens, wounded Louis XV with a knife. Damiens was tortured and then torn to pieces, but the frightened monarch issued an order for all possible measures to be taken against his "enemies." The *philosophes* loudly proclaimed that the Jesuits were at the bottom of the attempt—Damiens had been connected with their organization—and recalled the murder of Henry IV by a religious fanatic. Unfortunately it was decided, much to the delight of the Jesuits, that the principal measures would be taken against "subversive" books, their authors, vendors, and printers. The law proclaiming capital punishment or long galley terms for such offenders was revived. Le Breton was thoroughly frightened, and again only Diderot's persuasive eloquence prevented his assistant editor from running out. After all, he argued, the authorities had not been too dissatisfied with the last volumes, and they still had the protection of d'Argenson, Malesherbes, and other persons of influence.

For the moment, the *Encyclopedia* had fallen to second place in Diderot's interests. Inspired by Goldoni's comedy, *The True Friend*, he had written his first play, *The Natural Son*. Its publication aroused tremendous enthusiasm among the *philosophes* and a volley of hoots from the opposition. It went through four editions in 1757. Grimm, in his *Literary Correspondence*, called the work sublime and predicted that its author would soon become absolute master of the French theater. Fréron, on the other hand, prepared a stinging attack for his *Literary Year*, accusing Diderot of plagiarism. The "philosophic party" got wind of the forthcoming blast and indignantly pleaded with Malesherbes to prevent its publication. Tired of these endless squabbles, Malesherbes decided to attempt a reconciliation between the two men, and invited them to talk things over. Fréron, however, respectfully declined to participate in any such negotiations. Diderot belongs to a detestable group, he replied; he is a dangerous innovator. Besides, if he can no longer criticize the *philosophes*, what will he have left to write about in his periodical? Of course, if he were elected to the French Academy, then he might consider a reconciliation!

When Fréron's review came out, it was quite moderate in tone. He had a more subtle plan now: to publish a forged letter from Goldoni, supposedly thanking a friend for sending him Diderot's "translation" of his play. When Malesherbes again barred its publication, Fréron gave instead a detailed analysis of Goldoni's play, distorting it in such a way that Diderot really appeared to be a mere plagiarist and not a dramatic author.

Diderot's self-justification appeared, in November of 1758, in his *Discourse on Dramatic Poetry*. He refuted the accusation of plagiarism, showing the similarities with Goldoni's play to be few and superficial, less than some of Goldoni's own borrowings. At the same time, he published another play, *Le Père de famille*, (*The Father*).

As if these annoyances were not addition enough to his troubles with the *Encyclopedia*, Diderot had to contend with a sudden flare-up on the part of his brother. The abbé had also seen fit to become indignant over *The Natural Son*. He complained bitterly to their father about it and then wrote to Diderot, definitely breaking off friendly relations. The Philosopher tried to appease him and answered in a conciliatory tone. He expressed his fraternal love—an expression more diplomatic than sincere—and his regrets at having "unwittingly" offended. Finally he suggested that the abbé point out, for purposes of discussion, the parts that had displeased him. To this letter of pacification the abbé replied in a cold but moderate tone. "You propose a discussion on the passages I find reprehensible. Permit me not to accept your challenge; it would scarcely be proper between brothers." Besides, the last time he had made similar objections, he had been called a fanatic and the same procedure would probably be repeated. No doubt existed that Diderot had spoken of religion in an improper way.

Bowing to the wishes of his father, Diderot finally effected a reconciliation at the end of that year. The priest had been unrelenting in his rancor, and it was the philosopher who made all the advances, until peace was grudgingly granted.

To make matters worse still, a host of writers, self-appointed defenders of the faith, sought to make capital of the unfavorable position of the *philosophes*. Among these, Charles Palissot enjoyed the unique distinction of being at the same time their enemy and a friend of Voltaire. His comedy, *Queer People,* had poked fun at Rousseau in 1755. Now he became exasperated at the cocky intrusion of Diderot into the theatre. In 1757 he put out a violent satire, *Small Letters on Great Philosophers,* blasting *The Natural Son,* condemning the *philosophes* for their mutual flattery and their concerted criticism of all others.

But the hardest blow of all, and the most popular of the antiphilosophic diatribes, was the work of a lawyer, Moreau. His "Useful Warning," published in the *Mercure de France,* had been only another petty annoyance. Quite different was the famous *New Memoir for the History of the Cacouacs* which followed. Who were the *Cacouacs?* None other than the *philosophes!* Moreau condemns them as atheists, anarchists, immoralists, and egoists, all the more dangerous because of their superficial cleverness. In a little allegory he tells how his servant, after having turned *philosophe,* stole his master's watch, wallet, and snuffbox—reminding us of Diderot's own lesson in *The Sceptic's Walk.* The important thing, however, was not what Moreau had to say—he was one of a hundred—but his ingenious invention of the catchword, "Cacouacs." A perfect onomatopoeia, it spread like wildfire and injured the *philosophes'* reputation more than all the satires combined. It immediately suggested cacophony, the quacking of ducks, a bedlam of noise devoid of any meaning. There is no refutation of a sound, it has been remarked. The encyclopedists smarted and swore, but were utterly helpless. Soon the abbé de Saint-Cyr's *Catechism of the Cacouacs*, the abbé Guyon's *Oracle of the Cacouacs*, and innumerable others rolled off the presses.

When Diderot's mistress asked him to explain the meaning of the word "Cacouac" which she had heard so often, his reply betrayed his annoyance. "The *Cacouacs?* That's what they called, last winter, all those whose moral principles were built to the measurements of reason, who noticed the stupidities of the government, and discussed them openly, and who dragged Briochet, father, son, and abbé in the mud. All you have to ask now is who is *Briochet:* he was the first puppet-puller in the world. Now you will understand that I am the very devil of a Cacouac, that there is scarcely a clever or well-educated man who doesn't belong more or less to the clique."

Soon an open campaign against the *philosophes* became a pulpit theme. The queen, the dauphin, the Jesuits did their utmost to encourage it and satires flew more thickly than ever from many pens. D'Alembert, unable to take any more punishment, resigned, this time irrevocably. His prestige had been important. It was a severe blow, even though he had for some time been a recalcitrant co-worker, fearful of compromising his personal comfort and safety, and resenting what he considered inadequate compensation. Now he decided the time had come to call quits and run for shelter. In some ways, Diderot did not regret it; their relations had grown cool and he even suspected his co-editor of wishing to supplant him. But deep down, he bitterly resented d'Alembert's desertion. Despite this, the seventh volume appeared, containing d'Alembert's article on Geneva, which immediately stirred further controversy. It urged the establishment of a theater in Calvinist Switzerland, as an instrument of enlightenment and culture. It made other criticisms of that city, and of its pastors, and proposed certain reforms.

D'Alembert was chagrined by Diderot's decision to continue the *Encyclopedia,* and humiliated by its successful completion. (We may say as much for Voltaire who, in a disgraceful display of hypocrisy, turned about in fear of the court's disfavor, urged all the collaborators to resign as an "act of courage," and demanded the return of his own unpublished contributions.) D'Alembert's woes were increased by the cries of outrage stirred up by his article on Geneva, both in France and in Switzerland, among the clergy and at the court. Bitter protests from Geneva were followed, in 1758, by Rousseau's famous *Letter to d'Alembert on Spectacles,* in which he condemned the theater as a prime source of moral corruption. The upshot was the discomfiture of the *philosophes* and the glee of their foes, who rightly saw the "party" being torn apart by the desertion of d'Alembert and the defection of Rousseau. Grimm called the article—which Diderot had been reluctant to publish—a great blunder.

All in all, Diderot remained cooler in the face of attacks than his colleagues. D'Alembert protested furiously to any strictures on himself. Voltaire's sensitive vanity led him to enter a number of bitter polemical disputes and to write a hundred satires and diatribes in which he succeeded only in cheapening himself and defaming his own character. Diderot's life was relatively free from such exhibitions, possibly because he lacked a certain intellectual pride. He took little interest in the success of his works—although he was vain about their worth—or in the size of his audience and the diffusion of his ideas. He was satisfied, for the most part, to write for his small circle of friends. "I care little about glory. I can be praised without feeling vain or blamed without feeling hurt. Insults are not stones." Lacking an aggressive spirit, he was neither sure nor proud enough of his ideas to defend them. "I do not esteem myself enough to think I should defend my own cause." Sincerely tolerant, he welcomed honest criticism and was ever ready to enter into an honest debate.

As for personal attacks—"We must all go through that or else give up telling the truth." Unlike Voltaire, he realized that they reflected only on their authors; that his conduct and reputation were the best replies. He once remarked that by returning fire, he would lose his temper, which is disagreeable, lend himself to the malicious entertainment of the spectators, and save from obscurity the stupid writings of his enemies. He urged Voltaire to let his detractors yelp; they would be taken care of by their contemporaries and by the future.

But we must not paint the picture too white. Diderot felt no Christian meekness or love for those who would do him harm. Although his public reprisals, such as his satire of Batteux in the *Letter on the Deaf and Dumb,* were rare, he was capable, in his private writings, of pitiless irony and invective. The letters to his brother and the satire of his enemy, Palissot, in *Rameau's Nephew* are prime instances. And in the case of Rousseau, his animosity was so overwhelming, he could not keep it out of his published writings.

Diderot's unending rancor towards Rousseau arose from the quarrel that had been brewing between them. It reached a bitter and explosive head at this time. To the beleaguered philosopher this distressing episode came as the culmination of his troubles. The two years from the middle of 1757 to the middle of 1759 were undoubtedly the most harassed and unhappy of his life.

6

Extremely sensitive by nature, Diderot clashed at some time or other with almost all of his family and friends. Only two of his quarrels were serious, prolonged, and bitter. One was with his brother. The other, with Rousseau, became the most notorious and most significant quarrel of the century.

The "Citizen of Geneva," within the last few years, had been turning more and more antisocial. He found ever more unbearable the "hypocrisy" of the polite world, and the literary quarrels and cliques of Paris. He came to look upon the verbose philosophizing of his comrades as sophistry. By theory and by temperament, he felt compelled to make his life conform to his ideas. As this tendency became constantly more marked, he and Diderot began to get on each other's nerves, to have petty squabbles and sharp discussions. The little things, as when Rousseau began his "new way of life," in 1751, by selling his watch, had a cumulative effect. As awkward as Diderot was in formal company, as much as he loved nature and occasional solitude, he remained convinced that society was man's natural and happiest state; "he who does not enjoy its charms is a barbarian." In the *Encyclopedia,* he attacked the Cynics for affecting a rustic way of life in the midst of a sophisticated society, claiming that it led to an artificial and disagreeable virtue. Doubtless he had his friend in mind. While Rousseau could get along by himself, Diderot needed the company of others. Jean-Jacques, moreover, was utterly without a sense of proportion. An idealist, a dreamer and a neurotic, a seeker for absolutes, unable or unwilling to come to terms with life or with his own self, he became incapable of compromising with the necessities of social living. Jean Pommier has aptly speculated on a dialogue between the two friends, similar to that between Alceste and Philinte, in Molière's *Misanthrope.*

Even before this, Grimm had already developed a great personal antipathy towards the man who had been one of his earliest friends in Paris. Grimm was the first to see through Rousseau's vanity. On the day of the opening performance of his operetta, *Le Devin du village* (1752), the duke des Deux-Ponts approached Rousseau. "Will you allow me to congratulate you, monsieur?" "Very well," replied Jean-Jacques, "provided you make it short." Although differences of temperament and ideas were basic in their growing apart, there was an additional factor of resentment over Rousseau's influence on Grimm's mistress, Mme. d'Epinay, with whom he was in love by fits and starts. Grimm warned her of his "arrogance and ingratitude." In October 1752, both Diderot and Grimm wrangled with Jean-Jacques because he refused to solicit the king's favor at a court performance of *Le Devin du village*. But these were only preliminaries. The storm and the explosion were not yet at hand.

"The real subject of their quarrel," writes Diderot's daughter, "is impossible to relate; it was some social squabble, so complicated that the devil himself couldn't understand it."

Mme. de Vandeul is right about the complexity. There was, however, a succession of causes. So entangled is this affair, that literary historians are still divided into two bitterly opposed camps. According to the partisans of Rousseau, there was a plot among the Encyclopedists to discredit Rousseau's ideas by vilifying him personally. The champions of Diderot maintain that "Rousseau's unbridled imagination," aided and abetted by his mistress, Thérèse Levasseur, was alone responsible for the whole mess. We shall try to unravel the threads, and to speak impartially of both sides in the light of the evidence.

Rousseau left Paris in 1756 to live alone at the Hermitage, a small house on Mme. d'Epinay's estate. At that time open antagonism already existed between him and Diderot on the abstract question of society versus solitude. In addition, Diderot had allowed himself to intrude in what Rousseau considered his private affairs. Together with Grimm and d'Holbach, he had given financial aid to Thérèse Levasseur's aged mother. Rousseau objected to what he considered the unnecessary lesson in charity. But the philosopher continued his unwelcome sermons nonetheless. Doubtless discord was fomented by Thérèse's mother, a crafty, intriguing peasant who was more than a match for her simple daughter and her excitable, unrealistic lover. Rousseau discovered her to be carrying on negotiations with Grimm and Diderot behind his back. The partisans of Rousseau maintain that the real object of the subsidy to Mme.

Levasseur was to provide a way to meddle in his private life, probably because of Grimm's jealousy. Grimm, according to both Rousseau's and Mme. d'Epinay's accounts, also opposed her granting him a retreat at the Hermitage, so close to her home, alleging that solitude would blacken his imagination, exacerbate both his personal arrogance and his pride in the outlandish, unsocial philosophy he had proclaimed. Insofar as this was his motive (and we cannot be sure he had any other), Grimm was undoubtedly correct. Rousseau himself admitted that solitude led him to brood on his injuries.

Jean-Jacques was growing ever more sensitive and irritable. He complained of neglect when his friends left him alone and of being disturbed when they came to visit him. Never an atheist, he was turning to an emotional religion of his own. The personalities and "fanatical atheism" of d'Holbach and his group were so unbearable to him that he had broken with them all, by 1757, except Diderot and Grimm. When the "Holbachistes" began to circulate nasty stories about his solitude, Rousseau became convinced that they had formed a great plot to destroy his happiness. "Philosophers of the city," he cried, "if those are your virtues, I am glad to be vicious. . . . To love and to find ungrateful hearts, that is the only unbearable grief." He spoke of the days when Diderot, Grimm and he were poor but happy friends; "now they are famous people, I am still what I was and so we cannot get along any more." Yet he wrote to Mme. d'Epinay, in February: "I am living very happily here by myself, but if, *after Diderot*, I feel like seeing anyone, it is you."

When Diderot's *Natural Son* was published, Jean-Jacques came upon the line: "Only the wicked man is alone." Rightly or wrongly, he immediately took it as addressed to himself, and his heart was filled with rage and resentment. Actually, the idea was common enough at the time. Diderot had himself come across it again only recently, in an article, "Le Philosophe," that he had revised for the *Encyclopedia*. Mutual and bitter recrimination followed ("Oh, Rousseau, you are becoming wicked, unjust, cruel, ferocious, and I weep with sorrow at the thought of it"), but the affair was patched up. Diderot asked forgiveness in a letter (March 18, 1757), and promised never again to speak of his friend's solitude. Then, with his usual lack of tact, he concluded thus: "Adieu, Citizen! Just the same a hermit is a very peculiar kind of citizen!" This letter, wrote Jean-Jacques, pierced his soul. He made no secret of it, much to his friend's annoyance. "However much my letter hurt you," he answered, "I do not regret having written it; you were too pleased with your reply."

Another altercation followed, about Diderot's unwillingness to visit his friend (Diderot and his friends later claimed that he walked to the Hermitage once or twice each week—a patent untruth). In the course of this dispute, Diderot did threaten to walk to the Hermitage and also assured Jean-Jacques that his friends would not let Mme. Levasseur die of hunger, which enraged Rousseau almost beyond control. He wrote bitingly to Mme. d'Epinay about the many times Diderot had failed to keep his promise to visit him—only to break his own engagement, shortly after, to visit Diderot in Paris! This gave Diderot a chance to play the innocent victim and abandoned friend. "Oh, Rousseau!" he wrote, "You are becoming spiteful, unjust, cruel, ferocious, and I weep with sorrow." Then Rousseau admitted that *he* had asked Mme. d'Epinay to prevent Diderot's visit—in order to avoid a quarrel! "Besides, you wanted to come on foot; you might have fallen sick, and perhaps you would not have been too sorry." He answers Diderot's epithets with his own. "Diderot! Diderot! I see it with bitter sorrow. Living constantly in the company of spiteful men, you are learning to resemble them. Your good heart is becoming corrupted by their society, and you are forcing mine, by slow degrees, to detach itself from you."

Diderot finally got to the Hermitage in April. The quarreling friends were tenderly reconciled. In July, Jean-Jacques came to Paris and spent two days at Diderot's home. One of his motives was to get Diderot's advice about *The New Héloïse;* another (he claims, at least), to help Diderot by a show of union at a time when his friend was embroiled in Fréron's accusations of plagiarism. Diderot unwisely dragged him once again to the "synagogue of the Rue Royale." Rousseau returned to his solitude more bitter than ever. "Everyone is unbearable to me, beginning with myself." His emotional condition was scarcely normal; he was physically sick and a victim of nervous disorders.

He soon had another subject of annoyance. Grimm had been away during the summer, and as he had predicted, Rousseau utilized this time to meditate on his grievances. When Grimm returned in September, Rousseau was further offended by being moved out of the room at La Chevrette, where he was temporarily staying, for the benefit of his hostess' lover. The pique was heightened when he discovered a connecting door he had been unaware of, leading from that room to Mme. d'Epinay's.

Then came the trouble over Mme. d'Houdetot, the exquisite mistress of the soldier, poet, and *philosophe*, Saint-Lambert. Not long after she had become Mme. d'Epinay's neighbor, Saint-Lambert left for the army, and a tender, platonic friendship developed between her and Rousseau. But Jean-Jacques became too serious, too aggressively serious. Despite her coquetry and his violent transports, he failed to seduce her. Returning on leave, Saint-Lambert noticed a change in his mistress. He became suspicious when he learned that Rousseau had been urging her to break their liaison on moral grounds(!). This tactic Diderot later listed as one of Rousseau's "seven villainies." Doubtless Grimm had been the informer, for he and Saint-Lambert occasionally met in Westphalia, where the latter was stationed. Rousseau, however, rashly accused Mme. d'Epinay, and this she never forgave. The famous "day of the five notes" (August 31st) was the beginning of the end. Saint-Lambert, meanwhile, had asked Mme. d'Houdetot to detach herself gradually from Rousseau. Desperate now, Jean-Jacques begged Diderot to advise him what to do to avert her lover's anger. Diderot, probably at a meeting at the Hermitage, counselled a full confession. However, on September 4 or 5, 1757, Rousseau wrote Saint-Lambert an appealing letter, confessing nothing at all, assuring him of his loyalty, despite his moral disapproval of their affair. (This in face of the fact that he himself had been turning out a series of illegitimate children with Thérèse Levasseur!) Rousseau's sole purpose was of course to continue to see Mme. d'Houdetot.

Saint-Lambert's reply was most satisfactory. Although he did not take the moral lesson to heart, he suggested that he, Rousseau, and Mme. d'Houdetot form a *ménage à trois*. Rousseau was ecstatically joyful. (Echoes of this whole affair, and of the idyllic *ménage à trois*, found their way into Rousseau's best-seller, *The New Héloïse*.)

Almost simultaneously with these events came Mme. d'Epinay's crucial decision to undertake the arduous journey to Rousseau's native city, where she could be treated by the famed Dr. Tronchin. It was probably about October 18th, when Rousseau was still relishing the joy of his renewed friendship with Mme. d'Houdetot, that a letter from Diderot jarred his pastoral dream. It was Rousseau's categorical duty, wrote the officious philosopher, to show his gratitude towards his benefactress by accompanying her on this journey. He, Diderot, in his friend's place, would take a staff and follow on foot, if the places in her carriage were all taken. We can well imagine the comfort-loving Diderot doing this! Discounting in advance Rousseau's usual rejoinder that his conscience was his guide, he queried, "Is its testimony sufficient? Can we neglect completely that of other men?"

In his *Confessions,* Rousseau describes his reaction to this letter. Trembling with anger, he was (he says) unable to finish reading it. As soon as he could control himself, he dashed off a hot reply accusing Diderot of a plot, and rushed over to La Chevrette to have the matter out with his hostess. He found her with Grimm, and read the letters, with some additional discourse. Rousseau pictures this triumphant scene. "At this unexpected boldness in a man ordinarily so timid, I saw them both taken aback, stunned, unable to reply; I saw especially that arrogant man lower his eyes to the ground, not daring to confront the sparks from my eyes; but at the same time, deep down in his heart, he was swearing my destruction, and I am sure they plotted it before they separated." Another account puts the matter quite differently. At the end of the mad scene between the three, Rousseau burst into tears and promised to write an apologizing letter to Diderot, but again betrayed his word. Whichever version is true, the letter he did send was curt, cold, and haughty.

Why Grimm, at least, should have wanted Rousseau to accompany Mme. d'Epinay is not evident. Nor should we forget to mention that she and Diderot had barely met and were not yet on friendly terms. That Diderot was officious and unjustifiably impertinent, seems clear, if indeed, he was not acting, as is likely, at Grimm's behest. That Rousseau was hysterical and abnormally suspicious is also beyond doubt. "They are not friends, they are tyrants," he is reported to have shouted, as he stalked out of the room.

The same day or shortly thereafter, he wrote Grimm a calmer letter, but nonetheless bitter towards Mme. d'Epinay, justifying himself, accusing her of having enslaved him, and asking an opinion as to what he ought to do. His alleged motives for refusing to undertake the long journey were his own ill-health and the fact that Mme. d'Epinay had other traveling companions, who indeed took up all the places in her carriage. From a letter to Mme. d'Houdetot, we can see that the real and unconfessable motive was his love for her. To which we can add his aversion to being told what he should do. This refusal was another of Diderot's list of seven villainies.

Rousseau's refusal to accompany Mme. d'Epinay is further complicated by his later claim that he knew the real reason for her journey, but since he was not supposed to know it, he was in the false position of having to put forth other excuses, thus laying himself open for his enemies' trumped up charges. The "real" reason "he got from Thérèse who got it from the butler who got it from the chambermaid: Mme. d'Epinay was to have a child by Grimm, and Dr. Tronchin was to deliver her." Actually this rumor, if indeed Rousseau ever believed it (he did know that she had had a child by her first lover) was in all probability false. Mme. d'Epinay suffered from chronic abdominal troubles. But there is every reason to believe that Rousseau invented the calumny later, when he was writing his *Confessions*, in order to justify himself. For one thing, he himself had advised the ailing Mme. d'Epinay to consult Tronchin almost two years before the quarrel. Mme. d'Epinay was obliged to appeal to the police to prevent private readings of the *Confessions*.

On October 28th, possibly at Mme. d'Houdetot's prodding, Rousseau wrote to Saint-Lambert accepting his generous proposal of a *ménage à trois*. Reversing his stand on moral principles, he now confers his blessing on their liaison. However, he complains of Mme. d'Houdetot's joining the conspiracy to reduce him to slavery —she too had advised him to go with Mme. d'Epinay. "It seems there is a league among all my friends, to take advantage of my precarious condition and deliver me to the mercies of Mme. d'Epinay. My mind is made up, and I had rather be an ingrate than a coward." Actually, what concerned Mme. d'Houdetot was that some might "misinterpret" Rousseau's refusal to go to her own disadvantage. Consequently she had insisted that he write to Saint-Lambert, saying she had urged him to go. And in case he stayed, she wrote Rousseau, he was not to see her in Paris that winter. Her feelings toward him are expressed in her letter of October 26th: "If I had been able to form still another desire, it would doubtless have been to have, after a lover such as he, a friend such as you." Her advice to him, in her letter, is clearly that he should follow his own conscience.

On October 29th, Rousseau received Grimm's reply to his letter asking for advice. Grimm announced a brief delay in Mme. d'Epinay's departure (she was now in Paris), due to her son's illness. He denies that Diderot, as Rousseau had claimed, was just a mouthpiece for others (meaning himself), or that all his friends were plotting to make him leave. If Jean-Jacques would offer his company to Mme. d'Epinay, she would be pleased and doubtless answer "as she should." Here Grimm does not appear anxious for Rousseau to go with Mme. d'Epinay—this, according to Jean-Jacques, being part of the trap. Yet it is difficult to see why Grimm should have been enthusiastic about this trip. Thus while Diderot, who was not yet friendly with Mme. d'Epinay, urged him to go for reasons of high duty, Grimm hedged.

Instead of following Grimm's advice, Rousseau did exactly the contrary. If *she* had asked him nicely, and frankly, he wrote to Mme. d'Epinay, he would certainly have acceded to her request, despite the tremendous sacrifice involved. He tells her bluntly that there is a conspiracy against him, and that she is its head. "You have sought to reduce me to servitude, or to use me for your secret ends."

But on November 1st, the day after Mme. d'Epinay's departure, Rousseau received a second letter from Grimm. In the three days that had gone by since his earlier, hesitating letter, something had apparently changed his mind. It is this mysterious about-face that defenders of Rousseau seize upon as a clear indication that he correctly suspected a plot. For this letter is a ripping denunciation. He had always wondered, wrote Grimm, why Rousseau, desiring as he did to return to his native Geneva, refused to accept this opportunity.

> I did not then know your monstrous system ; it has made me shudder with indignation ; I see such odious principles in it, such villainy and duplicity! . . . I shall never see you again as long as I live ; and I shall hold myself fortunate if I can banish the memory of your actions from my mind ; I beg you to forget me, and not to disturb my peace of mind. If the justice of this request does not touch you, remember that I have in my hands your letter, which will justify, in the eyes of all decent people, the honesty of my conduct.

Unless we are to accept the plot thesis, we must find some other explanation for this abrupt about-face. This is not very difficult. Either Mme. d'Epinay had showed Grimm Rousseau's letter in which, instead of following his advice, he had bitterly denounced her, or he had heard (from Saint-Lambert or Diderot), of Rousseau's hypocritical reply to Saint-Lambert. Possibly it was the knowledge of both these letters that angered him. From another letter of Diderot's to Grimm later that month, we know that both men were aware of the deception he had practiced on Saint-Lambert, in contradiction to the promise made to Diderot.

Rousseau sent Grimm's letters back to him, with a brief note of rejection. ". . . Too late I have found you out. Here is the letter you have taken the leisure to meditate on; I send it back to you, it is not for me. You can show mine to the whole world and hate me openly; it will be, on your part, one less deceit." To Mme. d'Houdetot he wrote—whether brokenhearted, to justify himself, or to seek pity, it is hard to say—"all those I loved hate me."

So all was over between Rousseau and Grimm and Mme. d'Epinay. But more was still to come.

That Rousseau was at least in part sincere can be seen in his letter of November 4th to Mme. d'Houdetot. He is truly anguished at having received no news from Diderot. "I have written him insults, but we are accustomed to insulting each other, and to loving each other. He knows that I would redeem with my blood the pain that I give him . . . Oh, my Diderot, why do I not know you to be completely appeased?"

A letter from Diderot finally came. The idea that there had been a plot, or even consultation, is firmly rejected, and Jean-Jacques is taken to task for his attitude and his sophistries. Suppose he, Diderot, had been indiscreet, does that matter? "Am I not your friend? Haven't I the right to tell you everything that comes into my mind? Is it not my duty to tell you what I think is right to do? . . . It is certain that you have no friend left except me; but it is certain that I remain to you." This protestation only excited Rousseau's suspicions and led to a rigidly logical judgment, which he noted down on Diderot's letter. Grimm had just broken with him. Therefore Diderot either believed Grimm, and wanted to continue being the friend of a scoundrel, or was guilty of not defending Rousseau if he disbelieved Grimm. This also proved that every step was plotted between them, and that Diderot was either a coward or a traitor. The talk of friendship was only a hypocritical mask, the better to deceive him. Would it not have been a less harsh judgment to conclude that Diderot sided with Grimm, but genuinely desired to placate his other friend?

When their bitterness was somewhat soothed, Diderot went to visit Rousseau once again. He accused him frankly of hypocrisy and trickery in the d'Epinay and Saint-Lambert affairs, and condemned "the enormity of his actions." After a scene, there was another half-reconciliation. Diderot returned to Paris completely upset; he wrote to Grimm and described what had taken place. He was convinced that Rousseau was out of his mind, hardened in evil. "That man comes back to me right in the midst of my work; he upsets me, and I feel as if I had a damned soul beside me: he is damned, that is sure."

On November 21st, Rousseau finally had an answer to his letter of conciliation to Saint-Lambert, who was recuperating at Aix-la-Chapelle from a minor paralytic stroke. He is quite willing to accept Rousseau's reasons for refusing to accompany Mme. d'Epinay, although he should have preferred to see him act otherwise; but he bluntly scores Jean-Jacques' methods and principles. Ingratitude *is* worse than weakness. On the other hand, he does not doubt his sincerity, nor his accusations. Rousseau is justified in condemning the trickery that is obvious in Grimm's letters, and in denouncing Diderot's part in the affair. He is really to be pitied, rather than censored. "You are the craziest of the lot, but you are the least guilty." In this respect, at least, Rousseau had succeeded. Saint-Lambert was convinced of his honesty and suspected nothing of his secret passion for Mme. d'Houdetot.

The letters that followed between Rousseau and Mme. d'Epinay descend to painful depths of mutual recrimination. "I pity you," she wrote him on November 12, and he answered on the 23rd, "Our friendship is dead." Yet he asks permission to stay on at the Hermitage, as his friends had been urging him to do. This brought a caustic reply. "I only wish that your conscience were as tranquil as mine. . . . Since you wanted to leave the Hermitage and you should have, I am surprised that your friends have kept you there. As for me, I never consult mine about my duties, and I have nothing further to say concerning yours." What she should have written was that Jean-Jacques seemed to hearken to his friends' advice when it was to his convenience and advantage.

Early in December Diderot and Rousseau met for the last time—though they took leave of each other still on speaking terms and neither suspected it would be the last time. The encounter took place at the Hermitage. Many matters were vehemently argued—mostly Rousseau's accusations against Mme. d'Epinay and Grimm, but also d'Alembert's article on Geneva, and whether Rousseau should leave the Hermitage. Diderot's own statement that he went to see Rousseau in order to ask him why he had lied to him about his letter to Saint-Lambert is most dubious—that matter had not yet reached a head.

On December 15th, Rousseau did leave the Hermitage, and took up solitary residence at Montmorency. He so informed Mme. d'Epinay. *He* had never wanted to accept her hospitality in the first place, and at last he is free. She is right in saying he is to be pitied— who is not when he finds that he had entrusted his heart to false friends?

Recriminations such as these continued with increasing acrimony. In January and February, Rousseau complained to both Mme. d'Epinay and Mme. d'Houdetot that "people" were trying to paint him as a scoundrel in Paris. He is hurt, he writes the latter, that Diderot made no answer to his plea to abandon the *Encyclopedia* for the sake of his safety. "That is enough from him, this desertion tells me more than all the rest. I cannot stop loving him, but I shall never see him again as long as I live. You are the only one left me, you will abandon me in your turn when it suits you, I know men too well not to expect it." Rousseau's notes on the ensuing correspondence from Mme. d'Houdetot reveal that he was more and more convinced that there was a general plot against him, and a specific plot to get him to leave his retreat and return to Paris. This would be a confession of the failure of his ideas and cover him with ridicule. Nevertheless Rousseau sent Diderot a moving, though proud letter, on March 2, 1758, expressing his feelings of friendship and the hope that Diderot would not believe the rumors that were being spread against him. He appeals to him to reconsider, not to be Grimm's tool, and not to let their friendship die. He pictures himself at the point of death. "Perhaps then the proofs of my innocence will reach you; you will be forced to honor my memory and the image of your dying friend will haunt your nights. Diderot, reflect on it, I shall not speak of it again."

From March 23rd to the beginning of May, there was no communication between Mme. d'Houdetot and Rousseau. If it were not for what took place during that interval, his friendship for Diderot might conceivably have survived all the storms. But he was never able to forgive Diderot for causing a break between him and the woman he had loved. When Saint-Lambert returned to Paris at the end of March, he still suspected nothing of Rousseau's passion. But on May 6th, Mme. d'Houdetot wrote Rousseau an angry letter, reminding him how she had kept his love a secret, for his sake. "You have spoken about it to people who have made it public." The rumors finally had reached Saint-Lambert's ears, with unhappy consequences. From now on, she continues, there can be nothing more between them. However both she and Saint-Lambert realize that Rousseau was guilty of nothing more than weakness. "We are far from joining those people who are trying to defame you."

Was the gossip about Rousseau's secret love the result of a misunderstanding, or part of a plan to discredit Rousseau and cover him with ridicule? The second possibility cannot be completely ruled out, except by those historians who find all the truth on one side. For as we have seen in Mme. d'Houdetot's letter, Saint-Lambert learned of the affair from the common gossip of Paris. This seems to weaken the contention of Diderot's supporters: that his revelation of Rousseau's secret came about as the result of an indiscretion for which Rousseau's own double-dealing was responsible. When Saint-Lambert first became suspicious of Rousseau's affection for his mistress, Jean-Jacques, we remember, tried desperately to avoid a break, and asked Diderot's advice. Diderot's counsel had been to confess and to leave Mme. d'Houdetot—which Rousseau promised he would do, and, according to Diderot, later assured him, with much gratitude, that he had done. But we have seen that on September 5th, Rousseau wrote an entirely different kind of letter to Saint-Lambert, a letter which evoked the latter's generous proposal for a *ménage à trois*. (When Saint-Lambert later learned the true story, he termed it "an atrocious letter, that could be answered only with a stick.") Now, since Diderot "was left believing that a full confession had been made, his revelation to Saint-Lambert of Rousseau's ardent passion can hardly be qualified as an indiscretion, much less as a crime." We cannot, however, let Diderot off that lightly. In the first place, a letter from him to Grimm (March 2nd) proves that he already knew of Rousseau's real reply to Saint-Lambert, and that he had told Grimm about it. Furthermore, Diderot apparently revealed this secret to many others—if we are to follow Mme. d'Houdetot's impartial and trustworthy evidence. The excuse of a misinterpretation simply does not apply. Diderot had been gossiping about his friend's deepest secret.

Rousseau could stomach no more. He was sure Diderot had betrayed him. About the same time, he entered into a public but gentlemanly dispute with d'Alembert, replying to his article, "Geneva," with the famous *Letter to d'Alembert on Spectacles*. If our civilization is vicious, was its argument, then its most civilized aspect, the theater, is the most vicious of all. Significantly, he was writing this polemic at a time when Diderot, at Grimm's suggestion, was launching his brief career as a dramatic author.

The publication of the *Letter to d'Alembert* in September 1758 deepened the rift. In a famous footnote, he wrote, "I used to have an Aristarchus [critic], severe and judicious. I have him no longer, I wish to have him no longer; but I shall regret him ceaselessly, and he is missing a great deal more from my heart than he is from my writings." It was followed by a passage from *Ecclesiasticus:* "Hast thou drawn thy sword against thy friend? Be comforted, all may be as it was. Hast thou assailed him with wrathful words? Thou mayst yet be reconciled. But the taunt, the scornful reproach, the betrayed secret, the concealed attack, all these mean a friend lost." This public insult Diderot could never forgive. Even Saint-Lambert told Rousseau that he was revolted by the "atrocity" of Rousseau's thrust at a time when Diderot was being persecuted.

In fact, the personal quarrel became a part of the whole context of the struggle over the *Encyclopedia*. At this time of its deepest trouble, Rousseau had acted for its enemies, by publicly proclaiming that Diderot was a traitor and a false friend. Moreover, Diderot's defense of the morality and social utility of the theater, in the essay accompanying his new play, *Le Père de famille*, just published a month before, was undercut by Rousseau's effective polemic against the moral value of the theatre. This, too, was unforgivable.

Both men had been at fault. Rousseau, with his abnormal suspicions, his deceits, and his arrogance, had provoked quarrel after quarrel. Diderot, officious, meddlesome, bungling, and perhaps lacking in sincerity, had undoubtedly served, exactly as Rousseau charged, as the tool of Grimm, under whose spell and domination he had fallen.

Wherever the blame lay, their friendship of fifteen years was at an end. They never saw each other again. They went their separate ways, driven farther apart as time went on, these two men who had been such true friends. Rousseau trod the path of his paradox, of individualism, of mistakes and contradictions that led to tragedy and a broken life. He finally became the prey of a pitiful psychosis which made him consider himself the victim of a world-wide persecution plot—though it cannot be denied that his erstwhile friends ridiculed and abused him whenever possible, in speech and in writing. Diderot was to struggle not against the world, but within himself, as he felt his own personality more and more split between the paradoxes and inexorable materialism of his mind, and the impulses of his heart. His life was to be, in spite of certain regrettable episodes, an admirable and a happy one, with some beautiful chapters.

As the years that separated them grew longer, their rancor grew more intense. Diderot composed a point by point account of their quarrels. He attacked the paradoxes and contradictions in Rousseau's life and writings. Rousseau, the author of a French operetta, proved to the French that because of their language, they could never have an opera. After writing a comedy, *Narcissus,* he denounced the theater as corrupting. He held novels and love stories to be demoralizing, and wrote *The New Héloïse,* the most successful novel and love story of the century. He sent his children to the foundling hospital, but wrote a book, the great *Emile,* on the education of children. He became a Catholic when among Protestants, and a Protestant among Catholics. Diderot refused to believe in Rousseau's sincerity. He compared him to Don Quixote and other amusing fanatics and lovers of paradox. "Such is Jean-Jacques Rousseau, when he declaims against letters which he has cultivated all his life; against a philosophy which he professed; against the society of our corrupted cities, where he is dying to live, and in which he would despair to be forgotten." On the other hand, he never denied Rousseau's ability. When Helvétius called Rousseau wicked, Diderot objected. "You are calumniating him; he is not wicked *par système;* he is an eloquent orator, the first dupe of his own sophistry. Whatever revolution may take place in men's minds, never will Rousseau fall into disesteem." However when posthumous publication of Rousseau's *Confessions* was announced, Diderot suddenly changed his mind about his wickedness.

His personal letters abound in vindictive allusions to his erstwhile friend.

> He has lost all our common friends. I have kept them all. . . . He regrets me. I despise and pity him. He carries remorse with him and shame follows him. . . . His days are sad, his nights troubled. I sleep peacefully, while he sighs, weeps perhaps, and gnaws at himself. That, my friend, is because wickedness has its punishment. Sooner or later, limping Retribution catches up with the guilty one who flees before her.

Rousseau, for his part, remained the implacable enemy of all the *philosophes,* and attacked them frequently. "Wouldn't one take them for a troupe of charlatans, shouting simultaneously in the public square: 'Come to me, I alone am never wrong' . . . Haughty, positive, dogmatic, even in their supposed scepticism, knowing all, proving nothing . . . they find reasons only to destroy." He called Diderot a traitor, Grimm a scoundrel, d'Holbach a brute, and d'Alembert a knave. He accused Diderot of having played the role of *agent provocateur*, inciting him only in order to make him appear odious. He refers especially to some strong passages Diderot has made him include in the *Discourse on Inequality*, and speaks of others even more extreme that he had rejected.

Both Diderot and Rousseau tried to justify themselves in the eyes of posterity. The one who maintained his dignity and aloofness in this sordid affair was Grimm. In the *Literary Correspondence* he never spoke ill of Rousseau, though its secrecy gave him impunity to do so. When *Emile* was published, he wrote a biography of Jean-Jacques, adding these words that testify to his self-possession: "His private and domestic life would be no less interesting; but it is written in the memory of two or three of his former friends, who have maintained their self-respect by not writing of it anywhere." After Mme. d'Epinay composed her partly fictional memoirs, Diderot performed a considerable work of revision on them, designed to buttress his case. Much of what he put in was true, but other parts were fictional, even if, as his defenders contend, the fiction was not false to the spirit of things. Jean-Jacques, on the other hand, defended himself eloquently in his famous *Confessions*. He too alloyed truth with fiction; just what proportion of the fiction was intentional, and how much of it his seething imagination really believed, is a subject for idle argument. But it is amusing, in a distressing way, to recall that when word spread in Paris that Rousseau was to publish his *Confessions*, Diderot became highly alarmed— whether for fear of calumny or for fear of true revelations, the argument still rages. He countered Rousseau's blow by a bitter attack added to the second edition of his *Essay on the Reigns of Claudius and Nero*, in which he calls Rousseau a scoundrel and a hypocrite who calumniates himself only to make his calumnies of others more credible. "Detest the ingrate who speaks evil of his benefactors; detest the atrocious man who does not hesitate to blacken his old friends." Recalling that Rousseau had lost all his friends, in France and in England, he exclaims, "Too many honest people would have been wrong, if he had been right." He refers to Rousseau's own words, that he hated benefactors, because he hated to be grateful.

To put all the villainy on one side or the other would be to perform a purely partisan reading of history. The clash was not only of personalities, but of opposing philosophies and views of life. From the moment of Rousseau's first *Discourse* (1749-50), not long after the beginning of their friendship, a break was already inevitable. His way of living and thinking bred ever increasing tensions between him and his friends, until open hostility declared itself in 1756. He developed a philosophy that denied the world as machine, that rejected scientific progress and rational enlightenment as the key to the future—all the basic concepts of the Encyclopedists. Against these he held up a standard of emotion and intuition; frequently, the individual conscience as a guide to morality; a return from artificialities of civilization to simpler ways of living; an equalitarian but rigid social organization. To the objective world of science, he opposed the subjective world of the spirit. He warned against the dangers of the first and the neglect of the second. These are the two great thought currents that since the middle of the eighteenth century have split Western culture, the one leading to the scientific mentality and capitalism, the other to romanticism and other mystical or anti-rational movements. Rousseau, the heir of the Protestant theologians, prepares the way for Kant, on whom he exerted a deep influence, and àlso, by his concept of the State, for Hegel, Fichte, and modern egalitarian totalitarianism. The *philosophes*—at least most of them—deriving from Locke, lead to Saint-Simon and Comte, and to the liberal, open society. Paradoxically, Rousseau alone was the true revolutionary, for although absolute statism stems from his *Social Contract*, so does the cry for equality and popular sovereignty. Rousseau, not Voltaire or Diderot, was the idol of the French Revolution.

If we add to this irreconcilable opposition the complex personal problems and intrigues we have tried to follow, it seems inevitable that bitterness and underhand blows must have come from both sides. Since we do not have an objective knowledge of all the facts and motives, it is impossible to assess in any certain way the relative load of guilt and blame. We can only say, "It had to be."

In 1765, Rousseau, driven from Switzerland because of his religious ideas, sought refuge with Hume in England. Diderot hoped within his heart that Jean-Jacques would visit him, and, though he would not admit it, made soundings in that direction. "Paris is on his road and we await him." And a few days later: "Rousseau has been in Paris for three days. I do not expect his visit, but I do not hide from you that it would give me great pleasure; I should be glad to see how he would justify his conduct. I do well not to make easy the access to my heart; once someone has entered it, he does not leave without tearing it: it is a wound that never heals."

Rousseau never came. Perhaps it was better that way.

"Once someone has entered my heart, he does not leave without tearing it." Friendship was not a mere sentiment for Diderot; it was a passion. "When once I have said to myself, in my heart, 'I am his friend,' I would frighten you perhaps if I told you all that I have said to myself at the same time."

Few men have borne so high an ideal of friendship. He conceived of it as the communion of two hearts, in pleasure and in pain. This, in practice, became an ideal of service. He did not hesitate to demand considerable favors, but he was always prepared to accord as much or double. For his friends he performed an incredible amount of gratuitous literary labor; in their behalf, and without their ever knowing it, he frequently wrote spontaneous letters of praise or solicitation. He was a tireless giver of good advice, usually unasked for. "I like those who scold me and I scold those whom I like." He had a "pedagogical mania" that made him harangue unceasingly. Most of his friends accepted this quirk good-naturedly. Rousseau reacted violently against it.

Despite unhappy experiences with the temperament of Jean-Jacques, with the ungratefulness of his sculptor friend, Falconet, and Grimm's exploitation of him, Diderot declared he would rather make ingrates than falter in his generosity. Occasionally, when disappointed by the actions or attitude of his friends, he flew into a temper. He resented a harsh word from Grimm ("Since writing you the truth hurts you," he replied, "I shall not write to you at all"). A churlish outburst by d'Holbach called forth one on his own part.

> Made eloquent by their injustice, I made an abominable speech against friendship, painted it as the most unbearable of tyrannies, life's greatest punishment, and I ended with these words: "My friends, you whom I call my friends for the last time, I declare to you that I have no more friends, that I don't want any more and that I want to live alone, since I am so unfortunate as to be unable to make anyone happy by giving myself up without reserve to those who are dear to me." Immediately my heart

tightened, and I shed a torrent of tears. The marquis took me in
his arms and led me away to another part of the Tuileries, where
this scene took place, healed my wounds with soft and consoling
words, and then brought me back to have dinner with the friends
I had abjured. . . . We separated early and we all embraced each
other affectionately.

Part genuine, part acting, this scene reveals the idealism and
emotion that Diderot put into his friendship.*

7

Here a closer view of Mme. d'Epinay is in order.

Louise-Florence d'Esclavelles, known as Mme. d'Epinay, was
one of the most brilliant women of a century particularly prolific in
brilliant women. "It was the time," Sainte-Beuve has said, "of those
wanton and frivolous ladies who became at a certain point Mentors
and Minervas, and composed moral treatises on education during
the brief intervals of leisure which their lovers left them." Mme.
d'Epinay composed moral treatises on education, and loved three
men. She had a literary and philosophical salon, where she surrounded herself with many of the luminaries of Paris. In 1757, she
read Rousseau's *New Héloïse*. It gave her the idea of writing her
own life in story form—her "Memoirs," a brilliant picture of
eighteenth-century society—under the title, *Histoire de Mme. de
Montbrillant*.

She was born in 1725. An early marriage to her cousin, M.
d'Epinay, brought a harvest of shattered illusions. "She alone loved,
and that with the love of a boarding-school miss." A spendthrift and
roué, d'Epinay with callous cynicism soon urged her to take a
lover. She met Grimm in time to console her for the first lover,
Francueil, who had consoled her for her husband. There was no
scandal in all this. The feeling of the time was expressed by M.
d'Ette, who had acted as go-between with Francueil: "Only a
woman's inconsistency in her tastes, or a bad choice, or the publicity
she gives it, can injure her reputation."

Rousseau introduced Grimm to her. At the time, Duclos, the
novelist and *littérateur*, was trying hard, but in vain, to win the

* We cannot resist referring the reader to Jean Fabre's brilliant interpretation of the relations between Diderot and Rousseau, in "Deux frères
ennemis" ("Diderot Studies III," Geneva, 1961, pp. 155-213).

vacant place. She was struck by Grimm's gentleness and pride, by his intelligence, his shyness and sensitivity. Grimm gave her self-confidence and happiness for the first time; he guided her and gently dominated her. "He is perhaps the only man," she wrote, "with the faculty of inspiring confidence without bestowing it." She tells us that Grimm's carriage was not quite straight, that his nose was large and slightly crooked, which caused a lady to say, "Grimm's nose is turned, but always in the right direction."

Grimm's coldness was perhaps less insensitivity than stoicism. He was capable of writing to her, "How I long to hear from you! I do not know a single thing that you will do tomorrow; that has never happened before since I have known you." Yet when she wished to prolong a happy stay with him at Geneva, he reminded her that duty was more important than love. Grimm had a deep moral sense, within the framework of the time. He was worried that Mme. d'Epinay's children might discover their liaison. "Oh! how many times that fear has embittered the pleasure of moments passed with you!"

Duclos had sought a woman's vengeance for his rebuff by spreading malicious rumors about Mme. d'Epinay. It is curious that Diderot, who was so close to Grimm, seems to have believed these calumnies. We have one phrase Duclos wrote to him: "Your friend is very much in love with Mme. d'Epinay. She is a nice mistress to have, because you never run the risk of becoming seriously attached to her." For several years Diderot refused to meet her, try though she did, calling him "a bear hard to catch." It was not until 1759 that his resistance weakened. When they finally became friends they were enchanted with each other. "He exalts my head and my heart . . . He has given my soul a shock that has enabled it to enjoy all the good things that surround me." Through Diderot, she was introduced to the Holbachian circle and developed a close friendship for Mme. d'Holbach. Diderot himself became more and more devoted to her and often went to La Chevrette or La Briche for a change of scene. Their friendship stood the test of time. When he was sixty years old, she wrote to him, "To ask me not to forget you is almost an insult. I shall always remember you. Our friendship does not date from yesterday, and I cannot recall a single moment that spoiled its sweetness."

The unhappy quarrel with Jean-Jacques was over, but more trouble was in the wind. First came a series of bickerings with Malesherbes concerning certain passages in the dedication of *Le Père de famille*, especially the prayer to God, in the second act. After much emotional upset, Diderot had his way on the prayer, and the play, together with the *Discourse on Dramatic Poetry*, was finally published in November 1758.

Then came the mysterious and unhappy affair of the dedications. Shortly after the publication of *Le Père de famille*, there appeared a secret edition of two plays by Goldoni. One was *Il vero amico* ("The True Friend"), which Diderot had been falsely accused of plagiarizing in *The Natural Son*; the other was *Il padre di famiglia*, which had the same title as Diderot's new play, but no other resemblance to it. These were honest translations, done by two of Diderot's friends, Forbonnais and Deleyre. With each play, however, was a dedication, one to the highborn countess de La Marck, the other to the princess de Robecq, who had been mistress to the powerful duke de Choiseul. These dedications, satirical and offensive, appeared under the name of "Bleichnarr"—"pale fool," in German—an obvious parody of the name of Diderot's enemy, Palissot, whose *Small Letters on Great Philosophers* had so irritated him the year before. They amounted to no less than public insults. Malesherbes immediately started an investigation. He determined that the offending pieces had been slipped in by someone, and that the translators were innocent.

Diderot, called on the carpet, protested his innocence. But then, suddenly, he paid a visit to Mme. de la Marck, placated her with his eloquence plus a signed confession (the contents of which remain unknown, for she generously burned it). The lady then requested Malesherbes to drop the affair. This he refused to do, especially since Forbonnais insisted that the culprit be publicly declared, failing which, he and Deleyre would go to the courts and make the whole mess public knowledge. The upshot was that Diderot published a note absolving the translators, but admitting nothing. Malesherbes and all the others—except Mme. de la Marck and the princess de Robecq—remained in uncertainty as to who the real culprit was. Some accused Diderot. The weight of evidence (the German parody of Palissot's name, the fact that a lackey of Grimm's was spied dropping a copy of the translations at

Forbonnais' home, a recently discovered letter of Diderot's to Grimm) make it certain that Grimm alone was the guilty one. Diderot had acted to protect him and had taken the guilt upon himself.

The fact that Diderot—even if he did not actively connive to throw the umbrage of guilt upon two innocent men, on two friends of his—at least did nothing to remove this shadow from them until forced to; the fact that he did all this for his beloved Grimm, cannot be overlooked as indirect evidence in assessing his role in the quarrels between Grimm and Rousseau.

While all this was going on, disaster, so often staved off, gradually crept up on the *Encyclopedia,* and finally overtook it. The relentless pressure from the reactionaries had begun to take effect in a way not anticipated by Diderot. Frightened by the menaces of the government and dismayed by the barrage of satirical attacks, some of the best known collaborators deserted. Marmontel, the famous novelist and *littérateur,* and Duclos, who was also secretary of the French Academy and historiographer of the king, both washed their hands of a work which could bring them little glory and considerable grief. Voltaire was restrained from following suit only by Diderot's ardent persuasion. To the Patriarch of Ferney, always fearful of offending the court, it seemed that continued struggle could yield no useful result.

In December 1757, d'Alembert had resigned as editor and withdrawn from the enterprise. Diderot was not unhappy about this step. From the beginning, the two men had clashed frequently over their differing concepts of the work. As we can see by comparing d'Alembert's *Discours préliminaire* with Diderot's article "Encyclopédie," the former desired an orderly, Cartesian approach, emphasizing the certain, whereas Diderot was more interested in persuasion, propaganda, and freer scope for the imagination. D'Alembert insisted on open and direct expression of his ideas—a course of which the article "Geneva" was one unhappy result. Diderot, on the other hand, preferred the method of indirection, and wished to avoid criticism or censure from the authorities. For him the essential thing was to get the work finished and published, even if it was imperfect, while his co-editor thought the contrary. In addition to these intellectual differences, there was a strong personal rivalry for preeminence between the two men—and, after the unfortunate events we are about to relate, for leadership of the "philosophic" movement. D'Alembert hoped to regroup their

cohorts around himself and Voltaire, who grew to fear the radicalism of the atheistic materialists and thought it wiser to seek reform
by winning the adherence of the privileged classes, instead of
antagonizing them. It was part of this plan that led d'Alembert,
after the events of 1759, to favor continuing the *Encyclopedia* under
the protection of Frederick the Great, or failing that, to give up
the whole project. It is understandable that Diderot should have felt
great bitterness toward his friend; and this bitterness never died
out, even though they were genuinely reconciled when d'Alembert
fell dangerously ill in 1765.

Quite abruptly, matters took a serious turn. In the summer
of 1758, Helvétius published his work, *On the Mind*. Few books in
the eighteenth century caused so great an uproar, perhaps only
Toussaint's *On Manners,* d'Holbach's *System of Nature,* and
Rousseau's *Emile*. Helvétius proclaimed the extreme logical consequences of the sensualist philosophy. Man is formed entirely
through his sense experience; education and government can mold
him at will. Educators and legislators must realize that he is affected
only by his selfish interests, and make those interests accord with
those of society. Selfishness is the law of man, from each organ in
his body to his entire conscious being.

Helvétius had sketched an important utilitarian philosophy which
later influenced Bentham and John Stuart Mill. In France, the roar
of condemnation was frightening. Helvétius retracted, several times.
The tornado skipped him and struck the *Encyclopedia* with full
force. Helvétius' book, it was said, was only a systematic summary
of the larger work. Pamphlets rained thicker, and those of one
André Chaumeix especially were so influential that the Parlement
of Paris was finally moved to action, and prosecution began. The
Helvétius affair was directly responsible; but it merely climaxed
the persistent offensive waged by the Church, the reactionary influences at the Court and the writers in their service. The long,
constant, carefully maintained campaign had finally succeeded in
creating a hostile attitude among a large segment of the French
nation. As on previous occasions of persecution, the government's
immediate motive was to counteract unrest and criticism among the
people. Diderot, who was a sensitive observer, writes in 1758 of
"the discontent of the oppressed classes," of "the spirit of revolt,"
and general dislike for the government.

Before the Parlement, the king's attorney, Omer Joly de Fleury,
bitterly accused the *Encyclopedia* of attempting to destroy religion,

morals, and government. He demanded condemnation of the work. The verdict was delivered on February 6, 1759. Its surprising leniency came to the excited public as an anticlimax. Helvétius' book was ordered burned in front of the Palace of Justice; as for the *Encyclopedia,* its seven volumes were merely sentenced to be completely revised. The *philosophes* breathed a nervous sigh of relief as the tension suddenly broke. But the respite was not for long.

The devout party was not content. They would be satisfied with nothing less than total destruction of the work. It was easy for so powerful a group, after this verdict, to obtain revocation of the privilege. They took advantage of the public concern about free-thinking, which was quite real at this time, and of the fact that the Assembly of the Clergy was meeting to decide how much it would tax itself for the "free gift" so direly needed by the king. On March 8th, the *Encyclopedia* was completely outlawed by a decree of the Privy Council, and its privilege withdrawn. It was a staggering and unexpected blow. In vain, the publishers pointed to the false quotations in Chaumeix' influential volumes, which formed the basis of the attorney's accusation. In vain, they argued that no work could ever again be published by subscription. The decree replied that the benefit to knowledge obtained from the *Encyclopedia* was outweighed by the damage to morals and religion. The publishers were forbidden to sell any longer the volumes which had already appeared or to print any new ones, under pain of exemplary punishment.

Diderot had to face the facts. The second round had been lost. It looked as if the *Encyclopedia* was never going to be finished. It was all over with "the great work of his life."

CHAPTER 9

The
Arts

1

IN ENGLAND OF THE seventeenth and eighteenth centuries, the aristocracy and the rabble patronized the same plays and theatres. In France, where caste distinctions and feelings were sharper in all respects, the "literary" theater catered uniquely to cultured, refined tastes; those of more vulgar inclinations could seek amusement from harlequinades and gross farces at the Fairs. In the seventeenth century the pure ideal of neoclassicism flourished; a dozen great writers applied themselves to the study of man in the abstract and to analysis of the timeless qualities of human nature.

During the first half of the eighteenth century this situation gradually changed. Neoclassicism was slowly enfeebled by inferior imitators of Corneille, Racine, and Molière, and by the constant sniping of rebels and reformers. The new century was developing a social-minded attitude and an interest in problems of contemporary reality. Voltaire, a conservative in all things pertaining to literature and society, attempted to instill new life into the moribund classical theater by innovations borrowed from Shakespeare; but even he succeeded only in demonstrating that it was impossible to write great plays in a style that no longer reflected the intellectual and social atmosphere of the times.

In spite of all this, and in spite of innovators, the majority of eighteenth-century plays continued to be written in the tradition of neoclassicism, so strong was that tradition. The result was inevitable. A dozen or so decidedly second-rate plays are all that remain of a vast production. The only two great playwrights of the eighteenth century both broke sharply with tradition and created their own forms of expression. Marivaux devoted himself to the study of nascent love, in delicate comedies that reflect the atmosphere of the bourgeois home and the perfume of the aristocratic salon. Beaumarchais laid aside psychological and moral pretentions, in the *Barber of Seville* and the *Marriage of Figaro*, and concentrated on a breathlessly paced intrigue with political implications.

In the more serious genres, an entire new current developed. The middle class, after its rise to economic power, began to desire political and literary expression of its newly gained, self-conscious feeling of importance. Its tastes, which up to this time had been largely ignored, were reflected more and more in literature as the century grew older. In the theater dramatists such as Destouches and La Chaussée developed what was popularly known as "the weepy comedy"; in the novel, Richardson's popular stories had innumerable imitators. All these writers injected into literature three elements that particularly expressed middle-class taste: the love of a moral lesson, clearly indicated without any attempt at subtlety; a lachrymose sentimentality; and a background of contemporary realities and middle-class life.

The new trend in the theater was developing without consciousness of its own existence; it was little more than an instinctive groping. At this point Diderot stepped in. Uniting all the scattered new ideas and the forces behind them, he added some of his own and presented France with the *fait accompli* of a dramatic revolution, the realization of a bourgeois theater.

It was at a time when he had just completed a decade devoted mainly to scientific and philosophic problems (1745–1754). Now he found himself emerging from the clouds of speculation, his mind set at rest by his exploration of the great questions. He felt free to devote himself, for a space, to literary and esthetic work. From youth, Diderot had been keenly interested in dramatic theory, and as early as *The Indiscreet Jewels* (1748), he ventured to criticize the classical theater. He sketched a few dramatic plots which he eventually consigned to the wastebasket. Not until 1757 did he publish his first play, *The Natural Son.*

Although this play did not see the boards of the Comédie Française until fifteen years later, it was widely read and had considerable influence. It was, or was supposed to be the concrete realization of a new dramatic theory that he sketched simultaneously in the turgid and declamatory *Conversations on "The Natural Son"* which accompanied the play. The two works gave rise to innumerable discussions in which they were judged not only on their merits but according to the usual division of *philosophes* and anti-*philosophes*. Grimm had considerable influence on Diderot's dramatic thinking, although he cared less for the teaching of virtue than for realism and pathetic effect. It was he who urged Diderot to write *The Natural Son* (and almost all his other plays or efforts at plays) and who, together with Rousseau, had suggested revisions. It is not surprising then, to see him announce that within a few years his friend would be "the absolute master of the theater." Diderot felt so highly elated by this success that the very next year he published his second play, the *Père de famille.* It too was accompanied by an announcement of theory, the *Essay on Dramatic Poetry.*

Diderot declares openly that the conventional tragedy no longer satisfies the eighteenth-century public. Inspired by Destouches and La Chaussée, and by Lillo and Moore in England, he proposes a new genre, which he calls the *drama,* and into it puts the aspirations of the bourgeoisie. By a *drama* he means a serious play dealing with an everyday problem of the middle class. Although the problems Diderot proposes in his own dramas have a personal more than a social point, he is the true creator of the theory of the social play which was to flourish vigorously in the second half of the nineteenth century.

Instead of being a school for love, he holds, the theater should become a school for virtue. He urges not art for art's sake, but art for morality's sake: "Truth in art is morality." The theater can teach morals more effectively than the Church. This insistence is particularly interesting since it came at a time when Rousseau had joined with the Church to condemn the theater as radically immoral. The *drama* was also supposed to derive character from "social condition"—that is, from a person's occupation and social position in life. These professional traits were to be the heart of the play's psychology and motivation. This was a novel proposal, well in keeping with the social nature of Diderot's dramatic thinking, but completely theoretical and impracticable; even if the central figure is a magistrate, it is his character that will make a real, concrete person of him, not his calling.

Realism, or "truth," was the standard now; it led Diderot not only to suggest a new dramatic form, but a renovation of French theatrical conventions. Terrible situations were no longer to take place offstage; the strongest, most violent emotions were to be expressed, as in life. The action was to be energetic but simple; Diderot condemned artificial *coups de théâtre* and favored brief and expressive *tableaux*—such as family scenes. Furthermore, scenery, always neglected in the classical tradition of timelessness, was to be a vital part of the production. It was Diderot again who initiated the movement towards realistic staging; after him, settings grew more complicated and interpretative in the romantic period and became an integral part of the realistic and naturalistic play. Against this movement of a century and a half's duration there has been in our own time the suggestion of a reaction. Several plays have been produced without scenery—for the very purpose of securing the general value of classical timelessness, to which Diderot had preferred the effect of realism.

Diderot also turned his attention to acting, and there again condemned the traditional artificialities, especially emphatic, monotonous declamation and the custom of always talking to the audience. Echoing Hamlet's advice to the players, he demanded natural, expressive acting: "there is nothing good in this world except what is true; be true, then, on the stage and off the stage." Above all, he emphasized the importance of gestures and pantomime, which he held to be at times more effective dramatically than words. Garrick, whom he later knew personally, represented his ideal. To illustrate the importance of gesture, he related a little anecdote about the great English tragedian.

> One day some people were talking in his presence about pantomime, and he held that even apart from all discourse, there was no effect that could not be expected from it. Being contradicted, he grew warm in the dispute; driven to an extremity, he said to his contradictors, picking up a cushion: "Gentlemen, I am the father of this child." Then he opened a window, took his cushion, dandling, kissing, fondling it, and mimicking all the silly little ways of a father who plays with his child; but a moment came when the cushion, or rather the child, slipped from his hands and fell out of the window. Garrick then began to mimic the father's

despair. Ask the duke de Duras what happened. The spectators were struck with such violent consternation and terror that most of them withdrew.

Diderot's dramatic productions are startling by their infidelity to his theories. They are completely subjective and his own personality betrays itself in every line. Both plays consist of a complicated, fantastic plot, with a few weak *tableaux* and a goodly number of the melodramatic *coups de théâtre* he had condemned.

The Natural Son is the story of a perfect friend, a model of virtue, who sacrifices love and fortune for his companion, saves his life, his happiness, and the happiness of those around him—all this, in spite of being a natural child. Every character is a perfect example of virtue and self-sacrifice. Other romantic elements in the play are a "criminal love," a suddenly interrupted letter that reaches the wrong woman, and a brother-sister recognition. Diderot thought the play was excellent, full of life.

In the *Père de famille,* Diderot utilized his own quarrel with his father as the basis of the plot. His hero is Saint-Albin, the sentimental, passionate, and starry-eyed lover of romanticism. But whereas the intrigue of *The Natural Son* was based on a tangled knot of sentiments perplexing the four characters, here we have a son's resistance to his father's will, and also a villain—shades of Diderot's uncle, the canon—perfidious, treacherous, black in heart. The central figure is supposed to represent Diderot's theory of "social condition" as a substitute for character. He is the "père de famille" and harangues or soliloquizes constantly about the worries, problems and duties of a father. He is perfectly good, kind, and charitable, but is puzzled by his son's extravagant attitude. The end of the drama is equivocal. The father is opposed to Saint-Albin's desire to marry a divine and virtuous maiden, because she has the misfortune to be poor and of low birth. Logically, Diderot should either have favored the thesis of submission to parental authority and prevented the marriage, or else supported class equality and have the marriage take place in the circumstances that existed throughout the play. Instead, at the last moment, the "solution" is brought about by a puerile *coup de théâtre,* entirely exterior to the forces of the drama: the wicked uncle recognizes the sweet Sophie —so named for Diderot's mistress?--as the niece he has cruelly mistreated. Suddenly rich and of noble birth, she may now marry the hero.

Both plays are a complicated hodgepodge. They are immature and melodramatic in characterization, in their passionate ranting and copious tears, in the use of *coups de théâtre,* in the theme of the trials and triumph of virtue. They have the puerility of the worst of nineteenth-century romantic drama. Diderot's dramatic taste is epitomized in what he calls the type of situation he likes: a mother comes into the room and finds her husband stretched over the dead body of their only son. The *tableaux,* as Palissot correctly pointed out, are without interest and have nothing to do with the plot. All these features were nevertheless relished by the middle class of the time, and express the bourgeois side of Diderot's temperament and ideas. In the emphasis on a sound, even a Christian moral lesson, and in the general prevailing atmosphere, which is sickly with virtue, the eighteenth century bourgeois is everywhere evident.

In spite of their mediocrity, Diderot's plays had considerable influence. They began a school of "drama" writers of whom Sedaine was the best, and were even more popular in Germany, where they affected Lessing and Katzebue. More than three hundred *drames* were produced between 1757 and 1791, and the later melodrama derived from the new genre. On the other hand, critics of less bourgeois tastes mocked him mercilessly. Dramatist Collé called *The Natural Son* the biggest bore he had ever seen. "M. Diderot has no knowledge of the theater, or of society. He has not the slightest idea of the first rules of dramatic writing . . . And yet it is after this masterpiece that he has the impudence to publish a kind of poetics, and to play the blind legislator about things he has not seen, and which nature has probably veiled from him forever." La Harpe described the play as "a cold and pompous declamation, as unbearable to read as to see."

Here then is a curious situation. Diderot's carefully developed theory points toward the realistic problem play of the second half of the nineteenth century; but his own productions are a step in the opposite direction, leading, via bourgeois moralizing and sentimentality, to romantic melodrama. The spirit of contradiction again rules his work.

He never published another play. He sketched a few and got lost in their intricate complications; and late in life he wrote a much better play, Is He Good, Is He Bad? He also translated Moore's *Gamester.* For this lack of productivity, Diderot always blamed the time-consuming *Encyclopedia*—a rationalization that covered to his own satisfaction his lack of dramatic ability.

Shortly after his flirtation with the theater, Diderot became deeply absorbed in problems of painting and sculpture.

When Grimm first came to Paris, the abbé Raynal had been sending a literary newsletter to a group of subscribers at the court of Saxe-Gotha. This idea appealed to Grimm, and he later decided to exploit it more fully. Starting May 15, 1753 he sent out a biweekly report of the latest books and news to a select and secret list of German subscribers, which he entitled *The Literary Correspondence*. Who the subscribers were, we cannot say with certainty, except that they were limited to nobility. Frederick the Great (although he never subscribed) and King Stanislas of Poland also received copies for a time. The reports were sent out in manuscript form and delivered through the diplomatic mails. In this work Grimm maintained a high level of literary criticism—superior to any other of the time—and despite the security of secrecy, eschewed vicious gossip or calumny. Diderot was soon called upon to be a regular contributor. Whenever Grimm was traveling, which, as his diplomatic ambitions increased, occurred more frequently and for longer periods, the whole responsibility was thrown into Diderot's generous lap. Although it was a weighty and onerous one, he never failed to meet his deadline.

Since Diderot was a frequent visitor at the biennial art exposition known as the *Salon,* it occurred to him that Grimm might be interested in a description of them. In September 1759, he wrote to his friend and asked him whether that fitted in with the plan of his periodical. "Command; I obey you rather badly, but willingly." Grimm of course accepted, and on the 15th of the month Diderot's account was in his hands.

From then on, the *Salons* became a regular, biennial part of his routine. Between 1759 and 1783, he missed only the *Salon* of 1773, when he was in Russia. Only Grimm's correspondents and a few privileged friends knew of their existence; the first one was not published until 1795 and the last not until 1857. Diderot proclaimed to all his friends that he did not want to publish them for humanitarian reasons; his criticisms would snatch the bread from the mouths of poor artists. To Grimm alone he perforce revealed his true motive—fear of bringing upon his own head the wrath and enmity of those artists. On various occasions, Diderot's own words belie the reputation for uncompromising frankness and honesty which he carefully cultivated and which has become a tradition among his biographers.

Diderot was grateful to Grimm for making him work on the *Salons*. It impelled him to acquire a good knowledge of the arts and develop a ramified although disorganized esthetic theory. His tactic, as usual, was to study the arts at firsthand, to watch painters and sculptors and talk to them about their technique and their ideals. He frequented studios and became friendly with dozens of artists, including Chardin, Greuze, La Tour, and Falconet. Among them also was a certain Mme. Therbousche, a would-be painter of very small talent. Diderot obliged her by using all his influence to get one of her paintings accepted by the *Salon*. He failed, but she was grateful enough to paint his portrait. One day, after the head was completed, Mme. Therbousche complained that his clothing hid his neck. Immediately Diderot darted behind a curtain, saying not a word. A moment later he reappeared "as naked as a worm."

"I should never have dared to suggest it," she said, "but you have done well and I thank you."

The philosopher and the artist, lacking any false modesty, continued their conversation "with a simplicity and innocence worthy of the first centuries." Later, Diderot admitted that he had been a little worried about one thing: "As we do not command all the parts of our body (since the sin of Adam), there are some that want to when the son of Adam doesn't, and that don't want to when the son of Adam would like to."

Two or three artists with whom Diderot came into contact became his particular friends. One was La Tour, frank, honest, and blunt, a man whose wide intellectual curiosity led him to study literature, morals, theology, politics, and black magic. Diderot could admire him for an impulse such as overtook him at d'Holbach's, one day. The baron was showing them two pastels of Mengs. Then they sat down to table. Suddenly La Tour jumped up and left the room without saying a word. After dinner, the company found him rapt in contemplation of the pastels.

Another was Greuze, proud and easily offended, whose friendship Diderot did not long retain, thanks to his own lack of tact. After the Academy of Beaux-Arts accepted Greuze as a member, they rejected the painting he offered for the admission ceremonies. The humiliated artist placed the blame for this discomfiture on Diderot, who had been quite free with his unfavorable criticism of the supposed masterpiece. Greuze lost his temper, and they had a quarrel that put a sudden end to their friendship.

Then there was the sculptor Falconet, who was as petulant and quarrelsome a character as Greuze. In spite of this, Diderot became attached to him, possibly because of his high moral calibre and fondness for intellectual discussions. Falconet had a hated rival, Pigalle. When the latter exhibited his monument to Louis XV, Falconet went to see him. "Monsieur Pigalle, I do not like you and I think you reciprocate that feeling. I have seen your monument. It is possible to do something so beautiful, since you have done it, but I do not think that art can go a line further. That doesn't prevent our remaining as we are."

"There you have my Falconet," Diderot concluded.

Later Falconet went to Russia, to serve Catherine the Great. During their years of separation, the two friends carried on an ardent correspondence, interesting largely for a protracted debate on the desire for literary or artistic immortality. Falconet mocked it, while Diderot called it inevitable, necessary, useful, inspiring. Sometimes the debate became fiery and impassioned, but more often Diderot preferred a light, persuasive vein:

> Indeed, that posterity would be an ingrate if she forgot me entirely, I who have thought so much of her. . . . It isn't I, nor Peter nor Paul, nor John who is praising you, it is good taste, and good taste is an abstract being that never dies, its voice makes itself heard uninterruptedly, by successive organs that follow each other. That immortal voice will be stilled for you, doubtless, when you exist no more ; but that is what you hear now ; it is immortal in spite of yourself, it calls and will always keep calling: "Falconet! Falconet!"

Diderot's stand was only a reflection of his own desires. Almost indifferent to the praise of his contemporaries, in fact only too fearful of it, he preferred the more tranquil prospect of enduring fame among future generations.

Although the seventeenth century had theorized about the arts, particularly poetry, it was in the eighteenth that esthetics took form as a branch of philosophy. Since the English writers, and Shaftesbury in particular, had been concerned with esthetics, it is not surprising that Diderot, who took from Shaftesbury his initial concept of the linking between the True, the Good, and the Beautiful, reveals intense interest in that field even in his earliest writings. In the notes to the *Essay on Merit and Virtue,* and in the mathematical papers, where he becomes involved in the relation between mathematics, beauty, and esthetic pleasure, he is already deeply concerned with the theory of beauty. His thinking was brought to fruition in the article "On Beauty," which he wrote for the *Encyclopedia* in 1751.

This article contains Diderot's most original contribution to esthetic philosophy. He considers the idea of beauty as one aspect of all knowledge, developed in reaction to nature, motivated by utility. But as men reached higher levels of abstraction, and more subtle sensitivity, beauty became an evaluative relationship with nature, which he defines as "the perception of relationships." In his abstract discussion, Diderot is torn between his desire to avoid a completely objective concept of beauty, which would make beauty an absolute, existing in nature independently of man, as a form of truth, and the opposing subjective concept, which holds that beauty is an event in the mind, consequently without objective criteria. Although his reasoning is at times confused, he tends toward the "modified subjective view": the qualities that arouse the sensation of beauty in us are real and determinate, but beauty is not present unless a certain relationship comes to exist between the object and our own minds. This experience is not primarily emotional, although it may lead to emotion; it is rather intuitive and intellectual. Throughout Diderot's later writings, however, we find a sharp division between a subjective and objective view of beauty. He reaches extremes of objectivism when he defines beauty as perfect adaptation to function (the beautiful man is the one most perfectly adapted to his biological functions), extremes of subjectivism when he makes beauty depend on the momentary feeling or condition of the viewer. Dealing similarly with taste, Diderot recognizes on one hand its historical relativity; on the other hand he refuses to admit that good taste is a personal caprice, without objective foundation, and calls it eternal. There is no clear conciliation of these two positions.

From Diderot's ideas on the nature of beauty stem his theories on creation and creativity, which were developed in his writings on the theater and in the *Salons.* First, he gives us a general theory of imitation, strictly neoclassical, calling for objective representation of nature, and the choice and purification of select elements. By "purification" he meant the removal of individual "imperfections" and the presentation of general, eternal truth, according to an "ideal model"a timeless reconstruction of the essence of nature—which the artist forms by study. Just as he had urged for the stage, Diderot requires the artist to create the illusion of truth rather than to copy nature exactly; to start from observation, but to refashion what he sees in view of the impression he wishes to produce on the spectator. This is not the artist's personal impression, but one that will strike men of all ages and places as being true.

At the same time—and here is the more original and interesting part of his theories—Diderot advanced several ideas that were ahead of his age. These apply to literature as much as to painting and sculpture, for in the eighteenth century, it was commonly held that the same principles applied to all the arts.

The method of naturalism, developed a hundred years later, is already implicit in Diderot's theory of characteristic detail. The best way to describe a scene or a man is by a few precise, essential traits, for the mind cannot unify a mass of details, cannot portray the whole. As Leibniz had said, no two grains of sand are exactly alike; every being is distinguished by characteristic details. The impression of realism should be obtained by use of trivial circumstances that appear necessarily true—the artist need only put on a wart or a scar on a beautiful head to make the "ideal model" an everyday truth. Observation of nature, constant observation—and not imitation of the ancients, although he advises their study—is Diderot's watchword. "Great poets, actors, and perhaps in general all great imitators of nature . . . are busy looking, recognizing, imitating . . . I see them with their notebook constantly on their knees and their pencil in hand." Also prenaturalistic is Diderot's theory of physiological unity: the blind man, the hunchback, the porter, the pregnant woman bear throughout their entire bodies the signs of their occupation or condition; the body is a unit.

Symbolists, too, were able to find inspiration in Diderot's versatile mind. He advocates the use of alternate sound and silence on the stage, and also their theory of obscurity. "Clarity is good for persuasion, worthless for emotion. Poets, be dark." Then, contradicting his own theory of characteristic detail, he counsels the use of "suggestive" adjectives, such as "great," "terrible," instead of precise, limiting words. Poetry should be akin to music, which emotionally is the most effective of all the arts because it stirs the imagination by its vagueness.

There is also much romanticism in Diderot's esthetic thinking, although it is evident less in his theorizing than in his taste and in his critical reactions to actual works. We have seen that in the theater he enjoyed pathetic, melodramatic plots, drenched in intense emotion, rich in murders, deaths, and crimes. He confuses sublime with violent emotion, emotion that "shakes his insides"—uprooted trees, storms, men swept away—and speaks scornfully of "those people with a small refined taste, who are afraid of strong sensations." In paintings he enjoys Casanove's battle scenes, with their cracked skulls, transfixed chests, with dead and dying strewn over a scene of confusion and horror—or, at the other extreme, an innocent and idyllic pastoral scene. It was the romanticist in Diderot that led him to proclaim Shakespeare's genius, despite the bard's lack of good taste. "Admit that Shakespeare is an extraordinary man. There isn't one of his scenes that couldn't be made into something great, with a little talent. And then, what swiftness and what verse!"

Is the artist a true creator? Diderot sets out in his early writings with the neoclassical view, that the artist only imitates and recombines, clothing new objects with existing forms of beauty. The artist is the observer and recorder of significant forms and the facts of human emotion before the external world. At the most, some creativity is involved in the attainment of the ideal model. As Diderot's ideas evolve, he reaches a wider concept of creativity as the conscious production of images by the artist's imagination, under the directive impulse of an idea. In this act, the imagination does not merely imitate reality, but prolongs it by a process of analogy.

After Diderot's early writings, his emphasis on emotion and enthusiasm as the driving force in artistic creation rather abruptly gives place to a more rational position. His new view is expressed in his celebrated *Paradox on Acting*.

The word "paradox" deserves a brief comment in passing, for love of paradox is characteristic of most of Diderot's writings. Pride in his individualism, in his independent mind, instinctively rebellious to authority; a tendency to react to any position by finding truth may also be on the other side: these traits are perhaps at the base of his great love of paradox. He also considered paradox a way of exploring truth, and so, a means to knowledge. Much more than his published works, his conversation abounded in scintillating, often shocking paradoxes, for the heat of discussion was unchecked by considered judgment. He usually did not take them seriously, but a few did find their way into his writings. The most famous of these, by far, is the *Paradox on Acting*, written in 1773.

For more than twenty years Diderot had proclaimed the supreme value of passion and sensitivity as the sole sources of the sublime, in art, literature, and life. Even in acting, quite specifically, he had encouraged those traits in his dramatic essays. He complimented his young actress-protégée, Mlle. Jodin, on having a great quality that cannot be acquired: "a soul that becomes wild, profoundly moved, transported on the spot." Then he changed his mind. In the *Salon of 1765*, he declared that "sensitivity, when it is extreme, no longer discerns; everything excites it indifferently . . . Cold men, severe and tranquil observers of nature, often know better what delicate strings must be plucked; they create enthusiasm, without feeling it." At the base of this shift were Diderot's studies in physiology, which led him to realize the dominant role of the brain over the sympathetic nervous system.

This new attitude took definite form in 1769, after he had read a book about Garrick. He wrote a "review" of it, which he described to Grimm as a fine paradox. "I pretend that sensitivity is what makes mediocre actors . . . cold judgment and reason, sublime actors." Diderot now wants the actor to be "a cold and tranquil spectator of human nature"; this alone will enable him to imitate everything and play all roles. If his emotion were true, argues the philosopher, his performance would be completely different each night, and after ten nights, he would be exhausted. He does not deny to the actor all feeling, but wants it completely controlled by reason.

Diderot carried his new theory to its logical conclusion in *D'Alembert's Dream*, where Bordeu declares that sensitivity, "or the extreme mobility of certain threads of the nervous network," is the dominant characteristic of mediocre beings. Such a person is abandoned to every sensation, to internal tumult, and his reason and judgment are helpless.

The *Paradox on Acting,* one of Diderot's most popular and brilliant dialogues, was not published until 1830, and like *Rameau's Nephew*, was the cause of a literary quarrel over its authenticity at the end of the nineteenth century. It develops both the paradox expressed in its title and the wider implications about genius and mediocrity.

And why should the actor differ from the poet, the painter, the orator, the musician? It is not in the furor of the first emotion that the characteristic traits present themselves, it is in tranquil and cool moments. It is when, suspended between nature and their sketch, these geniuses cast their eye alternately on one and the other . . . Great poets, great actors, and perhaps in general all great imitators of nature, endowed with a beautiful imagination, keen judgment, delicate tact, sure taste, are the least sensitive of beings. . . .

In the great comedy, the comedy of life, the one to which I always return, the passionate souls occupy the stage ; the men of genius are in the audience. . . . Sensitivity . . . it seems to me, is that disposition accompanying weakness of the organs, a consequence of the mobility of the diaphragm, of the vivacity of the imagination, of the delicacy of the nerves, which inclines one to pity, to thrill, to admire, to fear, to become confused, to weep, to faint, to help, to flee, to shout, to lose one's reason, to exaggerate, to despise, to disdain, to have no exact idea of the true, the good and the beautiful, to be unjust, to be mad. Multiply sensitive souls, and you will multiply in the same proportion good and bad actions of all kinds.

When Diderot pronounced sensitivity to be the characteristic of a good heart and a mediocre mind or talent, he was not complimenting himself: "If Nature ever formed a sensitive soul, it was mine." And yet he preferred it that way, he finally decided. "Happy is he who has received from nature a sensitive and mobile soul! He bears within himself the source of a multitude of delightful instants that others are ignorant of." The man who has only intelligence, only genius, "lacks an organ," for there are things too subtle for the mind to perceive or express. The language of the heart is a thousand times more varied than that of the mind. It is not surprising that Diderot should select emotion as the best rule of life. His own temperament, his frequent emphasis on the natural goodness of human instincts led him to that conclusion.

3

In the field of art criticism, Diderot was an innovator whose work was of considerable importance. In spite of a few minor attempts previous to his, Diderot may be said to have originated art criticism in France with his brilliant series of *Salons*. These have not only influenced many later critics, especially Baudelaire, but still remain a masterpiece of the genre. This is true in spite of Diderot's often questionable or downright poor taste and frequent lack of true artistic feeling. He admitted his failings freely: "I do not guarantee either my descriptions or my judgments on anything. I am neither an artist nor even an amateur. As long as we have not handled the brush, we shall be only more or less enlightened conjecturers." But this unusual modesty was perhaps only a method of self-protection; Diderot did not hesitate, in his *Essay on Painting* (1765), to lay down technical principles of color, perspective, design, etc., although it is also true that he never dared to publish the essay.

Diderot put into the *Salons* all the emotion and enthusiasm of his reactions, and all his art as a writer. The basic attitudes of his theories are carried forward in his criticism; since they are so disunified, it is not surprising that his criticism is not based on any general principle. To a significant extent, however, he was able, as Dieckmann has put it, to free himself from the traditional esthetics, to open a new door for his great gift for the description, interpretation and evaluation of phenomena. The imprint of his individual taste is present everywhere. He cannot, for instance, dissociate art from literature, and insists that the subject and the composition must satisfy the reason, just like any tragedy. He compares color to style in literature and thinks that both arts must obey similar principles of order. In criticizing, he always asks first of the picture, "What does it mean? Where is its interest?" And he is likely to set down a comment such as this. "Beautiful, very beautiful composition, beautiful poem; affliction, sadness, sorrow rush towards your soul from all sides." Diderot has, it may be concluded, little appreciation of the esthetic experience in itself, divorced from the other emotions it may produce. His judgments are consequently often poor. He would not exchange ten Watteaus, he tells us, for one Teniers.

On the whole Diderot's taste is again characterized by elements which are either pre-romantic or representative of the bourgeois side of his temperament. He is attracted by compositions whose conception is bold and striking, whose appeal is obviously emotional, and which succeed in creating turbulent emotions in the spectator. He also admired the literal realism of Chardin. "You could take the bottles by the neck if you were thirsty; the peaches and raisins awaken your appetite and draw your hand . . . His paintings will be sought after some day." But his favorite artist was Greuze. Greuze was sentimental and moved him to tenderness and to tears. He liked *The Village Bride*, for example; "the subject is pathetic and one feels overcome with a sweet emotion on looking at it." Especially, Greuze took care, in many of his paintings, to point a clear and very Christian moral lesson; his series on the disobedient son, culminating in the latter's tragic punishment, stirred Diderot intensely, for reasons that are not hard to imagine. "Here is your painter and mine, the first among us who has thought of giving morals to art and of linking events so that it would be easy to make a story out of them."

He seems quite unable to conceive of any art not associated with some didactic or moral purpose. This aspect of his theorizing follows the subjectivist line of thinking; it places the value of beauty in the individual emotional effect, an effect of a particular nature, conveying a purely human evaluation of reality according to a moral scheme. In this he is again the typical bourgeois, sentimental and moralizing, not the bold rebel who praised the instincts of nature and derided Christian attempts to restrain them. Speaking of artists, poets and philosophers, he proclaims that they must be, above all else, excellent moralists, or else they will be dangerous corruptors. "I am not a Capuchin; yet I confess that I would willingly sacrifice the pleasure of seeing beautiful nude figures, if I could hasten the coming of the day when painting and sculpture, more decent and moral, will think of contributing, together with the other arts, to inspire virtue and purify our manners." This great service the arts, by their appeal to the emotions, can accomplish for mankind better than any preacher: "the kind of exhortation that is addressed to the heart by the intercession of the senses, aside from its permanence, is more within reach of the average man."

All this does not preclude Diderot's enjoying lascivious pictures himself, despite his theoretical disapproval. After criticizing a nude, he adds, "All the same, let me have her just as she is, and I do not think I shall waste time complaining that her hair is too dark." When he saw La Grenée's "Chaste Joseph" turning his back on the voluptuous wife of Potiphar, he commented drily, "I can't imagine what Jacob's son could have wanted; I wouldn't have asked for any better, and I have often settled for less." On seeing the same painter's "Chaste Susanna," he suggested that she could have caused the old men much more trouble if she had said "Go ahead." As he describes Greuze's portrait of Mme. de Gramont, he goes into a voluptuous ecstasy over the figure and face until his blood gets hot and he can hardly write.

In criticizing paintings, Diderot always looks for the dramatic thought. No fault is more unpardonable to him than a weak imagination. He conceives of the picture as a "still" in a play; for this reason, it is essential that the artist choose the right moment in the "action." Although he can be severe, he is always ready to let himself be carried away by the enthusiasm of his reaction, and to overlook technical faults when the picture as a whole moves him. When he dislikes a painting, he denounces it in no uncertain terms. "By Apollo, god of painting, we condemn master Parrocel, author of this miserable composition, to lick his canvas until nothing is left of it, and we forbid him to choose in the future subjects that require genius." Or he will even become violently angry. "Are you able to conceive that a man can be crippled in taste to the point of placing on her stomach a figure that has breasts, and to cover her buttocks? Hey! idiot! What then do you want me to see?"

Diderot was always teeming with ideas, and his ideas were always inspired as a reaction to something he read, heard or saw. When he feels that a painting has possibilities that the artist has not realized, he will offer suggestions for improvement, usually in conception, sometimes in technique. As early as his second *Salon* (1761), he starts to "remake" paintings, telling the artist how they should have been done, and in each *Salon* there are a few examples of this procedure. This would not be possible if Diderot did not "enter into" the painting, into its process of creation; so that criticism for him becomes at these times a re-creation. But Diderot could not remake the painting himself. In the case of literary criticism, he was able once to carry out his own criticism into a new creation. This was his famous tale, *The Two Friends of Bourbonne*, which he composed after writing a review of Saint-Lambert's *Two Friends*. However, Diderot does not intend this method to be a general prescription for art or literary criticism; he was able to follow it only because he too was a creator, because he was Diderot, with his individual personality and mode of reaction.

From the very first *Salon*, Diderot reveals his remarkable ability to make us see a picture through a word description and his keen eye for details and their fitness in the harmony of the whole. As time went on, he improved continuously. The secret of his method of describing paintings is simple; he animates them, makes them live, act, talk. Sometimes he is content with a simple, but vivid description; when a painting moves him, however, something like this review of Greuze's "Girl Weeping Over Her Dead Bird" may be the result.

What a pretty elegy! What a charming poem! A delightful painting, perhaps the most pleasing and the most interesting in the Salon. The poor little girl is facing us; her head is resting on her left hand; the dead bird placed on the upper edge of the cage, its head hanging down, its wings dragging, its feet in the air.

What a pretty catafalque this cage is! How graceful that garland of green that winds around it! Poor little girl! How grieved she is! How naturally she is placed! How beautiful her head is! How elegant is her coiffure! How much expression her face has! Her sorrow is profound; she is completely overcome by her grief. Oh what a beautiful hand! What a beautiful hand! What a beautiful arm! Look at the details of those fingers; and those dimples, and that softness, and that rosy glow with which the pressure of her head has colored the tips of those delicate fingers, and the charm of all that. We would approach that hand to kiss it if we did not respect the child and her grief. Everything about her is enchanting, even her attire. That kerchief around her neck is so natural! It is so light and supple! When you first see this work, you say: *delightful!* If you stop at it, or return to it, you cry: *delightful! delightful!* Soon you surprise yourself talking with the girl, and consoling her. This is so true, that here is what I remember having said to her.

"Why little one, your sorrow is very profound, very thoughtful! What does that melancholy and dreamy air mean? What! For a bird! . . . Come now, open your heart to me; tell me the truth; is it really the death of that bird that makes you meditate so sadly? You lower your eyes; you do not answer me. Your tears are about to flow . . . Well, I understand, he loves you, he swore it to you, and had sworn it for a long time. He was suffering so much: and how can you bear to see someone you love suffer?

Eh! let me continue; why close my mouth with your hand? That morning, unfortunately, your mother was absent. He came; you were alone; he was so handsome, so passionate, so tender, so charming! He had so much love in his eyes! So much truth in his words! He spoke those words which make your heart beat fast! . . . He held one of your hands; from time to time you felt the warmth of a few tears that fell from his eyes. And still your mother did not come. It wasn't your fault; it was your mother's. But there you are, weeping harder than ever. What I am telling you is not to make you weep. And why should you. He has promised to marry you; he will not betray his word . . ."

"And my bird. . . . You are smiling."

"Ah! my friend, how beautiful she was! If you could have seen her smile and weep! I continued: "Well, your bird! When one forgets oneself, can one remember a bird? When the hour for your mother's return approached, the one who loves you went away. How happy, content, enraptured, he was! How hard it was to tear himself away from you! . . ."

"And my mother?"

"Your mother? She came back right after he left; she found you dreaming, just as you were a little while ago. Your mother spoke to you, and you didn't hear what she said; she told you to do one thing and you did another. A few tears welled in your eyes; you held them back, or you turned aside your head to dry them furtively. Your distraction made your mother impatient; she scolded you; and that was an opportunity to weep without constraint and solace your heart . . . Shall I go on, little one? I fear that what I am going to tell you will renew your pain. You are willing? . . . Well, your good mother reproached herself for having made you sad; she went up to you, took your hands, kissed your brow and your cheeks, and you wept all the more. Your head bent over her; and your face, which was beginning to blush, see, just as it is now, hid itself in her bosom. How many sweet things that good mother told you! And how those sweet things hurt you!

"Meanwhile your canary was singing away for all it was worth, warning you, calling you, beating its wings, complaining about your neglect, all in vain . . . Neither its water nor its seed was renewed; and this morning the bird was dead . . . You still look at me; is there something else remaining for me to say? Ah! I understand; that bird, it was he who had given it to you. Well, he'll get you another one just as pretty . . . But that isn't all yet: you stare at me and your eyes are again filled with tears; what else can there be? Tell me, I can't guess."

"And suppose the death of that bird were only an omen? What would I do, what would I become? If he were ungrateful . . ."

"What madness! Fear nothing, my poor little girl: that is impossible, and will not be!"

What! my friend, you laugh at me! You make fun of a grave person who occupies himself in consoling a girl in a painting for the loss of her bird, for the loss of whatever you want to imagine? But don't you see how beautiful she is, how interesting she is! I do not like to make others sad; in spite of that, I shouldn't mind at all being the cause of her sorrow.

The *Salons* make delightful reading. As with so many of Diderot's works, their interest is heightened by many curious and brilliant digressions, touching on a wide variety of subjects. Should we obey the law always, or do what is best for the public good? Is the spirit of philosophy favorable to poetry? Or he may give us a brief and highly original dialogue on language and the imagination.

"My dear abbé, we have been talking for a long time ; you have understood me, I suppose?"

"Yes, very well."

"And do you think you have understood anything except words?"

"Most assuredly."

"Then you are mistaken ; you have heard only words, nothing but words. In discourse there are only abstract expressions which designate ideas, and concrete expressions which designate physical beings. What! do you mean that while I was talking, you were busy enumerating all the ideas implied by all my abstract words, that your imagination was working hard trying actually to portray the images linked in my discourse. You don't really mean that, my dear abbé ; I would have been at the end of my talk while you'd still be picturing to yourself my first figures."

"My word, you may be right."

"I am . . ."

"That is a surprising mystery ; I did get the complete impression . . ."

"It is the mystery of daily conversation."

"And will you explain that mystery to me?"

"If I can. We were children unfortunately a long time ago, my dear abbé. In infancy, words were pronounced to us ; these words were fixed in our memory, and their meaning in our mind, either by an idea or by an image ; and this idea or image was accompanied by aversion, hatred, pleasure, terror, desire, indignation, scorn ; for a considerable number of years, at each word pronounced, the idea or the image returned with the sensation that went with it ; but gradually we have used our words as we do coins: we no longer look at the design, the motto, the stamp, to recognize its value ; we give and take them by their shape and weight ; and so it is with words. We have left aside the idea or image, to limit ourselves to the sound and sensation. Without this abbreviation, we could not converse ; it would take us a day to say and to appreciate a long sentence. And what does the philosopher do, who weighs, stops, analyses, decomposes? He returns, evidently, to the state of infancy."

After an instant of silence and reflection, seizing the abbé by the arm, I said to him: "Abbé, what a strange machine a language is, and what a stranger one still the mind is! There is nothing in either one that is not related by some corner ; there are no signs, however different, no ideas however singular, that do not touch each other."

Diderot's taste in poetry is very much the same as in art. He favors Ossian, and Young's *Night Thoughts;* he appreciates "something enormous, barbarian, savage," the horror of a dark night, the terrors of a storm. His love of ruins and the emotions they inspire in him are thoroughly romantic. In the novel, Richardson is his god. His *Eulogy of Richardson* (1761) is a paean to the master, a passionate, enthusiastic recognition of his power to teach morality through emotion.

The *Eulogy of Richardson* is typical of Diderot's literary criticism. He is quick to condemn, quick to be carried away by a wave of enthusiasm. If there are one or two things that strike his imagination or stir his emotions, he is always ready to overlook the weak points. Why read to discover faults?

Diderot's esthetic writings are important for his theories on the theater and the arts. Time and again his ideas looked forward boldly to a renovation of art forms. Using the innovations of his contemporaries, Diderot created the drama; by his own genius, he created art criticism. In esthetics, he had a wealth of ideas. Mostly, they follow either the classical tradition or the newer theories that directed the thinking of the times towards graphic realism and stressed the emotional character of the esthetic experience. According to Bernard Bosanquet, all esthetic philosophies start from one of two standpoints. The first is to look for beauty according to causal laws or general truths in harmony with observed phenomena; the other wants beauty to respond to the individual's moral or hedonistic requirements. Both attitudes coexist in Diderot. Although his ideas are complex and disorganized, although they do not make a good esthetic philosophy, they are perhaps all the richer and the more fertile. Yet his esthetic thinking does not entirely lack unity. Regardless of his varying attitudes and precepts, he is always concerned with the imitation of beautiful nature, with conserving the truth of nature, and with provoking moral good in man. While nature's truth is objectively verifiable, it acquires esthetic significance only in the light of our perception of it and our conversion of it into purely human values. Art is the bridge between nature and man. And esthetic creation is the highest activity of the human mind.

CHAPTER 10

Diderot

chez

lui

1

THE AFFECTION and respect Diderot felt for his father, as well as the enduring attachment for his home at Langres, grew stronger as he entered middle life. He never missed an opportunity to demonstrate his feelings by sending gifts and good wishes, or by asking advice on financial matters. Of course he was equally prompt with unasked-for advice of his own, especially in matters of health. That these suggestions were not always tactfully put is scarcely cause for surprise. Apparently the philosopher did not approve of his father's arduous devotions, and in more than one little sermon he urged him to abridge them. "If it were certain that the most rigorous practice of Christianity shortened one's life, Christianity would be proven false in itself and unworthy of the God who has created man and commanded him to conserve himself. . . . Decrease your prayers and increase your charities. I should like to turn your piety towards charity, because I prefer you to climb up to an attic to warm some poor devil shivering with cold rather than get chilled yourself in a church. And those churches are full of people who pray and the houses full of poor who suffer; because everyone asks of God and no one gives to man."

In the Spring of 1759, Diderot was deeply upset on receiving unexpected news of his father's senility and ill-health. He confided his distress to friend Grimm: "My father will die, without having me beside him. Ten years from now, I shall seek his image in my memory, and shall not find it any more. Ah! my friend, what am I doing here? He wants me, his last moments are approaching, he is calling me, and I remain. There are still friends on earth, still lovers, but there are no more children." What is the part of mere rhetoric in this display of emotion? How much the genuine distress of the child who keeps delaying, thinking there is more time? Diderot felt that he could not leave Paris at that moment. It was then that the *Encyclopedia* was being condemned and his own arrest was a distinct possibility. To leave would be to run away, to acknowledge guilt, to endanger the whole enterprise.

This was a period of intense depression for Diderot—so much so that d'Holbach, alarmed, took him on a series of excursions in the country. At times this helped, but often the well-meaning Teuton got on his nerves. There were troubles with the Volland family, too, and we shall return to them in a moment. Physically, he was overcome with a general fatigue and poor digestion, and this did not help his morale.

On the ninth of June he wrote these words of grief to Grimm. "This is the last blow I needed to receive; my father is dead. I know neither when nor how. He had promised me, the last time I saw him, to call me in his last moments. I am sure that he thought of it, but that he did not have the time. I have seen neither my father nor my mother die; I shall not hide from you that I consider this a curse from heaven. Good-bye, my friend. You will give him some tears, will you not? Shed some too for your unhappy friend. Good-bye, dear Grimm, you know me, imagine my state. Other sorrows do not prepare for this one. Adieu. Adieu."

Grimm, in fact, had only recently stopped off to visit Diderot's father at the spa at Bourbonne, on his way to rejoin Mme. d'Epinay in Geneva. He had found him in improved health. Shortly after, Didier returned to Langres. Just as his neighbors were congratulating him on looking so well, he felt his eyes grow dim, his head become light. "I feel a little dizziness," he said. "But don't worry, it is nothing." He forced himself to continue the conversation. A moment later, he slumped back in his chair, dead.

Diderot left immediately for Langres. He wept when he rejoined his brother and sister, wept still more when he read the testament.

It was a document of piety and charity, and of good counsel. "My dear children, have a great love of God, love each other as the proverb says: 'like brother and sister,' and especially I recommend to you charity to the poor, particularly to our poor relatives." With them wept Hélène Brûlé, the same faithful servant, now grown old, who it is said had three times made the journey to Paris on foot, more than twenty years before, to bring the young rebel financial succor from his mother.

In sorrow Diderot received the calls of the townsmen, although he did derive some melancholy pleasure from meeting the men, now middle-aged, who had learned to spell with him, and whom he had almost forgotten. But most of his boyhood companions were dead; life expectancy in the eighteenth century was short. "Two things announce our fate to come," he reflected. "Ancient ruins and the brief duration of those who began to live at the same time as we. It is this secret feeling that makes their presence so dear to us; by their existence they reassure us about our own. It seems that they take us backwards, and we become young once more on seeing them." We can sense a cry of distress when he writes to Sophie, from Langres, "Love me; tell me that you do. Love me tenderly. Tell it to me often." Is he suddenly afraid of growing old alone, without love?

He went to church, probably for the first time in many years, to hear an old comrade preach. At the same time, always filled with an intense "party spirit," he noted with satisfaction that there were a goodly number of unbelievers in Langres, and that they were all respected citizens—an interesting comment on the penetration of "philosophy" in the provinces. "I am quite satisfied with the welcome of our inhabitants," he concluded smugly. "They have honored me in every way. It has been a round of endless visits and of repasts beginning with the day and lasting well into the night. I do not care for it, but one must be gracious and look glad."

Diderot took advantage of this visit and the emotion surrounding it to cement the pact of peace with his brother. There was an unpleasant family scene; the abbé complained that he showed favoritism to their sister, Denise, which Diderot stoutly denied. This was not pure hypocrisy, but also his usual facility for deluding himself. "I began," he writes to Sophie, "by undeceiving the abbé about a jealousy preconceived, I don't know how or why, that my sister was dearer to me than he." Then the abbé complained that Diderot had not spoken too well of him in his letters to their father;

to which the philosopher replied that he did not remember their contents, but that they were devoid of malicious intention. "My brother, if I have done anything wrong, even involuntarily, I beg your pardon for it." At this word Denise grumbled, "Such a speech is very humble for an elder brother."

The antipathy between Denise and the abbé was even sharper than that between the two brothers. Immediately on his arrival, Diderot was struck by their incompatibility.

"My sister is lively, quick, gay, headstrong, easily offended. I am the only man she has ever loved. The abbé. . . . would have been intelligent, but religion has made him cautious and cowardly. He is sad, silent, circumspect, and peevish. He carries with him constantly an uncomfortable rule by which he judges his own and other people's conduct. He is annoying and annoyed. . . . Gentle, easygoing, indulgent, too much, perhaps, it seems that I occupy between them a just mean. I am the oil that prevents those jagged machines from grating when they touch each other. But who will harmonize them when I am no longer here? That is a worry which torments me. I am afraid to bring them together, because if they should separate some day, it would be violently."

In spite of this character analysis and prediction, Diderot did persuade his sister and brother to try living together, in order not to have to sell the paternal home. He mollified the abbé with his protestations of affection, and won over Denise, who was tired of household cares, by arranging to have a poor friend of hers live with them. A compromise was effected between the abbé's love of good eating and Denise's more economical temperament. Finally all three embraced and mingled their tears.

"Will they be happy together?" Diderot asked himself. "Both are sensitive and charitable. But is that enough? I delude myself as much as I can on their diversity of character."

As for the inheritance, it was divided amiably and quickly, each trying to outdo the other in generosity. "Ah! if my father's soul were only with us, how happy it would be! It was all done in such a gentle, calm way, so gentlemanly like that you would have wept for joy." The farms and investments of the cutler were for the most part to be left intact, and the income from them divided three ways. As a result, Diderot now found himself in a rather comfortable financial position. He had fifteen hundred livres a year from his inheritance, a thousand from the publishers, two hundred "elsewhere"; then, if the *Encyclopedia* were ever completed, the eight or nine thousand livres he would have to invest would provide another four or five hundred a year, plus an additional five hundred from the projected sale of his library. "Calculate and you will find three or four thousand livres income a year, with which one can be very comfortable if he is not crazy."

At last Diderot had satisfied a desire for security that had preoccupied him ever since his marriage. After a bohemian youth, he had now attained his expressed ideal of middle-class mediocrity: "aside from the necessary minimum, an honest excess without which one cannot be happy." He also possessed a very bourgeois shrewdness in matters of finance. Wise management increased his wealth so that in 1766 he had an income of four thousand six hundred livres, representing a capital many times that. In his frequent struggles with his publishers, and those over his daughter's marriage contract, in the financial advice he gave to many of his friends and even to strangers, Diderot showed himself time and again to be a match for the sharpest adversaries.

In spite of his vaunted honesty, the philosopher did not hesitate to stoop to trickery and finesse, when the occasion warranted. Even before his marriage, he had tried with all his craft to wheedle a pension out of his father. Like a true bourgeois, his interest conquered his idealism. On one occasion, he paid a special visit to a wealthy aunt of his future son-in-law, and descended to the lowest flattery and hypocrisy to win her favor. "I am not too scrupulous in the matter of inheritances," he admits. "You see that I am a good politician." During this visit to Langres, he stumbled on a valuable library at the home of one of the townsmen, and tried to buy it for a mere song from the ignorant owner, who was unaware of its true value. But he overplayed his hand. Suddenly suspicious, the wary proprietor refused to sell at all, and the philosopher went away furious, mentally kicking himself for his bungling.

Finding it difficult to tear himself away from his family, Diderot prolonged his visit for two months. He enjoyed being in this town of his boyhood again. His father's tenant farmers paid their respects with tears in their eyes to the man who had always been so good and so generous. Sometimes Diderot was stopped in the street.

"Monsieur Diderot, you are good, but if you think you will ever equal your father, you are mistaken."

The vicar told him that "philosophy doesn't make men like that." Such statements made him feel proud.

The last days at Langres were filled with emotion and melancholy, with memories of his father and thoughts of his death. On August 14, Diderot informed Sophie that he had two more nights to spend with his family. "On Thursday morning, I shall leave this house, where, in a short interval of time, I have experienced many different sensations." The final hours were spent reading his father's papers, packing trunks with those of his things he might be able to use. "All these events, which link men to each other in so sweet a way, have cruel moments. Very cruel? I am wrong, I am at present plunged into a melancholy I would not change for all the noisy pleasures in the world."

On the very last night, the temperamental abbé caused a little family drama. Suddenly noticing that he was packing his trunk, too, Diderot asked him what he was doing. The abbé replied that he was offended because "he had not been informed" of his brother's departure. They were neglecting him, keeping things from him, plotting against him, they didn't love him—it was evident in the smallest things. He was so excited that he could neither eat nor drink nor talk. "I took his hands," Diderot relates, "embraced him, protested all I felt, perhaps more than I felt. His state filled me with pity. I trembled for the fate of my sister, who kept saying: 'See, that's the life he is preparing for me!'"

This remark and a few others from the impetuous Denise started things anew. When they sat down at table, brother and sister each moved off to one side, to the great astonishment of the servants who watched three silent beings, each ten feet away from the table; "one leaning sadly on his elbows, that was I; the other leaning back in her chair like someone who wants to sleep, that was my sister; the third twisting and turning in his chair, seeking a comfortable position." Finally Diderot sent the servants away and took the floor. "I reminded them of what they had sworn over the body of their dead father, begged them by the love they had for me."

At first even his eloquence had little effect.

"No, my brother, this man has been and always will be impossible to live with."

To which the abbé replied, "Let her go; even if we do embrace, she will not love me the more."

Diderot managed to drag Denise over to the abbé, peace was made and a cold supper eaten, during which he gave them a fine sermon. "I was moved. I do not know what I told them; but the end of it all was that they stretched their hands to each other across the table, that they seized them and squeezed them, with tears in their eyes, and after admitting their wrongs frankly, begged my pardon a thousand times and overwhelmed me with affection." A wonderful testimonial to the power of Diderot's eloquence!

This was the high point in Diderot's relations with his brother. The very next morning, the abbé came into his room and accused him again, but gently, of being partial to Denise, in spite of his efforts not to show it.

"What could I answer? That I had lived with him but little, that I did not know him as well as my sister, pretexts . . . that deceive only those who love us and who want to believe them; but what else could I say?"

Then the "terrible moment" came. To realize the emotions involved, we must remember the difficulties of travel and communication in the eighteenth century. After a round of tender embraces, the philosopher departed, choked with emotion, weeping, as was Denise, and worried about how the other two would get along together. He offered to mediate any dispute they might have, and they accepted, the abbé adding, however, that he trusted his equity more than his affection. This remark hurt Diderot. "There is not a man of his robe I esteem more than him. He is sensitive, although he reproaches himself for it; sincere, but harsh. He would have been a good friend and brother if his religion hadn't ordered him to trample on all those trifles. He is a good Christian who proves to me constantly that it is better to be a good man, and that what they call evangelical perfection is only the art of stifling nature, which might have spoken in him as strongly as in me." Diderot was obviously as blind and unjust as his brother in blaming the abbé's religion for his character. The two men were simply incompatible. The emotion of their father's death had brought them together, but only for a moment. They never saw each other again.

Peace did not last long. Just a year later, the quarrel broke out anew. Charged with leading the fight against impiety in his region, the abbé thought he should begin with his own family. He demanded that Diderot make a public retraction of his writings. The philosopher only laughed in scorn. Then, instead, in December 1760, he published another "Letter to My Brother," in which religion is maltreated and tolerance exalted. The result of these hostilities was a complete break.

Denise suffered patiently for three years. Finally, in September 1762, finding it impossible to go on, she and the abbé went their separate ways. The "damned saint" had made life intolerable for her, with innumerable petty quarrels, with his extravagance, and his sulking.

Diderot himself had several disagreements with Denise, concerning the management of their inheritance. On one occasion it was he who was suspicious and unjust, in accusing her of sacrificing him to the abbé, "who is not worth the clipping of my nail." The abbé had deliberately tried to cheat him. "In my eyes, he is the vilest, most unjust, tyrannical, and selfish of men." He reminded her of the abbé's ingratitude to her, of his conduct "unbecoming, I don't say a brother, a Christian, a priest, but a wild beast." Denise in turn accused him, with equal injustice, of trying to reduce her to beggary. To this the philosopher replied excitedly: "What have I ever asked of you? What have I required of you? What sacrifice have you made for me?" These were wild accusations, but it is not improbable that the abbé had been trying to undermine his sister's affection and trust.

Fortunately, such petty squabbles were only regrettable incidents that did not long disturb their affectionate relations. When Diderot went to Langres, it was to see Denise; and when she made the trip to Paris, on two or three occasions, it was only to visit her brother and his family. Diderot grew ever more attached to her; she represented to him his cherished home at Langres.

The strength of this attachment, and the influence it had, consciously and unconsciously, in the directing of Diderot's life—even his thought—on conservative, middle-class lines is difficult to exaggerate, although our precise knowledge is scanty. The links maintained by business and sentiment, by love and animosity, by correspondence and by journeys from both ends of the Langres-Paris axis became even stronger when he had to deal with his daughter's future in-laws, before and after her marriage.

On the stagecoach back to Paris, Diderot chanced upon two monks as traveling companions. Naturally, they began to talk of matters pertaining to religion. "It wasn't my fault," he relates, "if I didn't render them an important service, and free them from their inhuman prejudice, one that many other devout men have, that they must in all conscience destroy the enemies of God and the Church, wherever they met them. I tried to convince them that they served poorly a God of peace by murders, and that they preached ill a religion of love, with fire and sword in hand; that a Christian was destined less to spill the blood of others than to shed his own for them . . . When I noticed that my Fathers didn't have a proper respect for humanity or the docility towards my reasons that they deserved, and that it was still with repugnance that they spared unbelievers, I became impatient: 'Fathers,' I said to them, 'kill your own lice and leave to God the care of avenging his offenses!' I made up for this little brusqueness by the gentle and even respectful manner in which I treated them afterwards, but I didn't have a better opinion of monks. It seemed to me that these men had barbaric customs and ferocious hearts.''

2

Just before the depressing news of his father's death, Diderot had been greatly upset by an unexpected disturbance in his relations with Sophie Volland.

One day in April of 1759, the sky fell down on the two lovers. Diderot relates the incident with emotion and graphic conciseness. "We could scarcely wait to find each other again. I went there one day, and by the little stair. We had been together for about an hour, when we heard someone knock. Well, my friend, the one who knocked was she, yes, she, her mother. I don't have to describe the rest. I don't know what the three of us did. We jumped up, Sophie and I; her mother opened a secretary, put a paper in it, and went out. Since then, she speaks of going to her country estate, and this time with the child. They are going to take her away, to make her die of boredom. What a future!"

Mother Volland was determined to punish her "child," who was now only forty-one years old. She decided to take her to their country home at Ile-sur-Marne for six months of the year. Sophie's tears and melancholy, and Diderot's tears and pleading, made her change her mind a half dozen times. Diderot wrote her a violent letter, which she kept for three days before reading. When Sophie took sick and claimed she was going to die, Mme. Volland pretended to yield, but as soon as Sophie recovered, she ordered her to pack. Sophie immediately took sick again, but this time Mme. Volland, after waiting patiently for signs of recovery, insisted on the departure. This period of indecision was one of great stress and uncertainty for the desperate lovers. Diderot's unhappiness was reflected in his restlessness. "I am bored, I am bored, everywhere, except there; and it's drudgery even to go there. I am overcome with such a lethargy, that what I need is to be heard without talking, to have my letters done without writing them, and to arrive where I want to go without having to move. I read, but I don't know what I am reading about and I don't care."

To Grimm he poured out his heartaches. "The mother is a sphinx. Her soul is sealed with seven seals. She is the woman of the Apocalypse. On her brow is written, Mystery. . . . I was forced to tell her, 'I recommend to you her life; you gave it to her, do not take it back.' They are going to drag her away to the country. What will become of her there? And of me? My poor head is topsy-turvy."

He was as unable to understand Mme. Volland's lack of enthusiasm for her daughter's love affair with a married man as he was bewildered at his own wife's unending fury, when she discovered their liaison. He predicted confidently that in the country Sophie would die. Contrary to his expectations, she busied herself with farm occupations, and her health improved.

Sophie's melancholy was quite touching, as Diderot describes it. "Does she hear my step, when I arrive, she says to her sister: 'My sister, it is he.' I enter: she does not get up; she contents herself with smiling a little and looking at me with eyes in which I see the profound sadness that penetrates her. If I ask her: 'My dear, what are you thinking of?' she answers, 'I am thinking that you will all be happy when I am no more.' And then she gets up, and runs to the bathroom to weep with all her might." With all her grief, Sophie outlived the rest of her family.

In November the Vollands came back, and in spite of all the pother, the secret rendezvous were resumed, although less frequently than before. "The little stairway has not fallen, I still use it sometimes." The indignant mother could only shut her eyes. For a while Diderot's relations with Mme. Volland were very strained. He even invented a nickname for her. "Morphyse will always be Morphyse, a tangled skein of secrets and mysteries." As the years went by, however, and the lovers resigned themselves to their enforced separation, Diderot actually grew somewhat fond of the gruff mother. "Morphyse" becomes "maman," and then "la chère maman."

The concurrence of these events—disaster to the *Encyclopedia,* the death of his father, the agitation with Mme. Volland, and the subsequent separation from Sophie—produced, then, a prolonged effect of depression and melancholy. Between 1759 and 1765, Diderot seems to sense nostalgically the slipping away of his life. He looks more into himself. Feeling the sweetness of a gentle melancholy, he becomes less explosive, more relaxed. Doubtless his letters to Sophie, in which he describes minutely everything he sees, hears, feels, thinks, or does, were a major factor in his increased self-awareness and introspection. "I shall not kill a flea without accounting to you for it," he assures her. "I am carrying out without realizing it what I have a hundred times desired to do. How is it, I said, that an astronomer spends thirty years of his life at the top of an observatory, his eye applied day and night to the end of a telescope in order to determine the movements of a star, and nobody will study himself, nobody will have the courage to keep an exact account of all the thoughts of his mind, all the impulses of his heart, all his sorrows, all his pleasures, and numberless centuries will pass without our knowing whether life is a good or a bad thing, whether human nature is good or evil, and what makes our happiness or our unhappiness."

The image and personality of his father, instead of fading, grows even larger in his consciousness, and is associated with the thought of death. In November 1762 he writes to Sophie, "With age I am taking on the infirmities that my father had, and I think that the points of resemblance that were lacking are also coming out now. My face is wrinkling in the same places. I am getting hollows, prominences, individual marks where he had them when he died." In this new consciousness of himself, there is an increasing tendency for Diderot to look back into his past. Starting with *Rameau's Nephew*, the first version of which was composed in 1761, two years after his father's death, scenes and episodes of his childhood and youth appear more and more frequently in his writings. Not to mention such pieces as the *Journey to Langres* and the *Conversation Between a Father and His Children*, the evidences of his own experiences are apparent in the *Salons, The Nun, the Paradox on Acting,* and in many a page of *Jacques the Fatalist*.

When Diderot returned to Paris, after his visit to Langres, he found life there even less peaceful than with his brother and sister. His relations with Antoinette sank to a new low of misunderstanding and acrimony. Every week, sometimes every day, brought its distressing household scene. They were worlds apart, as incompatible as two people could be, and Diderot made no effort to bridge the gap. Apparently he was ashamed of her. To his friends she was nonexistent, and they never stopped to greet her when they visited him. Perhaps Antoinette was incapable of understanding Diderot, but he never tried to make it possible. In all their quarrels, he was always perfectly convinced that she was the terrible Xantippe and he the innocent martyr. That there was some truth to Diderot's complaints cannot be gainsaid. There is even a police report, uncovered by Professor A. M. Wilson's investigations, of a deposition filed by one of Diderot's neighbors, charging that Mme. Diderot had flown into a rage against her servant, kicked her, and knocked her head against the wall.

Once, when he was sick, Sophie committed the imprudence of sending a note directly to his house. Antoinette recognized the handwriting and the lackey. "There followed a domestic fire that is still throwing sparks. Really, that woman has a ferocious soul. Look at the circumstances in which she chooses to torment me. If she makes my house unlivable, where does she expect me to live?" So stormy was the outbreak, that he went in desperation to his wife's confessor, and pleaded with him to intercede and make her reasonable. After hearing Diderot's plea, the monk replied coldly: "Indeed, monsieur, you speak most eloquently." This reply exasperated him still further, and he shouted, "It is not a question of how I speak, but whether before another day I shall send a woman whom you have been directing for twenty years and in whom you must be interested, back to the poverty where I found her!" But the monk was completely unmoved. "Monsieur, vespers are ringing. You will excuse me. Your wife will come and we shall see."

"Read that, my friend," Diderot wrote furiously to Grimm. "Get married, and then when you are dissatisfied with your better half, go and speak to her confessor."

Frequently he sought an outlet in his letters to Sophie. "I am completely upset. You know how injustice and unreasonableness hurt me. Well, just imagine that I had to stand an outburst that lasted more than two hours. But tell me what advantage that woman will have when she has made a blood vessel burst in my chest or deranged the fibres of my brain? Ah! how unbearable life is! How many moments when I would accept the end with joy!" One of their scenes was so frenzied and passionate, that Diderot knocked his head against the wall in despair. Antoinette's ill-temper made everyone around her miserable. The poor servant, Jeanneton, was continually threatening to leave.

Finally, one quarrel was so violent and unbearable, that Diderot was prompted to a bold expedient. He refused to eat with his wife and had himself served in his study. "When we shall no longer see each other except in passing, I hope that we shall no longer have the opportunity or the time to fight. . . . She is beginning to feel the effects of this little divorce and is quite embarrassed as to how to forestall them without humiliating herself. The exhaustion of her funds, which is not distant, will bring reconciliation."

Eventually Diderot learned that the only recourse was to control his emotions, when he was able to, and to maintain an attitude of silence. "I don't dare speak to you of my health," he writes to Grimm. "Mme. Diderot, by her inflexibility, her ill-humor . . . is visibly killing me, herself, and her sister. That miserable woman, the most monstrous creature I know, mistreated me so for a month that I finally resorted to silence. For three days I didn't say 'yes' or 'no' to her, because for a 'yes' or 'no' I had a scene. She became so affected by my silence that the night before last she had one of her attacks." The attack ended his strike and he "went to her help."

Little wonder that Diderot was completely horrified on hearing that a friend of his, Suard, was about to get married. The sad, the delicate, the melancholy Suard! "His heart will be pierced with a hundred stings before a month is over!" When Suard came to see him, the philosopher hastened to impart the advice born of experience. "Weren't you once imprisoned in a cell? Well, my friend, take care lest you recall that cell and regret it." But apparently Suard had to get married. "It seems that there are reasons of honor and clumsiness," he informs Sophie. "They add that his wife is very pretty and that when someone is trying to show her that he loves her, nothing is easier than to push the demonstration too far. But my heart is sick; I haven't the courage to joke about it. The more I think of it, the more I am convinced that he is a doomed man. Grimm insists that if he hasn't drowned himself yet, it's just a matter of time."

During their brief periods of reconciliation, the philosopher sometimes had to assist at the parties his wife gave for her friends. These plebeian gatherings were quite different from the ones he was accustomed to, but he did his best. "I was very gay, I drank, I ate. After dinner, I played cards; I didn't go out at all. I was charming, and if you knew with whom! What faces! What people! What conversation!" Clearly, it was Antoinette's complete vulgarity of taste, more even than her ignorance and mediocrity, that repelled him.

When Antoinette was sick, the entire household was more upset than usual. Sometimes her acerbity sharpened with her indisposition. "I found my wife with fever and a sore throat. I did not dare to inquire about her health. The most solicitous questions bring such harsh answers from her that I speak to her only when absolutely necessary." At other times illness had a softening effect. Then Diderot would overwhelm her with attentions, and her good humor seemed to him a sad foreboding of her death. "But a symptom that frightens me more than any other is the sweetness of her disposition, her patience, her silence, and what is worse, a return of affection and of confidence in me." Yet he did not hesitate, with supreme lack of delicacy, to make fun of her condition in letters to various friends, especially to his mistress—and in that he was certainly guilty of bad taste. Among Nanette's diverse afflictions was sciatica of the thigh. "They have prescribed rubbing with a mixture of salt, brandy and soap," he writes to Sophie. "Several days ago this operation was being carried out. I was about to enter when my little girl ran to meet me, crying 'Stop, papa! stop! If you saw it you would die laughing.' Her dear mother was bent over the foot of her bed, her rump in the air, and the maid was on her knees rubbing her with all her might. It wasn't the case of the proverb which says that it's a waste of time to soap the head of a Moor, for Mme. Diderot is very fair, and it wasn't her head that was being soaped. The remedy has relieved her. I have been charged, once or twice since, with the operation and acquitted myself very creditably."

Diderot considered these attentions a great proof of his devotion and self-sacrifice. "The less one accomplishes his duty during the health of his wife, the more attentive he must be during her sickness. On Saturday I didn't leave the house. Yesterday I didn't go to the Baron's. I shall certainly not go to the Rue des Vieux-Augustins (Sophie's home) today, although I have given my word." Probably no one was more amazed at these attentions than Nanette. But on another occasion, when he had just returned after a month's absence, he stopped at home just long enough to leave his bags; then he ran right off to Damilaville's, without a word of greeting to wife or child. After all, he had to see whether there was a letter for him from Sophie. He returned at midnight and found his wife, from whom he had had no news during his absence, quite ill, but that did not stop him from having a gay time the next day and from leaving Paris again with his friends the day after. Although there was, on Diderot's part, an increasing desire to strengthen his family life, it was still a subordinate motive.

If Diderot made fun of Antoinette to his friends, he did not allow them to do the same. To a comment of Grimm's he replied that

"She isn't quite so ridiculous as you think." When Morellet mocked her publicly, Diderot told him brusquely to take a different tone or else keep quiet. "There are some rules even a professional jester like you must know. The first is that unless you are dealing with the most despicable of men, you must never expect him to allow you to vilify his father, mother, family, or friends. The second is that joking has its limits, beyond which the jester is no longer clever but merely impertinent." In these situations, Diderot was really defending only his own self-respect.

Aside from reproaching his wife for unbearable ill-temper, Diderot resented her hiding from him the letters she received from Denise, her harshness to their daughter, and her constant spying on him. He had to carry on most of his correspondence at Damilaville's house, where he did not have to fear "that Curiosity would approach on tiptoe and bend over my shoulder to read the lines I tried to screen from her." Most of all, he complained that marriage had ruined his career and wasted his talents, by forcing him to slave at the *Encyclopedia* instead of writing for the theater, for which he imagined himself highly gifted. "I arrive in Paris. I was going to take the gown and become a theologian at the Sorbonne. On my way I meet a woman, beautiful as an angel. I want to sleep with her. I sleep with her. I have four children with her. And there I am forced to give up mathematics that I love, Homer and Vergil that I always carried in my pocket, the theater for which I had an inclination; only too glad to undertake the *Encyclopedia,* to which I shall have sacrificed twenty-five years of my life." All this is pure self-delusion. It is also blindness to the importance of what was historically his greatest work. To us it seems far more true that his marriage saved him from a debauched and useless life. It was the stimulus and goad, however unpleasant, that he needed.

At least he was grateful to Anoinette for some things: for her economical habits and her sound common sense. He even consulted her during his negotiations with the publishers. He quotes approvingly to Sophie her opinion of the portrait Van Loo did of him, in the *Salon* of 1767: "Mme. Diderot claims that it makes me look like an old coquette who is trying to be cute and is still casting her eye about." As he grew older, home became calmer. His attachment to the comforts and closeness of family life increased. "I fooled around *en famille,* and it was a pleasure I found delightful." Occasionally he will even break out in praise of home, hearth, and family. In October of 1760, doubtless still sobered by the thoughts evoked by his father's death, he writes Sophie that after twenty-five, "one owes himself to his wife, his children, his friends." His only regret is that he did not do things differently—meaning, perhaps, that he had not picked a different wife. "Ah, if we could only begin again! That is a word of repentance that comes continually to our tongues. I have said it about all I have done, except, dear tender friend, about the sweet intimacy I have had with you."

The one source of joy at home was Angélique, who had been born in 1753. He was proud of his daughter's precocious intelligence, boasted about her to all his friends and repeated her clever remarks. "I am crazy about my little girl. What a lovely character! What a woman I could make of that child, if her mother would let me."

For a moment, when Angélique was eight, Diderot had been painfully disappointed in her. On returning home after a month's absence, he had found her lisping, simpering and smirking, prompt to cry and to put on fits of temper, disinterested in studying, her head full of silly puzzles. Of course, she was going through an "awkward" stage, but he ascribed it all to her mother's influence; "she is making her silly and vulgar; but one must have peace at home." Because of his irreligion, Antoinette had resolutely refused to let him have a hand in her education. But a year later, in 1762, realizing perhaps that her daughter was brighter than she, Antoinette suddenly gave up in despair and let her husband have complete charge. It was a job that filled him with enthusiasm. "To bring up a child of his blood according to the principles that were dear to him," one biographer has commented, "outside of superstition and only according to reason, to inculcate in her the love of the true, the beautiful, and the good, without having recourse to the promises and menaces of a religion, to make her understand that nature had arranged things so that vices were punished and virtues recompensed . . . could he dream of greater happiness?"

He decided that her education should include music, sewing, housework (a complete course), geography, history, moral readings, and poetry. No mathematics, languages or philosophy. His concept of history was similar to Voltaire's: "Men, their customs, opinions, manners, prejudices."

Among the first things he did was to give Angélique clavecin and harmony lessons. Here he combined charity with profit. A young German, Bemetzrieder, had come, as scores did each year, to ask for the philosopher's advice and help.

"Well, what do you know?" Diderot had asked him.

"I know mathematics."

"With mathematics, you will work hard and earn little." Diderot had good reason to know that.

"I know history and geography."

"You couldn't get your drinking water out of them. Parents aren't interested in giving their children a solid education."

"I have studied law."

"With all the merit of Grotius, you could die of hunger on a street corner."

"I know one other thing that everyone in my country knows: music."

"Well, why didn't you say so? Among a frivolous people like ours, solid studies lead to nothing; with the arts of pleasure, you can get anywhere. Monsieur, you will come every evening at six-thirty; you will teach my daughter a little geography and history; the rest of the time will be given to clavecin and harmony."

For this, "Bemetz," as Diderot called him for short, received board and five hundred livres a year. Later in 1770, they collaborated on a delightful musical work, *Lessons for the Clavecin*—the philosopher liked to feel that he had tried his hand at everything!

As for Angélique's moral education, he attended to that himself, and was proud of the results. He preached to her the most Christian virtues of modesty and chastity, explaining "the necessity of covering those parts of the body the sight of which would incite men to vice." To make his lessons more effective, he later had her take three anatomy courses with a famous woman anatomist of the time, Mlle. Biheron; these he considered the best preparation for marriage, and he boasted about them to his shocked and disapproving brother.

The results began to be evident when Angélique was about fifteen. Diderot wrote to Sophie that he was simply crazy about her. "She says that her mother prays to God, and her father does good; that my way of thinking is like socks, which we don't put on before everyone, but to keep our feet warm; that there are actions which are useful to us and hurt others, like garlic, which we don't eat, even though we like it, because it has an unpleasant odor . . . A few days ago I took it into my head to ask her what the soul was. 'The soul?', she replied; 'why, we make a soul when we make flesh.' " Evidently, Diderot had taken care of her philosophical formation!

One Sunday afternoon they took a walk together. Diderot decided to reveal to her "everything pertaining to the state of a woman," and began with this question: "Do you know the difference between the two sexes?" That having been explained, he went on to the subject of virtue, and explained to her the true meaning of gallant declarations made by young men.

"They mean: 'Mademoiselle, out of complacence for me, will you dishonor yourself, lose all social status, banish yourself from society, have yourself locked up in a convent, and make your father and mother die of grief?' I told her what she should and should not say, hear and not hear. . . . I told her everything that could be said decently, and she remarked that being informed now, a wrong action would make her all the more guilty, since she would not have the excuse of ignorance or curiosity. About the formation of milk in the breasts, and the necessity of using it for the nourishment of the child or of getting rid of it in some other way, she cried: 'Father, how horrible it is to throw into the toilet the food of your child!' . . . If I lost that child, I think I should die of grief. I love her more that I can tell you."

Once again, Diderot was ahead of his times.

They formed the habit of taking long walks together. Fear that Angélique might transgress the strictest rules of middle-class Christian morality prompted the fond father to many a lecture en route. In one of these, he launched into a discussion of the two rewards of virtue—self-satisfaction and the gratitude of others—and the two punishments of vice—conscience and the aversion of others. "The text was not sterile. We went through most of the virtues; then I showed her the envious man with his hollow eyes and thin, pale face; the intemperate one, with his dilapidated stomach and gouty legs; the debauched one, with his asthmatic chest and the remainder of several diseases for which there is no cure. . . ."

Diderot was completely opposed to Rousseau's denunciation of the theater. But when he wrote to his sister about the education of young ladies in convents, he sided with Rousseau—so great was his insistence on Christian morality since he had become a father. The theater, he judged, would corrupt their innocence of heart and pure morals, for the preservation of which they had been put into the convent.

In all, Diderot was a good and understanding father and had intimate contact with his child. He disagreed with Denise who scolded him for allowing Angélique to go to a ball when she was seventeen. "A girl of her age must enjoy her age. . . . Nothing is

innocent, even in church, when you bring a corrupted heart to it."
He declared that his only authority over his daughter was to make
her happy, and as for marriage—remembering perhaps his own,
and at any rate, thinking a century and a half ahead of his time—he
remarked that "the authority of a father is entirely subordinate to
the natural rights of the child." The philosopher understood children, and knew how to play with them. He and Angélique played
hopscotch, hot-cockles, hide and seek, blind man's buff, and coucou-
bay together, and incidentally he found it a good way to get in an
effective lesson on justice or grammar or logic. "We must make
ourselves little to encourage the little ones gradually to make
themselves bigger. We can tell them as valuable things over a doll, a
rag, or a straw cross as over the most important matters. . . . But
are there any trifles for them?"

Satisfied with a modest life for himself, Diderot wanted his
daughter to be rich. This desire not only cheered him in his labors,
but also led him to enter certain intrigues both before and after her
marriage. During long years, he accumulated her dowry and prepared for that event. A bad husband he was, but the love and care
he lavished on his daughter have some redeeming value.

Diderot enjoyed talking of his poverty and privations, but that
was only a part of his "philosophical attitude"; he was called "the
Philosopher" by everybody and felt that he had to maintain the
tradition of Diogenes. We have seen that ever since his marriage,
which closed the chapter of his bohemian days, he had labored
constantly to attain financial security. His middle-class tastes are
again evident in the importance he attached to comfort. "I need a
carriage, a comfortable apartment, fine linen, a perfumed woman,
and I could easily put up with the other curses of our civilized
state." He detested travel, and except on one famous occasion, never
went further than Langres, never even made the trip to Italy he
and Grimm had dreamed of. To the fatigue and inconveniences of
a journey, he preferred the solid comforts of home.

The only time Diderot left Paris with joy was to visit his friends
at Grandval, d'Holbach's country estate. There Mme. d'Holbach
gave him the best room in the house, where he could walk back
and forth between a good fire and a beautiful view. For this he was
always grateful to his hostess. "My comfort means a lot to me everywhere," he wrote to Sophie, "but most of all in the country."

At home Diderot worked hard, but saw to it that he had every
physical convenience. "I had a good foot-warmer placed under

my feet, and I took up my *Nun* which I scribbled at until eleven. At eleven, a little glass of red Malaga, the baron sent it to me, then a good pillow on which this bad head rested tranquilly until nine in the morning."

His study, it is true, was quite modest. An old rug, a large wooden table piled with books and papers that served as a desk, and some cane chairs constituted the principle furniture. A small Bergamo tapestry, two prints by Poussin, a pair of busts by friend Falconet were the principle ornaments. Diderot now occupied two stories of an apartment house in the Rue Taranne. The family living quarters had the fourth and his study and library the top floor. His collection of books had grown so, with the work on the *Encyclopedia,* and at the publisher's expense, that he needed several rooms to hold them. From floor to ceiling stretched the shelves. This was sometimes an inconvenience, as when he had to look high and low for a novel Mme. Duclos had asked to borrow. "I climbed up on two chairs placed one on the other; my chairs are narrow; all of a sudden they slipped and *patatras,* there was my searcher on the floor. I don't know how I didn't kill myself, and to make matters worse, I didn't find the book."

Later, in 1772, a revolution took place in his study. He had done Mme. Geoffrin, the *salonnière,* a great favor. In appreciation, she had most of his decrepit furnishings carted away. A new desk, comfortable leather armchairs, paintings and other fittings of a more luxurious nature replaced them. Among her gifts was an expensive scarlet dressing gown, destined to replace his shabby old blue one. This great change prompted a short personal essay, one of Diderot's most popular works, *Regrets on my Old Dressing-Gown,* a charming combination of loquacity and good humor, written in a tone of mock eloquence and hyperbole.

Why didn't I keep it? It was made for me; I was made for it. It fitted all the lines of my body without confining it; I was picturesque and handsome. The other, stiff, starched, makes me look like a mannequin. There was no duty to which its friendliness did not lend itself, for poverty is almost always obliging. Were a book covered with dust, one of its flaps was there to wipe it. If the ink refused to flow from my pen, it presented its side. You could see traced in long black streaks the frequent services it had done for me. Those long streaks announced the man of letters, the writer, the man who works. Now I look like a rich idler; nobody recognizes me.

Under its shelter, I feared neither the clumsiness of a valet nor mine, neither sparks from the fire, nor an overturned glass. I was the absolute master of my old dressing gown ; I have become the slave of the new one. The dragon who watched over the Golden Fleece was not more uneasy than I. Care envelopes me. . . .

I do not weep, I do not sigh ; but each moment I say: Cursed be he who invented the art of giving value to common cloth by staining it scarlet! Cursed be the precious garment I worship. Where is my old, my humble, my comfortable rag?

Usually the philosopher spent most of his time in his study. He had periods of laziness, to be sure, when nothing was done, and others when he worked by fits and starts. "In the absence of my friends, my days are much the same. We get up late, because we're lazy; hear our little daughter's history lesson and watch her play the clavecin; go to our study, correct proofs until two, eat dinner, take a walk, play some piquet, sup and begin all over on the morrow."

More often his days consisted of steady work—studying, writing, —from nine until two, dinner from two till three, and then, perhaps, an afternoon at the publishers, where he would revise manuscripts and proof for the *Encyclopedia*. For variety, there were the visits to Damilaville's office in quest of Sophie's letters, or an afternoon at the Salon. At seven he left the publisher's, not wishing to be annoyed by Le Breton's invitations to dinner. Previous ones had only irritated him; "they are miserly and set too much importance on a miserable dinner for me to accept it at that price." And yet Diderot enjoyed the gallant conversation of the very flirtatious Mme. Le Breton. Catching the philosopher staring at a piquant customer, one day, she turned up her nose and shrugged her shoulders: "Small eyes, big breasts, a provincial beauty. You act like a novice."

Evening might be spent at home, that is, if Diderot were in one of his working moods. He could work for ten days at a stretch, all day and evening, but was incapable of doing anything when laziness or the slightest annoyance overtook him. One such studious evening nearly ended disastrously, when he fell asleep at his desk and the candle set fire to some of his papers. Fortunately, he caught it in time, and spent an hour removing all traces, justly fearful of Antoinette's scolding tongue.

Most of Diderot's evenings were kept free for diversion in the company of his friends. A good discussion at one of their homes, a game of cards or checkers at Damilaville's might be his program.

He spent hours in cafés and restaurants, eating, sipping wine or coffee, discussing everything and everyone in the midst of a gay charivari. In 1765 the first eating place with the title of "restaurant" had been opened. It took is name from its motto, "Come to me all who suffer from the stomach and I will restore you." Diderot liked this new way of eating. "The hostess is really a very beautiful creature. Beautiful face, Greek rather than Roman, beautiful eyes, beautiful mouth, just the right plumpness. Tall and with a beautiful figure, an elegant and light walk, but ugly hands and ugly arms. Do I like restaurants? Yes, infinitely. They serve you well, not cheaply, but at any hour you want. The beautiful hostess never comes and talks with her customers, but they can go and talk with her as much as they like."

Walking was another of Diderot's favorite pleasures. By day and by night, alone or with friends, he loved as much as in his youth to stroll in the shaded lanes of the Tuileries, near the Palais-Royal, or along the quais above the Seine. He enjoyed picnics and excursions with friends of both sexes, and often went to the Bois de Boulogne, Meudon, or Saint-Cloud. These outings were featured by abundant food and wine and philosophical discussions. (Do men never reform? We have more knowledge than our forefathers, but are we better?)

Diderot was not very economical. He spent a good bit on entertainment, amorous or social. He liked to play cards, played poorly and lost regularly. Carriages were one of his favorite luxuries, and being rather absent-minded, he sometimes forgot them at the door and had to pay for a day's hire. He could not deny himself a book that struck his fancy, or a print; frequently he bought them and gave them away a few days later. To compensate for these extra expenses, he had to do extra work, for clubs, magistrates, any one who could pay him. He wrote lawyers' pleas, speeches to the king, whatever was asked for, just as he had once written sermons for a missionary.

One of the philosopher's great weaknesses was an overfondness for eating. His correspondence is full of tales of table debauchery, the regular consequences of which were attacks of what he thought was acute indigestion and what really was gallstones. One night he supped at the home of his friend Damilaville. The results are described to Sophie: "I am a glutton. I ate a whole meat pie; on top of that, three or four peaches, table wine, Malaga wine, and a large cup of coffee. It was one in the morning when I got home. I couldn't close an eye. I was burning up in my bed. I had the most beautiful indigestion." Another time he explains to her: "How I am suffering! More than ever, and I richly deserve it. I ate like a wolf. I drank wines with all kinds of names; a melon of unbelievable perfidy was waiting for me, and do you think it was possible to resist an enormous cheese? and then liqueurs and then coffee and then an abominable indigestion that kept me up all night, and which made me spend my morning between the teapot and another kind that it isn't proper to name."

Of course it was not always his fault. Once he supped gluttonously "out of sheer absent-mindedness." Another time he had a cold, and Damilaville persuaded him that the best remedy was good wine, good food, and good company. "And so on Monday, stomach to the table, back to the fire, I talked, disputed, joked, drank, ate, from one o'clock till ten. The night from Monday to Tuesday was terrible. I thought I would die."

His indigestions and other maladies furnished Diderot a host of intimate details with which he regaled his friends and correspondents, no matter who they were. His naïve egotism made him think that others were as interested as he in such personal data. At times these details appear incredibly coarse, but often they are unconsciously humorous. After his fall in the library, he vaguely described the consequences, largely the product of his imagination. "The first few days, my head felt peculiar. The next days, I felt a quick pain on the opposite side, and since then I have a constant desire to blow my nose, and a sensation of something blocked over my nose that is trying to fall."

He wrote to Hume about a gouty humor that began to make itself felt in his left arm. It developed into "colic of the intestines and finally a terrible inflammation of the ears, which kept me indoors the whole month of January, by the fireside. I came out of it with a deafness of a peculiar kind. I hear others talking quite well, but I speak so low that others can scarcely hear me. The sound of my voice resounds so strongly in my cavernous and sonorous head, that if it is just a little loud, it makes me dizzy." When he or his friends were ill, he always took great pleasure in analyzing the symptoms and discussing the remedies.

Many of his parties were in the company of Damilaville, whom he called "one of my three friends." Damilaville, a morose, sickly, and not too well-educated man, played an important role in the struggle of the *philosophes* against the Old Régime. He was connected with the tax office and used the official stamp to assure safe transport of otherwise censorable letters and packages. As Voltaire's agent, from about 1759, he was zealous in the distribution of his pamphlets and manuscripts. Diderot met him through d'Alembert, and thereafter went almost daily either to his home on the Ile Saint-Louis or his office on the Quai des Miramionnes, where he wrote his letters to Sophie and received her replies. Diderot's letters indicate that Damilaville was for him what he was for Grimm; that he liked him sincerely, but abused his good will and overwhelmed him with odd jobs and errands—all of which Damilaville performed without murmuring. It is noticeable that most of Diderot's letters to him are either requests for favors or excuses for breaking appointments.

Suddenly Damilaville became gravely ill, of a mysterious malady that puzzled the greatest doctors of France. Diderot willingly describes the symptoms—horrible swelling of the glands in the neck, armpit and chest—and the pitiful and ineffective remedies employed. It was Hodgkin's Disease, an incurable illness, at that time unrecognized. To see him waste away was heartbreaking. "I have suffered more," Diderot wrote to Sophie, "shed more tears than I could tell you."

His death, in 1768, was a severe blow to the "philosophic party." Not only was he irreplaceable in his fifth-column activities, but he had been the invaluable *agent de liaison* between Voltaire and others. His death effectively cut off those relations. No longer could Diderot write to him, "Please reserve for me and mine twenty-five copies of (Voltaire's) *Treatise on Tolerance*. They are all for the friends of the man and the thing. Their motto is also: *Ecrasez l'infâme.*" Diderot was inconsolable and so was Voltaire, who wrote to d'Alembert: "I shall regret Damilaville all my life. I loved the intrepidity of his soul. Damilaville is dead, and Fréron is still fat and prosperous."

Visits from friends and strangers frequently interrupted Diderot's work when he was at home. Most of the strangers came not to render homage, as they did to Voltaire, nor out of curiosity, like Rousseau's visitors, but to request his help, financial or advisory. He was well known for his charities and openhandedness; altruism was not only a part of his philosophy, but a profound need of his emotional, sentimental character. He felt that nature has put between all men "a bond of fraternity, which links us in a particularly sacred way to those who are unhappy." He never forgot his own penurious youth, and on occasions when he found it impossible to succor some of the needy who besieged him, he regretted it deeply. In these cases he frequently addressed his visitor to someone in better circumstances. He kept some of his poor relatives supplied with a regular allowance, and paid heavily to keep a girl "whose innocence was infinitely exposed at home" in a convent.

On several occasions the results of his good deeds would have shaken or destroyed anyone else's confidence in human nature. One young would-be writer was fed, lodged, and clothed by him for several years. When the protégé's first opus appeared, it turned out to be nothing less than a caustic satire of Diderot himself. The impudent writer actually came to him and presented him with the first copy. This insolence provoked Diderot's just wrath. "You are an ingrate! " he cried. "Anyone except me would have you thrown out of the window, but I am grateful to you for having let me know you as you really are. Take your work to my enemies, take it to the old duke d'Orléans." To this suggestion the satirist objected that he did not know how to write a good dedication. The end of it all was that Diderot himself wrote a dedication to the duke, who gave the satirist fifty louis. The story soon got out, the duke appeared quite ridiculous and the protégé quite contemptible.

Diderot was also completely taken in by a certain Rivière, young, handsome, eloquent, with the gift of ready tears—enough to endear him to the philosopher and to assure him assistance both financially and in his writing. One day Diderot questioned him about his family. Rivière sighed as one resigned to injustice.

"I have a very rich brother in the Church, but he hates me. When I was young I played a few tricks on him, and later I prevented him from becoming a bishop."

"How the devil do you prevent a man from becoming a bishop?"

"Nothing is easier. He was preaching before the king, and his sermons were eloquent; then I started joking about his talents and told everybody that I wrote all his sermons."

Diderot immediately offered to call on the abbé and try to patch things up.

"He may be a good man after all. But don't spoil my work with any new pranks."

The next day the visit took place. Diderot was received politely, but as soon as he announced the subject of his visit, the abbé interrupted him.

"Monsieur, a wise man never solicits anything without knowing the person he is recommending. Do you know my brother?"

"I think so; he has hidden from me none of the reasons that he has given you to complain about him."

"It is impossible, monsieur, that he dared to tell you what I am going to tell you."

Thereupon the abbé reeled off a list of acts unbelievably cowardly and vile. Diderot was so amazed and abashed by these horrors, that he started looking out of the corner of his eye towards his hat and cane. Fortunately, the abbé spoke too long, long enough for him to regain his equanimity. When the narration was finally completed, he had his reply in readiness:

"I knew all that, monsieur, and you still have not told me everything."

"Good heavens! What else can he have done?"

"You did not tell me that one evening, when you were returning from church, you found him lurking in your doorway; that he drew a dagger from beneath his coat and tried to plunge it into your breast."

"If I have not told you that, monsieur, it's because it is not true."

Then Diderot stood up, walked over to the abbé and took his arm.

"Even if that action were true, you still would not have the right to let your brother starve."

The lesson had prompt effect, and the abbé promised that he would take care of him. But the philosopher was not yet through. He returned to Rivière, told him what an abominable creature he was, and urged him to renounce his evil ways. As they were about to separate, Rivière stopped him.

"Monsieur Diderot, do you know natural history?"

"Oh, a little. I can distinguish aloes from lettuce and a pigeon from a humming bird."

"Do you know about the *Formica-leo*?"

"No."

"He is a very industrious little insect. He digs a hole in the ground in the form of a funnel, covers it on the surface with a thin layer of sand, and uses it as a trap for insects; then he takes them and sucks the blood out of them, and he says: 'Monsieur Diderot, I have the honor of bidding you Good-day.' "

A few weeks later, they chanced to meet again, in a cafe where Diderot had been driven to seek shelter from the rain. Rivière had the impudence to come over and ask how he was.

227

"Go away," was the philosopher's reply. "You are so wicked and so corrupt, that if you had a rich father, he wouldn't be safe in the same room with you."

"Alas," sighed Rivière, "I don't have a rich father."

Episodes like these did not shake Diderot's confidence in human nature or in good deeds. "I should rather be the dupe of a hundred hypocrites than hurt a single good man. I prefer to have spared a hundred guilty men, than to cast a shadow on an innocent one. More than once I have experienced the inconveniences of such a morality, but I shall not change it."

Even more costly to Diderot than requests by strangers were the constant services, mostly of a literary nature, demanded by his friends. His desk was usually piled high with the manuscripts they had confided to him for revision. "I spent my three-day holiday working like a galley slave for some good people whom I scarcely know, who have made an important discovery and to whom I can't refuse the service of writing it up." Statements like these are common enough in his letters. "Jobs for me follow each other without interruption, and I am beginning to become disillusioned about my dream of resting. The day before yesterday there was on my desk a tragedy, a translation, a political work, and a pamphlet, not to mention a comic-opera." For others, not for himself, he spends day after day at home, wrapped in his dressing gown. After this kept up for several weeks, he was exhausted. "The edition of the abbé Galiani, my plates, the slavery for Grimm, the *Salon,* and my own little affairs are overwhelming me. Sometimes I am so tired at night that I haven't the strength to eat, that is the literal truth."

"One of Diderot's beautiful moments," noted Marmontel, "was when an author consulted him on his work. If the subject was worthwhile, you should have seen him leap upon it, penetrate it, and in a flash, discover what riches and what beauty it could hold . . . His entire soul was in his eyes, on his lips." Grimm wrote, after Diderot's death, that he was "a rare man who would have immortalized himself by twenty masterpieces, had he known how to be miserly with his time and not abandoned it to a thousand annoying people." Grimm, however, should have been the last to make such a reproach.

Diderot himself does not seem concerned about this loss of time and effort. "It seems to me," he wrote to Hume, "that my time is better employed for someone else who asks for it than for myself." And when another friend, Naigeon, remarked: "You complain how short life is, yet you let yours be stolen," he replied, "It isn't stolen, I give it." Diderot's idealistic conception of friendship is again illustrated by his reaction to Grimm's offer to recompense him for the countless hours of labor he put in as substitute editor of *The Literary Correspondence.* "I rejected his proposal so firmly, that I hope he will never bring it up again. I am at his service every moment; but I consider services to friends in the same light as marks of honor; we tarnish them as soon as we associate them with reward."

When he revised a manuscript for some friend, he invariably remade it, and often as much as half of the final publication was his. Two of the works he thus edited were the abbé Galiani's *Letter on the Wheat Trade* and the abbé Raynal's tremendous *History of the Colonization of the Indies.* The latter, one of the most famous works of the century, was a bitter condemnation of the iniquities which made the story of colonization one of the blackest episodes in history. Raynal's work was widely read and had considerable influence. Many of its pages, and much of its eloquence have the unmistakable Diderot flavor. The recent release of Diderot's manuscripts from his descendants' vaults may now make it possible to determine which parts were his.

One foible marred his generosity. He liked to broadcast his good deeds—in conversation, in letters, and even in his published writings. He wanted everyone to recognize him as the good, the virtuous philosopher. In fact this desire is only one aspect of his vanity, a vanity most charming in that he was so completely unaware of it. With his faculty for self-delusion, he considered himself quite free from that failing—as from most of his others. His naïveté is sometimes amazing, as when he writes: "What does it matter whether I owe my estimable qualities to nature or to experience, so long as they are solid, and vanity never spoils them?"

Throughout his correspondence, we are amused by this ingenuous self-admiration. He is proud of his physical appearance, of his noble philosopher's head. Having hurt his ankle, at Mme. d'Epinay's estate at La Chevrette, he utilized the ensuing period of inaction to have himself painted by Garand. The result was quite gratifying. "I meditate on this canvas, I live on it, I breathe, I am animated; thought appears across the brow . . . you would be tempted to put your arms around it to hug and kiss it. Those eyes full of fire look off into the distance."

Of course he was enraptured by his own writings, and often spoke enthusiastically of the brilliant pages, the profound work or the moving drama that had flowed from his pen. To mollify Mme. Volland, he urged Sophie to tell her "that the highest respect in the memory of men is assured to me." This he sincerely believed. His correspondence with Falconet is testimony to the fact that if he did not publish his manuscripts, he expected future generations to accord him the glory and immortality that were rightly his.

Most of all Diderot esteemed himself for his noble character. When the dramatist Bret addressed a flattering letter to him, he had the modesty to accept only the praises pertaining to "the qualities of his soul." He boasts that the man does not live who is more honest than he. His veracity is equally unattackable: "Pillars of the Church have sometimes sworn just on my word." He even proclaims that his morals are irreproachable, forgetting that he deceived his wife and perhaps even his mistress. Sophie Volland, Grimm, and Diderot—what a triumvirate of virtue! "What three beautiful souls yours, mine, and his are!" The other two must not die, less he be the solitary voice crying in the desert.

Only once does he realize the fatuousness of what he is writing. "That's the way I am. I get excited for a moment and a moment later I am myself again, the frank, gentle, just, indulgent, honest, charitable, obliging man. Continue, if you please, this eulogy, for it isn't complete. I haven't said anything about my intelligence."

In his writings, Diderot seeks to maintain an attitude which may be resumed in the description of Dorval, in the *Conversations on the Natural Son:* "They had named him the Philosopher, because he was without ambition, because his heart was honest and envy had never touched its sweetness and serenity. In addition, he was grave in demeanor, austere, and simple in speech." Except when he spoke of virtue. Then, "you would have said that he was transfigured . . . His eyes expressed brilliance and sweetness. His voice had an inexpressible charm. His talk became moving, a chain of austere ideas and touching images that held you in rapt delight." Another characterization ends in these words: "He studied history, philosophy, morals, sciences, and arts; at fifty-five he was a good man, a cultured man, a man of taste, a great author and an excellent critic." But perhaps Diderot is not referring to himself. He was only forty-five.

This was the picture Diderot wanted to give to the public. Actually he was gay, ebullient and excitable in demeanor, eloquent and verbose in speech. All who approached him have reported that he was simple and unaffected.

Physically, Diderot was of medium height and husky build. His hair was wavy but sparse, and in public he frequently wore a wig. In the heat of conversation he might take it off and put it on his lap, or play with it. He had full, curved lips, a sharp acquiline nose, a very round chin and brown eyes, large and keen. This is how he saw himself in the mirror: "In a single day I had a hundred different countenances, according to the thing by which I was affected. I was serene, sad, dreamy, tender, violent, passionate, enthusiastic. . . . I had a high brow, expressive eyes, prominent features; my head was that of an ancient orator, with a kindly look that had something of the guilelessness, of the rusticity of ancient times." Meister has also left us a word portrait in which he compares Diderot's head in majesty to that of Aristotle or Plato. "His brow was high and bore the imprint of a vast, luminous, and fertile mind . . . the usual expression of his eyes [was] sensitive and gentle; but when his head grew warm, they sparkled with fire. . . . There was naturally in the bearing of his head—especially when he spoke with action—nobility, energy, and dignity. It seems that enthusiasm had become the natural state of his voice, mind, and features. In an unemotional situation, he was frequently constrained, awkward, timid, even affected; he was really Diderot, he was really himself only when his thought had transported him outside of himself."

Chapter 11

The
Last
Round

1

AT FIRST THE condemnation of the *Encyclopedia* had thrown the "philosophic" ranks into a disorganized retreat. Should they abandon the enterprise, fly to a foreign country, continue clandestinely at home? Proposals and conjectures followed each other confusedly. Even Diderot, distressed, harassed on all sides, discouraged by the defeatist attitude of his comrades-in-arms, for a brief despairing moment considered giving up his life's work. Tormented by domestic squabbles, saddened by the death of his father, he was pervaded by an immense longing for rest, by a desire to be forgotten, to return to a life of peace. Fortunately this natural reaction was only temporary. Before very long his fighting instincts took the upper hand, and he set himself once more to the task of rallying the remaining collaborators. He returned to the attitude of firmness with which he had answered Voltaire's advice to quit, or to fly to the protection of Frederick the Great. "To abandon the work," he exclaimed, like a soldier leading the charge, "would be to turn our backs on the breach and do what the scoundrels who are persecuting us want us to do. If you knew with what joy they have learned of d'Alembert's defection and the maneuvers they are using to prevent him from returning. . . . What shall we do, then? What befits men of courage: spite our enemies, attack them and profit, as we have already done, from the imbecility of our censors."

In March or April of 1759, Diderot called Jaucourt, d'Alembert, and d'Holbach together, at a dinner at Le Breton's home. After a hearty meal had put them all in good spirits, he explained his plan to continue the work secretly, to have all the remaining volumes published simultaneously and thrown suddenly on the public. It was a risky business. D'Alembert flew into a temper, spoke insultingly to Diderot and the publishers, and refused to participate in any such scheme. The most he would do was to correct proof on the remaining mathematical articles. While Diderot listened patiently to his tirade, d'Holbach could scarcely restrain his temper and twitched about nervously on his chair. His speech finished, d'Alembert left in a huff, and everyone felt relieved.* Plans were then worked out; the collaborators—now conspirators—encouraged each other and swore solemnly that this time they would continue fighting until the job was done.

But most of the old names were gone—the project was now too risky. And when Diderot went back to work, it was with the quiet determination of conspiracy: "the bolts on my door were closed each day from six in the morning until two in the afternoon." There was no zest and no joy; only exhaustion, depression, and loneliness.

For the publishers' resolution and courage Diderot had highest words of praise. A deciding factor in their attitude was the response to the royal decree requiring them to refund seventy-two livres to all subscribers, as the difference between the sum paid in and the value of the volumes actually published. Not a single request for such a refund was made, according to the traditional story. (Actually, many requests were received but only one was granted by the unwilling publishers, and that one to a persistent lawyer.) Instead, Le Breton succeeded in obtaining permission to indemnify the subscribers with the volumes of plates that were to accompany the text of the *Encyclopedia*. A new privilege was granted for this purpose on September 8. When a prospectus appeared announcing the forthcoming publication and the special reductions for old

---

* Much remains obscure in Diderot's relations with d'Alembert, from the beginning of the enterprise until its end. His own accounts, which we have largely followed, are unfavorable to d'Alembert. It is quite possible that he concealed some matters and presented a tendentious version of others.

subscribers, all wise Parisians immediately guessed that the work was being secretly continued. Even the Pope's unexpected excommunication had no effect whatsoever. The number of subscribers had now passed the four-thousand mark, and it became necessary to reprint the earlier volumes.

The only point that remained undecided for two years was whether the actual printing would be done abroad, in Holland or at Geneva. This course seemed safer and had the further advantage that Diderot's presence in Paris would deceive their enemies. In the end, however, they decided it would be simpler to do the printing secretly in Paris.

Scarcely had they returned to work when catastrophe nearly overtook Diderot again. Some rash *philosophe,* possibly Morellet, had written a reply to Chaumeix's mendacious but highly influential pamphlets. It was a sarcastic, insulting, and impious satire, called *A Memoire for Abraham Chaumeix against the Supposed Philosophers Diderot and d'Alembert.* It attacked not only Chaumeix but, as Diderot put it, "Jesus and his mother, the Court, the town, Parlement, the Jesuits, the Jansenists, men of letters, the nation, in a word, every respected authority and sacred name, dragged in the mud."

Once again the authorities were aroused. Someone denounced Diderot as the author and immediately all of Paris accepted this rumor as a self-evident fact. Malesherbes rushed to inform him that his personal safety was in danger, that his papers were about to be seized. Perhaps he even had the order to seize them. He urged him to hide or escape without delay, and the frightened philosopher did not wait long to comply with the warning.

"But what about the manuscripts?" he inquired frantically. "Where can we take them? What shall I do?"

"We must move everything to a safe place."

"But where?"

"To my house! They will never think of looking for them there!"

Thus the manuscripts were saved by the very man who was to be charged with seizing them, and this is not the least strange event in the history of the *Encyclopedia.* How Diderot must have thanked him and assured him of his eternal gratitude and the gratitude of posterity!

Later Diderot described to Grimm how the work had been interrupted.

"The baron was thumbing his books; the copyists, increased in number, were groaning under the gallows; the bolts of my door had been shut from six in the morning till two in the afternoon, and the work was getting along, when one of those events that we never expect threw me into great alarm. All of a sudden we had to take away our manuscripts during the night; I had to run away from home, sleep out, seek a shelter, and think of getting a post-chaise to carry me as far as I could go."

The next day, however, Diderot learned that a warrant for his seizure had not yet been issued. The first fright of the alarm quickly passed. He resisted the pleas of d'Alembert, d'Holbach, Turgot, Morellet, and Malesherbes, refusing to submit to their "odious plot" to throw the work into the hands of the Prussian tyrant. Instead he went directly to police headquarters and the attorney-general's office, to protest his innocence. He decided to show himself everywhere. To his friends who argued that in a criminal affair the surest way to plead was from afar, he replied courageously that "the most honest way is not to accuse yourself when you are innocent. Whatever the consequences of this adventure may be, they will find me at home." And at home he remained, despite his longing to run to Langres, as this was the time his father was reported near death.

Fortunately, the printers of the satire were discovered, and Diderot exonerated. The storm quieted down as suddenly as it had arisen, and work was resumed once more.

One October evening, six months after the dinner at Le Breton's, Diderot was taking his customary stroll in the shaded lanes of the Tuileries. Suddenly d'Alembert came up to him. After a somewhat embarrassed greeting, he abashedly explained that he was short of money and would be willing to contribute the articles he had originally promised, for the same compensation as formerly, provided they would ask him to do no more work as editor. Diderot told him bluntly that he had acted without courage or honor. He pointed out how generous Le Breton had been with extra bonuses and in lending him money and then tearing up the notes. To this d'Alembert could only protest feebly that he had put in extra time on the job. After the philosopher finished telling him what he thought of him, the matter was finally arranged and his articles promised for delivery within the next two years. When d'Alembert declared that he would write no more prefaces, Diderot retorted that they would not allow him to. "Your previous ones have drawn upon us all the hatred with which we are oppressed. Who is not insulted in them?"

Meanwhile Diderot had also arranged a new and satisfactory contract for himself. The unfinished work was estimated at seven volumes and his compensation was to amount to twenty-five thousand livres.

Grimm, who was traveling again, was charged with enlisting Voltaire's help. "Tell him that the whole thing will appear either here, with or without permission, or in Holland or Geneva, where I shall go. Add that I hope that in less than two years we shall throw the entire mass on our enemies and that he must help me to launch it vigorously and unexpectedly." Voltaire had performed considerable services for the *Encyclopedia,* soliciting articles, attacking its enemies, rallying powerful influences in its favor. Now, however, the sceptical patriarch of the *philosophes* had lost faith in the value and success of the enterprise.

Diderot hoped that the *Encyclopedia* would be completed by the end of 1760, but his calculations were much too optimistic. In 1760 and 1761, he put in two years of unremitting labor writing his own articles and editing the others. His correspondence reveals a series of disappointments and postponements. In November of 1760, he announced to Voltaire that the work was almost finished. A little later, he assured Sophie that if it were not done by Easter, he would be dead. He was mistaken on both counts. Then in September 1761, he exclaims, "That terrible revision is over. I have spent twenty-five days in succession at it, at the rate of ten hours a day!" Ten days later he wrote again to Sophie to explain where he had been on those beautiful autumn afternoons. "I was locked up in a dark apartment, burning out my eyes collating plates with their explanations, stupefying myself for people who would not give me a glass of water when they no longer need me and who even now find it difficult to act decently." Evidently, relations with the publishers were becoming more strained. A month later, Diderot's intense labor is unabated, as is also his discontent; the fruit of his work will only be "insults, injuries, persecution, worries."

Perhaps the greatest annoyance of all was the difficulty in getting his collaborators to show the same energy as he did. "My colleagues infuriate me by their slowness," he informed Sophie. "Those asses have such thick skins that my spurring them is of no avail; but if I didn't constantly keep the spur in their sides, they would stop entirely." The only exception was Jaucourt, but even his faithful efforts seemed inefficient to Diderot. "I no longer know when I shall leave this prison. The chevalier de Jaucourt's plan seems to be to keep me at it another year. For six or seven years that man has been surrounded by six or seven secretaries, reading, dictating, working thirteen or fourteen hours a day, and that position still hasn't tired him. . . . Do not fear that he will become bored with grinding out articles. God made him for that."

The heavy barrage of anti-philosophic pamphlets had not quieted down. It can well be said that the years between 1759 and 1762 were crucial and climactic, not only for the *Encyclopedia,* but for the entire struggle of ideas. The enemies of free thought redoubled their efforts, led by Berthier and the public prosecutor, Omer Joly de Fleury. Chaumeix was indefatigable in his publications. But of all these attacks only two were particularly annoying to Diderot.

First, Fréron created a fuss by accusing him publicly of stealing his plates from the dead scientist Réaumur's work on arts and trades. The Academy of Sciences, called in as arbiter, proclaimed the falsehood of the charge. Fréron called Diderot a hypocrite, Grimm a low flatterer, and the encyclopedic group as a whole, including Voltaire, "knaves, crooks, puppies, and scoundrels." The truth of the matter was that Fréron's accusation was substantially correct. There had been considerable plagiarism of Réaumur's plates, and were it not for these outcries, there would probably have been much more.

Then, on May 2, 1760, Palissot produced his famous comedy, *Les philosophes.* Under the name of Dortidius, Diderot was mocked as a pretentious fool and a hypocrite whose enthusiasm imposed on other fools. Rousseau appeared as Crispin, the valet who practices "return to nature" by walking on all fours and munching lettuce. This last trait received tremendous applause; in fact the whole comedy was a sensational success. Palissot had been prompted to write it by the princess de Robecq, his protectress, by the duke de Duras and other enemies of the *philosophes.* So anxious was the "devout party" to crush the "philosophic party," that various high ecclesiastics came ostentatiously to the theatre and applauded vigorously; one even praised the comedy in a sermon.

This was the hardest blow of all for Diderot to digest. It hurt to be mocked and maligned in public, to be the laughing stock of all Paris. It hurt bitterly, especially because he considered that he had earned the gratitude and respect of his fellow men. But he maintained his policy of not degrading himself, aided by Malesherbe's recommendation to keep calm and by his fear of compromising the *Encyclopedia*. "While this scandal was occupying all of Paris," wrote Grimm, "M. Diderot, whom that rascally Aristophanes had chosen for his Socrates, was the only person who paid no attention to it." Grimm's statement is a slight exaggeration. Diderot was upset and angry, and took revenge of a sort by calumniating Palissot in *Rameau's Nephew*, a work he left unpublished. The only open reply from the *philosophes* came from the pen of the rash Morellet, in the *Vision of Charles Palissot to Serve as Preface to the Comedy of the Philosophes*. Mme. de Robecq, who was dying of consumption, was cruelly insulted in it and Palissot accused of having turned his home into a brothel, with his wife performing the featured role. This time, however, Morellet was recognized as its author. A few days after its publication, on the demand of Mme. de Robecq, he found himself in the Bastille.

Palissot, who had the support of the powerful reactionary influences, was not yet through. Ignoring Voltaire's entreaties, he published a *Counsel of the Lanterns, or True Vision of Charles Palissot to Serve as Postscript to the Comedy of the Philosophes*, and later, in 1764, *The Dunciad*, in imitation of Alexander Pope. In both of these, Diderot was his special target.

As a counterattack on the "devout party," and in order to conciliate Diderot and the "radical" wing of his party, Voltaire conceived the idea of a campaign to elect Diderot to the French Academy. Election would amount to semi-official approbation and be the greatest possible triumph. He did not know that Diderot, because of his activities and notoriety, was *persona non grata* in every Academy throughout the land. He wrote several times to d'Alembert, a member of the French Academy since December 1754, urging him to begin the campaign and advising that Diderot seduce some influential, pious lady, go to church with her, and then the rest would be easy. As for the king, he could be appeased by saying that the Academy needed Diderot to complete its *Dictionary*. D'Alembert replied that the matter was utterly impossible; he knew that the king and the entire "devout party" would unite to prevent such a "scandal." Malesherbes also made soundings, and turned in a negative report. There is no doubt that Diderot was disappointed. In the *Letter on the Deaf and Dumb*, he was already pointing towards the Academy, and the article "Encyclopedia" was an almost open bid, hinting at his usefulness for the *Dictionary*. Not only would it have been a professional triumph; it would have meant the personal satisfaction of mortifying his jealous brother.

Whenever Diderot spoke later in life of his country's ingratitude, his exclusion from the Academy may well have been one of the thorns.

Besides, the *philosophes* were just then having their own party quarrel with the Academy. In May 1760, Lefranc de Pompignan devoted most of his reception speech to an attack on Voltaire, Diderot, and the *philosophes* in general. Voltaire, readily aroused, came back with one of his pamphlets,*The When*, published under the pseudonym of Clodoré, a useless disguise. The incorrigible Morellet followed with *The Yes* and *The Why*. Pompignan replied with a furious *Mémoire*. After failing to get the king's personal approval to publish it, he ordered it printed nonetheless with the inscription, "Approved by the King." When Malesherbes discovered this, he stopped the edition. A general rumpus ensued. The *Mémoire* was finally printed, without the mention of royal approval. Few bothered to read it, but the people of Paris had again been entertained by quarrels over the *philosophes,* who had been given more annoyance and unwanted notoriety. During all the excitement, Diderot alone remained impassively in his study, working on the *Encyclopedia* and reading Voltaire's *Universal History (Essai sur les moeurs).*

2

Amidst these attacks and his drudgery, Didèrot found distraction in various literary activities. His two dramas had not been produced after their publication, because the players of the Comédie Française, schooled in the tradition of more than a century, did not relish the new kind of acting they required. Then, towards the end of 1760, the *Père de famille* was produced at Toulouse and at Marseilles. It was so successful that the Comédie Française was finally forced to put it on, but not without considerable cuts and changes which distressed its indignant author. The premiere took place on February 18, 1761; it had seven showings, sufficient at the time to be considered a moderate success. This triumph, Diderot wrote, was won in spite of the actors, who were entirely disconcerted by the "natural"—more probably the emotional, melodramatic—acting they were called upon to do, and also in spite of a cabal organized by the "devout party" to belittle and impede the play.

The entire "philosophic party" exulted at the success of the *Père de famille,* and no one more than Voltaire, who graciously allowed performances of his own tragedy, *Tancrède*, to be post-poned in its favor. "Oh my dear brother Diderot! I yield you my place with all my heart and I should like to crown you with laurel! " He regarded the success of the play as a triumph of virtue over infamous calumny. It appeared to him another reason for pushing Diderot's election to the Academy. The philosopher's own reaction to his triumph is expressed in a letter to Voltaire.

> I am at the table of my friend Damilaville, and I am writing to you under his dictation that if the acting had corresponded more to the requirements of the play, the success would have been spectacular, and notwithstanding I shall have enough success to spite my enemies. Voices arose from the pit shouting: "What an answer to the satire of the *philosophes!*" That is the word I wanted to hear. I don't know what opinion the public will have of my dramatic ability, and I don't care, but I wanted them to see a man who bears profoundly engraved in the depths of his heart, the image of virtue and the feeling of humanity, and they have seen him. . . . Good-bye, my dear master, I know how much you have desired the success of your disciple, and I am touched by it. My affection and homage for all my life. They have just come back from the third showing. Success, despite the rage of the cabal.

Strangely enough, Diderot never went to see his own play.

3

From 1757 the battle of the *Encyclopedia* had raged unabated. On October 12, 1761, Diderot sounded the first exulting note of confidence in a letter to Sophie Volland. "Well, we have been excommunicated for over a year and a half now. It was the Lucca edition of our work that brought the Bull on us, and it is their hatred for us that provoked that event, now that they know every-thing is completed and that we shall appear, come wind and high water." The year 1762 was to bring the decisive turn in favor of the *philosophes*. They had steadily been gathering strength. In November of 1759, a friend of the new ideas, Sartine, was named police commissioner; this meant that they could work in relative security. As was customary, Sartine had to pursue his functions vigorously on the surface, while protecting the *Encyclopedia* secretly. When several peddlers of illicit books were caught, he had them pilloried, whipped, branded, and sent to the galleys. But the *Encyclopedia* marched on.

In addition to Malesherbes, other liberal nobles—even the marquise de Pompadour—had been affected by the steady encroachment of the new ideas. The prestige of the work, as well as even its importance as a major business enterprise, were felt by responsible people. But it was in 1762 that the campaign was won. Just as one battle can decide a war, so did the suppression of the Jesuits that year break the back of the obscurantist party. In 1761 the Jesuits had been expelled from Portugal, and this event had encouraged their enemies in France—the liberals and the far more influential Jansenists, masters of the Parlements and of the Sorbonne. The Jesuits had long been unpopular. They were accused of grasping ruthlessly for power, through their control of education and court confessionals and through diplomatic intrigues. In South America, they had carried out a conquest that was at once religious, political, and commercial.

The opportunity soon came for their enemies. The Society of Jesus had recently suffered heavy losses in its trade with Martinique, due to the war with England. A huge debt was incurred, followed by the scandalous bankruptcy of Father La Valette. Subsequent litigation reached the Paris Parlement. The Parlement did not waste its chance. First it ordered the Society to pay 1,502,000 livres. From there it went on to examine the Jesuit doctrine. It declared this doctrine opposed to Christian morality, murderous and abominable, dangerous to the monarch. Mme. de Pompadour now stepped in. She had owed to the Jesuits her supreme triumph, at the time of her greatest insecurity: her appointment as lady-in-waiting to the unfortunate queen. She took this opportunity to repay them by siding with their enemy, Choiseul, the king's minister. To the indignant dauphin, their principal defender, Choiseul replied, "Perhaps, Sir, I shall be unfortunate enough to be your subject some day; but I shall certainly never be in your service." On August 6, 1762, the Parlement issued a writ suppressing completely the activities of the Jesuits; and in 1764 the king's council ordered them expelled from France. The death blow was swift, and stunned the *philosophes* as well as their enemies. Bachaumont's journal notes the "excessive, almost indecent joy" of the bourgeoisie and the common people. Rejoicing among the *philosophes* was without parallel. "The middle of the century," commented d'Alembert, "seems destined to mark an epoch in the history of ideas through the intellectual revolution that appears to be in the making." Diderot wrote, "I seem to see Voltaire raising his hands and eyes to heaven, as he repeats the *Nunc dimittis*. There I am delivered of a great number of powerful enemies . . . Their system is only Machiavellism reduced to maxims. The most amusing of all is the joy with which the Jansenists are triumphing over their enemies; they do not see the oblivion into which they are going to fall." This prediction was accurate. Even more significant, the Parlements had destroyed another rampart of ecclesiastical sacredness and of the Old Régime.

There was one crowning irony. The publishers of the *Encyclopedia,* needing additional equipment, acquired the presses of the *Journal de Trévoux,* in whose columns their work had been attacked for so many years. This was a poetic revenge for Father Berthier's attempt to take over the *Encyclopedia* in 1752.

Discussion at Mme. d'Epinay's country home at La Briche, where Diderot was spending part of the summer, centered around the great news of the day. Someone quoted the complaint of one of the unhappy Fathers. "They are throwing us out! We are departing, despoiled of our clothes, our name, and our rank, from a house where we were surrounded by the hearts of our kings." "My Father," replied a wit, referring to the Damiens affair, "that's what comes from being too anxious to have Louis XV's."

Persecution of the *Encyclopedia* had aroused interest in it throughout Europe. In September 1762, Catherine the Great sent Diderot an offer to complete it at St. Petersburg under her full protection. A similar suggestion to go to Berlin again came from Voltaire, with the backing of Frederick the Great. Both were declined on the ground that the manuscripts were the exclusive property of the publishers. Besides it was too late, he told Voltaire. "At the very moment I am writing, the printing is being done, and I have some proofs under my eyes." Already, the first volume of plates had come off the press.

4

One brief dialogue came from Diderot's pen in 1763, the *Introduction to Great Principles* (published in 1798). Again it was a reaction to something he had read, this time to a dialogue in defense of religion which attacked the *philosophes* as moral nihilists. It includes the apologist's refutation and Diderot's final reply.

The first part of the work contains the dialogue written by a theologian, in which the "Sage" catechizes his "Proselyte."

"Do you believe that the divinity requires anything of men?"
"No ; except that they follow their instinct."
"What are, in your opinion, the duties of man?"
"He has none, being born free and independent."
"What do you think of justice and injustice?"
"They are purely matters of convention."
"Do you think that intelligent charity means to further one's own good, at any cost?"
"I believe it, for it is proven."
"Do you give up the vileness of humility and forgiving offenses?"
"I give them up."
"Do you promise to follow faithfully the voice of nature and the passions?"
"I promise."

The Sage then pronounces the Proselyte a disciple of Nature. "By the power that she gives you. . . . trample on *mores* and religion; make the people rise up against their sovereigns; free mortals from the yoke of divine and human laws."

Much of this nihilism was the very speculation that Diderot indulged in at times. But he would never accept it as a philosophy to live by, or for public broadcast. He replied in kind, giving his own version of the dialogue between the philosophic Sage and his pupil. This is an attempt at a "confession of faith" for his party. The fact that it is the duty of man to be happy implies "the necessity of contributing to the happiness of others, or in other words, to be virtuous." Forgiveness of offenses is the "sign of a great soul," although humility is rejected as involving an unnatural scorn of self. (Modern psychology would hold Diderot to be wrong; self-abasement, as well as self-assertion, is a natural tendency in man.) He still maintains that the passions always tell us the right thing, since they tell us to be happy. The objection to such an argument is obvious. Do they tell us the right way to be happy? But for Diderot it is our judgment that advises us badly and sets us on the wrong road. "It is reason, not Nature that deceives us"—how strange to find Diderot dissociating reason from nature! Again he sounds like that "sophist," Jean-Jacques. The major difference—Rousseau's emphasis on conscience instead of passions—is another point of confusion in Diderot's mind, and it is brought out in the later development.

It first appears as the result of a curious paralogism: the paths of virtue and happiness must be identical, he tells us, else it would be crazy to be virtuous. Clearly, happiness is paramount; therefore, the only way for Diderot to assure both is to make them interdependent. Almost desperately, he insists on their equivalence. "No, the path of happiness is the very path of virtue. Fortune may bring virtue reverses; but it can never take away that sweet enchantment, that pure voluptuousness that accompanies it." And it is here that he comes to the concept of conscience, without yet naming it. "The testimony of one's own self is the source of true good and evil; that is what makes the happiness of the good man amid persecution and misfortunes; and the torment of the wicked, amid the favors of fortune."

It is the theologian's refutation that forces Diderot to a still clearer statement. The weakness in Diderot's reasoning was only too evident. "Ah, dear sir," his opponent argued, "if you take what is written in your heart for the law of God, you make him write much foolishness. You will find written in it, pride, envy, avarice, maliciousness, lasciviousness, and the alphabet of all our vices." The good theologian had put his finger on the defect of romantic morality, and Diderot, like Rousseau, was quick to realize his error. For men are bad, as well as good (neither would affirm that man is essentially evil). And Diderot's reply is that by "heart," he means "conscience," not the passions. Actually he had specifically said "passions," as well as "heart," but we shall let him save face.

This concept of conscience, bound up with a formalistic ethics, is perhaps not Shaftesbury's theory of a moral sense, but a pre-Kantian idea of a moral reason or intuition in man, capable of perceiving moral axioms very much as we intuitively perceive the axioms of mathematics. Diderot has made a complete circle in this little work. He has started with a teleological ethics, modified to include society in the concept of man, arriving at virtue as the way to hedonic self-realization. Finally, by insisting on conscience as the innate and unfailing touchstone of moral good, he has reverted to formalism; for if conscience, and not the judgment, is what discerns the good, then conscience must work on an absolute or formal basis, perceiving the character of good in the action (as we intuit $1 + 1 = 2$), rather than in the goal of happiness.

For the rest, 1763 and 1764 were devoted entirely to the clandestine printing of the remaining volumes, although the secret was
not too closely guarded, with more than two score workmen
engaged on the job. Diderot was still revising—for the fifth time,
but his enthusiasm was mounting despite the work. The ten remaining volumes were coming off the presses in a steady rhythm. Then,
in November 1764, came the hardest, most bitter blow he had to
suffer, and the most unexpected. While he was by chance referring
to one of his favorite articles, "Saracens," he was suddenly staggered
by an unbelievable discovery. "Can that be the text of my article?"
he asked himself. "There must be a mistake." He rubbed his eyes
and feverishly reread the first paragraphs. No, there could be no
doubt. The cautious Le Breton, fearful of all the wrath of the law,
had pitilessly struck out every line, every paragraph that could
possibly give offense. Quickly, Diderot looked at the other articles,
hoping against hope that it was an isolated case. But no, the havoc
was general.

Since the manuscripts had been destroyed, he was unable to verify
the extent of the censorship, which was somewhat less serious than
he imagined. Still the damage was irreparable.

Diderot was uncontrollably furious, but beneath his rage, he was
heartbroken. The work of all these years, the days and nights spent
in slavery, the perils and alarms of persecution, the successful
defiance of the authorities—to have all this completely undone by a
traitor! He rushed to the printing office and a frantic scene ensued,
in the course of which Diderot's combined tears and imprecations
gave Le Breton a mighty unhappy half-hour. Le Breton had not
even told his partners of what he had done. When one of them,
David, whom Diderot called "a hard, miserly but just man," found
it out, he too upbraided the wily publisher for his "infamy."

A week after the discovery, Diderot wrote to Le Breton explaining that his duty forced him to complete his job, but at the same
time he unburdened his aching heart.

> You have plunged a dagger into my heart which the sight of
> you would only sink deeper. For two years you have deceived me
> like a coward. You have massacred like a brutish beast the work
> of twenty honest men who have gratuitously devoted to you their
> time, their talent and their nights, out of love for the good and the

true, and with the sole hope of seeing their ideas appear and getting from them some consideration which they have richly deserved, and now your injustice and your ingratitude have deprived them of that. But remember what I predict to you. Scarcely will your book appear, when they will go to their articles, and seeing with their own eyes the injury you have done them, they will not contain themselves, they will start to shout. Your subscribers will say that they have subscribed for my work and it is almost yours that you are giving them . . . Then they will learn of an atrocity of which there is no example in the history of books. Has anyone ever heard of ten folio volumes, secretly mutilated, truncated, chopped up, dishonored by a printer? . . .

I wept with rage before you ; I wept with grief at home, before your partner M. Briasson, and before my wife, my child and my servant. You have forgotten that it is not to the well-known, "safe" things that you owed your first success ; what people have looked for and will look for is the firm and bold philosophy of some of your workers. And you have cut it up, mutilated it, torn it to ribbons, without judgment, restraint or taste. You have made our work flat and insipid. You have banished everything that could have made its attraction, its piquancy, its interest, its novelty. You will be punished by financial loss and by dishonor ; that is your affair . . . At the end of it all, it turns out that the greatest harm we have suffered, the scorn, the shame, the discredit, the ruin, the mockery, came from its principal proprietor. . . .

On and on, page after page. Diderot made one request: to be allowed to recopy the text from the original proofs, so as to have one complete copy just for himself. Thereon hangs another chapter in the romantic adventures of Diderot's literary legacy. A few years ago, one bound volume of the original proof, with the censored lines crossed out, was discovered among the items advertised by a Paris bookseller. It had gone from Le Breton's hands into Russia. The Soviet government had sold it, with other collections, in Germany. From there it was purchased by the Paris bookseller, who sold it to Douglas H. Gordon, a Baltimore bibliophile.[1]

Diderot never forgot this "outrage." He could never speak of it without becoming excited. "He was convinced," writes Mme. de Vandeul, "that the public knew as well as he what was missing in

[1] The censored passages have been published by D. H. Gordon and N. L. Torrey ("The Censorship of Diderot's Encyclopedia," New York, 1947). One cannot conclude absolutely from this sample, however, as to the amount of censorship in the whole manuscript.

each article, and the impossibility of repairing the damage infuriated him even twenty years afterwards." Curiously enough, only a dozen people ever really knew of the expurgation, and not one of the collaborators ever complained or even mentioned the mutilation of his work.

As the end approached, Diderot grew more and more impatient, his enthusiasm completely destroyed.

> I shall scarcely go there any more, to that damned shop where I wore out my eyes for men who wouldn't give me a cane to guide myself with. We have only fourteen more sheaves to print, a matter of eight or ten days. In eight or ten days, then, I shall see the end of this enterprise which has occupied me for twenty years, which has not made me rich, which has several times nearly made me leave my country or lose my liberty, and which has taken up a life that I could have made more useful and more glorious! The sacrifice of our talents would be less common if it were only a question of ourselves ; we would resolve rather to drink water, to eat crusts and to follow our genius in an attic. But for a wife, for children, to what don't we resign ourselves? If I had to defend my merit, I wouldn't say to them: "I have worked thirty years for you," but I would say: "For you I have given up, for thirty years, my natural calling ; I preferred what was useful to you to what was pleasant to me."

This was in July. In August he again exclaims, "It will take me, I think, to the end of the week, after which I shall cry: Land! Land!" At least Le Breton has had the decency to make somewhat generous financial arrangements. "A bill for some books will be canceled. They will tear up one or two notes I have signed, and they will give me fourteen hundred and twenty-eight livres for the uncompleted last volume. All my debts will be paid off, and I shall walk on the earth as light as a feather."

Four months later, at the end of 1765, and nineteen years after its beginning, the immense work was at last completed. There still remained the perilous task of launching the ten volumes in the teeth of the authorities. The death of the dauphin in December was one encouraging event. Paradoxically, the *philosophes* now lamented his passing. The dauphin was a well-educated, intelligent, and politically liberal prince, although he was extremely devout and had sided with the Jesuits. Diderot recalled that he had disapproved of the exiling of Rousseau, whom he said was to be pitied, not persecuted. Voltaire praised him for knowing his tragedy, *Mahomet,* by heart, and for reading Locke on his deathbed. If the dauphin had ruled, instead of his weak and floundering son, Louis XVI, French history might have recorded another Henry IV. The Revolution might have been delayed or moderated. Probably it could not have been averted, for France had to molt the shell of the Old Régime, and the privileged classes were too shortsighted and selfish to bow to the march of progress.

In January 1766 this announcement was published.

> Samuel Fauche, bookseller at Neufchâtel in Switzerland, notifies the public that he has finished printing the rest of the *Encyclopedia,* whose manuscripts he had acquired after the publication of the seven volumes printed in Paris. The continuation begins at volume eight and contains ten volumes. Those who have the first seven volumes of this work are requested to get from the Paris publishers a note stating that they subscribed for the work. And the ten volumes will be delivered in sheets to the bearer, for the sum of two hundred livres.

The false imprint deceived no one. The publishers relied on the discretion of the subscribers to enable them to effectuate a quiet distribution, and a large number of copies were given out with the permission of Sartine, who in 1763 had replaced Malesherbes as director of publishing. But people began to talk, jestingly or indignantly, according to the stripe of their opinions, about the sale of a forbidden work. When the talk began to assume proportions of a scandalous defiance of the law, Sartine, who was afraid of the general assembly of the clergy, to be held that summer, issued an order forbidding further distribution without special permission. The clergy had always maintained that their "contributions" to the government were a voluntary gift, and now they threatened to discontinue their payments if pressure on the enemies of religion were relaxed.

Then Le Breton surprised everyone. Passing suddenly from extremes of prudence to boldness, he decided to defy this order and released copies to about two dozen subscribers at the Court, at their own request. Saint-Florentin soon learned of their defiance. He immediately issued a *lettre de cachet* for Le Breton's arrest, and another order for the recall of the copies which had been sent to Versailles. On April 23, a shadow from the past, none other than Diderot's old friend, M. d'Hémery, arrested Le Breton at his office and carted him away to the Bastille. Diderot would have had to possess the superhuman virtue of one of his own characters if he did not feel a certain satisfaction at the thought of Le Breton in the Bastille, despite the expurgation that was to have saved him from any such danger! The punishment was quite innocuous, however; it lasted but a week, and Le Breton was even allowed to bring his servant with him to assure his comfort.

In July, the nineteen-year-old chevalier de La Barre was condemned to have his right arm cut off and to be burnt alive for a blasphemous word about the Virgin—a punishment which the Parlement of Paris mitigated to mere decapitation and posthumous burning. The *philosophes,* who had been fighting for tolerance since the beginning of the century, were deeply shocked. Led by Voltaire, they protested vehemently in books and pamphlets. As usual, their protests provoked official reaction against themselves. When the king's attorney accused the encyclopedists of indirect responsibility for the crime—although none of their works was found in La Barre's library—the situation again began to look ugly, especially after their defiant publication of the *Encyclopedia.* Imminent danger of imprisonment hung once more over Diderot's head. Voltaire urged him anew to fly to safety and assured him of the welcome of Frederick the Great. Diderot thanked him but refused, replying with an indictment of the police state.

> I know well that when a wild beast has dipped his tongue in human blood, it can never do without it ; I know well that the beast lacks food, and no longer having Jesuits to eat, will leap upon the *philosophes.* I know well that its eyes are turned on me and that I shall perhaps be the first it will devour . . . I know well that we are enmeshed in the invisible threads of a net called *police,* and that we are surrounded by spies. I hear a voice at the bottom of my heart that joins yours and cries "Fly, fly" ; nevertheless I am retained by the most stupid and inconceivable inertia, and I remain. It is because there is beside me a woman already advanced in years . . . I am the father of a girl to whom I owe an education, and I also have friends . . . What do you expect me to do with life, if I can conserve it only by giving up everything that makes it dear to me?

No, a different way of life would have been impossible for Diderot. The thought of never returning to the dinners at d'Holbach's and the evenings at the Régence was unbearable.

Besides, he did not share Voltaire's enthusiasm for Frederick the Great. The two men never knew each other, but a genuine antipathy existed between them nonetheless. The king found the philosopher verbose and obscure; he called his writings insipid and not worth reading. "There reigns in them a conceited tone and an arrogance that revolts my instinct of liberty." If Frederick was referring to the *Thoughts on the Interpretation of Nature,* one can scarcely find fault with some of this criticism. Most of all, Frederick was to be furious at the open snub Diderot gave him by avoiding Berlin on his later journey through Germany, despite his invitation to call at the royal palace.

Diderot, in turn, freely admitted his hatred for the Prussian king, calling him a tyrant, "an ambitious and faithless politician, for whom nothing is sacred, a prince who sacrifices everything, even the happiness of his subjects, for his present power, the eternal troublemaker of Europe." Diderot's perceptiveness merits high credit because he, like others, had at first been beguiled by Frederick's pretention to the title of philosopher-king. In *The Sceptic's Walk,* the suggestion is made that a dangerous manuscript be published in the land of "that philosopher-prince whom you sometimes see, his brow crowned with laurel, walking in our alleys and resting from his noble labors in the shade of our chestnut trees; the one you recently heard scolding Machiavelli with so much eloquence and good sense." Diderot came to realize that Frederick was the most machiavellian and least liberal of princes.

The excitement over La Barre gradually cooled. Powerful figures at Court, including the duke de Choiseul and the duke de Richelieu, together with other influential men, such as Turgot and Malesherbes, were working in favor of the *Encyclopedia.* The end was unspectacular. The usefulness of the work became apparent, and common sense triumphed. Besides, its enemies were not nearly so strong as formerly. The Jesuits had been expelled, Chaumeix was a fugitive at Moscow, Fréron discredited. A new force, Freemasonry, found the *Encyclopedia* a basis for its own liberal doctrines, and put its weight into action. Soon public and official opinion offered no further obstacles to distribution of the completed work, and, a few at a time, Sartine issued special permits allowing each subscriber to get his copy.

Diderot was tired. "It is true that my head is weary. The burden I have carried for twenty years has bent me so well that I despair of ever straightening up again." The struggle had been long. And it had been an arduous one, both with the outside world and within his own camp—with d'Alembert, the publishers, the subscribers, and even with the collaborators. But his labors were not yet at an end. Five volumes of the plates had appeared, but as with the text, there were more than had been anticipated, and the remaining six were not completed until 1772. This type of work was less difficult and intense, but more tedious and wearisome, especially since Le Breton's treason had destroyed his enthusiasm.

Then another annoyance arose to plague him. For the sake of a lawsuit, one of the subscribers who had previously quarreled with Le Breton over some work of his own, Luneau de Boisgermain, sued for the reimbursement of his subscription price, on grounds that were purely technical. He claimed that the work had been announced as in ten volumes, and there were twenty-eight, seventeen of text, eleven of plates; furthermore, the format and type were not exactly the ones advertised—all this without consent of the subscribers who were "caught" after paying their first installments. The matter was serious. If judgment were awarded in his favor, the publishers would be completely ruined, having to refund the gigantic sum of 1,948,052 livres.

Diderot committed the unpardonable imprudence of receiving Luneau in his study and, worse still, of writing to him, urging him to prosecute vigorously people whose villainies he knew better than anyone else. Luneau immediately printed this letter in one of his briefs. Put directly into the case, the philosopher wrote a rejoinder for the publishers in which they were treated with as much scorn as their adversary. But Luneau, by printing it with tricky comments, again turned it to profit. This time Diderot was thoroughly aroused. He wrote a cold, logical reply, demonstrating the absurdity of Luneau's claims, arguing that he and not the publishers was responsible for everything in the work; the publishers were petty subalterns, mere tools who furnished the material means of production. "Yes, M. Luneau, you were cheated; but you were cheated as you would have been by someone who owed you only one écu and who gave you two." This memoir was not published— Diderot's friends persuaded him that it would be dangerous openly to admit being the editor of a forbidden work—but Le Breton's attorneys made good use of it. We can only imagine how unhappy Diderot must have been when the attorney for the defenders assured the tribunal that the final volumes—despite the freedom from censorship—contained nothing injurious to religion or to the government. "That part of metaphysics which might lead minds astray has been removed." The suit was prolonged for years, until, on August 14, 1778, judgment was given in favor of the defendant and Luneau was condemned to payment of costs.

The battle of the *Encyclopedia* was over. In spite of the Jesuits, the Jansenists, the clergy, the Parlement and a great part of the nobility and the Court—all the privileged classes—in spite of persecution, pamphlets, calumnies and decrees, in spite of sermons, satires and censors, the *philosophes* had won. It was really Diderot's victory, and a glorious one. The battle of the *Encyclopedia* is the heroic episode in his life, the noble episode that lifts it far above the self-centered lives of most of his fellow philosophers. Because of his limitless devotion to a cause, to an ideal, he alone was responsible for the inception of the great work, for its continuance and for its completion. His courage enabled him to face all perils, and obstacles seem only to have hardened his determination. His boldness and unshakeable resolution were revealed doubly. They were manifested first of all in the work itself, in his herculean labors and his tenacity in pursuing less diligent collaborators. Especially they were displayed at the hour of persecution, when his refusal to abandon the enterprise, to carry it abroad or to become demoralized make him a truly heroic figure in the history of thought and the fight for intellectual freedom. He surmounted the petty quibbling and the bitter betrayal of his publishers. Even his friends lost faith in the completion of their great project. D'Alembert and other collaborators abandoned the ship when it seemed to be foundering. Voltaire advised flight each time danger appeared. The enemy sniped at him constantly and three times seemed to have destroyed the work and endangered his personal liberty. But if he left the victory to the fanatics—and this is the core of his determination—who would re-light the torch? Most certainly, no other member of the "philosophic group" had the courage and devotion to adventure into such a death trap, nor was there a single one of them with the genius to carry out such an immense and pioneering project.

And so through it all, Diderot never swerved from his purpose: to serve humanity by a work of tolerance and truth. Posterity has justly honored Voltaire for his devotion and humanitarianism in the Calas affair, but it was a devotion that entailed no peril and brought him the acclamation he loved. Diderot's cause brought him peril, persecution, and calumny. It is doubtful whether Voltaire would have been capable of a devotion of that sort. Diderot's phrase about

Catherine the Great can be applied to himself: "nature has made obstacles only to distinguish great souls from common ones."

Diderot cannot be accused of venality in his courageous persistence. It is true that he had undertaken the work, back in the forties, to provide himself with a source of revenue. But after the death of his father, his financial situation, as well as his reputation had so improved that he no longer needed to worry, and he could easily have found other means to supplement his income. In reality, not many hours passed before an ideal purpose had submerged all other motives. That purpose was to denounce prejudice and to proclaim truth. "This work," he wrote to Sophie, "will surely produce in time a revolution in the minds of men, and I hope that tyrants, oppressors, fanatics, and the intolerant will not gain thereby. We shall have served humanity; but we shall be reduced to a cold and insensible dust for many years before we have any gratitude for it." When Voltaire encouraged him to crush their enemies, he replied that he did want to *écraser l'infâme,* but was interested still more in the constructive values of the work. It seems that Diderot's conception of the "philosophic spirit" was of a higher order than that of some of the other "party members." Their aim was the destruction of prejudice and privilege, of error, superstition, tyranny, and intolerance; it was a worthy one, and Diderot shared it. But much closer to his heart, as he himself indicates, was the work of laying the foundations for a better society and a better life. The discovery and diffusion of truth, the advancement of science, the moral regeneration of man were above all else.

The remainder of the story can be summarized in few words. When Le Breton surrendered the printing license, in 1773, Panckoucke published a *Supplement* composed of four volumes of text, one of plates, and a two-volume index. He had tried in vain to interest Diderot in this additional work, but Diderot was tired, and nursing the momentary illusion that he was going to edit a new and better *Encyclopedia,* under Catherine the Great's sponsorship. Later editions of Diderot's work were published in Geneva, Lausanne, and Yverdun. "Encyclopedias were now the order of the day," writes Professor Torrey. "The *Brittanica* was begun in England and the *Encyclopédie méthodique,* a rehandling of Diderot's work, was launched in France. Diderot's and d'Alembert's insistence on alphabetic arrangement, at first abandoned, finally triumphed. Larousse, the great French encyclopedist of the nineteenth century, paid a sincere tribute to Diderot in the Preface to his

Grand dictionnaire universel. But Diderot's purpose and spirit could not be recaptured. Other encyclopedias became mere colorless accumulations of fact, emphasizing the splendor of his work in blazing the trail to complete freedom of thought."

How far did the *Encyclopedia* succeed in carrying out its ambitious program? In science, it expressed and spread the new spirit of the age, the spirit of observation and experiment, and fought for its triumph over the scolastic and rationalistic schools of thought. It performed a fine job of vulgarization, popularizing the theories and applications of science, always holding out the promise of continuing progress, bending the reader's mind towards our destiny on this earth.

In the classification of knowledge of the technical processes of industry, and the campaign to win interest and respect for the trades and those engaged in them, the *Encyclopedia* led the thought of the century. Here the imprint of Diderot's bourgeois origins is dominant. "Put on one side of the scales the real advantages of the most sublime sciences and of the most honored arts, and on the other side those of the mechanical arts, and you will find that the esteem in which the ones and the others have been severally held has not been granted in just proportion to those advantages, that more praise has been given to the men who were busy in making us believe that we were happy than to the men who were concerned in causing us to be really happy. How queer our judgments are! We require that people should be usefully employed and we despise useful men." A thoroughly utilitarian and middle-class viewpoint that presages our own.

In its critical work, the *Encyclopedia* sought to substitute "nature for religion, reason for authority, tolerance for intolerance." Science, reason, tolerance: the work of the *Encyclopedia* is resumed in those three words. Its critical aspect does not represent the most radical tendencies of eighteenth-century thought; rather it repeats the generalities and criticisms that were acceptable to all but the conservative elements of the nation. In this way its propaganda was much more effective, since its aims appeared reasonable to almost all. The audacities, most often, are adroitly hidden in articles with innocuous titles or brought out by cross references. Thus, the article "God" is perfectly orthodox, but a reference to the article "Demonstration," if followed by the curious reader, will lead to contradictory conclusions. The insidious method of "impartial summary" of both sides, initiated by Bayle, was used especially in the attack on religion.

Still other expedients were to expose and praise the supposed beliefs of the Chinese and the Mohammedans, or to praise with willful overemphasis the doctrines of Christianity which to them seemed most irrational. Sometimes the writer would simply deny the very point he wanted to bring out: "eternal damnation is clearly revealed in the scriptures; therefore there is no point in inquiring through our reason whether a finite being can inflict an infinite injury on God." But no polemical expedient was as effective as the simple exposition of facts, such as the contradictions in the Bible and in the history of dogma and ritual. It was assumed that the disputed facts and interpretations would mark the Christian religion as man-made, just as surely as those with which it was compared. In all these ways, religions were attacked, tolerance preached, and a morality expounded which was independent of religion, based on human nature and social existence. Materialism and determinism were on the whole excluded, but Lockean sensualism is to be found again and again, and Lockean sensualism, in Arthur M. Wilson's words, was "corrosive and dissolvent to any religious authority based simply on revelation, and to any political authority based simply on prescription." As with science, the *Encyclopedia* resumes the thought of the century and continues its efforts towards an expressed ideal.

In the realm of politics, its theoretical pronouncements, especially those written by Diderot, appear bold enough: it condemns tyranny, proclaims the existence of a social contract, and the right to revolt against unbearable oppression. Whereas Montesquieu "forgot human nature in his study of social institutions," and Rousseau sacrificed the individual to the State, the *Encyclopedia* announced that the State exists only to guarantee and protect the rights of the individual; without them, man is no better than a beast. Laws must respect human nature, as well as climate, tradition, religion and economics. Aside from these generalizations, the *Encyclopedia*, when it turned to the realities of conditions in France, expressed the aspirations of the bourgeoisie. It upholds the monarchy, but not divine right, and intimates the desirability of a constitution giving expression to the wealthy and privileged classes of society. Governments, it maintains, are created by the needs and the will of men, and cannot be based on force. However, Rousseau's insistence on equality as a term of the contract is found only as a vague theory in one article, "Citizens." There is little against the privileges of the nobility and the clergy, nothing against the salt tax or exemptions from taxation, but other levies impeding commerce are condemned. Diderot wrote most of the political articles, and if he rebels at all against authority, it is in the direction of a new capitalist society of which political liberalism was one aspect. There was nothing dangerous in all this. To condemn fanaticism and despotism was no longer a novelty, nor to strive, as the encyclopedists did, for a more reasonable society.

The *Encyclopedia* contained valuable articles on the arts and letters, and contributed to the classification of the beaux arts. Most important, it laid the foundations, in a crude way, for the modern social sciences: sociology, anthropology, ethnology. It assembled facts, suggested hypotheses (now discarded) to explain them, performing the essential job of making erudition usable for later syntheses, and giving the initial impulse to organized, systematic investigations. Scientific determinism is preached: "laws are the necessary relationship that result from the nature of things." And everything is held to be submitted to natural laws. Nature and utility are the two poles between which the thought of the *Encyclopedia* flows. There are a number of articles in which the comparative method is employed as well as it could be at the time, on such matters as primitive religion, totemism, taboos, the matriarchate, etc.

There were bound to be innumerable shortcomings in this pioneer work. As yet, no concept of social facts existed, as apart from the individual and psychological fact. All human institutions and functions, notes René Hubert, are treated as a function of human nature, which is held to be a composite of sensations operating under the conditions of social living. There was little understanding of the primitive mind, little critical spirit, and an obsession with the requirements of rationalistic preconceptions. It was thought, for instance, that by means of comparative history and analysis, the origins of society, religion, government, law, and ethics could be determined. If we knew their origins, we could then discover their true nature and correct the "deviations" imposed by historical experience. Such a study would at the same time show, in the words of Daniel Mornet, that man's history is "a slow and continuous climb in which intelligence, submitted doubtless to physical nature, to man's needs and the changing conditions of material existence, slowly creates a happier and more enlightened existence." Here, as elsewhere, the typical contradictions of eighteenth-century thought are evident. The abstractions of rationalism supplement the limited findings of an approved experimental method. A relativism derived from a feeling for human diversity and the complexity of things often yields to an equally strong belief in a universal human nature, consequently, in universally valid truths and principles.

Despite these and still other shortcomings—uncritical compilations, plagiarism, lack of proportion—the *Encyclopedia* satisfied the intellectual needs and curiosities of the age. It was more than a compendium of knowledge; it contained living ideas, a positive faith, a critical and tendentious history of human progress. In addition to the four thousand, three hundred original subscribers, we must reckon with the seven editions that followed immediately and a total of forty-three editions, of all sorts, in twenty-five years. It was not only the greatest intellectual accomplishment of the eighteenth century; it was the most important work of the century from the viewpoint of the struggle for progress and for a new society. Michelet called it the Trojan Horse of the Old Régime.

Certainly, many pious folk used the *Encyclopedia* as a reference book, or a text for family reading, without being affected by its propaganda; and most who sought the propaganda had already been convinced. True, many other works expressed a more advanced stage of French thought. Undeniably, the influence of Rousseau's writings, and of Voltaire's, was more widespread. But the *Encyclopedia* was a great *machine de guerre*, expressing the new spirit and the aspirations of the time, epitomizing the Age of Enlightenment. Because of the resistance of its enemies, it united the *philosophes* in an almost solid party, united them in a common cause and a common endeavor. It became the symbol and the rallying point of their ideals. Around the *Encyclopedia,* the greatest and most crucial fight of the century was waged.

CHAPTER 12

Two
Novels

1

NOTWITHSTANDING HIS encyclopedic labors, in the early sixties, Diderot had found time to work on two of his most important literary productions. *The Nun*, his first genuine novel, is an intensely interesting work, partly because of its literary merit, partly because of its polemical value. Throughout the eighteenth century, in treatises, novels, and plays, the *philosophes*, and many believers as well, waged war against the convent system. The common practice of forcing daughters to take vows when there was no dowry for them, or in order to increase the funds held for an elder brother or sister, was attacked as barbarous. Education in the convent was condemned as the poorest possible preparation for life, and the superficial, frivolous, easy-moraled ladies who peopled the fashionable salons were eloquent evidence for the charge. Finally, stories of immorality within many of the convents became more and more common, until at the end of the century, any title of play or novel which suggested a convent tale provoked lewd snickers. Diderot, in his encyclopedic articles and elsewhere, attacked the convent as immoral, from the viewpoint of the enforced vows, and as anti-social, because of the rule of celibacy. He had a more personal reason, too, for his hostility. His younger sister, against the wish of her parents, had become a nun. Her order allowed relatives an annual visit. Once Diderot went to see her; she spoke with so much warmth and enthusiasm, that he went away persuaded that her mind was affected. Some years later, she died insane.

The immediate origin of *The Nun* was partly a true story, partly a hoax. The daughter of a jeweler, Suzanne Delamare, had been forced into the convent of Longchamps. Intensely unhappy, she had a petition made to the Parlement on her behalf, requesting to be released from her vows. Among those who interceded in her favor was the marquis de Croismare, a close friend of the *philosophes*. Croismare was an ideal representative of the type of man the eighteenth century produced—gallant gentleman, soldier, epicurean, freethinker, and philosopher, a lover of art, music, and literature. Unfortunately, his efforts were in vain; the petition was denied by judges fearful of breaking one of the principles on which the social structure rested—the right of a father to imprison his daughter in a convent. This much is true. The rest is a hoax played in 1760 by Diderot and Grimm on Croismare. They pretended that Suzanne had fled from the convent, and wrote in her name to her "protector," begging for his help. Followed an exchange of letters between the "ex-nun" and Croismare, intermingled with those of their supposed intermediary, Mme. Madin, the wife of a former army officer. All these letters were written by Diderot. Finally when the good marquis became too worked up over the pathetic letters of the unhappy, persecuted girl, in order to prevent the matter from becoming really serious, Diderot had to "kill her off." Not until 1768, when Mme. Madin expressed complete ignorance of the whole affair, did Croismare realize that he had been the victim of a hoax. The conspirators admitted everything, and the gallant marquis laughed with them.

After he had killed off his unfortunate heroine, Diderot felt inspired to complete the outline and make a novel of his little plot. He set to work in his usual manner, fired with enthusiasm, working at high speed. "I started to do *The Nun*," he writes to Mme. d'Epinay, "and I was still at it at three o'clock in the morning. I am winging along rapidly. It is no longer a letter, it is a book. There will be in it true things, pathetic ones, strong ones if I so wanted. But I do not give myself the time for it. I let my head go, and so I can scarcely control it." A friend, d'Alainville, visited him and found him in tears.

"What is the matter?" he inquired with alarm.

"What is the matter? I am sad because of a story I am writing."

Briefly, *The Nun* recounts the unhappy life of a girl forced to enter a convent. More interesting than the heroine herself (who serves novelistically as spectator, victim or witness, and whose innocence passes credibility) are the three Mothers Superior with whom she comes in contact. Her relations with them constitute the greater part of the plot. The first, kind and gentle, dies in "an agony of mystic despair"; the second, by subjecting Suzanne to the most savage cruelty because of her conscientious inability to conform, sinks to the level of a brute; the third, a lesbian, subjects her to revolting experiences, and "expires amidst the horrors of madness, remorse, and superstitious terror." The nun escapes, but her last adventures, written when Diderot had lost enthusiasm and was anxious to terminate the book, are of lesser interest.

The Nun is noteworthy because Diderot rises above the mere propaganda inherent in his theme of the "enforced vocation." This well-worn theme he completely recreated "by inventing a heroine who has no lover or desire to marry and who wants only liberty." At the base of the novel, Professor F. C. Green has commented, is Diderot's "ideal notion of human dignity. This can be maintained only in society and in freedom . . . Thus, *The Nun* offers tragic images of human lives that have been twisted and blasted by transplantation to a climate for which they were never intended by nature."

Even more interesting than the thought is the artistry. *The Nun* reveals Diderot as a psychological novelist, equal to any in the eighteenth century. His characters are consummate examples of his own method of rapid, realistic portrayal. He makes them live by putting them into action, by fusing word and gesture. He had a talent for painting people in action, for seizing the characteristic, distinguishing trait.

> She is a round little woman, yet quick and lively in her movements; her head is never still on her shoulders; there is always something out of place in her clothing; her face is not unattractive; her eyes—one of them, the right one, is bigger and higher than the other—full of fire and distractions; when she walks she throws her arms forward and backwards. Does she want to talk? She opens her mouth, before she has decided what to say; so she stammers a little. Is she seated? She wriggles on her armchair, as if something were bothering her; she forgets proprieties; she

lifts her wimple to rub her skin ; she crosses her legs ; she asks you something ; you answer her, and she doesn't listen.

Description of environment is concise and is given only as accompaniment to action, so that it acquires graphic value. We do not see Suzanne's cell until the "mob" of sisters tears it to pieces. Characteristically, Diderot prefers tableaux to descriptions, and *The Nun* has been properly described by Georges May as a series of tableaux: "Sister Suzanne saying 'no' at the moment of taking the vow; Sister Suzanne playing clavecin in the midst of other sisters; Sister Suzanne with a rope around her neck and a switch in her hand, macerating herself before the congregation; Sister Suzanne in the chapel holding off her superior and calling her Satan, etc. . . . It is by tableaux that Diderot imagined and composed." That this was conscious technique is proved by Diderot's own judgment on *The Nun:* "It is a work for painters to read and reread; and if it were not immodest, its proper epigraph would be *I too am a painter.*"

On the other hand, one cannot really speak of true characters, having organic personalities; they are rather an accumulation of traits and experiences—which is perhaps in accord with Diderot's theory of the personality as a flow of sensations and states, united only by memory. However, memory is precisely what is lacking in this novel. Although it is a *remembered* tale, it is told by Suzanne as if it were a current journal, with no anticipation of future events, no relating of the *present* of the story to the then *future*. Diderot does this to maintain curiosity and suspense; he wants the reader to discover her life as if she were actually reliving it, instead of relating and remembering it. She must therefore write as if she were rediscovering herself, all over again. Certain confusions in the details of the plot result from this method. On the other hand, there is a gain in immediacy and graphic realism.

But Diderot's chief esthetic aim is to affect the emotions of the reader by precise, realistic evocation, and by emphasizing the pathetic and the gruesome. He uses recurrent themes of illness, insanity, and death, with intervals of physical and mental torture. There are scenes of struggle for the preservation of the self, charged with both the pathetic and the dramatic. They are enhanced in tone by the play of light and darkness, which emphasizes the lugubrious and the macabre. In this regard, *The Nun* is one of the first of the "Gothic novels," and foreshadows Matthew Lewis'

The Monk, and the novels of Ann Radcliffe and the Marquis de Sade.

Diderot succeeds in putting genuine emotional power into his novel, and in maintaining a feeling of pity and awe. Again, he himself gives us the best discussion of his procedures. To attain this effect, the writer's technique must be that of the calculated lie. Certainly, he wants to be true, but he also wants to move, and "eloquence is a kind of lie, and there is nothing more contrary than poetry to the illusion of truth." The problem is then to ally truth with exaggeration, and this is how it can be done: "He will strew his narration with trivial circumstances closely connected with the action, strokes so simple, so natural and yet so difficult to imagine, that you will be forced to say to yourself: My word, that is true; things like that are not invented." There is certainly eloquence and emotion in *The Nun*, and never are "the little true facts" forgotten.

The influence of Richardson is visible throughout in the effort to arouse compassion through the heroine's self-analysis, and in the general tone of the work. In all his fiction, Diderot prefers unusual characters with strong passions who do as they want in defiance of obstacles and even risk their lives. But Diderot is not a mere imitator. Here, as in his other novels and short stories, he is an originator, experimenting with new techniques. Not only the graphic realism, but the portrayal of sexual deviation push back the still limited confines of the eighteenth-century novel. It is true that in the midst of the general currents of sentimental, picaresque, adventurous, and didactic novels, Duclos and much later the Marquis de Sade also dealt with abnormality. But only Diderot and Restif de la Bretonne united artistic power with penetrating psychological naturalism.

Diderot did not dare to publish *The Nun*. In 1780, he revised it completely and carefully. It did not appear until 1796, although it was known in Germany before that date, thanks to the manuscripts circulated by Grimm.

2

Diderot's literary masterpiece is a dialogue entitled *Rameau's Nephew*. Schlosser, the German critic, ranks its protagonist alongside Hamlet, Faust, Richard III, and Don Quixote. Goethe called it "the classical work of an outstanding man." Brilliant, full of paradoxes, it treats of a hundred topics, hopping from one to another, in a way that is only apparently without order, but that is disconcerting to one who approaches the author for the first time. It is a difficult piece, too, for the numerous allusions to contemporary events, people and ideas, requiring ample annotation for its full understanding. But despite the variety of anecdotes, satire, and philosophic discussion, *Rameau's Nephew* is not a potpourri. In the consistent personality of its protagonist, Jean François Rameau, nephew of the famous composer, Diderot holds fast to the highest esthetic unity; the episodic stems from him, serves to illuminate him, never dominates him.

Diderot knew Rameau well, having conversed with him often in the lanes of the Tuileries and in the Café de la Régence. He was a most unusual figure, a bohemian with startling ideas and a dramatic way of expressing them. Once started, he accompanied his talk with amazing antics and clownery. The strange fascination of this man was felt by a number of those who knew him, including such disparate characters as Grimm, Fréron, Cazotte, and Mercier, but by none so much as Diderot. For years the figure of Rameau haunted him, troubled him in some way, until he was impelled for once to leave writing of the tendentious type and forge a masterpiece that, despite the ideas it contains, stands up as a superb esthetic creation.

The reasons for this attraction are complex but not difficult to understand. Rameau was the man Diderot might have been—indeed had started out to be—were it not for the resurgence of his middle-class heritage, with its longing for security and respectability, its love of moralizing. In Rameau, Diderot saw the picture of his own youth, with the question that dominated all its days: where would the next meal, the next bed be found? It filled him with a combination of nostalgia for the irresponsible, adventurous, precarious *vie de bohême* he had given up, and horror, a fascinated horror at the sight of what he might have become. Rameau was an epical example of failure. The suspicion that he too was a failure undoubtedly tormented Diderot, for he longed for immortal fame among men. Had he written anything that would remain, after the glory of a day had passed? In 1767 he reassures himself that though he has as yet written no masterpiece, he has undiminished confidence that some day he will. "When? Tomorrow, perhaps, and who knows what I can do? I feel that I have not yet used half of my ability. Up till now, I have only fooled around." Besides, Rameau was so much like him, in so many ways. The same taste for paradox, the same intransigent materialism of his radical mood, the gift for enthusiastic conversation and gesture, even a similarity in physical appearance.

It was easy for Diderot to identify himself—or rather, one side of himself—with this monster. That was deeply troubling. So easy, that time and again in the dialogue, Diderot lends him his own ideas. Rameau not only becomes the conveyor of his mordant satire— satire of his personal enemies, satire of the degeneracy of French society, and of the fundamentally immoral character of all human society—but the mouthpiece for some of his favorite theories. It has even been suggested, by Professor Jean Fabre, that Rameau was Diderot's conscience, the living reproach of a man who dared to live the ethics his reason taught him, who lied but did not build his life on a lie, who was true to his innermost nature in defiance of convention. Was this not one of the reasons for his resentment of Rousseau's way of living? Lionel Trilling suggests that Rameau was the *id*, Diderot the *ego*. In Rameau's bohemian escapades and materialist paradoxes, Diderot has put the most original part of his own complex personality, so that he is forced, in the dialogue, to defend himself, for having led a moral, conventional life.

Two facts testify to the special nature of *Rameau's Nephew*, in the repertory of Diderot's works. It is the only one of his un-published writings that he kept from even his closest friends (until he eventually gave the manuscript to Grimm), which seems to point to the intimate nature of its exploration. It is the opus that he worked on longest and reworked the most, the actual composition extending from 1762 until 1777 or even 1779. In none other of his writings, with the possible exception of *Jacques the Fatalist*, are the symphonics of a complicated, polyphonal structure so carefully worked out, narration, satire, philosophy, pantomime intertwining and balancing each other. Diderot was, in the first place, etching a portrait, and its accuracy is amply attested to. But the portrait was gradually transformed from a merely individual likeness to the esthetic creation of a supreme literary type, in the great tradition of a Sancho Panza or a Becky Sharpe, combining universal value with the concreteness of a living individual. A man who had failed in his efforts to attain heroic stature in the realm of amoral living was endowed with a stature and a symbolic content he never had in life. This is literary creation, in its truest sense, something Diderot was usually unable to accomplish out of his own mind exclusively.

Rameau himself is a figure of startling reality. Physically, men-tally, and morally, his portrait is clearly drawn, or rather he is made to breathe and act and talk. He comes to us as the parasite raised to heroic proportions, far surpassing his prototypes in Plautus, Terence, and Lucian, the parasite plumbed in all the depths of his misery, "close to the tragic when he clowns, never more clownish than when he tries to be serious." Rameau is the man who lives by his vices, playing the jester, the fawner, the hypocrite, the pander, debasing himself in order to give others the satisfaction of despising him: "never false, as long as it pays me to be true; never true, as long as it pays me to be false." These others, the powerful of the earth, are the ones who control the means to satisfy the motive of all human conduct—the desire to masticate. These others are worse than Rameau, he himself explains, for they have all his vices, but veneer them with respectability, while he is unashamedly sincere in confessing his vileness. "You know that I am an ignoramus, a fool, a madman, an impudent, lazy cuss, what our Burgundians call a thorough scoundrel, a crook, a glutton. . . . It is hard to be a beggar, when there are so many rich fools at whose expense you can live. . . . My only merit lies in having done in a systematic way, out of proper understanding, out of a reasonable and true view of things, what most others do by instinct."

Vileness, yes, but with an awareness and a pride that almost lifts him above it. The only scorn he has for himself is when he feels that he is not doing as well as he should in plucking the ripe plums, or that others like him have succeeded better in the game of wits that life is. For his pride lies in surpassing all others of his kind. He boasts of his inventions—more than a hundred different ways of seducing a girl, in front of her mother, and even making the mother an accomplice. Rameau's greatest sorrow was the loss of his wife. On thinking of her, he enters into a rapturous, lecherous description. "But alas I've lost her; and with her all my hopes for fortune. I had taken her only for that, I had told her my plans. . . . Sooner or later she would have had the *fermier général*, at least." But the dream is gone, the hope of reversing the roles. If only that could happen, he would know how to command, and be fawned and waited on, and eat, and roll on pretty women—"we'll have all kinds of vices; it will be delightful."

And yet, with all Rameau's cynicism and bravado, there is in him a sense of failure as a human being that raises him to a tragic level. Part of his tragedy lies in his effort to reach sublime heights. "If it is important to be sublime in any field, it is most of all in evil. You spit on a petty thief; but you can't refuse respect of a kind to a great criminal." But his longing to be respected even in this way was not achieved. There is a subtle "double-play" here. Despite the epic character Rameau does attain in Diderot's pages, we are given to understand that in his actual life Rameau had some ineradicable traces of decency. Referring perhaps to the fact that he did not "profit" from his wife's beauty, Diderot accuses him of vacillation and of not having attained either complete unity of character or perfection in evil. Then he gives way to despair at not having been able to accomplish anything great as a musician, at having failed in everything. His failure as a parasite resulted from a sense of dignity that stubbornly refused to die even in him. "There must be a certain dignity attached to the nature of a man, and nothing can stifle it. It is aroused by a trifle. Yes, by a trifle; for there are other days when it means nothing to me to be as vile as you wish . . . I am willing to be abject, but I don't want to be forced to it. I am willing to forego my dignity . . . You laugh? . . . Everyone has his dignity; I am willing to forget mine, but when I want to, and not on someone else's order." We remember that Rameau had turned an inheritance over to his father. We feel that his pride in his very abjection is a desperate if perverted effort to save himself from the most intolerable of human situations, that of despising oneself. Cynics and parasites were common enough in the decadent world of eighteenth-century Paris. Some were brutal and extreme, some equally rational. But Rameau distinguishes himself from all the others by his soul-searching and his anguish.

When the story is over, we know Rameau. We have heard him and we have seen him; heard him in pages of scintillating dialogue, seen him enact his ideas and roles in the most brilliant pantomime that has ever been set down in the pages of a book. To hear him tell of how he seduced a girl, for a price, and then portray the nuances of the art of flattery, to watch him enact a dozen satirical pantomimes, is to realize that Diderot himself has accomplished a literary performance nowhere else equaled. The art of pantomime he had always been enamored of, and it played a large part in the theory and technique of his dramas. But pantomime was wasted in the wooden, garrulous abstraction of his plays. In the living model of Rameau, it was able to come to life and animate a character who is ethically of universal significance, if esthetically particular and unique.

To follow the modulations of Diderot's reactions to the unfolding of Rameau's personality is an interesting chapter in itself. The moralist is quick to decry the frankness of his vice.

"You are a lazy good-for-nothing, a glutton, a coward, a soul of mud."
"I thought I told you all that."
"The (material) things of life have their value, of course; but you are not aware of the value of what you are sacrificing to get them."

Sometimes the wrath is tempered, despite himself, with laughter. "Twenty times a burst of laughter prevented my anger from breaking forth; twenty times the anger that rose in my heart ended with a burst of laughter. I was amazed by so much wisdom, and so much vileness; by ideas alternately so true and so false; by so general a perverseness of feelings, so complete a turpitude, so uncommon a frankness." At another time admiration alone will prevail, for Rameau's candor, his consistency, his profound understanding of human nature.

One result of the portraits of the two speakers, "He" and "I"— a result Diderot was certainly aware of—is the dissociation and confrontation of the two tendencies that are notable throughout his life and work. Rameau is the materialist, whose consequent ethics is complete amoralism. This parasite, musician, and buffoon is "a sort of Nietzschian *avant la lettre,* who deliberately lived beyond good and evil, and professed a distressingly plausible creed of selfishness and immorality."

The materialism of the *Thoughts on the Interpretation of Nature,* and the subsequent philosophical works, could lead to only one logical conclusion: life is a meaningless accident. As Diderot says again in *Rameau's Nephew,* whatever is, is necessary, and therefore is neither good nor evil—an idea he may well have taken from Spinoza. From this theory, two different conclusions are drawn, by each of the protagonists. Rameau remains at the level of natural fact and natural morality. Considering man only on the biological or organic level, he justifies vices as natural, condemns virtues as unnatural. The only law is the struggle for existence and survival of the fit. We not only hear this argued, we see it enacted in Rameau's picture of the "menagerie" of parasites at his patron's house, and of the patrons themselves, a corrosive etching of human vileness that knows only the law of the jungle.

Rameau defends this situation throughout. "Virtue" is "an old word devoid of meaning." Everyone lives for himself. The dead man does not hear the bells. Higher values, such as knowledge, have no *use*. Certainly, people do not mind being honorable, except when it comes to their professions or business; as "universal grammar" has exceptions, or idioms, so does "universal conscience." The lesson Rameau reads from *Tartuffe* is precisely the one Rousseau had warned against: to be a hypocrite, but more cleverly. In morals, there is nothing true or false except as interest dictates; "virtue" is often vice, and "vice" is virtue. He who is fleeced or cheated is as deserving of his misfortune as if he put his hand in the tiger's cage. "That is all written in the tacit pact." The only god to be worshipped is money, for it alone brings happiness and power. How one gets it is meaningless in the historical perspective; success alone has meaning, and a rich villain is more respected than an honest beggar. Rameau is strongly reminiscent of the great figures of the Spanish picaresque novel, of Lazarillo de Tormes, or Quevedo's Pablo the Sharper. All of life's motives are egotistical and base. The world is a hunting wood. There are no duties, no rights. Honest labor is for fools.

The character of Rameau's remarks, and of Diderot's reaction to them, is best illustrated by a section of the dialogue.

HE—Ah, there you are, *monsieur le philosophe*. And what are you doing among all these loafers? Do you also spend your time pushing wood? (That is what they scornfully call chess and checkers.)

I—No, but when I have nothing better to do, I enjoy watching for a while those who push it well.

HE—In that case you rarely amuse yourself; except Légal and Philidor, the rest don't know what it's all about.

I—You are hard to please, and I see you spare only sublime men.

HE—Yes, in chess, checkers, poetry, eloquence, music, and other baubles. What's the use of mediocrity?

I—Very little, I agree. But you see there must be a lot of people trying in order to discover the genius. He is one of the crowd . . . But what have you been doing recently?

HE—What you and I and everybody else does, good, evil, and nothing. And then, I've been hungry, and I ate, when I had a chance to; after eating, I was thirsty, and I drank, sometimes. Meanwhile, my beard grew, and when it came I shaved it off . . . That's the way you are, you philosophers, you think that the same happiness is made for everybody. What a strange vision! You decorate that queer idea with the name of virtue, and you call it philosophy. But are virtue and philosophy made for everyone? Imagine the world wise and philosophical; admit that it would be devilishly sad. Here! Long live the philosophy of Solomon: drink good wine, gorge yourself with delicious food, roll over pretty women, rest in soft beds—the rest is vanity.

I—What! To defend one's country? . . .

HE—Vanity! There are no more countries: from one pole to the other I see only tyrants and slaves.

I—To serve one's friends?

HE—Vanity! Do we have friends? And even if we did, why should we make ingrates of them?

I—To follow a career in society and do one's duty?

HE—Vanity! What does a career matter, as long as you're rich, since we take up a profession only to become rich? Do one's duty, what does that lead to? Jealousy, trouble, persecution.

I—To take care of our children's upbringing?

HE—Vanity! That's a tutor's job.

I—But suppose this tutor, penetrated with your own principles, neglects his duty, who will suffer for it?

HE—Well, it won't be I. Maybe my daughter's husband, or my son's wife.

I—But suppose they dishonor themselves?

HE—No matter what you do, you can't dishonor yourself when you are rich. . . .

I— . . . What makes those social butterflies so delicate about their amusements is their profound idleness. Since they never get tired, they can never relax. Pleasure is always a business for them and never a need.

HE—Good! A need is always disagreeable.

I—They wear out everything. Their senses become dulled, boredom overcomes them. I don't despise sensual pleasures. I have a palate too, and it is flattered by delicate food and delicious wine; I have a heart and eyes, and I like to see a pretty woman, I like to feel under my hand the roundness and firmness of her breast, to press her lips against mine, to expire in her arms; sometimes a good debauchery, in the company of my friends, doesn't displease me. But it is infinitely sweeter to me to help an unfortunate person . . . to give some useful advice, to read something delightful, to walk with a man or a woman dear to my heart, to spend some instructive hours with my children, to write a fine page, to perform the duties of my profession. . . .

HE—Then, according to you, we should be virtuous people?

I—To be happy, certainly.

HE—Still I see an infinity of good people who are not happy and an infinity of bad men who are.

I—That's what you think.

HE—As long as I can be happy with the vices that are natural to me, I'd be very queer to torment myself like a damned soul to twist myself into somebody I'm not. All that to give myself a character that doesn't belong to me, some very estimable qualities, I'll admit it for the sake of argument, but which would be painful for me to acquire and to practice, which would lead to nothing, maybe to worse than nothing. People praise virtue but they hate it, but they fly from it, but it freezes them, and in this world we've got to have warm feet. And then that would always make me ill-tempered, and I've got to be gay, funny, clownish, amusing. Virtue makes itself respected and respect is annoying. Virtue makes itself admired, and admiration isn't very amusing . . . To cut it short, I don't care for your kind of happiness or that of other visionaries like you.

I—I can see, my dear fellow, that you don't know what it is, and that you're not even capable of learning.

HE—No, God damn it! And so much the better. It would make me die of hunger, boredom, and maybe even remorse.

The morality represented by Diderot himself in the dialogue accepts the denial of transcendental good or evil. But it finds in man a universal experience and a universal nature: physical and emotional needs, structure, feelings. His preaching of virtue is based on the need for happiness that derives from this common nature and experience. The assumption of the "moral" Diderot is the one we have noted before—that virtue and happiness are equivalent, vice and happiness exclusive. Morality is based also on the love which experience teaches us to have for other men, on the desire for reputation and immortality on earth. This is what he terms the "moral fibre," and again it brings to mind Rousseau's moral intuition and Kant's moral reason. Both Rameau and Diderot proclaim a "human" philosophy, but the identity of terms conceals a fundamental incompatibility. "Human" for Rameau refers to man's needs as contrasted with the impersonality of the cosmos. "It is natural to be hungry . . . and I think that not to have enough to eat is not a good order of things." For Diderot "human" refers to hyper-organic values, or what is specifically *human* and non-animal. An ethical view is pitted against amoralism, or at best, an evolutionary morality.

This does not imply that Rameau is to be sweepingly condemned.

His cry for food is a demand to satisfy what is certainly the most basic need and right, without which the higher values cannot begin to function. As he contends, "the voice of conscience is very weak when your insides are complaining." Diderot, with his full stomach, does not realize this, and minimizes the importance of the organic life. It is Rameau who brings up the fundamental ethical problem of distributive justice. "This is a hell of an economy, with men who have an excess of everything while others have a stomach as nagging as themselves and nothing to put under their teeth."

But Diderot reveals tellingly that human nature is more than brute desire. "Everything that lives," declares Rameau, "seeks its good at the expense of whoever it may be"; if we brought a savage into society, he too would want wealth, women, feasts, and luxuries. Yes, replies Diderot, in a passage Freud has quoted, if we left the savage to himself, "he would twist his father's neck and sleep with his mother." Man is more than animal and has more than simple organic needs and modes of living. True, these others may not be "innate," may derive from experience, but the universal law is established nonetheless—as Plato showed in his theory of the cardinal virtues.

Diderot's role in the dialogue is not a literal one. It involves an esthetic transmutation or *diminishing* of his real self into his personage, "I," even as his adversary is augmented. His place in the esthetic whole is to bring out the character, attitudes, and ideas of personage, "He." Whether it be for this reason, or because of the pragmatic weakness of his philosophic position, Diderot (as we shall continue to call him, for the sake of convenience) does not succeed in imposing his philosophy of virtue, and his abstract moral system appears inadequate face to face with the dynamic vigor and existential realism of his opponent. There are men whom vice does make happy and whom virtue would make unhappy. The wicked are not always punished, but often are admired.

It also appears that the moral problem, for the consistent determinist, is philosophically unsolvable. No matter what twist is taken, there can be no morality without responsibility. We are reduced to considering punishment as the primitive mind does—as a social survival mechanism in which the factor of moral responsibility is simply not taken into account. Diderot once more attempts to escape the impasse by insisting on the modifiability of man, and the influence of law and education. It is these influences that prevent the child from strangling his father when he becomes an adolescent. Of course, what he really means by his word "education" is the development of the social and spiritual levels of the human personality. With specious reasoning, he had insisted, in the letter to Landois and the article "Modification," that necessity is the very guarantee of such modification. "The less a being is free, the more sure you are of modifying it." However, we all know that laws and education have often failed to make men social beings. And the determinist must admit that if an individual is not free to reject modification, neither can he help himself from not being "modified," or sufficiently modified.

Twice Diderot is led to admit—and gladly, for this is his opinion as a humanist—that the human individuality is an element that cannot be overcome by "education." Modifiability is strictly limited by the inherited possibilities. This idea nullifies his "social morality." From another viewpoint, such a system of social sanctions, based purely on what is useful to the group, leads to the absolute tyranny that Rousseau was to fall into in his *Social Contract*. However, while complete social control is one possible deduction from materialism (as in communism), and there is a hint of this in his principle of modification, Diderot never develops such a theory. On the contrary, in the person of Rameau, in the *Voyage to Bougainville,* and in other pieces, his materialism leads to an opposing conclusion: an anarchistic, typically Sophist claim for the primacy of the individual, heralding the revolt of his instinct against social discipline.

> The child of nature abhors slavery;
> Implacable foe of all authority,
> He rages at the yoke, constraint maddens him:
> Liberty, that is his wish; his cry is liberty. . . .
> Nature has made neither servant nor master;
> I wish neither to give, nor to receive laws.

Diderot's problem was indeed unsolvable. His defense of genius and individuality is based on a pluralistic philosophy that invests primary reality and significance in the individual. This pluralism is at times humanistic, at times anti-humanistic in some of its materialistic conclusions. But no less dear to him was a quite contrary belief in the primacy of the whole. "The system of the individual must not be preferred to that of the species," he writes in the article "Particular." And to Falconet: "For the individual passes, but the species has no end, and that is what justifies the man who sacrifices himself." Here, then, we have a distinctly monist philosophy; the individual is inseparable from the whole, in which alone he can find his meaning.

Diderot has properly been called the greatest experimenter in morals before André Gide. With Rameau, as with Saunderson, in the *Letter on the Blind*, he has used a monster as a concrete instance with which to challenge an abstract philosophy.

From a broader perspective, *Rameau's Nephew* marks the beginning of a new and critical phase of Diderot's work. Alongside of his cosmological and scientific speculations, he will embark on a whole series of works which are literally *experiments* in morals. They include all his remaining dialogues and short tales, and his important novel, *Jacques the Fatalist*. In all of these, Diderot tests abstract ethical theories in the light of real persons and real situations—or else unusual characters who embody extreme attitudes—in order to determine their truth and viability. Both interlocutors in *Rameau's Nephew* defend systematic reductions or formulations of behavior and of values; both viewpoints are shown to be inconsistent or unworkable. In many of these writings, we meet characters who are distinguished by their *greatness*, especially by their greatness in evil. This is another problem, and a relevant one, which fascinated Diderot. Even as men in general rise above the first or mechanical level of nature to a human socio-moral level, does not the "exceptional" individual become a legitimate "exception" to the second level? Aren't the normal rules and restrictions of morals meant for normal men? Are they not obstacles to greatness, which the great man will hurdle and ignore? Perhaps. But then he must be truly great, or else he will be crushed. And Rameau (like Gousse and Friar John in *Jacques the Fatalist*), though he thirsts for such greatness, lacks it, both in imagination and in effective action. To be great as a parasite is a contradiction in terms. The renunciation of dignity cannot be a road to the conquest of dignity. Also, at bottom, there is too much of a desire for bourgeois security, too much infiltration of moral feelings, even in Rameau, for him to be consistent, great and successful in evil.

Finally, in this series of moral experiments, Diderot comes to grip with the deepest problem of his time and of ours: nihilism, or the challenge to the legitimacy of any moral restrictions or distinctions. Having thrown off a Christian, or supernatural morality, what new basis of authority (or authorization) could be found that would justify restricting the aggressive demands of the ego? This is the inner problem and meaning of most eighteenth-century writings on ethics, and of Diderot's. In these works, then, he uncovers—as in Rameau, and in Rameau's picture of human society—the persistent nihilism of human nature, which is veneered by a secondary mask of culture, or moral behavior. Human life and actions all appear suddenly absurd, as we confront naked existence in its meaninglessness. They are reduced to what Rameau calls "the pantomime of the positions," the vile, hypocritical posturings of the *persona*. If Rameau attains greatness at all, it is in pantomime—not in life, but in an imitation of life; not in the sphere of moral experience, as a man, but in the sheltered realm of esthetic experience, as a clown. His performance is not only without dignity and moral value; by incorporating absurdity as its very essence, it denounces the absurdity of our values, of our acts, of our existence.

Later, in the *Refutation of Helvétius,* Diderot will admit his failure to accomplish what he would have liked, more than all else, to have done during his lifetime: to find an intellectually persuasive justification of moral values. He will have to settle for the level of life, which has its own truth, realities, and requirements. His "moral experiments" all show that these do exist and that they are beyond the grasp of discursive reason. On this level, he will, as always, preach moral virtue as the foundation of social welfare and of individual happiness.

Rameau's Nephew, unpublished during Diderot's lifetime, enjoyed the most amazing of all the romantic adventures undergone by his manuscripts. It is doubtful that Naigeon, Diderot's literary executor, possessed a copy, for he did not publish it, and when his library was sold, in 1819, it contained no manuscript of *Rameau's Nephew.* Meanwhile, in 1804, Goethe had translated and published a copy of the original manuscript given to him by Schiller, that had somehow come out of Russia, where Diderot's library had gone after his death. It was not until 1821 that *Rameau's Nephew* was published in French, by two men, de Saur and de Saint-Geniès, who claimed to have the authentic manuscript. What they had done was merely to re-translate Goethe's translation, with many mistakes, changes, and interpolations. This falsification lasted until 1823, when Brière published his edition of Diderot's works, with a fairly authentic but imperfect and bowdlerized text of *Rameau's Nephew,* taken from a copy of the original manuscript given to him by Diderot's daughter. De Saur and de Saint-Geniès had the temerity to deny the authenticity of the Brière edition. Believing that attack is the best method of defense, they boldly accused it of being a translation of the German edition. A controversy followed that aroused the entire French reading public. Finally, Brière appealed to Goethe himself. He replied that the Brière edition seemed to him authentic, and the translators were discredited. In the course of the nineteenth century, several other copies were found, permitting the establishment of a more exact text. From Leningrad came the "original manuscript," sent there with his library—but which now turns out to have been a copy of the original (a slight case of deception on the part of Diderot's daughter?). And finally, in 1891, on the quais along the Seine, Georges Monval, leafing through volume 186 of a collection of tragedies and miscellanies, stumbled upon the real original, in Diderot's autograph. Ironically, the three-hundred volume collection in which it was found had been assembled in the first half of the nineteenth century by a minor French diplomat with a passion for collecting, a passion he sometimes satisfied in devious ways that made publicity undesirable. In all probability, Diderot had given the manuscript to Grimm, who had kept it after the author's death, taking it to Germany when he left France in 1792. Why or how it disappeared from Grimm's library is a mystery. But the manuscript's travels were not yet at an end. The curious American scholar can now consult it in the J. Pierpont Morgan Library in New York.

CHAPTER 13

Life
Among
the
Philosophes

1

TWICE A YEAR OR MORE, Diderot sought refuge from the unending war and the confining atmosphere of the Rue Taranne. At the country estates of Mme. d'Epinay and the baron d'Holbach—the inner sanctums of "philosophy"—the most rebellious and radical elements of his personality could blossom in a hospitable and nourishing soil.

Diderot and Mme. d'Epinay had become such good friends that she found herself confiding all her troubles to him. He would console her from time to time for Grimm's "brutalities," and when he could not visit her, send her the intimate details of his indigestions. Occasionally Diderot found her weeping bitter tears. Grimm was bored; he didn't see her except when he had to; when he saw her, he remained moodily silent; worse still, he deceived her with little lies. In truth, Grimm always remained faithful to her. But as he became absorbed in his *Literary Correspondence,* and later in diplomatic activities that required frequent travel in Germany and Russia, he neglected her more and more. For a Frenchman love can dominate all; for a Teuton there is more serious business in life.

The philosopher tried to soothe her feelings with consoling

words: "But he is young, but he is faithful, but you love him." Yet, when Grimm failed to come to her, after a long absence, despite his promise, he could find no words of consolation. "Does he still love me?" she asked him. "What the devil could I answer to that? You can't tell the truth; you simply have to lie. Let us allow her to keep her illusion; the moment of her disillusion would perhaps be her last."

Diderot grew accustomed to spending a week or two either at La Chevrette, or at the less pretentious La Briche. Himself almost a rustic by birth, his love of the countryside developed instinctively. To the formal gardens of conventional, classical taste, he preferred nature untouched by man. Evidently, La Briche was preferable to La Chevrette: "The house is small, but everything around it, the waters, the gardens, the park, has a wild appearance. That is the place to live, and not in that sad and magnificent Château de la Chevrette. Immense ponds, with steep banks covered with reeds and swampy grasses; an old ruined, moss-covered bridge that crosses them; groves where no gardener's scythe has cut; trees that grow as nature pleases . . . that is what I enjoy."

Life in the country was simple, intimate, refreshing: "conversations, serious or jesting, walks, alone or together, much reading, thinking, silence, solitude, and the rest." In the morning, he generally stayed in his room, reading, and writing to Sophie. A long dinner was followed by a chess game and a walk. After a rest, there followed an hour or two of conversation, supper, some more conversation "and thus an innocent and sweet day will end during which we have been busy and amused, during which we have meditated, learned, and loved."

Sometimes they were joined by other guests. One day they were surprised by Saint-Lambert, his mistress Mme. d'Houdetot, and various friends. This was the occasion for a party dinner, after which the company gathered in the salon to hear some music, to wit, clavecin and the voice of a young girl, whose modesty, innocence, and charm delighted Diderot. "Who would dare to change anything in that masterpiece," he murmured, as he looked at her with an appreciative eye. "It is so perfect." But his libertine neighbor, M. de Villeneuve, was not of his opinion; he replied that when he met innocent girls, he liked to instruct them. At six, a party of hunters returned, and dancing ensued to the tunes of a violin.

When Diderot sprained his ankle, the occasion was utilized to paint him, and sitting directly opposite him, Mme. d'Epinay. "She is represented with her breast half-uncovered; some scattered curls hang over her neck and shoulders; the others tied with a blue ribbon that circles her brow; her mouth is half-open; she is breathing and her eyes are full of languor. She is the image of tenderness and voluptuousness."

A frequent caller at La Chevrette was the parish priest, a jolly old fellow with the most unusual physiognomy, which Diderot, with his talent for caricature, described for Sophie. "He praises with his nose, he blames with his nose, he prophesies with his nose . . . anyone who understands the nose of the curé has read a great moral treatise." Then there were the dramatist Saurin, whose declarations of love were gently but firmly turned down by Mme. d'Epinay, and their old friend, the abbé Raynal. Diderot's favorite dramatist and disciple, Sedaine, was also among the privileged few. Diderot enjoyed telling how he had rushed up, wild-eyed with excitement, to congratulate Sedaine on the success of his play, *The Philosopher Without Knowing It*. When he threw his arms about his neck, with tears in his eyes, Sedaine withdrew a pace, looked at him coldly, and commented: "Ah, Monsieur Diderot, how handsome you are like that!"

Diderot's stays at d'Holbach's estate, Grandval, were more frequent and longer. There the company was gayer and more numerous, the discussions more vigorous, and the food beyond compare. The proprietor of Grandval was really Mme. d'Aine. German by birth, she was the mother of d'Holbach's first and second wives, and an inimitable Rabelaisian character. At fifty, she preserved intact the spirit of youth.

One night, suddenly remembering that the fire had not been put out, she got out of bed and went downstairs clad only in her night gown, with a little night-lamp in her hand. As she was coming down, she was met by one of their guests, Le Roy. He was a gallant young man who enjoyed staying up late and reading alone by the fire in the immense livingroom. Diderot described their encounter, for Sophie's entertainment. "They see each other. Mme. d'Aine runs away; M. le Roy pursues her, grabs her by the waist and kisses her. And she starts to cry, 'Help! Help!' The kisses of her ravisher prevented her from speaking clearly. 'Help, my sons-in-law! If he gives me a child, so much the worse for you!'" By the time help arrived, Le Roy had fled to his room and the object of his pursuit was found in considerable disarray. Diderot decided that it was quite amusing to see a white, plump woman, almost naked, in the arms of an insolent and lascivious youth. This incident monopolized the next day's conversation. Some of the company declared that Mme. d'Aine had called too soon.

Another time, the "mad Mme. d'Aine" performed a still more astonishing feat. They had been in the midst of a humorous and libertine conversation when the parish priest, who did not hate women, arrived and sat down vis-à-vis Mme. d'Aine. Invited by his posture and the width of his spread, she took an armchair, drew it in front of him and cried: "Abbé, watch out!" and in a jump she was astride his lap. The abbé did not get angry, but held her. "You should have seen the maidservant's face, innocence and modesty itself. She opened her eyes wide, looked at an enormous pool on the floor, and exclaimed: 'Why, madame!' 'Yes, yes, I did it; I'm wet and so is the abbé; quick; shoes, stockings, petticoats!'"

Mme. d'Aine was withal a perfect hostess, constantly preoccupied with her guests' comfort and entertainment. Diderot was quite fond of her. "If she sees that you like a dish, the next day you get it, and so on. She plays cards although she doesn't like to, walks, although she doesn't like walking; she loves to gossip and keeps quiet when we are reading. Then she has a bizarre and frank gaiety that amuses us from morning till night. She always inserts into our philosophy some silly remark that makes it bright."

Le Roy, Mme. d'Aine's assailant, had a fearful reputation as a Don Juan, and mothers locked up their daughters when he called. He made the whole company laugh with his after-dinner anecdotes. One of them told how Saint-Evremond, the seventeenth-century freethinker, fell asleep between two women who were quarreling over the relative beauty of their eyes. They awakened him to act as judge, and asked, "According to your opinion, monsieur, which are the most beautiful?" Saint-Evremond, rubbing his eyes, yawned, "The most beautiful? . . . small and wrinkled ones."—"Small and wrinkled eyes the most beautiful? you don't mean it."—"Oh, you are speaking of eyes!" At this Mme. d'Aine burst out laughing, while d'Holbach's wife looked hard at her embroidery and pretended she hadn't heard.

Mme. d'Holbach, who was the sister of d'Holbach's first wife, was a lovely and charming woman, of whom almost all her guests became enamored. When Diderot told her gallantly that he thought more of her than any of her other admirers, she coquettishly invited him to her toilette the next morning. In the intimacy of the boudoir, before the freshness of her youth, the grace of her movements and her little grimaces, it was a rude test, and only his unattackable fidelity to Sophie and the sacredness of friendship saved the philosopher's virtue—or so he wrote to Sophie. Even while she worked at her embroidery, he feasted his eyes upon her. "Oh, how beautiful she was! What a complexion! And what a costume! A lovely coiffure and a kind of little girl's dress of red taffeta, covered with a transparent white waist through which you could see, here and there, the color of pink."

During one of Diderot's sojourns at Grandval, "the delicate Suard" made a persistent attack on Mme. d'Holbach's virtue. Her resistance was determined, even heroic, but Suard refused to be discouraged. At the same time, in order to avoid the baron's suspicions, he pretended to be courting Mme. Necker. While d'Holbach laughed loudly at his complete lack of success and pretended despair, his own wife finally succumbed to Suard's mastery of the art of seduction. For a while they had quite an affair of which d'Holbach remained blissfully ignorant. Some months later, the lovely mistress of Grandval became seriously ill, and "languished" without any interest in life. The baron made no connection between his wife's sudden illness and Suard's simultaneous announcement of his forthcoming marriage.

But another time it was not so simple. Mme. d'Epinay had complained to a friend of the familiarity between Grimm and "la piquante baronne." The friend talked and the baron was furious. Until Diderot, with much effort and persuasion, was able to smooth ruffled tempers, there was high tension between the baron and Mme. d'Epinay, and Grimm refused to go to Grandval. This episode reveals how the extreme *liberté d'allure*, the principal charm of this rather dissolute society, became painful as soon as suspicion was aroused.

Diderot was the favored guest at Grandval. Everything was done to entice him and to keep him there. Without his conversation the house seemed dead. He alone could shake the baron out of his fits of sullen moodiness and save the entire household from their effects. D'Holbach often made life miserable for everyone by his tyranny and his cutting, humiliating remarks. Diderot wondered how one man could be so unpleasant, and so generous, good-hearted, and intelligent; how one man could be at the same time a bitter misanthrope and a tireless distributor of charity; how in one moment he could delight everybody with his charm and sociability and then distress them with his temper. He predicted that some day d'Holbach would be entirely alone. "What a sad old age awaits him! How I pity those who won't be able to get away from him!" Many was the gay conversation in which the baron placed the only discordant note, and many the conversation in which his unleashed wit and good humor were without equal. "He is original in his tone and in his ideas. Imagine a gay, piquant, indecent satyr, in the midst of a group of chaste, soft, and delicate figures. Such he was amongst us." At other times, he was simply unbearable. "He complains without suffering; he is brusque, pouting; he wants to eat and he doesn't want to, he wants to be alone and he doesn't, he rebuffs you if you try to be nice and growls at you if you don't. . . . We are awaiting the end of our slavery."

The art of social living is often said to have reached its apogee in the eighteenth century. In Diderot's letters we can see that society live again at Grandval, with all its delicacy and all its liberty.

They have put me in a small, separate apartment, quiet, cheerful and warm. It is there that between Horace and Homer, and the portrait of my sweetheart, I spend hours reading, thinking, writing and sighing. That is my occupation from six in the morning until one. . . . We dine well and at length. The table is served here as in the city, and perhaps even more sumptuously. . . . After dinner, the ladies sew ; the baron dozes on a couch ; and as for me, I do what I please. Between three and four, we take our staffs and go for a walk ; the women in their direction, the baron and I in ours. We take very extended excursions. Nothing stops us, neither hills nor forests nor quagmires, nor plowed-up fields. The spectacle of nature pleases both of us. On the way, we talk of history, of politics, of chemistry, of literature, of physics, or of morals. Sunset and the freshness of the evening bring us back to our house, where we scarcely arrive before seven o'clock. The women have already returned and are already changed. There are lights and cards on a table. We rest for a moment ; then we begin a game of piquet. . . . Ordinarily supper interrupts our game. We sup. On leaving the table, we finish our game. It is ten-thirty. We chat until eleven. At half-past eleven, we are all sleeping—or should be. The next day, we begin again.

Diderot enjoyed nothing more than the long walks across field and country, stick in hand, with one or two friends for company and good conversation to cheer the way. Bad weather, unless it was actually storming, could not keep them indoors. "We follow the crest of the hills, at the risk of being swept away by the wind. For two days, the barometer has been below the tempest reading. It seems that my head is wild in the high winds." He feared neither thistles nor thorns nor dung—which he said smelled much better than a perfumed woman. He enjoyed the fields and rivers and lakes and hills, watched the wagons loaded with hay and wheat amble across the farms "I am a rustic and proud of it." A pre-romantic in so many of his emotions, acutely sensitive to beauty in all its forms, Diderot did much more than merely look at nature. Nature calmed him, he became lost in revery, and, like Rousseau, fused his entire being with the earth around him. "It is a persuasion that we breathe, an example with which we conform by a natural inclination to harmonize with everything we see. The immobility of the trees stops us; makes our eyes and our soul get lost in the expanse of a plain; the steady monotonous murmur of the waters rocks us to sleep. It seems that everything lulls us in the fields; we share the revery of the Being who formed the disorder of this scene."

Diderot loved good eating, and the table at Grandval was eminently satisfactory to his epicurean tastes. "I still have eight days to spend here," he informs Sophie. "Pray to God that I don't die of indigestion. Every day they bring us from Champigny the most furious and perfidious eels and then little melons, and then sauerkraut, and then partridge with cabbage, and then partridge squabs cut open and broiled, and then *babas,* and then meat pies and then pies, and then twelve stomachs you need, and then a stomach in which you put enough for twelve. Fortunately, we drink in proportion and it all passes."

When rainy days kept the household confined, billiards, cards, and reading were among the favored distractions. Diderot dreamed of Sophie and wrote her minute accounts of all that was said and done. "Mme. d'Holbach is wearing out her eyes sewing; Mme. d'Aine is digesting, sprawled across some cushions; Father Hoop, his eyes half closed, his head perched between his two shoulders and his hands clasped to his two knees, is dreaming, I think, of the end of the world. The baron is reading, wrapped in his dressing gown and lost in a nightcap. As for me, I walk up and down mechanically. I go to the window to look at the weather, and I think the skies are dissolving into water, and I am filled with despair. Is it possible that I have already lived for two weeks without hearing from you?"

Hoop—"Father Hoop," Diderot called him, because of his melancholy—probably was John Hope, a Scottish surgeon and intellectual who later founded the "Select Society" of Edinburgh, in company with Adam Smith, David Hume, and Allan Ramsay—all frequenters of the Holbachian circle. Diderot met him in October 1759, when Sophie had been carried away by her wrathful mother and he had gone to Grandval to console himself with good company and philosophy. Hoop—to use Diderot's transcription—had studied in Paris many years before and had returned for the same purpose. He was welcomed by d'Holbach, who had once taken some courses with him at Leyden and who may have thought that Hoop, like Diderot, could help him in his own work.

Hoop's travels as a ship's doctor to the four corners of the globe had only deepened his cynicism and hypochondria. To Diderot he was an example of the typical Englishman, driven to wandering, and frequently to suicide, by melancholy—or more exactly by that fashionable malady of the body and soul called "spleen." During one of their long walks Father Hoop himself explained to the philosopher the symptoms of that woeful disease. "For twenty years I have felt a general restlessness. Sometimes it is like a weight dragging me forward that would pull me from a window into the street, or into the bottom of a river if I were on the shore. I suffer from somber ideas, sadness, and boredom; I am uncomfortable everywhere, I don't want anything, I try in vain to amuse myself and to keep busy; the merriment of others depresses me, I suffer at hearing them laugh or talk. Do you know that kind of ill humor we feel, on awakening, after having slept too well? That is my usual state. Life is tasteless to me. The least variations in the atmosphere are like violent shocks. I can't stay in one place, I must go without knowing where."

While Diderot listened with fascination, Hoop admitted that he had been on the point of committing suicide.

Hoop was well-read in addition to being well-traveled; he had thought deeply on the problems of life and was a keen student of history. All told, he was an invaluable man in a discussion. On one of those rainy days, d'Holbach, tired of his reading, tried to stir up a little conversation. He picked on the Scotsman.

"Well, old mummy, what are you ruminating about?"

"I am ruminating on a very hollow idea."

"And that idea is?"

"Is that at a certain moment Europe came within a hair of seeing the pontificate and royalty united in one person and of falling again under a sacerdotal government."

"When and how was that?"

"It was when they deliberated whether or not to allow priests to marry. The Fathers at the Council of Trent, attached to miserable, petty concerns of ecclesiastical discipline, were far from realizing the importance of the matter."

"My word, I don't see it any more than they."

"Listen. If they had allowed priests to marry, isn't it certain that the sovereign could have made himself a priest, and united in his person the ecclesiastical and temporal power?"

A long discussion followed on the consequences of such an eventuality on knowledge, oppression of the people, hieroglyphic writing, and other matters. "And if all that had taken place, my daughter," was Mme. d'Aine's comment, "you would sleep with a priest and make little priests."

One October day, Diderot left early to visit a "poor devil" who wanted his advice on some financial project. When he came home, it was cold and windy. After three games of *trictrac* with a lovely lady, he, Father Hoop, and the baron pulled their chairs around a stout log and began to philosophize on pleasure and pain, the good and the evil in life. The melancholy Scotsman said he did not care about his.

"That's why I gave you a room overlooking the moat," put in Mme. d'Aine. "But you don't seem in a hurry to profit from my attention."

"Perhaps you don't like to drown yourself," added the baron considerately. "If you find the water too cold, Father Hoop, let's have a duel."

To which the Scotsman replied: "Gladly, my friend, on the condition that you will kill me."

Visitors to Grandval would regale the company with the latest gossip from Paris, and frequently they brought some savory anecdote. One is told of the eccentric and miserly old M. de Bacqueville. It was said that he had his wife seduced by a friend so that he could surprise them together and get rid of her. Only recently he had hanged a vicious horse in his stable, to serve as an example to the others.

Father Hoop frequently dug up a tale from the rich storeroom of his experiences. He told of his old obstetrics professor who would worry, during difficult deliveries, about the child dying without benefit of baptism. To prevent such a catastrophe, he baptized it before delivery. "First he pronounced the formula: *Child, I baptize thee;* then, taking a mouthful of water, he applied it suitably and blew as hard as he could. Wiping his mouth with a towel, he would say: 'It takes only the hundredth part of a drop to make an angel!' "

Then there was Marchais, a sailor, who horrified the philosopher with his account of the hardships of life at sea. "Ah, dear friend, what a picture! The skin wrinkles and blackens, the lips dry up, the muscles bulge and harden. They eat only hard tack and salted meat. Often they lack water, and then there are tempests that keep you between life and death for twenty-four hours."

This account certainly did not decrease his aversion to travel. With his usual tactlessness, he asked Marchais how old he was.

"Thirty years old."

"Thirty years old! You look at least like forty-five!"

Diderot must have been thinking of the intimacy and charm of Grandval when he said that Rousseau was a barbarian. "By *barbarity,* I understand that sombre disposition which makes a man insensitive . . . to the charms of society."

Contemporaries have left us ample testimony of Diderot's prowess as a conversationalist. "His face shining with the fire of inspiration," writes Marmontel, "Diderot spread his light in all minds, his warmth in all hearts; he who has known Diderot only in his writings, has not known him. His discussion was animated, perfectly sincere, subtle without obscurity, varied in its forms, brilliant in imagination, fertile in ideas and provocative to his listeners. You could let yourself go for hours at a time. . . . I have experienced few greater intellectual pleasures."

Diderot was complacently aware of his talent, and his power to create an effect. His satisfaction bubbles over in a letter to Sophie.

I seemed extraordinary to them, inspired, divine. Grimm didn't seem to have eyes enough to see me, nor ears enough to hear me. Everybody was astonished. I myself felt a contentment within me that I can't express. It was like a fire burning in my depths that seared my breast, spread over them and set fire to them. It was an evening of enthusiasm of which I was the hearth.

One of the amusing features of Diderot's conversation was his occasional tendency to turn it into a monologue, preventing by a continuous flow of eloquence any possibility of reply. That this trait has been exaggerated is apparent, for the discussions at Grandval were usually many sided and Diderot proved himself a good listener as well as a good talker. Nevertheless, the following account of a "conversation" with him, written by a young visitor, is priceless, even if exaggerated.

He doesn't appear any more surprised to see me than to see the return of day. He spares me the trouble of stammering clumsily the purpose of my visit. He apparently guesses it from the great air of admiration with which I must have been covered. He also spares me the long meanderings of conversation which it seemed absolutely necessary to lead to the question of verse and prose. Scarcely has the question been broached, when he gets up, his eyes are fixed on me, and it is quite clear that he no longer sees me at all.

He begins to speak, but at first so low and so quickly, that although I am right next to him, although I am touching him, I can scarcely hear and follow him. Little by little, his voice rises and becomes distinct and sonorous ; at first he was almost motionless ; his gestures become frequent and animated. He has never seen me before this moment ; and when we are standing, he puts his arms around me ; when we are seated, he slaps my thigh as if it were his.

If the rapid and fleeting associations of his talk bring up the word "laws," he sketches for me a plan of legislation ; if they bring up the word "theater," he gives me five or six plots for dramas or tragedies to choose from. As for the tableaux which it is necessary to put on the stage, where scenes without dialogue are to be heard, he recalls that Tacitus was the greatest painter of antiquity, and he recites or translates for me the *Annals* and the *Histories*.

But how horrible it is that the barbarians have buried under the ruins of architectural masterpieces such a great number of the masterpieces of Tacitus! Thereupon he becomes moved over the loss of so many beauties which he regrets and weeps as if he had known them. At least if the monuments which have been dug up in the excavations at Herculaneum could uncover a few books . . . and this hope transports him with joy. . . .

And thereupon he expatiates like an Italian engineer on the methods of excavating in a prudent and successful way. Letting his imagination roam over the ruins of ancient Italy, he recalls how the arts, the taste, and the politeness of Athens had softened the terrible virtues of the conquerors of the world. He transports himself to the happy days of Lillius and Scipio, where even conquered nations attended with joy the triumphal celebrations for the victories that had been won over them. He recites me an entire scene from Terence ; he almost sings several songs of Horace. Finally he ends up by actually singing a song full of wit and grace which he composed himself as an impromptu at a supper, and by reciting to me a very pleasant comedy of which he has had a single copy printed to save himself the trouble of copying it.

Many people then enter his apartment. The noise of chairs pushed forward and backward disturbs him in his enthusiasm and his monologue. He picks me out in the midst of the company, and comes to me as someone whom you find again after having seen him with pleasure a long time ago. He remembers that we have said some very interesting things together about laws, the drama and history ; he has realized that my conversation was very profitable. He urges me to cultivate a friendship whose worth he has felt. On separating, he kisses me twice on the brow, and tears his hand from mine with genuine sorrow.

Diderot's conversation was not always philosophical. It was often gay and often licentious, enlivened by incisive wit or amusing fancy. His comment on the dimensions of the parish priest, for example, was quite pointed: "You could kiss him for three months without stopping, without ever kissing twice in the same spot." There was ever on the tip of his tongue a dozen shocking paradoxes. He outraged Sophie's mother by a series of witty diatribes against marriage: marriage was a vow as crazy as any other, with the one difference that instead of promising to keep your body locked up in a large cell, "you promised to keep a small part of it locked up in a small cell." He might throw out a strange idea, at Grandval, that would keep the whole company in discussion until midnight. "We prepare carefully for the planting of a seed, or a tree, prepare the earth, choose the weather and season; why then do we produce a human being without any forethought or preparation?"

The one annoying quality of Diderot's conversation was his mania for preaching. In his letters and *viva voce,* he was unable to overlook an occasion for moralizing. Grimm received a sermon on the necessity of always following his conscience. To another he might thunder from his imaginary pulpit: "Woe to you if the practice of virtue isn't familiar enough to you, and if you are not rich enough in good deeds to be proud of them, to compliment yourself constantly on them, to be fanatical about them." If there was anything Diderot was fanatical about, it was virtue, and yet how often did he deny its very existence!

2

Diderot would have been perfectly happy at Grandval were it

not that he missed Sophie and Grimm so keenly. He gave many hours to his cherished correspondence with Sophie, filling his letters with expressions of his undying passion and with a detailed account of the day's events and conversation. "One always presses to his heart the one he loves and the art of writing is only the art of stretching out one's arms." Separation was their cruelest enemy. "When I see you again, how I shall embrace you! How I shall rest on you! How I shall seek the one I love! Ah! If only nobody is there to prevent me! But we cannot count on that." If only they could be rejoined! If only they could, "no propriety, no respect could stop me. I would jump on you, hug you with all my strength, keep my face attached to yours until my heart could beat again. Even on talking of that moment, on imagining it, I feel a thrill in all the parts of my body, almost a fainting. Ah, my dear one, how I love you, and how you will see it, when we are returned to each other!" Or another time: "When I am in your arms, it seems that I have never loved you so much as at that moment. But it is an illusion. How is it that the memory of happiness is as strong as gratification itself? Can we compare past transport with present intoxication? I await you to decide."

It was not only to Sophie that Diderot penned these intense expressions of his love. He confided his feeling to Grimm and other friends. To Falconet he writes: "I could see my house burn down, without being upset; my freedom threatened, my life compromised, all sorts of misfortunes come upon me, without complaining, as long as I had her. If she said to me, 'Give me your blood, I want to drink it,' I would slake her thirst until I had none left to give." Even discounting the share of rhetoric and auto-intoxication in this somewhat gruesome expostulation, the sincerity and intensity of feeling remain striking.

His letters to Sophie are a precious document. One can only regret that of five hundred and fifty-three letters, three hundred and sixty-six were destroyed, and others mutilated, by his censorious descendants. Rarely, if ever, has a man revealed so completely his life, emotions, ideas, and interests. Rarely has a reader felt more personal contact with an author.

The extraordinary charm of Diderot's correspondence results partly from the intimacy and intensity of the emotions it contains, partly from the natural, sincere expression, the artlessness and lack of order. "I talk while writing to you, just as if I were beside you, with one arm on the back of your chair." The variety of subject and tone is probably unsurpassed in epistolary literature. Diderot's letters reflect faithfully not only his sensitive, changeable temperament but also the entire social background with which he was in constant contact. They are the best picture of life and customs among the *philosophes*, rich in humorous anecdotes and descriptions, as well as in the faithful reporting of philosophical discussions.

Entertaining, too, are the abstract questions which the two lovers enjoyed debating in their letters. Why are there beautiful old men and no beautiful old women? It is because women are made only for our pleasure, Diderot argues. "When they no longer have that attraction, they have lost everything; no accessory idea makes them interesting, especially since women no longer nurse their children. Formerly, in sorrow, a mother could tear her clothes and plead with her son by the breast that had nourished him—but no longer. If an old woman could have a beautiful head, it would be spoiled by the rags that cover it. We go with bare head; you can see the forest of our white hair [Diderot was practically bald]; a long beard makes our face respectable [Diderot was beardless]; under a wrinkled skin we keep our firm muscles. The soft, round build of women that makes them attractive in their youth, also makes them collapse, flatten, hang, in their old age."

Another knotty issue arose when an unmarried woman of Diderot's acquaintance asked a friend of his ("not himself, of course") to make her a mother; should he satisfy her and be unfaithful to his mistress for just once? (The question of infidelity to his wife was too unimportant for consideration.) A warmly contested discussion followed. Another woman living in poverty with six children was offered a lucrative position for her husband at a price, as Diderot puts it, "that you can guess." Her dilemma was further complicated by the fact that she already had a lover, and would have to be unfaithful to him as well. The poor woman was in a most perplexing situation. Diderot advises her yielding. "Should she refuse him a quarter hour of pleasure in exchange for security for her husband, education for her children, a comfortable position for herself?" A most practical viewpoint! "How things are done in Paris! A job is vacant, a woman solicits it; she lifts her skirts a little, lets them fall again, and there's her husband, formerly clerk at one hundred francs a month, now M. le Directeur at twenty thousand a year. What connection is there between a just or generous action and the voluptuous loss of several drops of a fluid? In truth, I think Nature is concerned neither with good nor evil, but only with two ends: self-preservation and the propagation of the species."

Whenever Sophie's letters failed to arrive on time he was upset in a way more befitting an adolescent than a man of forty-six in love with a woman of forty-two. He walked up and down distractedly. Wild conjectures traversed his tormented mind. "If this continues, I shall go mad. Can that M. Gillet [their intermediary] be a scoundrel?" And Diderot threatens to prosecute him. Or perhaps the fault is Sophie's. "Don't you love me any more? Tell me the truth. Could something have happened to you that you are ashamed to tell me about? Then shouldn't you admit it to me? Do it sooner rather than later. But I am mad; it can be nothing like that." What joy when the long awaited letter finally arrived! "I am sure that on receiving it, my hands trembled, my face was distorted with emotion, my voice quivering."

Sophie, too, was jealous about her lover and concerned about his fidelity—a fact that distressed him exceedingly: how could anyone doubt his constancy? She meant so much to him. "With you, I feel, I love, I listen, I look, I caress. I have a kind of life that I prefer to all else. If you hold me in your arms, I enjoy a happiness beyond which I can conceive nothing." Still she wants to be constantly reassured: "He tells me tender things, he thinks them, but does he tell them only to me?"

Again they seem like two adolescents, as they build an imaginary château and dream of the idyllic life they will have there together. He kisses her letters because her hand has touched them, and places a kiss at the end of his, so that she can do likewise. But at times his compliments—despite his vaunted knowledge of feminine psychology—are amazingly awkward: "Good-bye, my dear, I kiss your brow, your eyes, and your dried-up little face that pleases me as much as a nice plump one. As if that is important at forty-five!"

In his transports of passion, Diderot practically never praises Sophie's beauty, but only her mental and moral qualities. He is already the pre-romantic seeking to idealize his love, and at the same time, the classicist, justifying it by reason. "I love you more and more every day, because of all the virtues I discover in you. Time, which despoils others, makes you more beautiful."

This idealism is by no means incompatible with baser desires. The praise of Sophie's virtue may lead to a precise invitation. "The more I esteem you, the dearer you will be to me. The more virtues I show to you, the more you will love me. It is this idea that consecrates caresses . . . What pettiness in the transports of ordinary lovers! What charms, what elevation, what energy in our embraces! Come my Sophie, come! I feel my heart growing warm." It would be unjust to minimize the purely physical emotion Diderot put into his love for Sophie. His letters abound in exquisite expressions of affection and tenderness. "Do you sleep sometimes like me, with your arms open? How tender your looks were yesterday. Ah, Sophie! You did not love me enough if you love me more today. I kiss you. Oh, I kiss you well, do I not? And it is always the same pleasure for me, always."

Even Grimm recedes before her image. After a long absence, he is about to see Grimm again—but he is also about to see Sophie: "It seems that there is only one thing in the world left for me. I love Grimm; in any other circumstances my heart would have leaped at the very thought of recovering him; with what impatience I should have awaited that dear, dear friend! I scarcely thought of him. It is you, it is you alone who fill me. You annihilate all else in my heart and mind. Is that how you love me? Is that how you wish to be loved?"

He asks her passionately why she believes that he loves her, when he has found so few ways to express his love. "Have I lived beside you? Have you seen me make your happiness the sole care of my days? Have I served you in sickness? Consoled you in sorrow? Succored you in poverty? Have I envied all those who approached you to fix your hair, to dress you, to serve you? Do you know the hundredth part of my passion? Only I know how much I love you. You will never know."

All the emotion of his heart was poured into this love for Sophie. It was a complete love, and at the same time "as pure, as ideal as the ethereal love of Dante, Petrarch, or Lamartine." It was one of the beautiful chapters in his life.

3

Next to love came friendship. Each time that Grimm, who was growing ever harder and more ambitious, ever more the ruthless climber, left on one of his diplomatic junkets, Diderot was filled with melodramatic sadness. "I had foreseen this event. The foreboding of sorrow rarely deceives men. You will not die in my arms. I shall not die in yours, do not expect it, my friend. Some shock will come that will throw us a thousand leagues apart . . . It is midnight. What new affliction will tomorrow bring? Good-night, my dear, my only friend." Diderot corresponded almost as ardently with Grimm as with Sophie, and suffered almost as keenly from his silence. "For Heaven's sake, cruel man, send me a note, as big as your nail, just to tell me you are well and miss me. . . . Tell me anything that comes into your head, as long as I have something to read."

When the moment of reunion finally arrived, he was suffocated with happiness. "With what emotion we embraced! My heart swam. I could not talk, nor could he. We kissed without saying a word, and I wept . . . I love him, and I am tenderly loved. *C'est tout dire* . . . We were up to dessert when they announced: 'It is Monsieur Grimm!'— 'It is Monsieur Grimm!' I repeated with a shout; and I jumped up, and I ran to him and I threw myself at his neck! . . . They treated us like a lover and mistress." *I wept,* but not Grimm! Another time, when Grimm arrived unexpectedly, Diderot was so overcome with emotion, he was unable to eat or to speak. "He was next to me. I clasped his hand and looked at him."

These are certainly extreme expressions of friendship. But the conclusion of one scholar, that there may have been a homosexual relationship between the two men, is utterly baseless and malicious. If there were any psychological peculiarity, it seems rather to have been a dominance of one personality, and a self-abasement of the other. When Sophie Volland objected to Diderot's assertions that Grimm was superior to him, he replied, "I console myself for his superiority by recognizing it. I am vain about the victory I have won over my vanity." He blamed only his own weaker will for Grimm's ascendancy. But the measure of devotion was large. In 1762, when Grimm almost lost his sight, Diderot became agitated, and warned Sophie, "Be careful to say no ill of the man I love most." He almost wished Grimm would become blind, so that he could prove his devotion.

Whenever Grimm left on one of his lengthy journeys, Diderot "put on the shop apron," that is, did Grimm's work of editing *The Literary Correspondence.* He assumed this time-consuming burden at intervals from 1757 to 1772. Nothing was too much to do for Grimm. He stayed up half the night finishing an article, took work with him to Grandval, offered to review all the new plays, even refused an invitation for a stay at La Briche. Time and again he wrote to Sophie that he was completely worn out because of Grimm's work. One job was not completed until he had spent four days in uninterrupted drudgery. "Grimm's shop will be well furnished when he returns . . . I am overwhelmed with fatigue. What consoles me for the fatigue and annoyance is that I am relieving my friend, sparing his eyes." For all this, Grimm apparently showed little gratitude. Once he timidly expressed concern about his friend's time, but was easily silenced by Diderot's more generous reply: "If you truly love me, you will have no regret for my time. What better use of it than to give it to my friend? Isn't that your way of thinking? Take care; or you will begin to resemble that wicked Rousseau, who fears those who enjoy serving him."

Such devotion can be explained only by the intense emotion Diderot put into friendship, and Grimm was the man he had chosen as the great friend of his life. To him he had to give all within him, from him he could keep nothing. "My tender, my only friend," he wrote in 1772, more than twenty years after they had met, "you have always been, you will always be my dear and only friend, even if you killed me with your own hand, for I should prefer to suppose that it was for my own good, rather than impute the slightest wrong to you. I feel bound to you so strongly that I have never separated your actions, good or bad, from mine. It is impossible for me to feel the slightest feeling of gratitude for your favors. Whatever you think, say or do, it is I who am talking, thinking, doing. For twenty years, I have felt myself one in two persons."

At intervals, when his good nature was outrageously abused by the work heaped on him for the *Salons* or *The Literary Correspondence,* Diderot did revolt against Grimm's tyranny. The protest was generally sent to Sophie, however, not to the offender. "I have just received from Grimm a tyrannical letter that hurts my too sensitive spirit . . . He wrote that if it isn't ready tomorrow, I shouldn't bother to finish. I shall avenge myself for this harshness, in a way that befits me. I worked all day yesterday and today. I shall spend the night and all day tomorrow, and at nine o'clock he will receive a volume of writing." At rarer intervals, Diderot dared to express his exasperation to Grimm. Then it was always he who suffered and who yielded, after waiting in vain for Grimm to take the first step. Grimm was protected by an armor of insensitivity, and Diderot knew it. "All you need do is affect an indifference which you know I cannot bear, and I am always the dupe of that ruse." Once when this happened, he wrote to Mme. d'Epinay, complaining of the unhappiness and agitation Grimm had caused him. "He has wounded me mortally . . . I met him twice; it is impossible that he didn't see how sick my soul was. He entered without making the least sign to me; he remained without noticing me. He left without saying a word to me. The man must have the soul of an Hyrcanian tiger." Yet throughout their quarrel, he did not cease for a moment doing the work that Grimm had loaded on his desk, work which brought him neither profit nor fame.

It would be unfair to paint a one-sided friendship. Their loyalty was mutual. Grimm praised and defended Diderot. He called him "the most perfectly moral man I know," and to Diderot's ears there could be no higher praise. Wherever he went, in his literary-diplomatic activities, he stirred interest in Diderot's great enterprise. In days of trial, Grimm gave him moral support, sound advice, and helped in the correction of proof. Because of Grimm, Diderot wrote his magnificent *Salons.* Through Grimm's *Literary Correspondence,* Diderot developed as a critic, and circulated three of his major works that were unpublished during his lifetime: *Jacques the Fatalist, The Nun,* and *D'Alembert's Dream,* with the result that his literary reputation was established much earlier in Germany than in France. Through *The Literary Correspondence,* these works reached the mind of Goethe.

But there is one black mark against Grimm's loyalty. When Stanislas, king of Poland, tried to arrange a personal contact with Diderot, whose work he admired, Grimm's answer was an outright refusal and a scornful estimate of his friend's accomplishments. "Instead of utilizing his time to share the glory of genius with Voltaire, Diderot wastes it writing scrap for these sheets *(The Literary Correspondence)* or giving it away to all who are bold enough to demand it. I dare say to Your Majesty that he will die unknown." This was worse than treachery, it was ingratitude. We should be glad, for Diderot's sake, that he never learned of this double-dealing by the man he loved most.

4

At the gatherings of the clan in Paris, at d'Holbach's "synagogue" in the Rue Royale, the company was more carefully restricted to the encyclopedic clique. Consequently, the emphasis was on political, religious, and metaphysical discussion. Many was the tirade in favor of atheism. "The baron made a remark which had occurred to me long before him: it was about the strange trick by which the religion of a man who had spent his life, and lost it, preaching against temples and priests, was full of temples and priests."

There was a stream of foreign guests at the "synagogue," among them Wilkes, Hume, Sterne, Beccaria, Garrick, Franklin, and Priestley. It has often been told how Hume remarked at one of their dinners that he did not believe a genuine atheist existed. It was a rather imprudent statement.

"Count how many are here," d'Holbach told him.

"Eighteen."

"I am fortunate enough to be able to show you fifteen atheists at once. As for the other three, they are agnostics."

The group was much impressed by a description given them by the baron de Dieskou, who had fought in Canada, of the savagery of the Iroquois. But that did not destroy their faith in man's natural goodness, in the idyllic, viceless life of primitive peoples: the blame was easily pinned on religion. "Vengeance is for that unfortunate people a religious virtue."

It was at d'Holbach's, writes Morellet in his *Mémoires,* "that you could have heard the freest, liveliest, and most instructive conversations that have ever taken place. There is no boldness in politics and religion that was not advanced and discussed pro and con, almost always with subtlety and depth . . . It was there that I heard Roux and Darcet expose their theory of the earth, Marmontel the excellent principles which he has assembled in his *Elements of Literature* . . . Galiani tell long stories in the Italian manner, Diderot treat a question of philosophy, art or literature, and by his abundance, his eloquence, his inspired air, captivate our attention for a long while . . . It was there that Diderot, Dr. Roux, and the good baron himself established dogmatically absolute atheism. We were a goodly number of theists there, too, and not at all ashamed of it, and we defended ourselves vigorously."

Great excitement was created among the "philosophic" clan, in the Fall of 1768, when Christian VII, king of Denmark, expressed a desire to meet them. Baron de Gleichen, the Danish special envoy, was charged with the arrangements, and a reception was held at the York Hotel, where the king was staying. Among the eighteen guests were Diderot, d'Alembert, d'Holbach, Condillac, Duclos, Helvétius, Grimm, and the abbé Morellet. The king spoke to each one individually and to d'Alembert expressed surprise that there should be ecclesiastics among them. To our philosopher he remarked:

"M. de Gleichen is a good friend of yours."

"Sire, it is in virtue of that title that I have dared to appear before Your Majesty."

"I hope that you see each other often."

"His conversation," interrupted Gleichen gracefully, "instructs and enlightens me."

It was about the same time that Diderot, ever the true friend, praised Gleichen warmly in a letter to Grimm and added generously, "you will like him better than me."

After Diderot, the best conversationalist of the group was the abbé Galiani, a philosopher and wit who for eight years was the delight of the Paris *salons*. He was small and chubby, and endowed with the eloquence of word and gesture natural to Neapolitans. A typical man of the eighteenth century, Galiani was well versed not only in history, economics, and law, but also in Greek, Latin, French and English literature, mathematics, the natural sciences, and archeology. Diderot had a large hand in the revision of his *Dialogues on the Wheat Trade*, and he was convinced posterity would place that work on a shelf beside Plato and Pascal.

In his profound pessimism and Machiavelian cynicism, Galiani resembled d'Holbach more than any of the other *philosophes*. He carried his erudition very lightly. At Grandval, he was inexhaustible in his witty remarks and a treasure on rainy days. "When he tired of reasoning, he told us tales. I'm crazy about that abbé; he almost always grasps the oldest things by some secret corner that no one has seen. He would make a good character in a comedy." Indeed, in *Rameau's Nephew*, Diderot has compared the extravagances of Rameau with those of Rabelais and the "stories in action" of Galiani. "They are three storehouses which have provided me with comic masks that I place on the faces of the gravest persons."

Galiani's complete lack of sentimentality was the only thing about him that displeased the philosopher. He was shocked to hear Galiani admit that he had never wept in his life, that the loss of his father, brothers, sisters, and mistresses had not cost him a tear.

Another point of disagreement was the existence of God. Galiani, having heard Diderot expound his theory of atheism, made a date with him for the following Thursday, at which time he promised a rebuttal. The offer was eagerly accepted, and the entire company was on hand at the appointed hour. After dinner and coffee, the abbé sat down in a comfortable armchair and crossed his legs. As it was rather hot, he held his wig in one hand, leaving the other free for gesticulation.

"Let us suppose, messieurs, that he among you who is most convinced that the world is a work of chance is playing dice, not in a gambling house, but in the most honorable home in Paris, and that his opponent gets a seven twice, three times, four times, and keeps on constantly. After the game lasts a while, my friend Diderot, who is losing his money, won't hesitate to say: 'The dice are loaded, I am among cutthroats!' Ah, philosopher, what are you saying! Because ten or twelve throws have left the dice box in such a way as to make you lose six francs, you believe firmly in an artificial combination, in a well-organized swindle. And on seeing in this universe so prodigious a number of combinations, a thousand and thousand times more difficult and more complicated and more lasting, and more useful, you do not suspect that the dice of nature are also loaded and that there is up there a great thief who makes a game out of catching you! "

But to Diderot, Galiani's "artificial combinations" were merely the workings of nature's great and necessary law.

"This world," he retorted, "is indeed only a mass of molecules loaded in an infinity of different ways. There is a law of necessity which works without design, without effort, without intelligence, without progress, without resistance, in all the works of nature. . . . This beautiful order which enchants you in the universe cannot be different from what it is."

"Yes, the universe is a great machine," replied Galiani, "which moves and works of necessity, but of how many wheels is that machine composed? That is what no one knows. In a word, are there other minds, aside from the human mind?"

But this great problem was an enigma to Diderot, too, and he had no illusions about possessing the answer to it.

Galiani returned to his native city in 1769, and never saw Paris again. Diderot always regretted him. "Good-bye the good stories; good-bye the always original, frequently profound and gay reflections."

Often d'Holbach and his friends would purposely stimulate Diderot's intellectual fire by calculating remarks. They did this partly for the fun of it, partly because they could pluck for their own writings many of the ideas they provoked. The contrary, in a sense, was also true. On a man as impressionable as Diderot, the influence of his milieu was bound to be considerable. Conversations were a major source of inspiration to him, both by the direct provocation of his ideas in the course of discussion and by his sensitivity to opinions expressed by others. After a conversation with Mme. Duclos, he wrote to Sophie that he was filled with it for several days. "I could not tell you the ideas it has inspired in me." He reminded Grimm about a little walk they had taken together in the Bois de Boulogne; it had slipped out of Grimm's mind but its effects were still working on Diderot. "I warn you that whether you were joking or serious, I've thought a great deal about it; that I owe to it almost all the moments of relaxation I have enjoyed since; that it has taken root, and that it is within a hair's breadth of becoming a settled project."

There is no doubt of the strong reciprocal influence between Diderot and d'Holbach. On the philosopher, that influence was in the direction of pessimism and atheism. Against d'Holbach's pessimism he broke many a lance in favor of mankind. Once he defied the baron to find in history any scoundrel whose life, in spite of the appearance of happiness, did not offer evidence that he was really unhappy in direct proportion to his wickedness; or of any good man whose happiness, despite apparent unhappiness, was not proportionate to his virtue. But another time Diderot took from the mantel a volume of Voltaire's *Universal History,* and in less than twenty pages read of a hundred horrible crimes. It was d'Holbach's turn to crow. "Such is the sublime nature, the innate beauty of the human species, its natural goodness! " And all the poor philosopher could do was confide his distress to Sophie. "Quick, quick, my friends, let us run away to the woods, to Peking, to Avignon."

D'Holbach's successful use of history to confound Diderot's deepseated but shaky optimism could be annoying. "The baron is killing himself reading history, and it only warps his mind and embitters his heart. He retains only the atrocities of man and nature. He learns in it to despise and to hate his fellowmen more and more. Does he encounter some pages black enough to make one tremble? He takes a secret joy in regaling me with them. It is certain that if everything resembled what he showed me, it would be unbearable."

So profound was Diderot's need for a positive stimulus, for a point of opposition against which he could hurl his ideas, balance them with all possible contrary conclusions and then be provoked to finding new arguments or analogies, that he often created imaginary conversations in the solitude of his study. From some of these resulted his great dialogues, "Thoughts," and "Letters," in which he pursued a line of thought only so long as it was interesting. or fruitful, and then followed the tempting digression indicated by a natural association of ideas. In imaginary discussions his mind found the full-blooded exercise it needed, exulted in its talent for paradox, for developing both sides of a question in an effort to explore it to its ultimate recesses, and to find, if possible, not on which side truth lay, but how much of it lay on each side. "As for me, [I] busy myself more with forming clouds than with dispelling them, more with suspending my judgment than with judging."

This method of working does not lead to a systematic spirit or to methodical control. Diderot's thought was usually the reaction of the moment to a specific stimulus, and the stimulus and reaction may at different moments be quite contradictory. One of his criticisms of Helvétius was that he reasoned with inflexible rigor. Diderot prefers what he terms "internal force," the "secret order" of life. Too much order and method denote "a mind that is too tranquil, too much master of itself. The spirit of invention is agitated in a disorderly fashion; it searches. The methodical mind arranges, orders, and supposes that everything has been found." According to Pierre Mesnard, Diderot was dominated by the sympathetic nervous system, by organic needs and sensitivity, so that his thought is a palpitation of ideas, a running from one to the other, a series of emotional contrasts and reactions to accepted ideas. This description is largely true. It does fit the composition of his works in their first form. But we must not forget that he was capable of the patient labor required by the *Encyclopedia*, and of painstaking revision of his own writings.

When his thought on some question had been stimulated, when a sudden idea for a book or a play had come to him, Diderot was usually filled with his inspiration; he concentrated on it everywhere, at home, in the street, even among friends. Its grip was relentless. Night and day he could not take his mind off it. Then, when some definite conception had evolved from the agitation of his thought, he would set to work, with relentless intensity. At other times such a period of incubation was unnecessary; he would simply sit at his desk, and in a few hours, from the warmth of his imagination would come some scintillating dialogue.

Second to the influence of d'Holbach were the conversations with Father Hoop and the abbé Galiani. From the latter, Diderot may have absorbed some parts of Vico's theory of history. The conception of history as an essentially repetitious cycle, each phase—each civilization—composed of periods of growth, stability, and decline, fitted admirably with his own dynamic theory of transformism as the great law of the universe.

With Hoop he could satisfy still another craving of his mind.

Typical of his cosmopolitan century, one aspect of his universal curiosity was focused on the civilization of foreign lands. Hoop had traveled everywhere, and Diderot pumped him for information about the customs and the literature of England and China.

One is impressed, in Diderot's conversations and letters, by the sincerity of his cosmopolitanism. More than mere curiosity, it was a vital part of the "philosophic" ideal. "What! Are not justice, good deeds, humanitarianism, moderation, patriotic heroism worthy of our admiration and praise in all times and places, at Constantinople, Peking, London, ancient Athens, or modern Rome?"

The ideal of cosmopolitanism was but one aspect of his much larger idea of humanitarianism: between all men there exists an unbreakable bond of human brotherhood. He longed for the final extinction of nationalism; the hatreds engendered by it seemed to him the principal cause of war—man's most bestial, degrading occupation—and the principal barrier to perfect understanding and cooperation between all mankind. "Shall we never see the end," he wrote to David Hume, "of those national aversions which narrow the exercise of virtue? And what does it matter to me that a man is born on one side of a strait or the other? Does he not have the same needs? Is he not exposed to the same suffering, avid for the same happiness? I find Polyphemus more excusable for having eaten Ulysses' companions than most of these little Europeans, less than five and one-half feet tall, who have two eyes, resemble each other in every respect, and who devour each other nonetheless. I flatter myself that I am, like you, a citizen of the great city of the world." The noble and eternal thought of Shylock's speech becomes in Diderot's mind the symbol of his ideal of cosmopolitanism and tolerance.

Among the friends who were not guests at Grandval was Jacques-André Naigeon. Diderot, sixteen years his senior, had been attracted to him at first by his wit and irreligion. "That effervescent Naigeon is delightful," he wrote shortly after they had met, on the occasion of a picnic. Naigeon had been a painter and sculptor before becoming a "philosopher." He occasionally helped Diderot in the work of describing the *Salons,* and also made himself useful by collecting subscriptions for the *Encyclopedia* and performing similar subaltern jobs. He took advantage of his usefulness to attach himself to Diderot, whom he sometimes annoyed by his irritable temper and fanatical hatred of everything connected with religion or the Church. With the help of d'Holbach, whose dogmatism was closer than

Diderot's to his own, Naigeon wrote *The Philosophic Soldier*. A few years later he persuaded Diderot to sign a paper making him his literary executor. For one reason or another, Naigeon neglected to publish several of Diderot's manuscripts. Those he did publish, however, were on the whole carefully edited, with notes born of his own dogmatic atheism.

Diderot's relations with Voltaire form another episode. Through long years, during which the two men never met, their mutual sympathy grew strong and at times even emotional. Voltaire, in his joy at Diderot's fight against a common enemy, in the fellowship of their common humanitarianism, was always writing praises of his co-worker and using his influence in behalf of the *Encyclopedia*. He avoided criticism of Diderot, and if he did not relish the *Père de famille*, he can scarcely be blamed for that. In spite of his personal opinion, his elation at the success of Diderot's play, considered as a triumph over the calumnies which had been heaped upon him, was limitless and sincere. It was then that he began his campaign to put Diderot in the Academy, an idea he at last abandoned with great reluctance. His constant advice, his offers to protect Diderot in exile were appreciated by the philosopher, who wrote to him, "I feel all the gratitude I owe you, and from here I throw my arms about your neck."

Diderot freely praised Voltaire's works. In addition to admiring their artistic value, he too rejoiced, in a common "party spirit," each time some new play or pamphlet overwhelmed their enemies. The thought of Voltaire's great age once made Diderot exclaim with intense regret, "Why must he die! "

Diderot's enthusiasm, from the sixties on, was centered about Voltaire's humanitarian work in favor of Calas and other victims of fanaticism. In accordance with his belief that "a beautiful action is worth infinitely more than a beautiful page," he considered these efforts to be Voltaire's crown of glory. "Oh, my friend, what a noble use of genius! That man must have a soul, *sensibilité;* injustice must revolt him and he must feel the charms of virtue. What are the Calas to him? What reason does he have to suspend work that he loves, to busy himself with their defense? If there is a Christ, I assure you that Voltaire will be saved."

Diderot was ever insistent that the *philosophes'* work should be more than one of negative criticism. "Ah, big brother, you do not know how these scoundrels who constantly do evil and imagine that they alone can do good, are suffering to see you the friend of men, the father of orphans, and the defender of the oppressed. Continue to do great work and good deeds, and let them burst of spite. *Adieu,* sublime, worthy, and dear anti-Christ."

With all this, Diderot never hesitated to criticize Voltaire when he felt that criticism was earned. He did not share "the Patriarch's" attitude of overlooking all else in favor of the "party." "I admire Voltaire as one of the most astonishing men who have yet appeared. But I am not always of his opinion." He felt compelled to judge Voltaire's literary work as impartially as that of any other author. He was lavish in his praise, but not overawed by Voltaire's fame and reputation. He was proud of this independence of judgment and liked others to recognize it. Perhaps to preserve this independence, he kept Voltaire at a distance, and sometimes did not reply to his communications.

If, later on, he became annoyed with Voltaire on religious grounds, it would be erroneous to interpret this as intolerance of his deistic beliefs. Diderot's vexation sprang mostly from Voltaire's "hypocrisy" in building a church and going to mass. The fact that he wanted to discuss or debate their opposing beliefs, or to convince Voltaire, is not equivalent to intolerance.

In the 1760's, the ideological differences between the two men, which both had tried to gloss over, turned into tactical differences, and developed into what has been called "a civil war" among the *philosophes*. Voltaire and his friend d'Alembert disliked the atheism of Diderot and d'Holbach, but were even more concerned by the latter's slashing attacks against political oppression. Voltaire wanted reform and a modern State, but would have no truck with democratic notions or revolutionary ideas. He thought it was insane to engage in a frontal attack on the civil authorities. The wise tactics, he held, were to win over the "establishment" to their side. On both these issues each group tried, over a period of years, to convince the other, but unsuccessfully. Voltaire and Diderot were really in rivalry for the leadership of the movement. In the end, each went his own way, without open expressions of antagonism or an open breach of unity.

Diderot was guilty of a diplomatic concealment of his unfavorable criticisms. He always boasted about his great frankness; but, as has been evident, his accommodation to realities at times when his own interest is concerned might be termed hypocrisy by a severe critic, by a friendly one, clever diplomacy. It is understandable that he should have carefully avoided writing his true opinions to

Voltaire, whose sensitive vanity was often the very subject of his criticisms. Diderot did not wish to pass judgment on Voltaire's play, *Tancrède,* but when their common friends, Damilaville and Thieriot, practically forced him to, he completely transformed the criticism he had sent to Sophie. A work "founded on the point of a needle, which moves clumsily," full of faults of detail—although redeemed by many beauties—becomes, in his letter to Voltaire, the source of "transports of admiration and joy," and so on.

What annoyed Diderot more than anything else were Voltaire's petty, violent, often coarse attacks on those who had wounded his hypersensitive vanity by criticism or satire. These diatribes not only lowered Voltaire in his esteem, but offended him by cheapening the entire "philosophic" group in the opinion of the public. Such tactics transgressed his own idealistic conviction that irreproachable conduct was the highest duty of the *philosophes* and their most effective weapon. Party spirit inspired Voltaire's generous attitude to Diderot, and party spirit contributed to Diderot's critical attitude. Voltaire's satire of a rival dramatist, the *Eulogy of Crébillon,* vexed the philosopher particularly. "It is the truth, but the truth offends in an envious mouth. I cannot forgive a great man such pettiness."

Diderot admired Voltaire sincerely, that is most evident. On the other hand, he had no particular affection for him. This was not because Voltaire was "too great to be loved," as has been said. There was no jealousy in Diderot's heart. He could scarcely be expected to love a man whom he had never seen, with whom he had no intimate relations whatsoever. Diderot was the truest and most unselfish of friends, but the assumption that he ever considered Voltaire as a friend is erroneous. For that matter, no genuine personal affection is visible in Voltaire's attitude either. Their relations were solely on a basis of "party" cooperation, and friendship, in the true sense of the word, is not really in question. To anyone reading their letters, the gulf between them appears immense; common interests and admiration produced mutual sympathy, but there was a complete lack of personal contact.

Differences of character, especially, made a true friendship impossible between the two philosophers. Voltaire was a mocking, at times malicious ironist, dry, egoistic, unemotional, essentially an aristocrat. Diderot's sentimentality, emotional enthusiasm, fundamental generosity, and more vulgar middle-class outlook were at the opposite pole.

Intellectually they were almost as far apart. Voltaire was at once more and less a sceptic than Diderot. Essentially a conservative, his scepticism halted before certain beliefs he thought necessary to preserve a well-ordered society; destruction of fanaticism and certain economic and administrational abuses were his limits. When Diderot's rationalism was on the march, it did not halt until the ultimate consequences of his relentless logic were reached. Voltaire was more sceptical, however, in the consistency of his attitude, for Diderot frequently abandoned his rational criticism and scepticism, in things pertaining to real life, and abided by a traditional code of sentimental bourgeois values.

Both men agreed on a universal, natural moral law, but Voltaire's belief was rationalistic, whereas Diderot based his theory on the identity of biological organization and social needs of the human race. In literature, too, they formed a contrast, Voltaire ever looking backwards for his models, to seventeenth-century classicism, while Diderot, ever foreshadowing the future, was "a romantic apologist of strong emotions and Shakespeare," and at the same time the first theorist of realism.

If Diderot's writings are more complicated and contradictory, it is partly because Voltaire's were the product of cool reason, directed towards a single effect, generally that of persuasion and propaganda. He, too, knew emotion and torment, but they were rationally controlled, and found a safety-valve in irony. His lucid, elegant style, his telling wit were perfect instruments for his type of mind. Diderot's works, like Rousseau's have the quality of being more obviously felt and lived, as well as thought. Behind the idea vibrate an intense personal emotion and the torment of search, which Voltaire sublimates into a more impersonal art.

These were some of the differences that prevented the two great philosophers from feeling an intimate bond of sympathy. There were ties, strong ties between them, but not of an intimate nature. They were joined by their common battle against fanaticism and Christianity. In a more important and more positive way, their mutual love of tolerance created a bond.

No man in history has served the cause of tolerance better than Voltaire; yet, possessed of his prejudices and hates, he was not the most tolerant of men himself. To a certain extent, his tolerance was really hatred of religion and the Church, that is, a form of intolerance. There is also the question of racial bigotry. For the Jews, Voltaire had only hatred and calumny, though he was opposed to their persecution; he seized every opportunity for vituperation, a field in which he was unequalled. Contrary to Voltaire, Diderot praises Moses as a great legislator, and lauds the Jews for their monotheistic ideal. To Falconet, who had been traveling in Germany, he wrote that he was "glad and little surprised" to hear that the Jews were not "so disagreeable as they are painted to us." On the other hand, Diderot did not, any more than most of the *philosophes*, demand a more humane treatment for the Jews, or make their civic emancipation part of his program for reform. The unsavory anecdote of the Jew of Utrecht, which he inserted in *Rameau's Nephew*, had originally involved a Dutchman, and Diderot's transformation of his protagonist into a Jew, though doubtless motivated by a desire for heightened effect, pandered to the common prejudices.

Of all the *philosophes*, Diderot was the most truly tolerant. He respected all shades of opinion, from atheism to piety, provided they were sincere. Truly undogmatic, he was always open to persuasion. ("I am not a tyrant of opinions, all my friends will tell you that. I give my reasons, and I wait; and I have noticed several times that after a while my adversary and I had both changed our opinions".) Tolerance and open-mindedness were fundamentals of Diderot's personality, and came largely from his intuitive tendency to see some truth on all sides of a question, from his rare ability frequently to remain undecided. If truth is too difficult for the human mind to grasp, if there is always some right on both sides, what reasonable man can persecute his fellowmen for not sharing his own opinions? Who can be sufficiently sure that he possesses the truth?

Tolerance, with Diderot, like cosmopolitanism, was part of a large ideal of humanitarianism. His reactions to children, old people, peasants, mothers, his ever ready charity, his suffering at their sufferings, all reveal a profound love of his fellow men. This attitude manifested itself consistently, in the smallest and most distant things. On hearing that two book peddlers, completely unknown to him, had been condemned to the galleys, he was deeply distressed. "When they get out, what will become of them? All they can do is to become highway robbers. Degrading punishments take away every resource from a man; they are worse than capital punishment which takes away his life." His deep sympathy for the unhappy and the oppressed, for the people of France, are striking. He had a generous heart, and one cannot help loving him for that. He could not deny even to wrongdoers the bond of human fellowship. "It is so good to forgive. We relieve ourselves of such a heavy burden! After the generous forgetting of past wrongs, there is the flattering hope of better action in the future. The more I examine myself, the more I am convinced that in our youth there is a decisive moment in our character. I do not know what it hinges on, a word perhaps, a circumstance, a little misfortune or a little success. A slight gust of wind blows those feathers to the good or bad side, and almost irrevocably."

Humanitarianism was one of the great movements of the eighteenth century, and it was Voltaire's humanitarian actions that did most to win Diderot's sympathy. Voltaire belonged to the first half of the century, and his humanitarianism was largely intellectual, based on ideas of justice and opposition to fanaticism, though it could evoke deep indignation. The bourgeois current of sentimentality to which Diderot belonged—at least *part* of Diderot— made its humanitarianism an emotional, frequently a weepy affair. Diderot put all his heart into his love for all men, and the comment of Jean Thomas is amply justified: "It was Diderot who communicated to his whole century the spontaneous love of humanity, the need of substituting for the abstract notion of general man, such as La Rochefoucauld and Racine painted, the living reality of the fleshly being, moving in his weakness, admirable in his universal curiosity."

CHAPTER 14

The
Philosophy
of
Materialism

1

AFTER THE PUBLICATION of *Thoughts on the Interpretation of Nature,* in 1754, Diderot had turned his back on philosophical questions and focused all his extra-encyclopedic attention on the theater, the novel, and the arts. Then, about 1763, the tide of his interest began to turn. Problems of universal scope once more became dominant in his mind. From 1763 to 1772 he wrote three philosophical and scientific works; four others touching on moral problems were completed in the following three years. Included in this period are a group of masterpieces: *D'Alembert's Dream, The Supplement to Bougainville's Voyage, Rameau's Nephew, The Paradox on Acting,* and *Jacques the Fatalist.*

What caused the sudden change in direction, back in 1754, is more or less evident. The first torments of his revolt against religion and the search for some new ground to stand on had consumed the preceding ten years. In that interval Diderot had sketched for himself a fairly satisfying metaphysical and moral philosophy. With his mind put at rest by a materialistic theory of evolution, his attention was suddenly claimed by the theater; then, immediately afterwards, by his enthusiastic involvement with the problems of the fine arts;

and finally, by purely literary work. A decade of philosophy (1745-54) was thus followed by a period of literary and esthetic production.

What caused his reversion of interest, in 1763, is less clear. The clue may lie in his deepening thought on biological matters. His readings in Bordeu, Robinet, Haller, and Toland provided fresh fuel for his explorations, which were to absorb a third decade.

Another clue may lie in his more resolute atheism during this period. Back in 1749 the question of God was just a "ball for philosophers." It had no connection with human welfare, or with morals, which are based on needs inherent in all men. Scientifically, the concept of God was sterile—only after we know the nature of matter and of life can we begin to discuss the question of God reasonably. He refused equally to believe or to deny what lies beyond the knowable.

> I am no more than an ignorant person who has the frankness and the courage of his ignorance. . . . Infinity does not concern me in the least. When and by whom was the world created? Where do we go after death? What shall we become? All these problems, which you judge of capital importance, do not deprive me of any sleep. Never has anyone, in hundreds of thousands of centuries, succeeded—I do not say in solving—but even in clarifying these matters. Therefore! God, the soul, future life—I neither believe nor disbelieve in them! I eliminate these questions, I confine myself to the present life, and I consider, with Spinoza, any meditation about the Beyond and about death as useless, vain and depressing.

Morals are the key to Diderot's change of attitude. When the idea of God no longer seemed indifferent to morals, he could no longer be indifferent to the idea of God.

As early as 1760, he had begun to shift to his new stand. The inhumanity of the Iroquois he had attributed, under the influence of the d'Holbach clan, to their gods. "Who has inspired in them vengeance and treachery? The gods, my friend, the gods." And his general conclusion: "There is not a single country, not a single people, where the command of God has not consecrated some crime."

It is probable that d'Holbach's influence was paramount in the dogmatization of his attitude. "Last Saturday," he wrote to Damilaville in 1765, "was taken up by the baron in discussing certain points of philosophy on which we did not agree, such as this one for example, whether the belief even in a good and charitable God was not a source of corruption in morals." He urges Damilaville to combat Voltaire's deism, by reciting to him all their arguments— "our catechism," he says, thereby indicating again the influence of the d'Holbach milieu. And among the arguments of the catechism is this apologue:

> Recall to him my fable about the misanthrope who had taken refuge in a cave where he meditated deeply on how to avenge himself in the most terrible way on the human race with which he was displeased. He said to himself: 'I must find some notion to which they will attach more importance than to their lives and on which they can never be in agreement.' Instantly he ran out, crying 'God! God!'. His voice was heard from one pole to the other, and men began to dispute, to hate each other and to murder each other. That is what they have done ever since that abominable name was pronounced, and that is what they will continue to do until the end of time.

In the crystallization of this important question in Diderot's mind, the cruel martyrdom of two innocent Protestants, in quick succession, must have been a decisive factor. The most notorious act of religious persecution in the eighteenth century, one that aroused the conscience of France and of Europe, was the Calas affair. Falsely accused of killing his son in order to prevent his conversion, Jean Calas, an honored merchant of Toulouse, was broken on the wheel in 1762. Just two years later, Pierre-Paul Sirven, condemned to death on a similar charge, escaped only by fleeing to Geneva. Calas and Sirven were rehabilitated, the former posthumously, through the devoted efforts of Voltaire. Both of these barbarities had a profound influence on Diderot; to him, as to Voltaire, they seemed a justification of the motto: *Ecrasez l'infâme.*

It is not entirely surprising, then, that Diderot, to whom morality and the love of mankind were the very purpose of life, who had once thought the existence of God "indifferent" and immaterial, should now exclaim with the passion of a fanatic: "I would sacrifice my life perhaps, if I could annihilate forever the notion of God."

Religion, with its "superstitions," its hatreds, and its priests, appeared to him even more evil than the idea of the Deity. "Everywhere a God is admitted, there is a cult; wherever there is a cult, the natural order of duties is reversed and morals corrupted.

Sooner or later, there comes a moment when the notion that has prevented the stealing of an écu causes the slaughter of a hundred thousand men." Of all religions, Christianity, he held, was the worst:

> the most absurd and most atrocious in its dogma; the most unintelligible, the most metaphysical, the most entangled and consequently the most subject to divisions, sects, schisms, heresies; the most fatal to public tranquillity, the most dangerous for sovereigns because of its hierarchical order, its persecutions and its discipline; the dullest, most disagreeable, most gothic and saddest in its ceremonies; the most puerile and unsocial in its morals, considered not in what it has in common with universal morality, but in what is particular to it and constitutes evangelical, apostolic and Christian morality; the most intolerant of all.

Fortunately, his fanatical moods, when he was ready to make the great sacrifice, were few, the result of a moment's passion. For one thing, he was sceptical enough about the possibility of moral progress to admit that little could be done about the matter, except to decrease intolerance. "In general, we do not know how a prejudice takes root among a people, and still less how it ceases." Atheism, was his final conclusion, in 1775, "can be the doctrine of a small school, but never that of the great number of citizens. . . . The belief in the existence of God will remain forever."

Even more opposed to fanaticism was his natural temperament. In one of his most radical dialogues, *The Conversation of a Philosopher with the Maréchale,* he admitted the possibility of his being wrong, but expressed his hope that God, if he did exist, would not punish him for a sincere use of his God-given reason. The question reduces itself again to the conflict between his inexorable rationalism and an emotional heart that rebelled against the conclusions of his intellect. At the very time that he was, intellectually, most firmly tied to atheistic materialism, he wrote to Sophie these significant lines: "Atheism is close to being a kind of superstition, as puerile as the other. . . . Nothing is indifferent in an order of things which is tied together and conducted by a general law; it seems that everything is equally important. There are no great or small phenomena. If I believe that I love you of my free will, I am mistaken, it is nothing of the sort. Oh, what a fine system for ingrates! I am maddened at being entangled in a devilish philosophy that my mind can't help approving and my heart refuting."

The supreme dialectical statement of Diderot's materialism is his famous trilogy, *A Conversation between d'Alembert and Diderot, D'Alembert's Dream,* and *The Continuation of the Conversation* (1769). Diderot and d'Alembert are the interlocutors of the first part of the dialogue. In the continuation, and also in the final part, Diderot replaces himself by his friend Bordeu, the eminent physician-scientist, who had given him much information and influenced his thinking—perhaps in order to lend to his words the weight of a professional scientist. A note of piquancy is also added by the addition of d'Alembert's mistress, the passionate Julie de Lespinasse, who was later to break his heart by leaving him for a more virile lover. However, Yvon Belaval has conjectured that Diderot really had Sophie Volland in mind when he wrote this part of the dialogue. This trilogy, generally called for simplicity's sake *D'Alembert's Dream,* is a scintillating imaginary dialogue; its indisputable literary merits, combined with its freshness and bold-ness of thought, have given it a first-line position among Diderot's works. Developing fragmentary ideas from Lucretius, Maupertuis, Buffon, La Mettrie, Toland, and Bordeu, he welds the most advanced and integrated system of materialism in the eighteenth century. It was another masterpiece that he did not dare publish. Doomed to remain unprinted until 1830, it had no influence on his contemporaries' thought.

While at work on the trilogy, he referred to it with enthusiasm in his correspondence with Sophie. "It is impossible to be more profound or more crazy." A few days later, he was slightly more explicit. "It is of the greatest extravagance and at the same time, the most profound philosophy; there is some cleverness in having put my ideas in the mouth of a man who is dreaming: it is often necessary to give to wisdom the appearance of folly, to obtain admission for it."

The problem of life and questions of human psychology dominate *D'Alembert's Dream.* Bordeu sets forth the subject as "the general sensitivity of matter, the formation of the sentient being, its unity, the origin of animals, their duration, and all the questions pertaining to these."

Ever since the beginning of Diderot's inquiries into the meaning of things, in the *Philosophic Thoughts,* the question of life had seemed crucial to him. If life needed a God to create it, then God was the explanation for everything. If atheism and materialism were to be accepted, then life had to be proved self-creative. This involved the possibility of inorganic matter becoming, under proper conditions, "organic," by which he meant "living." That is why the theory of spontaneous generation played an important role at the time. In the *Philosophic Thoughts* it was rejected, in the deist's argument. From the time of the *Letter on the Blind*, Diderot apparently accepts it, implicitly at first, then openly in the *Dream*. This change of view, necessitated by his materialism, was made possible by Joseph Needham's "discovery" of "infusoria," aquatic life that could then be accounted for only by such a theory.

In 1754, in the *Thoughts on the Interpretation of Nature*, Diderot had sought the link between inorganic and organic matter, concluding that the difference was one of organization. By 1761, he had changed his mind, and he wrote to Sophie Volland that no inert body could be made to live by any attempt to reorganize it; life must be the unique property of a special kind of matter. But by 1765, he had returned to an idea already suggested in the earlier work. Sensitivity is an inherent property of matter, along with motion (force or energy) and extension. "Sensitivity is a universal property of matter," he writes to Duclos, "inactive in dead bodies . . . activated in those same bodies by their assimilation with a living animal substance. That is what the phenomenon of nutrition proves every instant. . . . The animal is the laboratory where inert sensitivity is made active." Just as a compound of two elements (as we would say today) has a new structure, and different properties, so can the inorganic become organic.

D'Alembert's Dream pushed this materialistic line of reasoning to its logical conclusion. Borrowing an idea from the English deist, John Toland, Diderot asserts that flesh can be made from marble, and marble from flesh. This is being done continuously in the life cycle. As there is "inanimate" and "animate" force (potential and kinetic energy), so marble has inactive sensitivity. "And to expound before the Academy the process of the formation of a man or an animal, one need employ only material agents, the successive results of which would be an inert being, a feeling being, a thinking being, a being solving the problem of the precession of the equinoxes, a sublime being, a marvelous being, a being growing old, fading away, dying, dissolved and given back to the soil."

But so far Diderot has accounted for transformation into life only by the assimilative action of an organism that is already living. The question of the origination of life still remains. Indirectly he tackles the problem by means of the old question, whether the hen or the egg came first. From a metaphysical viewpoint, considering all things in essence, there is no exit from the closed system of hen-egg. But Diderot considers nature as a dynamic force, a process of movement and change, therefore of creation. Things not only exist; they come into being and disappear. Before either hen or egg, there was something else that was neither one of these. "If you are worried by the question, which came first, the hen or the egg, it is because you suppose that animals were originally the same as they are now. What madness! We can no more tell what they were originally than what they will become." The creative process is mechanical. "Beyond a certain limit of complexity," says Bordeu, "mechanism becomes organism." Or, as Diderot put it in the *Elements of Physiology*, "The difference between a feeling and a thinking being is only a matter of organization."

This explanation is still considered scientifically sound. Philosophically, it is less satisfactory, especially since it is not clear whether the difference is conceived as one of degree or of kind. On the one hand, his unique substance has two, or more, different *kinds* of sensitivity: inert, living, moral, etc.—and he would have to show that organization can produce such qualitative differences. On the other hand, his attempt to avoid this difficulty by postulating a universal "inert" or potential "sensitivity" falls into the difficulty of panvitalism. His theory actually combines both ideas, with the emphasis on process and development, on the emergence of unexplained novelty accompanying new complexities of organization. He attributes to matter sensitivity, of one kind or degree, and to organization the power to bring into being, out of the lower level, a new and distinct realm of being. On the one hand, the idea of emergence breaks through the limits of mechanism, on the other, the process itself is purely mechanical, and in the *Refutation of Helvétius,* he again specifically limits it to "physical agents." There is only the recombination of atoms, and the laws of physics and chemistry. He thereby implies that quantitative changes are accompanied by qualitative changes, such as the emergence of organism, life, and behavior (what Jules Bordet calls "ingenuity and the gift of achieving an end"). This will again be apparent in his discussion of the mind. Two questions, at least, remain, and still remain to science today. Why do predictable quantitative changes produce unpredictable qualitative changes? Do new properties emerge, or only new effects of properties already present?

More directly, he tries to resolve the question of life's beginning by referring to Needham's recent "proof" for spontaneous generation. Applying it rather naïvely, he speculates that the elephant may have suddenly sprung up from an atom, as the product of fermentation. Size itself is no problem. "The miracle is life, sensitivity, and this miracle no longer is one. When I have seen inert matter become sensitive, nothing can astonish me." He then takes a hint from Lucretius and puts it in more modern form. "Do you see this egg?" he inquires of d'Alembert. "With this you can overthrow all the schools of theology, all the churches of the earth. What is this egg? An unperceiving mass, before the germ is introduced into it." The germ itself is only a nonliving fluid. But the union of these two nonliving units, he declares (following Descartes, Maupertuis, and Buffon), acting by "heat generated by motion," creates "active sensitivity," life, memory, consciousness, passion, and thought. But is the chicken that results from this purely mechanical development a machine? The answer is ambiguous. "Little children will laugh at you, and philosophers will reply that you too are a machine." Whatever the chicken is, so is man. The difference between animal and human is then one of degree, not of kind. This thought persists in a later dialogue, *Conversation with the Maréchale,* where one interlocutor says that animals are machines, and the other rejoins, "And man, too, who is simply a somewhat more perfect animal than the others."

This reasoning was brilliant for its time and has persisted in scientific thought. Spontaneous generation—in a more sophisticated form—is now accepted. But do machines evolve? And the enigma is not only the production of life from egg and sperm, but even more, that there should be an egg and a sperm. When Diderot speaks of life originating from inert matter, "organized in a certain way," the whole mystery lies within the quotation marks. Why did matter organize "that certain way," and what is the distinguishing factor? Is the cause the "comfort" or "stability" the molecule seeks? Is this a satisfactory explanation of the complexity, specialization, coordination and purposiveness of life? While most biologists now hold to his view, others will not accept it. Haldane feels that no mechanism can bring about organic maintenance and reproduction. There is a difference between "structure and activity" and "living structure and living activity" which is an organized metabolic activity controlling structure. Diderot may have found the answer, but the question is still an open one, although the breaking of the genetic code apparently confirms his physical-chemical explanation of the life processes.

Diderot and the other eighteenth-century materialists insisted that man is not an exception in the universe, physically or biologically, in his origin, his functioning, or his end. Our hungers, our struggles, our innermost instincts and impulses, as well as our anatomy, physiology, and molecular structure, are identical with those of all nature.[1]

In the universe of living and lifeless matter, man is the crowning accomplishment of a long series of trials and errors. Diderot's theory of transformism applies to all manifestations of nature. It applies to the solar system and to life. "Who knows what species of animals have preceded us? who knows the species that will follow ours? Everything changes, everything passes, only the whole remains. And what about man, you will ask me? Yes! man, but not as he is now; first, a certain something, then something else; and then, after a few hundreds of millions of years and as many 'somethings,' the two-legged animal that bears the name of man." Evolution is not a phenomenon Diderot would consider by itself, in the realm of biology. It is rather one aspect of the constant flux which is basic to reality.

But how do these transformations come about? To his previous ideas of trial and error, and survival of the fit organism, Diderot now adds a new concept, borrowed from La Mettrie. The more senses, the more needs, says d'Alembert. "Organs produce needs, and reciprocally, needs produce organs," asserts Dr. Bordeu.

"I have seen two shoulderblades lengthen," testifies Bordeu, "in default of two missing arms, shape into pincers and become stumps. Suppose a long succession of armless generations, suppose continuous efforts, and you will see the two sides of that pincers extend, extend more and more, cross behind the back, turn forward, perhaps develop digits at their extremities, and remake arms and hands. The original conformation becomes degenerate or perfected by necessity and habitual function. We walk so little, work so little, and think so much, that I do not despair of man's ending up by being only a head."

Evidently, Diderot takes for granted the hereditary transmission

[1] For a similar view, see Dr. Hartman's article in the "Scientific American," January 1950.

of acquired characteristics. But just as his earlier idea of fitness does not anticipate the Darwinian competition, so this new theory does not really foreshadow Lamarck, since there is as yet no mention of an ever-changing environment as the stimulus to adaptation. An internal dynamism accounts for all changes, just as internal viability determines survival. *D'Alembert's Dream* had no direct influence on Lamarck, for it was not published until a year after his death. But the theory of transformism, sketched by Maupertuis, Diderot, and Buffon was adopted by the group of encyclopedists, and their discussions directed the attention of scientists in England, France, and Germany to these hypotheses. Lamarck was a student of Buffon and a contributor to Naigeon's *Methodical Encyclopedia* (1785).

The discussion turns back to the unity of nature:

> Do you not agree that everything in nature is connected, and that it is impossible for there to be a gap in the chain? . . . There is only one great individual, the whole. In this whole, as in a machine, as in any animal, there is a part you will call such and such; but when you call that part of the whole an individual, it is by as false a concept as if, in a bird, you gave the name of individual to a wing, to a feather in the wing. . . . What is a being? The sum of a certain number of tendencies. Can I be anything else but a tendency? No, I am going towards an end. And species? Species are only tendencies to a common end which is particular to them. And life? Life, a succession of actions and reactions. Living, I act and react as a mass; dead, I act and react as molecules.

It is not easy to decide whether or not Diderot really conceives of the universe as an organic whole, as he appears to in this passage. An organism involves functional interdependence, as well as new properties and a new "reality" of its own, distinct from the sum of all its parts. At other times, Diderot emphasizes the structure of the universe as one of self-sufficient particulars—a pluralistic universe whose unity is purely a causal interrelationship. He writes in this same work that nature's dynamism rests solidly on the fact that "everything is connected; if you imagine a new phenomenon or bring back a moment of the past, you are creating a new world." And in the *Principles of Matter and Movement*, "an atom moves the world . . . since the atom has its own force, it cannot be without effect." Here we have, at most, something like the harmony of Leibniz, in a universe of self-sufficient monads.

More important is Diderot's insistence on the organic character of organizations of matter in living forms, involving the creation of organic wholes that go beyond mechanical combinations. D'Alembert is tormented in his sleep by the baffling question of the organic unity of an animal, as contrasted with a mere aggregate. The living whole, in Diderot's thought, is more than a sum of its parts. What is it that makes this system *one*? The difference is comparable to that of contiguity and continuity. In living forms, continuity is a "melting" of one into the other, as a result of which, in addition to the sensitivity of each individual part, there is a new sensitivity of the whole. Each of the parts may itself be a similar aggregate— again we see his central concept of a pyramiding of structures. This "continuity" is equivalent to, and is maintained by constant action and reaction. "Everything cooperates in producing a sort of unity that exists only in the animal." Diderot now borrows an analogy from Bordeu. Whereas a cluster of bees form a contiguous mass, our organs are like separate animals living in a continuous relationship, under the laws of unity and identity. Diderot is unable to tell us how or why such an organic unity develops, or to account for its uniqueness in terms of his general view. Nor does he attempt to explain the relation of laws governing its peculiar function to the laws of the nonorganic physical world. But, like Maupertuis, he feels that the harmony of the whole is maintained by a collective consciousness whose presence is felt in every molecule of the organism. Yet he fails to draw the final philosophical conclusion from organism: that an atom may behave differently when it is part of a man, being to an extent determined by the whole.

A large portion of the second dialogue is given over to questions of psychology, and from that third viewpoint the problem of unity is further explored. Mlle. de Lespinasse expresses her wonderment at the consciousness we all have of our unity and self-identity. Bordeu explains that it consists in the constant relating of all our impressions to the brain, which is like the spider in the web. The power of memory is basic to all the operations of the brain. On memory alone hinges our persistence of identity through constant change in our bodies and psychological states. The psychological unity, Bordeu continues, may be broken by disease, or heightened to the exclusion of peripheral sensitivity, as in the case of the intellectual who forgets pain or the martyr who is consumed serenely by the flames. (A phenomenon that would seem to indicate an independent psychological realm, linked to the physical.)

In sleep, the psychic unity of consciousness is gone, the central control relaxed. Senses act on the brain without their being acted upon, and the brain must receive their messages. Dreams result from some irritation or temporary disorder. But in this disorder, the mind is active too, and we sometimes have logical dreams. In quiet sleep, all consciousness of identity is lost, but not so in dreams— one can never dream he is someone else. We can add to this explanation Diderot's theory of the "jumps" made in our minds by the unexpected "harmonics of thought"; as early as *The Indiscreet Jewels,* he had attributed the characteristic of dreams to the *rapprochement* of unrelated objects and ideas, forming a new and strange whole.

To Descartes, Buffon, and others, man was different from animals because of his soul and his power of thought. Thought, explains Diderot, is the result of a certain type of matter highly specialized in its sensitivity. Between the mind of man, the ape, and the earthworm, the only difference is one of degree. The "soul" is only consciousness, and this Diderot explains as "a nexus of sensations, volitions, impulses, and what not, a tumultuous chaos of stimulated and accessory ideas." Thought, like identity, depends on memory, which itself results merely from a certain organization of matter. To be more exact, the chain of the process is sensation, impression, memory, thought. Since reflection requires thinking of more than one thing at a time, which, strictly speaking, we cannot do, Diderot develops an analogy, suggested by La Mettrie, with the resounding of vibrating strings.

> It is this vibration, this inevitable resonance, which holds the object present, while the mind is busied about the quality that belongs to that object. But vibrating strings have yet another property, that of making other strings vibrate; and that is how the first idea recalls a second, the two of them a third, so that there is no limit to the ideas awakened and interconnected in the mind of the philosopher. This instrument makes surprising leaps, and an idea once aroused may sometimes set vibrating a harmonic at an inconceivable distance. If this phenomenon may be observed between resonant strings that are lifeless and separate, why should it not occur between points that are alive and connected, between fibers that are continuous and sensitive?

Diderot's terms are not modern, but the thought is. In the words of a scientist of our own day, "All the gradations of feeling and action of which we are capable are provided by variations in the frequency of nerve impulses and by the number of nerve cells stimulated," through a system of "pulse-frequency modulation." [2] This description, which is analogous to Diderot's, is undoubtedly correct from the scientific viewpoint of measurement. But measurements are descriptions of reality, not explanations. Thought may well depend on matter, but is not necessarily equivalent to the motions of matter. Although there is a quantitative similarity, is there not also a qualitative difference between "pulsations" and a feeling of love, hate, or jealousy? Is there no essential distinction between the mechanical memory of an electronic robot and the "understanding" that enables us to be conscious of the process we are performing, to comprehend it, to build value judgments upon it?

The philosopher of organism contends that the scientific method of analysis deals only with abstracted aspects, while reality is a whole. D'Alembert glimpses this objection in somewhat different terms. He accuses Diderot of making of the philosopher's mind a being distinct from the instrument, "a musician who listens to the vibrating strings." And Diderot, in pointing out d'Alembert's error, approaches the modern theory of epiphenomenalism. The philosopher, he explains, is an instrument that has the faculty of sensation; consequently, he is both the instrument and the musician. "We are instruments endowed with feeling and a memory; our senses are so many keys that are struck by nature around us, and that often strike themselves." A harpsichord with sensations, with the ability to feed and to reproduce, would be a living harpsichord.

In this last statement, we again see Diderot's failure to penetrate to the root of the problem of life. That a harpsichord would be living if it fed is a facile assumption. But why should a harpsichord feed? Why does anything feed? Only because it has "need-satisfying behavior," and this unexplained need and behavior is the crux of the problem.

Once more the discussion turns to problems of biology. In La Mettrie, Diderot had found, in addition to a mechanistic psychology, an interest in physical abnormalities.

Following the more original work of Maupertuis, Diderot points out that defects may skip generations. "It takes two to make a child, as you know. Perhaps one of the agents repairs the vice of the other, and the defective network is reborn only when the

[2] W. Gray Walter: "An Imitation of Life," *Scientific American,* May 1950.

descendant of the monstrous race predominates and dictates the formation of the network." This problem is connected with that of the differentiation of the organs in the fetus. With remarkable prescience, he turns to malformations as the best clue to the process. He concludes that if "the thread" (read: "chromosome") that forms the eye were excised—no eye would develop. These "monsters" show the role of chance error and argue against biological finalism.

Near the end, d'Alembert and Mlle. de Lespinasse recapitulate.

D'ALEMBERT: So there is everything reduced to sensitivity, memory, organic movement. . . .

MLLE. DE LESPINASSE: According to your principles, it seems to me, that by a succession of purely mechanical operations, I could reduce the greatest genius on earth to a mass of unorganized flesh, to which would be left only momentary sensitivity, and that we could bring back this shapeless mass from the most profound state of stupidity to the status of a man of genius. One of these phenomena would consist in mutilating the primitive skein of a number of its threads, and in scrambling the others; and the inverse phenomenon would consist in restoring to the skein the excised threads, and in leaving it to a successful development. Example: I remove from Newton the auditory threads, and no more sensation of sound; the olfactory, and no more sensation of odor . . . I cut out or mix up the others, and there goes the organization of the brain, memory, judgment, desire, aversion, passions, will, consciousness of self, and there is a shapeless mass which has retained only life and sensitivity.

Restore all these, and everything will be just as it was: "I have again my man of genius—and without the interference of any heterogeneous or unintelligible agent." And so Diderot makes of life a machine, in which, theoretically, we could make modifications, taking out parts or putting them in, as in any machine built by man.

And yet, with all his materialism, his denial of the soul and of immortality, Diderot wrote to Sophie: "It seems to me that as long as I enjoy good health, I shall think like Father Hoop; but that at the last moment, perhaps, I would buy the happiness of living once more with a thousand years, with ten thousand years of Hell. Ah! dear friend, we would find each other again! Isn't it sweet to exist, and to find again our father, our mother, our sweetheart, our friend, our wife, our children, everything we have cherished—even in Hell! " Always the fight, the fight between mind and heart!

"Liberty" is the magic word that leads the characters in Diderot's dialogue to his innermost preoccupation, morals. Bordeu immediately declares that there is no free will. "Will is always born of some external motive, some present impression, some reminiscence of the past, some passion, some project." Our actions are the necessary effect of a cause which is highly complicated yet a unity: ourselves. We depend on our organs, and most of all on our heredity. We depend on the entire previous history of our lives (our impulses are "the result of all we have been from birth to the present moment"), with all the influences implied by that history. We depend finally on all of history before us—on the experience of the race. These influences can be modified, but not suppressed.

Actually, all he has done is to stipulate a motive for every action. But "free will," or freedom of the self, does not mean that our acts have no causes, or that our desires are free. Freedom, if it exists, lies in the conscious control we have over the passage of impulse into action. The strongest motive we must obey. It is not determined, however, by a mechanical competition for nerve paths, but selected by the Self, by an operation of the mind, by our own decision. The mind is capable of creating or being its own cause. The act of choice is an act of self-creation.

Yet we must realize that determinism was an inevitable consequence of the effort to reintegrate man into nature. Great impulse had been given to this view by Newton's discovery that everything in the universe, large and small, is regulated by laws. Eighteenth-century philosophers did what Newton had refused to do; they considered these laws as complete and sufficient explanations of reality. There was no room for anything distinctive in man, no ground for considering him a special being. "It would be most singular," wrote Voltaire, "that all nature, all the stars, should obey eternal laws, and that there should be a little animal five feet high, who, in defiance of these laws, could always act as he pleased according to the whim of his caprice."

Before necessity's motivation, concludes Bordeu-Diderot, morality disappears. There can be no responsibility, and no meaningful moral qualification, for a necessary action. This amoral conclusion is completely logical, and no way out of it has ever been found. And Diderot again sketches a social morality, based on modification through example and punishment, to induce behavior considered desirable by society—the only criterion of right or wrong.

The ultimate conclusions of a *natural* morality are reached in the sequel to the dialogue. This brief addendum is an attack on conventional sexual conduct and sex laws, which controvert the nature of things and public good. All abnormal sexual practices are defended. Pleasure and profit being the only criteria of our actions, when there can be no profit, let there at least be pleasure. And let no one speak the word "unnatural." "Anything that is can be neither against nature nor outside of nature."

"Evil" is the result of the same natural laws that cause "good." "The words 'good' and 'evil' have no more application to the universe than to a machine in which one part would wear out another . . . At each moment, we can say of the universe that everything in it is as it must necessarily be; nothing to blame, nothing to praise." This absence of values in the universe again assigns the status of man to that of another incident in nature's planless productions. Diderot derides providentialism, in the *Salon of 1767*. Suppose a grain of sand blows into your eye. "What does that matter to nature? Did she make this landscape to your order? . . . Come, my friend. Let's not act so important. We are in nature; we are in it sometimes comfortably, sometimes uncomfortably."

The implications are clear. In nature, there is only living. And in the inexorable struggle for existence, any idea of "good" or "evil" changes completely with the viewpoint: to the preyer and his victim, and to the bystander who is helped or harmed by either one, the simple and necessary action of self-preservation may be given entirely different moral values, whereas nature attaches to it none at all. We may extend this to the other egoistic drives.

In nature, the law of force is the only "justice" or "morality." For civilized man they are matters of convention or personal interest. With the only possible morality a human one, based on man's social needs and physical nature, Christian morality necessarily appears vicious to Diderot, for it attempts to turn the current of instinct into artificial channels created by the taboos of a mystical doctrine. The logic of materialism does not allow him to realize that this morality, whether or not it be the best for man, is an effort to transcend the "natural," to realize what is most "human" in us.

This whole view of man's life, anticipating Freud's mechanistic-naturalistic approach, represents Diderot's decision to accept the brutal facts, and not look for consoling answers. Since there is only matter and its laws, the psychic life is reduced to the physical and the physiological, and ethics is reduced to social utility. But it still allows man to become greater, writes Paul Vernière, through his brain, by gaining dominion over his own reality.

D'Alembert's Dream is characterized by a spirit of scientific positivism and by bold imagination; its limits are those of the knowledge of the time and of Diderot's viewpoint. The eighteenth-century climate of opinion accounts for the entire range of his ideas, although he is often a step ahead. The Encyclopedists, according to the great physicist Ernst Mach, believed they were close to a final explanation of the world by physical and mechanical principles. This was a natural exaggeration of the power of new knowledge, a natural tendency to overlook the logical chasms which lie between physics and life and thought. Dampier points out that they naively took the phenomenal world as real. "How can the motion of senseless particles produce consciousness, or, in the alternative, what is the endowment of matter itself with sensation but an assumption of the very thing to be explained?"

Diderot has succeeded in outlining a complete materialistic system. It applies to the cosmos, with its monism and dynamics of change within the unity of the whole; to life, in its origin, processes and evolution; and to man, in his physical, mental and moral activities. The whole dialogue, writes one scholar, "develops from the effort to dispose of the difficulties inherent in a supernaturalistic interpretation of the universe." Not only is it doubtful whether Diderot has disposed of these difficulties; it is clear that he has only substituted the difficulties inherent in a materialist interpretation of the universe. Later, he will realize this. Even at this point, there is, throughout the dialogue, a feeling for life as a vital process, distinct from the mechanics of the nonliving. "His materialism," writes Sainte-Beuve, "is no dry geometrical mechanism, but a confused vitalism, fruitful and potent, a spontaneous, unceasing evolutionary fermentation." His concept of the universe as a Whole belongs to an idealist school of philosophy, for the materialist sees only discrete units in fixed points of time and place. His concept of organic unity likewise envisages the whole as more than the mere sum of its parts. Finally, he defines life as behavior, as action directed towards an end, a concept that involves choice and rejection in natural process.

In the *Salon of 1767*, Diderot summarizes his materialistic view of nature. "This world is only a mass of molecules, loaded like dice in an infinity of different ways. There is a law of necessity that works without design, without effort, without intelligence, without progress. . . ." Compare his view with that of Whitehead:

> Evolution, on the materialist theory, is reduced to the role of being another word for the descriptions of the changes of the external relations between portions of matter. There is nothing to evolve, because one set of external relations is as good as any other set of external relations. There can be merely change, purposeless and unprogressive. But the whole point of the modern doctrine is the evolution of the complex organism from antecedent states of less complex organisms. The doctrine cries aloud for a conception of organisms as fundamental for nature . . . The organism is a unit of emergent value . . . Thus in the process of analyzing the character of nature in itself, we find that the emergence of organism depends on a selective activity which is akin to purpose.

Diderot was closer than anyone in his time to a feeling of organism, but he had opted for a materialist system that prevented development of its fullest conclusions.

3

In 1770, a short series of thoughts, *Philosophical Principles of Matter and Movement* (published by Naigeon in 1792) were intended as a definitive statement of his views on matter. It presents the usual materialist position, that obtained until demolished by quanta, wave mechanics, and relativity. Matter, eternal and uncreated, is stipulated as the sole constituent of the universe. It is indestructible, possesses extension, mass, and definite location in space and time. The question of motion and initial impulse is solved, following Toland, by the denial of absolute rest. Movement is as much a property of matter as mass, essential, uncreated, equivalent to the force inherent in matter. This motion, or energy, is either kinetic ("active") or potential, held in dynamic equilibrium. The linking of energy to matter was necessary to a materialist philosophy, in order to eliminate God as prime mover. It was a step toward the present-day dissolution of matter into energy, which completes the circle from Descartes, for whom matter existed without energy, as extension. It was also necessary in order to account for Diderot's dynamic, evolving universe. In this process of constant change, interaction, and recombination, the only thing that does not change or die is the elementary unit of matter, because the energy that it contains and that keeps it going is eternal.

The problems of biology, which interested Diderot more than physical questions, continued as a subject of investigation. Between 1768 and 1780, he jotted down a series of notes on his reading and thinking in the field, most of them stemming from the work of the great physiologist, Albrecht von Haller.

Much of the speculation deals with.the unity of the living body. Surmising the importance of the glandular system, he has a clear vision which approaches our twentieth-century view that we think not with the brain alone, but with the entire body. Man is a fantastically, incomprehensibly complicated creature. Yet he is essentially a machine, of a special and higher order. "The will is no less mechanical than the understanding . . . a pure, simple, and passive machine . . . he has not produced even a single act of his will. He has thought, he has felt, but he has acted no more freely than an inert body, than a wooden automaton that might have performed the same acts as he. . . ."

"The difference between the machine of flesh and the machine of iron or wood, between man, a dog, and a clock is that in the latter all movements, which are determined, are not accompanied either by awareness or will." But since awareness and will are mechanical, there is no qualitative difference between the living and non-living. (Awareness, however, creates a new way of being in the world.)

How then shall we consider a spark that lights up one of the pages of the *Elements of Physiology,* one of those flashes of illumination we meet in all his works? In *D'Alembert's Dream,* he had insisted that life is a pure phenomenon of physics and chemistry. Now he speaks, briefly and vaguely, it is true, of a "vital principle," almost coining Bergson's famous expression of more than a century later.

"As long as the vital principle is not destroyed, the most bitter cold could not freeze the fluids of an animal who is exposed to it . . . Without life nothing can be explained, nor without sensitivity, and living and sensitive nerves. Without life, there is no distinction between the living man and his corpse."

There is only one other passage at all like it, one in which he says that irritability is different from any other "force" in nature, is life itself. The influence of Haller is evident: for the Swiss physiologist had held that irritability and sensitivity are the unique and distinguishing properties of life. By the "vital principle," Diderot means that mysterious, incomprehensible cooperation of all the organs, in a new and distinct whole, which constitute life. Death is the extinction of the same "vital principle" that permits life, the end of the marvelous unity of the body. The ultimate mystery of life consists precisely in that vital force that *animates,* creating the unity and the continuity of the life process. Diderot had attributed life to a special organization that changes the type of sensitivity in matter. But does that account, as he asks, for the difference between the living man and the corpse?

Pursuing his idea, Diderot compares the life of the organ with that of the whole animal:

> Self-interest is born in each organ from its position, its construction, its functions; it is then an animal subject to comfort and discomfort, to comfort that it seeks, to discomfort of which it tries to rid itself. The difference between the organ and the whole is that the whole foresees, the organ does not. The whole experiments, the organ does not. The whole avoids ill; the organ does not avoid it, it feels it and tries to free itself from it.

Continuing his thinking about evolution, he clarifies his idea of selection, adding the significant element that was lacking in his earlier formulations. Selection must not be understood as a tendency toward perfection and beauty, but as a purge of beings ill-adapted to the material environment, which consists of certain combinations of matter. If the environment were suddenly changed, the most perfect and beautiful beings might suddenly become imperfect and ugly, and would perish, unless they could re-adapt themselves. But movement, and therefore change, is the law of the universe, from the smallest combination to the greatest mass; it applies equally to the individual, the species, and the universe. Since our environment changes constantly, the species must also evolve. It is absurd to suppose "that there is on the surface of the earth a being, an animal who has always been what he is now . . . Only the molecule can remain the same." From this struggle to adapt oneself and to survive, Diderot concludes that "the world is the house of the strong." In this way he gives us the theoretical foundation for the evolutionary morality that is one possible terminus of materialism.

He also embarks on a lengthy discussion of memory, its nature, power, and connection with imagination and reason. He defines it as "a faithful chain of sensations awakened in the same succession in which they were received, a property of the brain." He describes the subconscious memory, calls it a storehouse of forgotten impression. "The sound of a voice, the presence of an object, a certain place, and all of a sudden an object—what do I say—a long period of my life is recalled. I am suddenly plunged into pleasure, regret, or affection. This power [of memory] is wielded either while one is relaxed *(dans l'abandon de soi)* or occupied. The organ of memory seems to me to be always passive; it recalls nothing by itself; it needs a cause to set it to work. . . . I am inclined to believe that all we have seen, known, or heard *. : .* exists in us without our realizing it." The importance of this theory in twentieth-century psychology and literature needs no comment.

Not all of Diderot's scientific ideas are so brilliant. He accepts, quite naturally, many of the errors of his time, but his limitations only make his vision the more remarkable. On the problem of fertilization, he held that the sperm cell does not enter the egg, but exudes a vapor that acts as a catalytic agent. To determine the existence of pregnancy, Diderot suggests the vaginal insertion of garlic, before retiring; if the odor is perceptible from the mouth, the following morning, then a pregnant condition does not exist. He believes in prenatal influence, and the predominance of the father in heredity.

4

In *D'Alembert's Dream*, Diderot had sketched the theory of a materialist ethic to which he had already given a body in *Rameau's Nephew*. Now he was to unfold the vision of a "natural" society, operating according to some of his principles. The *Supplement to Bougainville's Voyage, or a Dialogue between A and B*, composed in 1772, is one of his most radical pieces.

Under orders of the king, Louis-Antoine de Bougainville accomplished the first French circumnavigation of the globe between 1766 and 1769. His account of it, appearing in 1771, created a great deal of comment, especially the parts dealing with the moral notions of the Tahitians. Diderot conceived the idea of a "supplement," a clever fiction similar to Saunderson's supposed conversation in *The Letter on the Blind*.

The *Supplement* portrays a society with practically no sexual restraint of any kind. And it is a happy state, without rape, seduction, jealousy, hate, crimes of passion, or the idea of sin. The only morality is the eternal law of nature which commands that the individual seek happiness, and that the general welfare be preferred to individual welfare.

Such is the glib statement of "natural," or primitive society that Diderot presents in his dialogue. As with Montaigne, primitive life is an excuse for dwelling on the relativity of religious and moral values and for criticizing our own civilization by a comparison with the life of the happy savages. The upshot of the dialogue is that neither religion nor "sexual morality" exists in nature. The critical phase leads to a final philosophical evaluation of the meaning of morality and of the worth of progress and civilization.

The religious discussion is not of exceptional interest. The ship's chaplain attempts to convert his Tahitian host, Orou, but the primitive's naive answers reduce to absurdity every doctrine and argument the priest can muster. It is only too obvious that Diderot's savage is reasoning with the precise logic and incisive irony of an eighteenth-century rationalist. This phase is a purely polemical invention. Bougainville himself had clearly set down a truth that applies to all primitive peoples, as well as to the inhabitants of Tahiti: he found them to be superstitious believers in good and evil spirits, and prostrate before the absolute authority of their priests. In fact Diderot's picture of the primitive mind is consistently false, although the sin is more often one of ignorance or of romantic imagination than of deliberate invention.

The dialogue between Orou and the chaplain occurs only as interludes in the principal discussion, which is between A and B, two Frenchmen who have read Bougainville's account. A and B conclude that the most natural and most agreeable act in life has become a great source of vice and of suffering, because civilization has attached to it such artificialities as marriage, fidelity, modesty, flirtation, and jealousy. In this part, Diderot is enjoying the intellectual game of pushing his rational amoralism to its extreme logical consequences.

Diderot's radical notions on the sexual act stem from an ethics that was at odds with itself, consisting of distinct trends which were never thought out to harmonious conclusions. He naively blames Christianity for attaching "the names of vices and virtues to actions that were not susceptible to moral qualifications." Such a view can only be predicated—as indeed it is—on a conception of the sex relationship as a purely biological act, having as its sole signficance the "voluptuous rubbing of two membranes" and perpetuation of the species. It is not true that incest, free-love without jealousy are any more "natural" than the feelings he condemns. Here Rousseau was keener than Diderot, recognizing that as soon as people live together, habit evokes the *natural* feelings of possession and jealousy. Intent on the evil consequences of the civilized sex relationship, Diderot overlooks the essential fact that it has transformed the entire value of the sexual act, changing it from a nonselective animal urge to a human passion we call "love," a source of psychological and spiritual fulfillment.

Diderot's "natural system" includes only one side of man's nature, since man's personality is social and consequently moral, as well as animal. We can therefore question the naturalness of a "natural system" that bestows *moral* approval on intercourse between father and daughter, mother and son. Even among the most primitive people, there is rigorous regulation of sexual intercourse. This Diderot was forced to concede.

Diderot's derogation of marriage is resumed in a line to Sophie Volland: "The indissoluble vow of marriage makes and must make almost as many unhappy people as there are married people." His profound aversion comes partly from his rational immoralism, but first and foremost from his own bitter experience. It often seems, in his correspondence, that the idea of marital fidelity is incomprehensible to him. The sin of infidelity, he explained to Sophie, "is a fault less reprehensible than the slightest lie."

In the *Supplement*, derision of marriage is cast in more rational form. Marriage is a form of the idea of property, a concept offensive to the dignity of man and contrary to the law of change. But once more he disregards the good in the moral relationship which has superimposed itself on the biological. This relationship has a higher worth, despite the conflict it engenders, in that it alone allows realization of the hyperorganic values that grow out of complete fulfillment of the sex drive. The idea of possession is not the crude material possession of the body. Violation of the rule does not, as he thinks, itself refute the principle, its worth or indeed its necessity, but underscores the difficulty of its realization.

On the other hand, Diderot was faced in France with an unreasonable legislative situation that allowed no divorce and gave women no rights. Furthermore, in his attacks on marriage, and on celibacy, he was under the universal illusion, not dispelled until Malthus' work, that the most pressing social need was to increase the population. Children were considered future tillers rather than future consumers.

When the discussion broadens to the general ethical problem, we come upon the same basic errors: preference for a lower level over conflict at a higher level, and a confused evaluation of the word "natural." This word is sometimes taken to mean the "instinctual," organic and egoistic; sometimes the preference of moral good and general welfare to instinct and pleasure. Most important of all, Diderot fails to realize, or refuses to acknowledge that the conflict involved in man's effort to surmount the instinctual or animal level of existence is the essence of his humanity. "There existed a natural man; we have introduced within that man an artificial man, and within the cavern there is continual warfare throughout his life." It is typical of the century to see Diderot substituting for the good-evil Christian dualism, an equivalent "natural man–artificial man" dualism, so contrary to his profounder idea of an amoral universe and a relativist, humanistic morality.

What Diderot is attempting to formulate is a social definition of virtue that will not contradict a "natural" (instinctual) morality. "Civil law must be only the statement of the law of Nature." To attempt such an impossible feat was again characteristic of eighteenth-century rationalism. "On birth we bring only a similarity of organization with that of others, the same needs, attraction towards the same pleasures, aversion for the same sufferings— which constitute man as he is and should serve as foundation for the morality that suits him." The physical basis, which dominates the implications of Diderot's words, is irrefutable. But again he over-simplifies. Man is more, far more, than he here allows, else he is not man. If to live with others is as much a part of human nature as our physical urges, then man is as naturally moral as he is immoral. The "human" triumph lies in controlling and directing our instincts, not in passively yielding to them.

When Diderot declares that there is no rule other than the general good and the private good, he leaves the content of "good" completely undetermined. This rule would suit a totalitarian as well as a democrat. Consequently, he is able to justfy adultery and incest, since they lead to private pleasure and to social good in the production of children. Even the most primitive morality could not stand before such a criterion. What is "useful" for the individual? Diderot fails to distinguish between immediate utility (stealing, fornication) and ultimate utility in the light of the total nature of man and his complete self-realization. What is good for the collectivity? Again we must have a complete view of its life, or we fall into the error of the totalitarians.

Diderot condemns laws that are contrary to natural instincts as lacking the power to modify our conduct. The fallacy of his plea for sexual freedom here becomes most evident. If laws only sanction instincts, then there is no need of laws at all. What about our other aggressive drives, towards possession and destruction? What meaning does his final conclusion have? "You will find men subjected to three codes, the code of Nature, the civil code, and the religious code, and obliged to infringe alternately upon these three codes which have never been in agreement." And indeed, how could they be in agreement, for if we understand "Nature" as Diderot here does, to follow its code would make the other two superfluous.

It would be ill-advised to consider Diderot's moral ideas in the light of a system. It is noteworthy that he never had the courage to approach his greatest project, a treatise on morals. The reason is evident. In morals, as in many other fields, Diderot was divided against himself; at different times, or even simultaneously, his thought followed widely divergent lines.

The lack of sexual restraint advocated in the *Supplement* is in complete contrast to his preachings elsewhere. The exaltation of modesty and virtue in the *Salons*, in the heroes and heroines of his plays, and in real life, to his daughter, would meet the hearty approval of any Christian. At those times he uses the word *vice* to describe an act he elsewhere terms natural and good and which he calls vicious to restrict! Even marriage, and marital fidelity, on which he heaps abuse and condemnation, are avenged at other moments. In the *Introduction to Great Principles* he defines marriage as "a debt which everyone must pay to society." After his daughter's wedding, he wrote to her that the very suspicion of infidelity on her part would crush him with grief and destroy all his esteem for her; "I should die to have to blush for it."

Diderot had one morality in which he abandoned his objective rationalism and followed the sentimental bourgeois impulses of his heart. It was the Christian morality of some of his writings and much of his life. At the other extreme was the ethical theory of Diderot the rebel, the atheistic materialist who insisted on a complete and almost anarchic liberty for the individual. This was the morality of *D'Alembert's Dream*, the *Supplement to the Voyage of Bougainville*, *Rameau's Nephew*, and of his own amorous escapades. Between the two, but in a sense part of the first, was a reasoned theory of social virtue as the source of individual happiness.

This philosophy is most satisfactory when expressed teleologically as a form of utilitarianism—the well-known "enlightened self-interest." Often it finds expression in a formalistic belief in the conscience—a much more emotional faith than Kant's moral reason, and attached to the current of bourgeois sentimentalism. It was only Diderot the rebel who called virtue and remorse "puerilities" and "prejudices." To the other Diderot, nothing in the world was dearer than those same puerilities and prejudices.

The ultimate question in the *Supplement to Bougainville's Voyage* is the worth of progress and civilization. Of the many abstract questions that captured the imagination of the eighteenth-century mind, few were more popular or more important. On it— with Diderot's stimulation—Rousseau had won his scandalous success and founded the most influential philosophy of the time. Its vogue was partly a result of explorations in Oceania and travel journals such as Cook's and Bougainville's, more deeply a reaction to the spiritual and political decadence of the age. Clothed in the garments of rationalism, primitivism expressed the eternal romanticism in man, the longing to escape from the artificiality and dessication of an ultra-refined and formalized society. Polemically it was an excellent means of satirizing foibles and abuses, and as such was utilized by the most civilized of eighteenth-century writers, Voltaire.

In his zeal to sketch a utopian version of life on Tahiti, Diderot even gilded the glowing account of Bougainville. The picture is essentially the one given by Rousseau in the *Discourse on the Origin of Inequality,* the work in which Diderot exercised the greatest influence on his sometime friend. Without the evils of property and love, with no desires beyond the "natural" ones (still considering man to be "natural" only in his organic functioning), and with a beneficent climate eliminating struggle for these, the fortunate Tahitians, Diderot declares, have only to lose by the introduction of civilization and "progress." Civilization would mean the end of all this; new needs, complications, corruption, and strife—not to mention new diseases.

Property appears to Diderot, as to Rousseau, the mainspring of society, the source of strife and warfare. The need to fight and unfavorable natural conditions led to the progress of knowledge. Once started on this fateful journey, there was no stopping place, and man was carried far beyond the stage where he can be happy, "to knowledge and depravity." The less knowledge, the less artificial morality and vice. In the final summing up, "A" inquires, "should we civilize man or abandon him to his instinct"? (A meaningless question, of course, since man's "instinct" leads him to civilization, of whatever level he can attain.) "B" replies: "If you wish to be his tyrant, civilize him . . . and let natural man be forever chained to the feet of moral man." Since there is no real progress toward happiness, the decision is that "the more men are civilized, the more vicious and unhappy they are." Anarchism thus sets up a natural-moral antithesis, and prefers the natural.

Bougainville himself had taken a more objective view. He admitted that there was neither liberty nor equality on Tahiti, but cruel tyranny and abject submission. And he concludes about primitive people that as soon as there is more than one family, "interests become complicated, individuals try to dominate by force or fraud. The name 'family' changes into 'society,' and were it established in the woods, were it composed of first cousins, an attentive mind will discover in it the germ of all the vices to which civilized men have given names . . . It follows from the same principle that in societies called civilized, virtues are born of which men still close to the state of nature are not capable."

In the light of Diderot's other writings, many have questioned the seriousness of his condemnation of civilization. They have stressed his polemical intent, and his love of paradox. And indeed, Diderot, recalling how he suggested this idea to Rousseau, says he intended it only as a paradox. He was certainly not an obscurantist, and had great faith in the progress of science. While the *Supplement* again offers a pre-Freudian view of the energy of the individual and its forced repression under social conditions, elsewhere Diderot, like many post-Freudian psychiatrists, sees civilization as the developer of individual energies in skills and activities that provide greater satisfaction and welfare, and a longer span of life. When it pleases him to attack Rousseau, he writes, in the *Refutation of Helvétius*, "Rousseau believes that society serves only to deprave human nature; and you [Helvétius] believe that only good social laws can correct nature's original vices. . . . All is bad in the cities, but all is worse in the woods." And he adds, in Voltairean style, "Yes, monsieur Rousseau, I prefer refined vice in silken garb to savage stupidity in an animal skin." As for man being naturally good, he recognizes more realistically that he is born with "organic and natural tendencies . . . to harm himself and his fellow men . . .

to justice or anger, to respect or to scorn of laws." But he does not retreat on the sexual question. He still insists it is futile to make what is unnatural honorable. The sexual organ will never have "any instinct other than its own. It has its object like the eye, and the legislator who would order the eye, under pain of ignominy, to look only at certain important objects, would be crazy." One cannot help thinking of Don Juan's line, in *Man and Superman*, "I saw then how useless it is to attempt to impose conditions on the irresistible force of Life, to preach . . . virtue, honor, chastity."

It would be an error to conclude that the *Supplement* is no more than a paradox. The Tahitian utopia was rather an illusion, a hope, even a profound longing. Fundamentally, Diderot—that is, Diderot the rebel—was an unconscious anarchist. Happiness cannot exist without virtue, but, he inquires, in *The Temple of Happiness*, can civilized man be virtuous? "I am convinced that there can be no true happiness for the human race except in a social state where there would be neither king, nor magistrates, nor priest, nor laws, nor thine, nor mine, nor *propriété mobilière*, nor *propriété foncière*, nor vices, nor virtues; and that social state is devilishly ideal." This deep tendency in Diderot is confirmed by his interest in the curious system of Dom Deschamps, an obscure Benedictine monk who seriously hoped to do away with property, organized society, and law. The true paradox of the *Supplement* lies in the meeting of this illusion of his romantic nature with the logical conclusion of his most extreme rationalism.

The *Supplement to Bougainville's Voyage* deserves an important place in the history of primitivistic writings, since it points up more sharply and rationally than most others, and certainly with less reserve or reticence, the conflicts involved. The ingenuously perceptive savage and the wise old man were standard equipment in writings of this type, and are as usual turned to satirical ends. The themes are the customary ones. It is in his frank and uncompromising crystallization of the issues, carrying the discussion to final logical conclusions, that Diderot has made a contribution.

Although the *Supplement* had no influence during the eighteenth century, Professor Chinard has shown how it affected the "physiological school of love" in the nineteenth, including Schopenhauer, Maupassant, and Zola, by its conception of love as an organic appetite and instinct rather than a feeling. The early nineteenth century witnessed a keen discussion on this subject. Many reacted against Diderot's crude view of human nature, Stendahl, among others, proclaiming that "love is the miracle of civilization." Chateaubriand's *René* reintroduced the idea of sin (or innate evil) in man, and of "the internal struggle that Diderot and his group had tried to suppress." Psychiatry has confirmed Chateaubriand's view. In terms of Diderot's transposition into natural and artificial man (in which "natural" is falsely associated with "good"), philosophers have generally seen in this conflict not merely the torment, but the triumph of man.

5

The disconcerting quality of Diderot's thought is largely due to the one profound cleavage that runs through his life, thought and personality: the recurrent struggle within himself between heart and head, between bourgeois temperament and rebellious mind. His inexorable rationalism led him to atheism, materialism, determinism, amoralism, anarchy. His bourgeois sentimentalism led him to virtue, moralizing, humanitarianism, and the defense of property rights. His heart resented the conclusions of his mind, because temperamentally he was an enthusiastic optimist. His rationalism destroyed virtue and morality, but without them he could not live. When it was a question of practical living, his fundamental bourgeois realism most often dominated the rational logic of revolt.

Setting out all over again from the question of God, Diderot had spent a decade building a well-rounded philosophy. He had developed an explanation of the universe, of life, and of man—both as an animal and as a thinking being—in the light of a complete and radical system of materialism. Man has been put in his place, a dual place, partly in the animal world, partly in the social world. In the contrasting impulses and needs of this dual existence lies the source of his problems and torments. If Diderot is sometimes contradictory, even confused, let us not censure him too severely. At least he has had the merit of appreciating, better than any other man of his century, the complexity of life, of truth, and of right.

CHAPTER 15

Wherein
Some
Changes
Occur

1

OF THE MANY CHANGES that occurred in Diderot's personal life between 1769 and 1772, as he approached his sixtieth year, probably the saddest was the slow death of his love for Sophie Volland. For twelve years they had loved each other tenderly. Then, due partly to the chill of age and still more to the inconstancy of his temperament, Diderot's feelings gradually lost their emotional quality, and their love affair settled down to a purely intellectual and habitual relationship. This cooling-off process can be followed in his letters, now less frequent and less lengthy. The declarations of love, once so tender and so ardent, which he felt compelled to continue, become brief, artificial, devoid of the fire of sincerity. "Bonjour, Mlle. Volland. I think we still love each other . . . I shall keep for you, Mlle. Volland, my first feelings, as long as I live."

There was another reason for Diderot's growing indifference towards the woman whom he had once claimed to prefer to wife, child, and even to himself. He had fallen in love again, for the fourth time. The object of his last flame was Mme. de Meaux. Forty-four years old in 1769, of illegitimate birth, Mme. de Meaux had been at the very same time as Mme. Duclos, the mistress of Damilaville.

In a word, Diderot had replaced his friend, after his death in 1768, and Mme. de Meaux was thus enabled to continue her "philosophical" love affairs.

In this episode of his relations with Sophie, as in his premarital quarrels with Antoinette, Diderot displays a certain weakness of character. Lacking the resolution to admit the truth, to break with her, he chooses the easier and more degrading course of simulating unbroken constancy. He shows himself incapable of making the difficult decision and lacking in moral courage. It is somewhat distasteful, after the amorous pages of the earlier letters, to read Diderot's ineffective attempts to pretend a continuance of the same relationship. "That is very nice, my sweet friend," he writes in 1769. "You tell me all about the way you spend your time, your amusements, your harvests. You assume that I am interested, and you are right." Sophie was not long in suspecting that "the eternal love" of her friend had vanished. But even when she frankly accused him of indifference, in October 1770, Diderot could not bring himself to admit it, and instead tried weakly to persuade her of the contrary. There is something sad, if not something ignoble, in the dragging out of this liaison, after all love was dead.

The *affaire* with Mme. de Meaux was a swan song, the last attempt of an aging man to recapture and taste once more the fleeting pleasures of love. How much of Diderot's virility remained is questionable. Three years before, on his fifty-fourth birthday, he had assured Sophie of his fidelity in these terms: "You cannot imagine how virtuous a man is when he is fifty years old, and with what courage he refuses a pleasure that he is no longer in a condition to enjoy. Even if a young woman were disposed to hear me, can I forget how little I have to say to her?"

There is scant doubt, however, that Mme. de Meaux became his mistress. When the philosopher made a trip to the spa at Bourbonne, in August of 1770, it was not for his health, but to rejoin his new love, whose absence caused him cruel pangs of regret. She had gone there to accompany her daughter, the attractive Mme. de Prunevaux, who was suffering from the aftereffects of childbirth.

At Bourbonne, his joy was completely spoiled by the arrival of a certain M. de Foissy, a polite, courtly, and good-looking gentleman of thirty-five. It seems that de Foissy soon triumphed in the hearts of both mother and daughter. At first Diderot was unaware of the rivalry, and blissfully returned to Langres, where he wrote the *Conversation of a Father with his Children* and *The Two Friends of Bourbonne,* two of his best shorter works. When Diderot finally realized what was going on, he suffered terrible torments of jealousy. Desperately anxious to find out which of the two women de Foissy loved, he purposely encouraged his rival's advances, only to receive a still greater blow. De Foissy was interested in Mme. de Meaux and not, as he had hoped, in her daughter.

At first Diderot made a show of taking his defeat philosophically. He would not bother the two lovers any longer; instead he would seek consolation in the recovery of his liberty. "I have carefully tested myself," he wrote to Grimm on October 15. "I am not suffering! I shall not suffer." But five days later, he is insane with jealousy, although he pretends to be upset less about his mistress' inconstancy than about her insincerity. Mme. de Meaux had told him, "I love you, I love only you," and then she had said the same thing to his rival. "And my happiness, and my tranquillity, what becomes of them in all this confusion? If they had planned to drive me crazy, could they do any better? . . . Does a woman allow herself such an amusement at the age of forty-five?"

All his references to the loss of his time and liberty, to motives of sincerity and decency were only pretexts and rationalizations. Diderot was suffering. He was suffering the jealousy of a man of fifty-seven who is overthrown in favor of a younger rival. It is hard to feel any sympathy for him, despite the intensity of his anguish.

Once again he displays the same weakness of character. Lacking the resolve to break with his mistress, he gradually resigned himself to the rival, and outstayed him. In that way his friendship with Mme. de Meaux continued almost until the end of his life, in fact until the end of hers. On the first of January 1778, he sent her this little poem:

> My Portrait and My Horoscope
> Sent to Madame de M . . .
> New Year's Day 1778

> Spoiled child of nature,
> Such was I made, I think, in a moment of intoxication,
> Such without remorse have I remained!
> Postponing from day to day the counsel
> Of sad reason, of austere wisdom,
> Past my sixtieth year, cap and bells in hand,
> I follow with bent back the droll battalions

Of its turbulent rival,
And sometimes in my shaking head
You can hear the bells of Momus ringing.
   Near you I could have played
A more decent role, if not so sweet:
   I mean that of laughing at fools,
   When it is past the season to be one;
   But for this role, it is perhaps necessary
To have common sense, to be you.
   At my age it is difficult
   To pass under new laws
   And you have, wise Lucille,
At least fifteen years further to mock me.
   Yes, for fifteen years, you may be sure,
Swelled with old sighs, scorched with old desires,
I shall feel this octogenarian heart
   Beat for your slightest pleasures.
   But when on my sarcophagus
   A great disconsolate Pallas
   Will point out to passersby
   The engraved words: *Here lies a wise man,*
   Do not, with indiscreet laugh,
   Belie weeping Minerva,
   Disgrace my honored memory, by saying:
Here lies a fool . . . Guard well my secret.

2

The year 1769 was an exciting one in French politics. As a result of Louis XV's high-handed administration of justice, the Parlements again rebelled against his tyranny. In open defiance, they deprived the duke d'Aiguillon, governor of Brittany, of his "rights and privileges as a peer." This court order, and others, were broken by the king, who announced that he held his crown from God and that the legislative power belonged to him alone. When the Parlement refused to sit, it was exiled by an edict of chancellor Maupeou. Never was the populace more excited, more defiant. Again the cry of "Estates-General" rang out. When the provincial Parlements made common cause with the Parlement of Paris, their fate was sealed, and Maupeou instituted courts of his own to take their place. The echo of this agitation runs through Diderot's correspondence. "This is the end of constitutional government in France," he cried, with thousands of others. But the king held firm, backed by the new favorite, most vicious of all the line, Mme. du Barry. He silenced talk of the Estates-General by threatening to execute the first person who mentioned that body to him. It is apocryphically related that at this menace Mme. du Barry silently placed a portrait of Charles I upon his desk.

Diderot had no love for the Parlements, which he quite justly accused of being intolerant, thoroughly corrupt, opposed to all reform, and supremely selfish. Bad as they were, however, they were the only safeguard against tyranny, the only limitation on the monarch's absolutism. "In one moment, we have jumped from the monarchic state to the most perfect despotic state."

One good effect, at least, resulted from the king's arbitrary action. The unanimous cries of protest, coming from all ranks and all parts of France, showed that the principles of liberty were at last spread throughout the land. This, Diderot held, was the work of the *philosophes,* and it seemed to predict the dissolution of the old regime. "The spirit of our century is liberty. The first revolt against oppression, authority and prejudice, violent and immoderate, was against the tyranny of religion, the most formidable and most respected barrier. From then on it was impossible to halt. As soon as men have turned menacing glances towards the majesty of heaven, they will not fail, a moment later, to direct them against the sovereigns of the earth. The cable that holds and enchains humanity is formed of two cords; one cannot give way without the other breaking." Thus, in a brief but magnificent passage, he expresses the entire direction and meaning of the march of ideas in his century.

Not all the events of this post-encyclopedic period were unhappy. Diderot derived considerable satisfaction, in August 1769, from the performance of his *Père de famille* at the Comédie Française. In the dozen years since his formulation of a theory of the drama, the French public had become more receptive to the sentimental, moralizing, bourgeois play, and Diderot's success was the outstanding dramatic event of that year. Wrote Bachaumont in his secret Memoirs: "This very pathetic drama has produced the usual effect, of tightening the heart and causing abundant tears. You could count as many handkerchiefs as there were spectators; women became ill, and never did a Christian orator in his pulpit produce so theatrical an effect."

Bachaument's last remark once more confirms the identity of Diderot's practical morality and Christian ethics. The success of the *Père de famille* also proves the importance of *moment* and *milieu* and the change of values from generation to generation.

Diderot was overwhelmed by the acclaim of his friends and pleased at the discomfiture of his enemies. After the triumph of the first night, the enthusiastic actresses surrounded him and hugged and kissed him; this, he wrote, was one of the little profits of success. Even Antoinette, ashamed at hearing her husband's play praised by all the neighbors, finally weakened and took Angélique with her to see it. She refused to give her husband the satisfaction of a favorable comment, but Angélique whispered to him that her mother had wept as much as anyone else. The only shadow that passed over this bright scene, he wrote to Sophie, was the absence of his three friends, Damilaville, Grimm, and herself. "How everything is arranged in this world! Of all those whom I should have wanted there, and whose head would have been turned by this success, one is dead, the other abroad, and you are in the country."

Two years later the Comédie Française decided to try the *Natural Son* again, hoping it would have the same success. But the *Natural Son* was even more ineffective dramatically and more ranting in style than the later play, and this time Diderot had to swallow a humiliating failure. Bachaumont's comment is again typical of the general reaction: "this drama has appeared unbearably dull ... . The moment was not favorable for the author, and the ridicule with which he had recently covered himself in the affair of the publishers against Luneau contributed not a little to disposing the public unfavorably towards his play."

One result of Diderot's theatrical fame was to increase the number of social invitations from ambitious salon women. Had he desired to push himself in society, nothing would have been easier. But he was as timid and awkward as ever, and did not dare to venture outside the "philosophic" milieu. The last time he had widened the sphere of his social activities had been in favor of the rising Mme. Necker, whose husband was later to take a prominent place in the succession of Louis XVI's ministers of finance.

Mme. Necker held open house on Tuesdays and Fridays, just as Mme. d'Holbach did on Thursdays and Sundays. Conversation at her home was more worldly and refined than at Mme. d'Holbach's, and never irreligious or vulgar. It was there that seventeen philosophers gathered together in April 1770 and decided to honor Voltaire with a statue, which Pigalle was commissioned to execute. Diderot soon fell under the ascendancy of his hostess' charm, intelligence, and soft blue eyes. Her influence was a peculiar one on him. Diderot's coarse and irreverent pleasantries were displeasing to her, as they had been, without his realizing it, to other refined—and important—people. She tamed him, and taught him a sense of restraint. This he freely admitted, and with gratitude. "It is regrettable to me," he wrote to her, "that I did not have the good fortune of knowing you sooner. You would certainly have inspired in me a sense of pureness and delicacy that would have passed from my soul into my works." All of his letters to Mme. Necker are filled with an unparalleled respect, approaching almost to reverence. "I dare to believe that the purity of your soul would have passed into mine, and I too should have become an angel."

Mme. Necker was by no means averse to discussing philosophical problems, however.

"Monsieur Diderot," she said one evening, "did you not say that it was possible to explain thought by sensations?"

"Why of course," interrupted Naigeon. "Certainly, with the greatest clarity."

"All nature," explained the philosopher, "is only a graduated series of sensations. The stone feels, but very feebly; the plant feels more than the stone; the oyster more than the plant, and so on until man."

Diderot turned out several short stories and a novel between 1770 and 1773, years when he was also writing so many important philosophical works. The first was the touching and perfectly fashioned story of *The Two Friends of Bourbonne*. The second, *This Is Not a Tale*, containing the no less moving account of a heartless lover and a heartless mistress, and the unhappiness they bring to their true friends, renews the moral problem and the esthetic strategy of the Pommeraye-Hudson diptych, in *Jacques the Fatalist*. Here Diderot has earned another title to fame. He may justly be considered a creator of the modern short story, a form of writing characterized by utmost concentration of all means towards a single effect. Both these stories are masterpieces of realism, of deft, incisive characterization, of dramatic effect, produced through a close-knit construction and economy of means. They emphasize his contribution to the replacement of the abstract, psychological analysis of classicism with creatures of flesh and blood whose physical being and little quirks are all noted, and who are endowed with movement—gestures, attitudes, speech—all fused in action.

A word must be said about one of Diderot's most brilliant

dialogues, *The Conversation of a Father with his Children,* which he published in 1773. This is another "moral experiment." Here the problem of moral judgment is applied directly to the anarchistic individual who sets himself up against law and order, claiming to be an exception, not to satisfy his own egoism, this time, but in order to do justice in a case where the law, in its rigidity, is powerless. Diderot realizes that such a self-declared "superior" individual puts himself not only above the law, but above civilization, that he is indulging in an anarchism destructive to the necessary forms of social functioning. "Isn't the reason of the human species more sacred than that of a legislator? . . . It seems that we have to go around in circles for centuries, from folly to folly, from error to error, to reach the point to which the first spark of judgment and instinct would have led us straight off." We are brought face to face with an agonizing dilemma: civilization and morality may find themselves in opposition. The accomplishment of right may require an act destructive to the structures of organized society. The result of this experiment is an impasse in which coexisting human requirements are found to be incompatible. "I would not be too upset, he answered me, if there were one or two citizens like you in the city; but I would not live there if they all thought like you."

Another story, *Mme. de la Carlière* (1772, published in 1779) is related both to the basic moral problem and to the folly of giving too much importance to marital fidelity—a theme already explored in the *Supplement to Bougainville's Voyage.* Mme. de la Carlière is an extraordinary woman, who has the kind of uncompromising single-mindedness and "greatness in being" we find in the characters Diderot chooses to exemplify his moral experiments. She demands of her husband an absolute, one of which human nature is perhaps not capable. When he fails her, she prefers her destruction to compromise with life on its own terms. How shall we judge such a character—admire her or condemn her? Diderot makes us see how the public judgment varies, and is in any case irresponsible and unfounded. Guilt is shown to lie not formally in an act, but in circumstances that vary and that usually cannot be known. The lesson of the story is symbolized when the magistrate rips up his gown, a gesture of defeat.

3

As early as 1759, Diderot had conceived the project of selling the large and valuable library he had accumulated during his work on the *Encyclopedia*. He loved his books and needed them, but realized that unless Angélique were provided with a substantial dowry, her chances of making an advantageous marriage were slight. Several abortive negotiations were carried on, but he was unable to get the price he considered just.

Here it was that Diderot's good angel entered his life. Catherine the Great, "the Semiramis of the North," ascended the throne of Russia in 1762. Following the example of her fellow tyrant, Frederick the Great of Prussia, she immediately became a patroness of artists and philosophers. Her generosity, intelligence, and tolerance attracted to her court, as to Frederick's, many Frenchmen who were keenly aware of the indifference, if not of the persecutions, of their own government. To d'Alembert she offered the post of tutor to the grand duke Paul. To Diderot, through the intermediary of Voltaire, she offered asylum in Russia for his encyclopedic enterprise. Both proposals were politely refused.

Catherine's ambassador, prince Dmitri Galitzin, and her director of buildings, General Betzky, eventually informed her of Diderot's desire to sell his library. Both Betzky and Galitzin frequented the salon of Mme. Geoffrin, and it was there that Grimm had succeeded in interesting them in his friend's needs and intentions. A report was sent to St. Petersburg. On March 16, 1765, Betzky wrote to Grimm that her majesty was unable to see without emotion "that this philosopher, so famous in the Republic of Letters, found it necessary to sacrifice to his paternal love the objects of his delights, the source of his work and the companions of his leisure." Consequently, continues Betzky, as a mark of her favor and as an encouragement to the continuance of his career, her majesty has commissioned him to buy Diderot's library for fifteen thousand livres, on the single condition that he keep it for his own use until it pleased her to ask for it. In addition, he would receive one thousand livres each year for the rest of his life, in payment for his trouble as "librarian."

What was this library for which Catherine was willing to pay such a handsome sum? We know only that it contained two thousand nine hundred and four books, consisting of classics, scientific, philosophic, and documentary works. Were Diderot's library available today, it would constitute an invaluable treasure for scholars, for it would clear up the sources of his writings, his borrowings and his originality, and supply invaluable marginal comments in his own hand. Unfortunately, the entire library has vanished. On their arrival in St. Petersburg, his books were placed in a separate room in the Hermitage Library. At some later date, they were transported to the Imperial Library (now the Public Library), and either scattered and lost among the general collection, or else erroneously sold as doubles. Only a few odd volumes have been identified. This disappearance is peculiarly in keeping with the fate of Diderot's manuscripts.

Diderot was thoroughly excited on learning the good news. As a loyal French subject, he made a request to Saint-Florentin for permission to accept the foreign monarch's offer, and after consulting with the king, the minister, on May 1, issued the requested authorization.

Scarcely was the matter settled when Galitzin came to tell him of a new offer from Catherine. This time she wanted to buy his manuscripts.

"My manuscripts? I am sorry, Monsieur, but that is no longer possible."

"And why not?"

"Because I have already sold them."

"Sold them?"

"Certainly. I sold them with my books."

"Monsieur, that is charming, and I shall report the matter as you put it."

This was done, and Her Majesty replied that she was not surprised at this generous action, and that she would not forget it. When Diderot's pension, the following year, was delayed for several months through the negligence of a clerk, Catherine made her noble gesture and sent him, as an advance pension for the next twenty-five years, twenty-five thousand livres. In all, then Diderot received forty-one thousand livres. He had made a wise move in being generous with his manuscripts.

Diderot was overcome with enthusiasm for his benefactress. He wrote a poem in her praise. He begged her to make use of his talents in some way, hoping at the same time to put to shame the French Academy which had found him *persona non grata.* "Let me acquit my obligation, and let me use the sacred fingers of our sovereign to tweak the nose of our Forty Immortals." His gratitude and his praises were boundless. "Great Princess, I fall down at your feet, I stretch out my two arms toward you." His emotion was shared by the entire philosophic clan. Voltaire and d'Alembert both wrote letters of thanks to the generous monarch. Catherine, whose motive undoubtedly was to dazzle "the Republic of Letters," must have been quite satisfied, perhaps even a little surprised, at the enthusiastic reaction her gesture had provoked.

In return for Catherine's magnanimity, Diderot became a sort of unofficial agent for her, purchasing important art collections at auctions, usually with the advice of his artist friends; some of his most important acquisitions were made at the sales of the famous Crozat and Choiseul collections. In addition, when she needed technical experts, he made various personal recommendations, some of which were turned down and others accepted. His outstanding success, in this line of activity, was the sending of Falconet to St. Petersburg, to create a monument to Peter the Great. After the contract was signed, Diderot, ever faithful to his friends, informed Betzky that Falconet was obtaining no financial gain from the enterprise, and urged that he be covered with honors and treated with every possible consideration. Falconet set out for Russia in September 1766, and stayed there many more years than he had expected. But the choice turned out to be a wise one, for his equestrian statue of Peter the Great remains today his outstanding work.

Diderot's most resounding failure, as "personal adviser," occurred a year later. When Catherine needed an economist, he sent her a young man with the euphonious name of Pierre-Paul Le Mercier de la Rivière. A follower of Quesnay's physiocratic school, and former *intendant* of Martinique, La Rivière had written a book on the *Natural and Essential Order of Political Societies,* which Sartine had asked Diderot to censor. (Strange as it may seem, Diderot performed the function of official censor several times!) Knowing very little about economic theory, he found La Rivière's book a revelation, and since he agreed with its ideas (the defense of private property is the object of all legislation; the single tax on land alone is justifiable; truth is the best weapon against tyranny, etc.), he immediately wrote to Falconet, with his usual enthusiasm, that La Rivière was the greatest economist alive. "It is he who has discovered the secret, the true secret, the eternal and immutable secret of the security, duration, and happiness of empires." Under the stimulus of his pressing advice, La Rivière was sent for, but soon after his arrival turned out to be a real fiasco. A theorist entirely out of contact with realities, La Rivière could think of only one thing— his great project. This was nothing less than the complete transformation and modernization of feudal Russia. His plans for the creation of a class of bourgeois entrepreneurs and a class of free workers, "proprietors of their persons and of their work," were completely unwelcome in a "régime of servitude," and the unfortunate economist was soon asked to leave. Still more displeasing was his impertinent, superior attitude, which evoked Catherine's dry comment to Voltaire: "He assumed that we walked on all fours, and had very politely taken the trouble to come from Martinique to train us to walk on our hind legs."

This was in 1767. The following year brought Diderot another mission. At Mme. d'Epinay's or at d'Holbach's house, he had heard Claude de Rulhière, former attaché at the French embassy at St. Petersburg, read part of his *Anecdotes on the Revolution of 1762*. This was a relation of the crimes and intrigues by which Catherine had seized the throne, so well done that Diderot, frightened on behalf of his protectress, wrote an excited letter to Falconet, who lost no time in turning it over to her. The philosopher had advised Rulhière to suppress the work. Convinced that his advice would not be followed, he wrote to Falconet that it would be better for it to be published with Catherine's consent. "Our Sovereign appears in it as a 'master woman,' as a *gran cervello di principessa.*" Catherine, through her minister, Khotinsky, informed Diderot that Rulhière's account could have no truth in it, but suggested that he buy up the manuscript just the same. Meanwhile, Rulhière, who was counting on her to buy it for a handsome price, had agreed to Diderot's request not to publish it for the time being. When Khotinsky saw Diderot, the philosopher was quite upset that the matter had taken on the proportions of an affair of state, and he claimed to be completely ignorant of Ruhlière's whereabouts. Thereupon Khotinsky found out the address for himself. His visit and one made together with the embarrassed philosopher were unsuccessful, however, for the author insisted that the empress make a direct request for his manuscript. Although the negotiations were fruitless, Ruhlière was afraid to publish his book, and it did not appear until 1797, when both he and Catherine were dead.

With a satisfactory dowry assured for his daughter, Diderot next set about finding her a husband. First he broached the matter to Vialet, Mme. le Gendre's would-be but unsuccessful lover, and received a humiliating rejection. Then came a series of lengthy negotiations with the family of Caroillon de Vandeul—friends of his father—and these were destined to meet with eventual success.

It was in March of 1770 that Caroillon made the journey to Paris, to sue for the hand of the fair Angélique. Quite properly, he spoke to the father first. The philosopher listened gravely, forewarned and forearmed, and then took the floor, feeling all the importance of his position.

"Your wishes are not at all unbecoming. I shall not prevent two families, linked by our fathers, from being united by our grand-children. I shall not speak to you of wealth, because, without despising it, it is not what I esteem the most. Before all else I put intelligence, morals, an honest position, and health. I think you possess most of these advantages. But I am only the father of my child. She has a mother to whom she belongs even more than to me by the perils of her birth and the continuous cares of her upbringing. The matter is grave enough to consult her opinion, and I shall speak to her. Besides, it is not enough for my daughter to please you. You must please her, too. My daughter will not hesitate to tell us her opinion, because while she is sensible enough not to be stubborn about a match we would disapprove, she knows that we are good enough not to force her to a marriage that would be repugnant to her."

These were merely pompous words. Diderot's mind was already made up. The match appealed to him. Angélique, too, like most young ladies of the time, was probably chafing under the severe confinement imposed by worldly custom, and readily gave her consent. To girls of the eighteenth century, leading an almost cloistered existence, marriage was liberation. As for Mme. Diderot's opinion, despite her husband's high-sounding words, it seems to have carried little weight. She never approved of her proposed son-in-law, for reasons that are not clear.

Since Angélique was only sixteen, a three-year engagement period was decided upon. During this time Caroillon was placed "under observation." At times father Diderot was quite irked by him, especially when he failed to find a job, for he did not wish his daughter to go through the same bohemian period of struggle and privation that he had shared with Antoinette in his own youth that now seemed so far away.

Still more vexing was the acrimonious question of the marriage contract, entailing the amounts to be contributed on both sides and the terms under which they would be held, or used, by the husband and wife. The matter was settled only after a number of stormy debates, the account of which, as given in Diderot's family letters, is quite distasteful. Once again, the philosopher showed himself an astute bargainer, worthy of his middle-class origins. In the course of the transactions he was frequently exasperated by the Vandeul family's failure to supply the financial information he had requested, and still more by Caroillon's own bargaining propensities. "That young man understands his interests too well to be in love. If he proposes to make of my daughter a money speculation, he is mistaken. I will find him out, and when I do, I will treat him as he deserves. If he continues, Angélique will despise him, and good-bye to love." The marriage nearly foundered (Diderot thought the first contract cheated him, Caroillon's family thought the second one cheated them), but eventually an acceptable compromise was reached and the courtship pursued.

Most delicate of all was the task of winning the consent and benediction of Diderot's brother, the ferocious abbé. Since breaking off relations, in 1760, they had maintained a stubborn silence, the philosopher refusing to retract his writings and the abbé refusing to yield an inch. In 1768, Diderot at last attempted a reconciliation. The abbé, interpreting this as a sign of weakness, added a second condition for an armistice: he insisted that Angélique must finish her education in a convent, in all probability to counteract the iniquitous paternal influence. The thoroughly indignant author of *The Nun* replied that he was neither hypocritical enough to retract his writings nor stupid enough to comply with the second demand. He had given Angélique a perfectly good and moral education, he declared with complete sincerity, and to put her into a convent at this late date would lead gossips to suspect a misstep on her part.

In the spring of 1770, after one fruitless offer to be of service to the abbé, he tried a second time for a reconciliation. He asked Denise to inform their brother that Angélique was engaged. Here most assuredly, is the clue to Diderot's eagerness to patch things up. The abbé was well off, and the prospect of his wealth being left to the Church instead of to his own daughter was, to say the least, distressing to the bourgeois father. Diderot was thinking of the inheritance, then, when in all his wrath he wrote to Denise, in May 1763, that "even if the abbé had as much gold as a mountain, he could not make me simulate for a minute a feeling I do not possess."

In May of 1770, he wrote directly to the abbé. The information is meager. Apparently he became furious at receiving no answer to a first letter, and then thinking better of it, promptly sent the abbé a second one. "Why have you remained so long estranged from your sister-in-law, your niece, and myself?" And he brazenly denies having broken his promise not to write or talk against religion, adding with greater truth: "I have not and have never had the mania for proselytizing. I think for myself and for myself alone. I let others have their own opinions." Then he adds:

> The same conditions you once proposed to me, you propose them to me today. Allow me first, my dear abbé, to point out to you that one proposes conditions only to a subaltern, and that I am not yours . . .
>
> Morals, morals, my dear abbé, that is the only basis on which men are permitted to judge each other in this world. We must abandon the rest to the pity, the justice, and the decision of God. Flee the wicked man, even if he hears as many masses as are said in all the churches of the kingdom ; embrace the good man, whatever his way of thinking . . .
>
> Now admit it, dear friend, if I had been as intolerant as you, while you hated me on your side I should have hated you on mine ; for after all, if diversity of opinions authorizes hatred, I had the same right to it.
>
> If you come to Paris, as I hear, you should bring sister with you. You know of Caroillon's *démarche*. It will be wise for us to talk about it together. You must know the young man better than I. Good-bye, and come soon. You could not come too soon.

This scarcely diplomatic letter was not likely to placate the irate abbé. He never came to Paris, and in July, it was Diderot who stopped off at Langres, on the way to the spa at Bourbonne. There, in spite of two humble letters and the intercession of family friends, the abbé refused even to see him, and after two weeks Diderot left in disgust, feeling that he had done all he could, and perhaps more than he should. So fierce was the abbé's stubborn rancor, that he even estranged the friendly negotiators who were trying to bring the two brothers together.

Still Diderot did not abandon all hope for a reconciliation: the stakes were too high. Two years later, on August 21, 1772, another letter went out to the recalcitrant brother. It resumed the aim and the results of the last visit, firmly pinning to the abbé the blame for its failure, frankly accusing him of injustice.

> But you know how impossible it has been for me to force your door, and with what harshness you made the mediation of your own friends futile. If you can justify this conduct to yourself, I congratulate you . . . If the most important affair of my life, the

happiness of my only child, has been arranged without your partici-
pation, I hope at least that you will not have the injustice to
complain about it . . .

Even if I were guilty of genuine wrongs, humanity, reason, and
religion should have long ago brought you to forget . . . But
just tell me, abbé, even if you have solid reasons to complain about
me, what have your niece, your sister, your sister-in-law, the
mother, son, son-in-law, and all the rest of the two families done,
for you to envelop them in your hatred? Be that as it may, I ask
your benediction for the young couple, and they both solicit your
prayers and intercession with heaven for the happiness of their
union.

Then Diderot concludes with his usual tact and diplomacy:

Good-bye, abbé. Keep well ; and rest assured that you will find
me at all times such as I wish you to be, a good brother and a
good friend. Any one else but you would have come to Paris to
unite the two children.

Perhaps the irascible abbé did not deserve any better. At any
rate, the nuptial benediction was not forthcoming. The abbé
claimed, after a conversation with Caroillon, that his religious con-
victions were not all they should be, even though his own friend,
the abbé Gauchat, a well-known theologian and anti-*philosophe*,
expressed himself as quite satisfied on that head. In reality, what
he could not forgive was that Angélique had not received her
education in a convent.

Angélique and Caroillon de Vandeul were married on September
9, 1772 without the blessing of their uncle, and with the disapproval
of Mme. Diderot. As the great day drew near, the philosopher was
overcome with emotion, a mixture of joy and sadness, and also
annoyance at his wife's refusal to allow any of his friends to attend
the ceremonies. Even Grimm, who had brought so much music
from Germany for Angélique, was no exception, and Diderot had
to invoke his presence by mail. "Holy prophet, raise your hands to
Heaven tomorrow, between five and six in the morning, and draw
down its blessing on all."

The event left him quite downcast, and the weeks that followed
were melancholy ones. Without Angélique's chatter, the house
seemed so empty, so lonely. Grimm and his sister were his confid-
ants, and to them he freely unburdened his grief. "My poor sister,
I couldn't say that I am happy . . . I have no more child; I am

alone, and my solitude is unbearable." Diderot was a "family man"—when he was not in the arms of a mistress—but he was still paying for an earlier mistake which deprived him of the usual consolation in such cases. "Parents who lose their children find each other again, talk to each other and solace each other. The mother still has the company of the father, the father that of the mother. There is nobody here any more. We wander about, Mme. Diderot and I, one around the other; but we are nothing to each other. How can you speak to a woman full of ill-humor and ready to burst out for a trifle?"

So unyielding was her disapproval, that Mme. Diderot refused to visit the young couple, and received them with such coldness that Angélique often went away with tears in her eyes. Father, on the contrary, found his only consolation in visiting "the nest of the young birds" and in showering gifts upon them: an earthenware pail, a silver coffee service, six cords of wood, candlesticks, forty pounds of coffee, utensils for an entire kitchen. These and others followed in rapid succession. It was not very difficult to get gifts, and money, from him. When Caroillon hinted that he needed a desk, the good father forbade him to buy one and promised to take care of it. And, of course, the harpsichord and harmony lessons were continued. Diderot's philosophy on the subject was sound. "All the expenses I can spare them, I spare them. *Que voulez-vous*, my dear? Whatever they get during my lifetime, they'll have that much less afterwards, and isn't it better to help them at a difficult moment than to wait until they no longer need anything?" And then he adds, with a father's joy: "They love each other tenderly. They try to please each other in everything."

His paternal pride found cause for satisfaction, too. "She's really a wonderful little wife. Before two months are up, she will do her domestic routine just as if she had never done anything else all her life . . . They seem to be comfortable at home, judging from the little anxiety they show to go out."

Diderot was no less proud to observe the fruit his moral lessons had borne. He was dining at his daughter's, one night, when some impudent young man, seated between them, embarrassed one of the ladies with an impertinent remark. Quickly the philosopher's daughter pulled the offender's sleeve and whispered in his ear: "Monsieur, it does not suit me that ungentlemanly things be either said or done in my house. Kindly remember it." Bursting with pride, Diderot took Angélique aside after dinner and kissed her. "Courage, my child, when you've given insolent wretches their desserts three or four times, you won't see any more of them."

Despite all this, Diderot remained sad for several months. His normal tendency towards weepy sentimentality became, as he admitted to Grimm, even more exaggerated. "Good-day, my friend, good-day, my dear friend! My soul has become so sorrowful that I see nothing, hear nothing without emotion. Everything affects me. I cried when I opened your letter, I cried when I read it, and I'm crying while I'm writing to you. There's no reason for it, I tell myself, but I don't cry any the less. I shall never forget the moment of the ceremony; my child, who lacks neither reason nor courage, lost her head and felt ill several times. I'll let you guess what became of me. Only her mother retained self-possession. Yet she loves her daughter. Tell me then how so much harshness can be allied with a certain sensitivity. Good-day, my Grimm. You will always remain to me, won't you?"

Later Diderot analyzed for his friend the causes of his agitation. "I shall even tell you confidentially that I have discovered a good platitude at the bottom of my heart, that is that not all my grief was solitude. Would you believe that this pain was mingled with that of no longer being loved alone? How can those ridiculous feelings be found in a good heart? Who would believe that a sensible father could feel such a stupid jealousy? This discovery, which I have laughed at, has relieved me a great deal."

There were other torments for the poor philosopher, however. While the young couple were tasting the first joys of marriage and the delights of setting up house, Diderot was attending to the more practical business of finding a job for Caroillon. This was no easy task, but after utilizing every connection he possessed, including the decisive influence of the powerful duke d'Aiguillon, Caroillon was finally given an important post as manager of the forges of the count d'Artois.

No sooner was that settled than the devoted father had a new source of worries. Caroillon has suddenly turned out to be frivolous. He makes fun of the expensive music lessons to which Diderot treats Angélique. "That little fop," the philosopher complained to Grimm, "wants his wife to be dressed like a doll from early morning, and wants her to spend the day decorating herself to please him. He's trying to make a little fool out of my child, a silly impertinent woman who will soon know only how to put on a pompom, smirk, slander, and smile. Nor is that all. He thinks that she hasn't enough dresses; she needs one, I suppose, for every hour of the day, in order to satisfy the vanity of my little florist who would like his little tulip to adorn herself differently every minute for his diversion."

To all this Angélique, serious and sensible, objected. Quite a reversal of the usual situation! And Diderot continues his lament: "I had accustomed the child to reflection, to reading, to the pleasures of a retired life, to contempt for all the frivolities which evaporate the entire lives of women." How will it all end? Diderot makes the dire prediction that if this state of affairs keeps up, his daughter's morals will be menaced, that she will succumb to temptation like the other social butterflies. What a horrible thought for the author of *Bougainville's Voyage!* To prevent the shipwreck of family morals, he wrote a long and eloquent letter to his son-in-law, but on rereading it, decided not to send it after all.

A few months after her marriage, Angélique had a miscarriage. The following year a girl was born, but did not survive long. And then in June 1775, a son Denis-Simon, came to gladden the entire family. Soon after this event, several other forges were confided to Caroillon's management, so that he was later enabled to purchase a position as government treasurer, and with it, the title of squire. He made several wise investments in farms, in the Langres region. Finally, as the industrial revolution was making its way into France, he founded a textile mill, thereby assuring the fortune of his line. His descendants prospered and became pillars of conservatism. They learned to be ashamed of their radical ancestor, and carefully relegated his papers to the secrecy of a moldy backroom.[1]

The happy couple were also destined to receive a tidy sum from the Diderot family. Shortly before their marriage, Aunt Denise had suggested assigning her own wealth to them. To the doting father, ever planning for the financial stability of his offspring, this was a most welcome suggestion, but he replied with peasant-like craftiness: "As for the rest you will do on your side whatever you wish. I have never proposed to you that you alienate your wealth in favor of your niece; it is an idea which has come from you alone. Persist, or don't persist, you will be none the less dear to me. You have thought, quite justly, that the abbé might frustrate her of her grandfather's wealth, and you have thought that it would be nice

[1] They have been rescued recently by the Diderot scholar, Dr. Herbert Dieckmann.

for you to make up for it by a gift. If you decide to change your mind, we shall love you none the less."

Denise did persist, to Diderot's everlasting joy and gratitude. "The benefactress of my child is mine," he wrote to her on September 25th. "After what you have done, you need have no scruples about using my revenue as if it were yours. Use it then. Take care of yourself. Spare yourself nothing." This letter was signed: "Your brother, the only brother who remains to you." The offer was sincere, for he repeated it in October of that year, in December 1776, and a last time in November 1778. Thus two thirds of the little fortune, so painstakingly accumulated by the honest labor of the good cutler of Langres, was assured to his descendants in the Vandeul family.

On September 25th, the same day he expressed his gratitude to Denise, Diderot decided to make another gesture towards his brother. The shrewd abbé had suspected mercenary motives in the recent attempts at reconciliation, and had not hesitated to say so. Diderot's vanity, his conception of himself as a viceless paragon, could not bear such an accusation. He indignantly denied it, with the transparent nuance of hypocrisy—or self deception—not infrequently found in his letters.

> Dear abbé:
>
> You have written two very wicked letters, one to your brother, the other to your niece . . . In the letter to your niece, you preach to her hatred of her father. Ah, abbé, traverse the entire surface of the earth ; appeal to all men, and if there is a single one to whom this action does not appear atrocious, I shall deem you the finest man in all the world.
>
> One more thing. You attribute to a motive of interest the advances that I have always made to you, and the patience with which I have suffered your behavior. You must, my friend, put a very high price on money, since you think it capable of leading a man who has more than he needs to insincerity and baseness. Get rid of that idea. I will not be here any longer when you commit the injustice of disinheriting my grandchildren. What does it matter to me, then, if you trample on the laws of blood and the most sacred customs of society?

After an eloquent plea in favor of tolerance, in the course of which Diderot formally withdraws his promise—about the observance of which he had so frequently perjured himself to his brother—never to attack religion, he closes: "We await you with open arms. You

Diderot

will return to us whenever you wish; whenever you are tired of tormenting yourself."

Unrelenting, the abbé replied to this peace offer with cold irony and hatred. This time Diderot gave up the struggle. This time he meant to tell his brother all he really felt. The letter he sent, on November 13, 1772, is a remarkable document of about twenty printed pages. Diderot reproaches the abbé for his wrongs: his animosity; a letter of hatred written to Angélique; his injustice towards her; his shameful and ungrateful conduct towards their sister, and his harshness towards her friend.

Monsieur l'Abbé:

I am never in a hurry to write to you, because I am still less in a hurry to receive your answers. You are bursting with bile and you are of a deathly sadness. When one has a pure heart and a tranquil conscience, one should be light and gay . . .

So then, my tone displeases you very much? I have however no other with the most touchy men in the city and the Court, and it has seemed to me up to the present that they accepted it. You would like me to become angry and put myself in accord with you. That is not possible. Each of us must keep his role; I must tell you gay truths that hurt you, and you must retort with good coarse insults that make me laugh . . .

You are pretty old to start learning spelling and French; and you would have to begin there. Believe me, stay ignorant; limit yourself to charity; do it the least ostentatiously you can; . . . and put an end to a scandal that honest people have excused up till now only by the disturbance of a nerve or some incurable sore in your *pia-mater*. We call *pia-mater* one of the membranes which serve as envelope to the brain. Your joking is insolent and heavy; nevertheless, keep on joking. I prefer you a clown to a sad maniac . . .

I know, yes, monsieur l'abbé, I know, and I know well, that you have made two unhappy creatures, whose name you would not dare to pronounce if you did not have a heart of bronze, shed tears of blood . . . Why, wretch that you are, why didn't you leave them peacefully, rather than persist in making them suffer, in order to avoid the shame of leaving them! And you believe in God! And you allow yourself to do things like that! This trick is of a different color from the one you used to chase a poor old woman from her home. I blush about the other. This one has made me shudder. Prostrate yourself; beat your brow against a stone; and try to obtain from the One who will judge you some

day not to be treated as you have treated your father, your sister,
her friend, your sister-in-law, and your niece . . .

The conditions which you set for our reconciliation were to put
my daughter in a convent! You lie, you lie against your conscience.
Never were you imbecile enough to make such a law, because you
knew I would never be imbecile enough to accept it. You lie ; you
lie then, priest of the Lord.

I promised you not to write or speak against your opinions.
I have kept my word. I have not written a line about religion.
I have not said a word about it, except with bishops and doctors
of theology . . .

Unleashing a wave of fury, Diderot boasts of his atheism, attacks
the immortality of the soul, and finally condemns the abbé as
a sanguinary fanatic, a thief, an ingrate, and a villain. Then he
continues:

I don't impose silence on you. Write, preach your best ; denounce our doctrine ; show its falseness, if you can ; draw from
it such conclusions as you wish. But no personalities ; no insults ;
no calumnious imputations ; no persecutions ; no dragonades ; no
prisons ; no dungeons ; no burning at the stake. That is the doctrine
of the Gospel, which I have read more and better than you . . .

You speak very lightly of a book (the *Encyclopedia*) which you
have not read, which you are not capable of understanding . . .
With all its faults, four thousand five hundred copies of it have
been printed, and not a single one is left in the bookseller's shop.
And yet it is not a book that costs one *écu* . . . They are re-
printing it at Lucca, at Lausanne, at Geneva. Your books are
incontestably better ; but those sublime productions are like the
vases on your altars: sacred they are because nobody touches
them . . .

Do you imagine all good enclosed in the little handful of
Catholic Christians? And what about Protestants then? And
Lutherans? And Quakers? And Moslems? And Chinese? And
the Infidels of past and present time? Believe, master Pierre, that
Cato was as good as you, and that there is at Constantinople or
Peking some poor damned soul who is worth more than you or me.
I do not know whether at the last judgment you will be scolded
for the reasons you say, but before that departure, you will
certainly see yourself a bad priest, because you have had a fierce
heart, unjust conduct, a proud, inflexible, implacable character,
the fury of a persecutor ; a bad Christian, because you have called,
if not the fires of heaven, at least the fires of earth against your

opponents ; a bad citizen, because you have professed and followed principles disruptive to any society, to any family ; a bad son, because you saddened your father and betrayed his last wishes ; a bad brother, because you have tormented your brother and made your sister weep ; a bad man, because you have been an ingrate, a liar, a slanderer, false, suspicious, avid for scandal, unbearable to your superiors, to your inferiors, to your equals . . .

Diderot's anger falls, exhausted. He concludes with a final invitation to reconciliation, but this time it is the abbé who must make the sacrifice of his pride.

Monsieur l'abbé, I am not at all your servant. I am a good philosopher, sensitive to outrages, to insults, injustice, harshness, and infamy ; but quite ready to welcome his brother, without bitterness, without reproaches, without resentment, when it will please him to step forward. Until that moment, *peace and silence*. No more letters to receive. No more answers to make.

Fortunately, we possess the abbé's reply to this philippic. It matches the philosopher's in irony and bitterness, but falls short in eloquence and style. He objects to Diderot's insults and ill-treatment, accuses him of trying to arouse hatred against him in the family, excoriates him for his role in their financial dealings. Let us read some of his own words:

I am most obliged to you for having given me the definition of *pia-mater*. You have spared me the trouble of looking it up in my dictionary. I am still more obliged for your teaching me that the infallible way for a girl to obtain the rare privilege of acquiring modesty is to take three courses in anatomy ; I should certainly not have found that in my dictionary. I have leafed through it in vain to find out whether it is a good and solid answer to reply to all the reasons one puts forth: "You lie impudently." It says nothing about that . . . I shall not mention the supposed proposal of putting your daughter in a convent ; you would only say, "you lie, you lie"—that is your war cry. You repeat it on each page, so you must often be at a loss. You do not eulogize your daughter when you say that she perhaps knows more than I. You have doubtless forgotten that a few sentences back you reproach me for being so stupid, but so stupid that I do not realize that I contradict myself from one line to another. You do not realise that you yourself follow my bad example. I am bursting with bile . . . You are very brave to despise a barbarian, a madman, a wild beast. Oh!

how modest you are to place yourself in the class of the most respected men of all classes of society! No, I do not take it back! If they resemble you, I am proud to be mad in their eyes . . . I admit that I am not able to understand your book. What consoles me, is that I am not alone . . . Once you tried to get me to do a part of your work [for the *Encyclopedia?*]. That reminds me of a robber crying 'Stop thief' after he has waylaid some poor wretch . . . You were doting already when you wanted to keep your marriage secret, doubtless out of disinterestedness, and at the same time wanted me to baptize your child publicly.

I admit that I was wrong to challenge you. I know you will stop at nothing. You are right not to scribble any more papers. Eight sheets of scribbling is too much. Furthermore, I know neither Greek nor Hebrew, and one must be Greek at least to feel the weight of your reasoning, the strength of your replies, the sweetness of your compliments.

The letter bears neither a salutation nor a signature. Diderot, however, never read it. He wrote on the envelope: "If I were sure of finding my brother in this letter, I would open it, and I would not read it without shedding tears of joy. But I prefer to send it back unopened, and spare myself two sorrows: one of hearing, the other of replying to unpleasant things."

Again, as in the Rousseau quarrel—as in any quarrel—it would be sheer partisanship to lay all the blame on either one's head. But it is difficult to feel any sympathy for the narrow and fanatical abbé. These were the last relations between them, but one feels that Diderot, the family man *par excellence*, never ceased regretting the schism in his own family—and the loss of the abbé's inheritance.

CHAPTER 16

A Philosopher Queen

1

NOT LONG AFTER the beginning of their relations, Catherine began to press her protegé, through Falconet, Betzky, and Galitzin, to be honored guest at the court of St. Petersburg. It was flattering to the great monarch to be surrounded, like her rival in Prussia, by luminaries from Paris, the hub of Western culture. Moreover, it was altogether fitting and proper that he render in person the thanks and homage he poured out in his letters. Diderot was quite embarrassed by these suggestions, since he did not dare to refuse nor did he desire to accept. Alone among the *philosophes,* he had always avoided travel. "Travel is a fine thing, but you have to have lost your father, mother, children, and friends, or never have had any, to make a business of wandering over the surface of the globe. What would you say of the owner of an immense palace, who spent his life going up and down from attic to cellar, from cellar to attic, instead of sitting quietly in the midst of his family?" He hedged constantly and cleverly. In some letters he took pains to assure Falconet that they would soon meet again: "I will squeeze you in my arms. The wishes of a sovereign such as the empress, of a benefactress, are orders by which any soul, sensitive or not, must feel honored. Once in his lifetime, one must see such a woman, and I will see her."

Diderot pierced Frederick the Great's philosophic mask and saw the tyrant beneath; but either he was still fooled by Catherine's posing as a liberal and "philosophic" monarch, or more probably, he again allowed interest to dominate sincerity. Admiration, as well as gratitude, he exclaimed to Falconet, would drive him to St. Petersburg. "I shall want to see her, that woman despot who one day takes it into her head to say to her subjects: 'We are born to live under laws. Laws are made to make men happy. Nobody knows better than you under what conditions you can be happy. Come, then, and teach them to me.' History has no record of an action such as this, and it should be transmitted to remotest posterity."

Just when it appeared that he was about to give in to all the coaxing, the wily philosopher would pull in his neck. No, his health, or his wife's, would not at the moment permit the journey and long absence. And then he has his daughter's education to complete, and her health was not so good either. He even blew upon the dying embers of his love for Sophie in order to find a convincing pretext. After all, he could not think of leaving her, for she would die, she loves him so. Falconet would not want him to be so heartless. "Speak, my friend, speak. Do you want me to put death in the breast of my love?"

It was not until the Spring of 1773 that his resistance finally collapsed, under a barrage of invitations from Falconet and Catherine herself. The *Encyclopedia* was finished. His daughter was married and settled. He was free, and further excuses would seem ungrateful. He suddenly made up his mind to risk the great adventure. Once the journey was determined upon, preparations were completed rapidly. With many eloquent and tearful good-byes, and not a little posturing, he bid farewell to wife, child, and Paris early in June. Mme. de Vandeul records his departure as of May 10, but her dates are usually inaccurate, and Diderot's note to Naigeon, confiding his manuscripts to him, is dated June 3rd. Grimm had left for the same destination in March, but intended to spend some time in Germany before accompanying the margrave Caroline of Hesse, whose younger daughter was to marry the tsarevitch, to St. Petersburg. He hoped incidentally that despite their mutually expressed dislike, he would have the opportunity of presenting his philosopher friend to Frederick the Great.

Diderot did not go directly to Russia, either. His first stop was at

The Hague where he remained for two months as the guest of his friends, prince and princess Galitzin. It was a happy and tranquil period, devoted to the quiet pleasures of conversation, walking and study. At The Hague Diderot's romantic soul discovered the beauty of the ocean. "When I go out, I always walk by the sea, which I have not yet seen either calm or agitated; the vast uniformity, accompanied by a certain murmur, inclines you to reverie; it is there that I dream well." He spent fruitful time on various pieces—the *Paradox on Acting,* a revision of *Rameau's Nephew,* and a commentary on Helvétius' posthumous work, *On Man.* He began a brochure, *A Voyage to Holland,* into which he put his painstaking and detailed observations on the political, economic, and cultural life of the country. If Diderot was not a great traveler, he was a keen one. He noted such things as the abundance of foxes and the rarity of wolves and boars, the methods used to clean houses, the coarse food and drink of the populace, who obtained from beer "a heavy and prolonged intoxication." The men he found to be sensible, business-like, and democratic; the women, homely.

On the 20th of August, Diderot at last tore himself away from his charming hosts, and in the company of Catherine's chamberlain, Narishkin, set out for St. Petersburg. It was late in the season, but fortunately they had a stout carriage and encountered good weather. He was supposed to spend a week at Berlin, but since Narishkin was anxious to arrive in time for the grand duke's marriage, they decided to go by way of Dresden and Leipzig instead, thereby incurring the displeasure of both Frederick and Grimm. Diderot was not sorry to have missed the encounter. The instinctive antipathy between the two men had increased with time. Frederick was so piqued at Diderot's obvious repugnance to meeting him that he had one of his parasites, the philosopher Formey, compose a diatribe against his character and writings. This seemed the signal for a flock of satires, among them one by Luneau de Boisgermain.

It was a long and a hard trip. Diderot twice fell ill, once in Westphalia and again within two hundred miles of St. Petersburg, the victim of what he believed to be a violent intestinal colic. "My stomach was hard and taut. I suffered everything it is possible to suffer, but much washing, from top and bottom, finally brought about a kind of cracking within me, like that of several rings separating from each other."

After forty-one days of travel, the weary philosopher reached his destination, on October 9th, more dead than alive, as he promptly informed his wife. "Try to imagine, if you can, the state of a man tormented by a violent colic, rolling over the worst roads. At each jolt—and every instant brought a more or less strong one—if they had plunged a knife into my stomach and sawed through my intestines, they would not have hurt me more."

Dropping Narishkin at his home, Diderot continued to Falconet's residence, where he expected to stay. He had been looking forward to their reunion with genuine enthusiasm, and with his usual candor, assumed his friend felt the same emotion. "What a day! What a moment!" he had written, announcing his departure. "I shall rush into your arms, we shall cry excitedly: it is you . . . yes, it is I . . . here we are at last! . . . At last here I am!" But Falconet, who was no longer in favor with Catherine and Betzky, was turning sour. When the sick and weary Diderot knocked at his door, Falconet turned him away with the excuse that his son's unexpected arrival from London had taken up all the available room. For a moment he felt desperate. This was a turn of events he had not reckoned on. After considering for a moment taking a room in an inn, a thought he could scarcely bear, he decided instead to ask for temporary refuge at the home of Narishkin. A note was rushed to him and only a few minutes later a carriage rolled up.

"Tell me frankly whether my presence will inconvenience you, or your brother, or your sister-in-law," pleaded the unhappy philosopher. Narishkin and his relatives all assured him of the contrary, and there he remained, a welcome guest till the end of his stay. For this hospitality he was eternally grateful.

It is painful to think of Diderot, who hated travel and loved the comforts of home, on that first night in St. Petersburg. Here he was, after six weeks of discomfort and torture, unhappy and alone in a foreign city. It is painful to think of him groaning as he put on his cherished night cap, pulled the comforters about his ears, and sought the consolation of sleep in this strange bed in a strange land.

He awoke the next day, to the peal of bells and the booming of cannon, all in honor of the wedding of the grand duke Paul Petrovitch and princess Wilhelmine of Hesse-Darmstadt. He felt his loneliness and misery even more keenly. He thought of his two friends in St. Petersburg, of Falconet, who had turned him away, and of Grimm, who did not seem in a hurry to visit him, and wondered what the next months were to bring; wondered even how Catherine would receive him.

While Diderot was making his arduous journey to the North,

trouble was in store for him at home. In Helvétius' recent work, *On Man*, the dedication to Catherine II was followed by a preface that aroused the ire of many patriotic Frenchmen. It called France a degenerate nation, scorned by all of Europe, whose only hope lay in being conquered by a foreign country. The duke de Noailles, terming it an insult to France and to Catherine, accused Diderot of having written or inspired it, or at least of having expressed similar sentiments at The Hague. Louis XV, through his foreign minister, the duke d'Aiguillon, sent a protest to Catherine, claiming that her minister, Galitzin, had taken charge of spreading the infamous work. The protest was rudely rejected. The Russian court denied complicity and tartly pointed out that several books published in Paris were far more insulting to Russia. The French rejoinder that they were not dedicated to the king of France and that no minister was involved in their distribution fell on deaf ears. Fortunately for Diderot, his government decided to drop the matter there.

Catherine received her guest without delay, and their first conversation immediately cheered him up. "I have found her such as you painted her to me in Paris," he wrote back to princess Dachkov, "the soul of Brutus and the charms of Cleopatra. If she is great on the throne, her charms as a woman would turn thousands of heads. Nobody knows better than she the art of putting everyone at ease."

Diderot's description is trustworthy, despite his enthusiasm. Catherine was indeed one of the most remarkable women in history's pages. How remarkable she was, he did not even begin to suspect. He knew little or nothing of her private life. Catherine, a pretty German fraülein, had been married young to the grand duke Peter, heir to the throne of the Russias. Peter turned out to be an ugly brute, eccentric and degenerate; he tormented his wife in private and insulted her in public. At the end of a year of marriage, she was still a maiden.

The lonesome princess had only two friends at court. One was the conceited Leo Narishkin, later Diderot's traveling companion; the other, the gallant Sergei Soltykoff. Both offered her their amorous services, and she finally succumbed to the advances of Soltykoff. In his arms she tasted the delights of love and her ardent temperament developed into a boundless craving. Soltykoff was followed by a succession of lovers, thirteen in all. Among them were Stanislas Poniatowski, poetic, morbid, and fatalistic; Lieutenant Gregor Orloff, a reckless gambler, "forever lying between two beds or seated between two bottles"; and the notorious, one-eyed

Potemkin, an uncouth, thick-lipped, sensual soldier whom she called her "Cyclops."

Orloff was known as a prolific begetter of children. Catherine had two bastards by him and one by Soltykoff. Peter, who had winked his eye at his wife's affairs, suddenly grew sensitive. He decided to send her to a nunnery—but first to parade her through the streets with a sign on her back, "Mother of the Bastard."

He never got a chance to carry out his plans. A sudden revolution, engineered by Catherine and her friends, swept him off the throne, and a few days later he was killed in a drunken brawl. Catherine was probably guiltless of the murder, but she shed no crocodile tears over his loss.

Now she was free, the most powerful woman in the world, empress of Russia. Now she could roll in the deepest debauchery and satisfy her remarkable sensual appetite. Not for nothing was she called "the Semiramis of the North"! She lost no time in making Orloff a count and Poniatowski, a little later, king of Poland. It is Poniatowski who has left the best description of her. "She had black hair, a dazzlingly fair skin, a brilliant complexion, large eloquent blue eyes, long black eyelashes, a Grecian nose, a mouth that seemed made for kissing, a trim waist, not too small . . . a soft and pleasant voice; and a laugh as merry as her disposition."

In spite of her escapades, Catherine took her regal job with utmost seriousness. Just as she dominated her lovers by her virile will and superior intelligence, so she controlled the politics of her country. Her one idea was to increase the power and importance of Russia. Cynical at heart and ruthless in method, she crushed everyone who ventured into her path, and defeated or destroyed Sweden, Turkey, and Poland. Internally, her hope was to modernize the Russian administration, but she did little to counteract the procrastination of the conservative Assembly of Notables. At first she declared herself opposed to serfdom, but at the end of her reign the serfs were worse off than before. She paid great lip service to the philosophic ideal of liberty, but in practice she was a cruel autocrat.

This was the woman the naïve, idealistic philosopher was hoping to tutor, the "Scarlet Empress," cold and satanic. Yet they had some things in common—their sensuality and their gluttony, their love of conversation, and zest for life.

His arrival was followed by several days of parties, balls, and feasts in honor of the newly wedded couple. It was Diderot's first taste of court life, and with his characteristic *gaucherie,* lack of poise and self-confidence, he was none too happy. *"Hé, ma bonne,"* he complained in a letter to Antoinette, "do you think, however comfortable I may be here, that I would not be better off at your side? Am I made for court life, and is court life made for me?" He must have been quite unhappy to make such a large concession.

When the celebrations were ended, Catherine took Diderot under her protecting wing. She made it a habit to receive him almost every afternoon at two, alone in her study, and frequently their discussion lasted until five. From the first day he was completely captivated by her informality and charm. She gave him carte blanche to say anything he wanted, and he assured princess Dachkov that he took full advantage of the offer, speaking everything that came into his head: "wise things, perhaps, when I think I am being mad, and perhaps very mad ones when I think I am wise." Evidently, Catherine enjoyed his *sans gêne.* "The empress is delighted, that is the essential thing," wrote Grimm to count Nesselrode. "Besides, he takes her hand, shakes her arm, knocks on the table just as if he were in the midst of the synagogue in the Rue Royale."

The table referred to by Grimm has become famous. "Your Diderot is a very extraordinary man," Catherine reported to Mme. Geoffrin. "I can't get out of my conversations with him without having my thighs bruised and black and blue; I have been obliged to put a table between him and me to shelter myself and my limbs from his gesticulation." To anyone who is acquainted with the formality, veneration, and distance that surrounded a Russian monarch, there is an inconceivable, unreal note in this familiarity. But Diderot remained Diderot, even in the company of a great monarch. One chronicler relates that he was accused of grabbing the arms of his two neighbors at table, while he talked ceaselessly and continued to eat at the same time. This is just one example of the innumerable apocryphal and malicious anecdotes that sprang up about his visit to Russia. Many of them were inspired by the hostility of the court nobility. According to another of these tales, Catherine tired of his preaching atheism to her courtiers, and asked the great German mathematician, Euler, to silence him. Euler is said to have approached Diderot before the entire court, and declared gravely:

"Monsieur, $\dfrac{a-b^n}{a} = x$. Therefore, God exists. Reply."

Then Diderot, "for whom algebra was Hebrew," is supposed to have blushed and stammered, while the entire assemblage laughed heartily. In fact, so ashamed was the defeated philosopher, that he requested immediate permission to leave for France. This story itself is doubtful, and none of its allegations is true. Catherine did not tire of Diderot, he did not seek to leave until he was ill and homesick, and, especially, he was an able mathematician.

Other current falsehoods were to the effect that he had come to Russia only to extract further gifts from his benefactress, that she had merely wanted to be amused at his expense, and that as soon as she saw him, she was anxious to be rid of him.

Quite to the contrary, their conversations went on all through that winter. Diderot assailed her with questions about every aspect of Russian life, political and economic organization, including such things as "the quantity and composition of the population, the nobility, the clergy, the free peasantry; the Jews, monks, and nuns; agriculture, the bread, wine, lumber, cattle trades," etc. Intensely interested in obtaining information, he filled his notebooks with facts and observations, questioned those with whom he came into contact, and with a cosmopolitan, open-minded outlook, made a genuine effort to rid himself of any and all prejudices.

It cannot be said that Catherine replied to his frank questions with equal honesty. She was never averse to lying or hypocrisy, and before the philosopher she was playing a role, that of the good monarch. When he asked her about the pernicious effects of serf-dom, she boldly replied: "I do not think there is any country in which the farmer loves his land and his home more than in Russia." She even cited provinces where the peasants had turkey every day, and disdained so common a dish as chicken. Lies, vague generalizations, or clever joking were often Catherine's answers to her questioner's embarrassing queries. He was, she thought, completely fooled by her artfulness. Perhaps he was. Certainly, he naïvely wrote all his friends at home of the wonderful things—indeed, the miracles—she was about to perform in her desire to correct abuses. Nor does he seem to doubt that Catherine took all of his "philosophical" ideas with absolute seriousness.

While Catherine was not genuinely interested in reform, Diderot was completely unrealistic. When he reasoned about politics, men were simply theoretical entities which he modified at will. Certainly, many of his criticisms and suggested reforms seem sound to us today; but they were proposed without a thorough knowledge of the conditions in Russia and of the resistance that made their realization even more impossible, without revolution, than in France. His illusions and idealism amused the empress, sometimes annoyed her, as when she interrupted him one day in the midst of one of his beautiful excursions.

> "Monsieur Diderot, I have heard with the greatest pleasure all that your brilliant mind has inspired in you; but with all your great principles which I understand quite well, one would turn out fine books and bad work. You forget, in all your plans of reform, the difference between our positions: you work only on paper, which suffers everything; it is smooth, simple, and opposes no obstacle to your imagination or your pen, while I, poor Empress, I work on human skin which is a great deal more irritable and ticklish."

The Philosopher, quite abashed at this scolding, replied meekly:

> "I may have been indiscreet, thoughtless, but I have here, on my left side, a severe censor which assures me that I have been neither false nor wicked. I am a philosopher just like any other, that is to say, a well-born child who stammers about important matters."

On this latter point Catherine expressed full agreement: "Sometimes you seem to have the head of a man a hundred years old, at other times that of a child of twelve."

Finally, aware of her disagreement with many of his proposals, Diderot had to admit that "the eye of the philosopher and the eye of the sovereign see quite differently."

Despite all this, the numerous legislative projects drafted by Catherine are proof that she paid some heed to his reports to her. None of these projects was carried out.

It is not surprising that Catherine's opinions about her protégé, as expressed to her correspondents, are a mixture of eulogy and criticism. "His is an extraordinary head; the temper of his heart should be that of all men," was her comment to Voltaire. But after his death, she wrote to the count de Ségur, "I have spoken to him often and at length, but more out of curiosity than with profit." Her displeasure was due to her discovery, among Diderot's papers, of his "Observations on the Instructions of her Imperial Majesty to the Deputies for the Drawing-up of Laws." Remembering her wrath at the criticisms of his own protégé, Le Mercier de la Rivière, who had the temerity to proclaim that everything in Russia "would have to be undone and redone," he had thought it more prudent to write down his observations and keep them among his notes. The decision was a wise one.

The frequency of their meetings bears witness to the enjoyment Catherine must have derived from them, even if she did not take them more seriously than as a form of intellectual exercise. She enjoyed Grimm, too, although less than Diderot. "I see them very often," she wrote to Voltaire, "and our conversations are unending . . . I could talk with them all my life without getting tired. Diderot has an interesting imagination, and I classify him among the most extraordinary men who have ever existed."

Once, when their discussion became rather heated, she stopped short with this remark:

"You are a hothead and so am I. We interrupt each other, don't hear each other, and say silly things."

"With this difference, that when I interrupt Your Majesty, I commit a great impertinence."

"Between men," she graciously replied, "are there impertinences?"

One of the curious episodes of Diderot's Russian sojourn was the French government's attempt to utilize him to effect a *rapprochement* between the two countries—while continuing, at the same time, to suspect him of unpatriotic sentiments. He was approached by Durand, the French ambassador at the court of St. Petersburg, and asked to use his intimacy and influence with the empress. Diderot's first reaction was to refuse, for he visioned himself caught between Scylla and Charybdis, that is, between Catherine's anger and the Bastille upon his return home. Durand persuaded him that it would be wiser to change his mind, and he finally brought to his protectress, very delicately and timidly, the project of an alliance, accompanying this proposition with an even larger dose of flattery than usual. But Diderot, the dreamer, could not hope to persuade the wily Catherine of anything she opposed, and all he accomplished for his worry and his pains was to be laughed at again for what she called his childish ideas.

In addition to the round of court festivities and receptions, and the private parties to which he was often invited, Diderot saw Grimm whenever possible. It was his greatest joy, and a fortunate coincidence, at a time when he was thousands of miles from all he loved, to have his dearest friend as a companion in exile. "And Grimm," he wrote home, describing their excited reunion, "of whom I take leave in Paris, wondering whether we shall ever see each other again, traverses one arc of a circle ending at St. Petersburg, while I traverse the other . . . With what violence we rushed into each other's arms! We remained a long time hugging each other, letting go, taking each other again, hugging again, without being able to speak."

He also saw Falconet from time to time, and had completely forgiven him his cold reception, despite Antoinette's rancor at the treatment accorded her husband. He even attempted to soften her anger. And yet before he left Russia, for some unknown cause, he had irreconcilably fallen out with Falconet.

There was exciting news from home, too. He had become a grandfather. He immediately dispatched a long letter of urgent advice to Angélique, and followed it at short intervals with others. "Beware of spilling your milk. You need only one atom of that cursed leaven to corrupt the whole mass of humors; and then just try and purify it. Listen carefully: as long as the slightest odor of milk is exhaled from your body, keep to your room, keep yourself warm, and perspire."

Thus the winter slipped by. Diderot and Grimm were made members of the Imperial Academy of Sciences. But even with Catherine's friendship and a full calendar of social activities, he was not too happy. The nobility did not treat him kindly. He had won the admiration and sympathy of some, but many others were shocked by his informal manners, suspicious of his radical ideas, most of all jealous of the favor he enjoyed. His show of disinterestedness irked the courtiers and they sneered at it as a hypocritical mask. Perhaps they were not entirely wrong. Although Diderot felt genuine gratitude, generous friendship, and idealized enthusiasm for his benefactress, that did not exclude a sense of realities. The two moods took turns in dominating him. It must have been a "practical" day when he wrote one letter to a friend boasting of his complete disinterestedness in his relations with Catherine, and another to his wife, assuring her that despite his diplomatic request that she give him nothing further, he confidently expected her to continue her subsidies and gifts. And even when he was in the enthusiastic mood, his exaggerated praises of Catherine often do not ring true. When she requested his critical opinion about a comedy she had written, he hastened to assure her that it was a most splendid work. "I can affirm to Your Imperial Majesty, to whom I have promised the truth, that the greatest sovereign of Europe will be, when she wishes, the greatest comic poet of her nation." Or as he wrote another time, "Madame, the simplest words of Your Imperial Majesty are not of a nature that they can be forgotten by the man, gifted with ordinary sense, who has had the happiness of approaching you and hearing you." Such courtly and gallant exaggeration is scarcely a matter for serious condemnation, but it is none the less striking in a man who boasted of his uncompromising frankness— and believed in it.

Ill at ease at court, Diderot soon became homesick, and then he began to await impatiently the end of his stay. He missed the jovial dinners with his comrades in arms, and their philosophical discussions; he even missed his wife. And most of all, perhaps, he longed to see his new grandson. Curiously, he had forseen all this. In the *Salon of 1765*, he imagines himself in Russia, thinking nostalgically, almost tearfully, of the life he has left behind. First, Grimm's house: "That is where the one I cherish lives; perhaps he is thinking of me at this moment; he misses me." Then, the home of Mme. d'Epinay: "How often have we lunched in that little cottage. That is where gaiety, enjoyment, reason, confidence, friendship, sincerity, tenderness, and freedom reside." Then, d'Holbach's house in the rue Royale-Saint-Roch: "That is where honest and clever people meet. That is where conversation is solid, where we talk of history, politics, finance, belles-lettres, philosophy. That is where people esteem each other highly enough to contradict each other, where we find the true cosmopolitan, the man who knows how to use his fortune . . ." The only ironical part is the end. For the last stopping place in his imaginary tour is the Rue des Vieux-Augustins, the home of Sophie Volland. "There, my friend, words would fail me. I would lean my head on my two hands, some tears would fall from my eyes; and I would say to myself: 'She is there; how can it be that I am here?' "

He still corresponded with Sophie, but the tone rings hollow and forced. "Are you trying to drive me to despair? I haven't heard from you for a century; did you perchance not receive my last letter? Mademoiselle Volland, if you knew all the cruel visions that obsess me, you would take care not to let them endure; tell me only that you are well, and that you love me; let me see your handwriting once more." The letters are no longer addressed to her, but to her family, "Mesdames et bonnes amies." They conclude,

"I greet you; I embrace you; accept my respect and eternal and tender friendship."

When Diderot became ill again, with "intestinal colic produced by the water," he could stand no more. He threw out broad hints to Catherine that he might wish to be leaving soon. The empress, loath to see her conversationalist and entertainer depart, put off giving her consent. As the end of the winter approached, however, she realized how natural was his impatience, and ordered a special carriage made for him, in which he could recline without being cramped. He was greatly relieved to hear that his comfort was to be carefully provided for.

Early in March, the word was given. Diderot packed excitedly, and then went to bid Catherine farewell. With his usual display of virtue, he begged her to belie his calumniators by making him no further gifts.

"It will be sweeter to me to be believed, when I eulogize your great qualities, than to have more money."

"Are you rich?"

"No, madame, but I am content, which is better."

"What shall I do for you then?"

"Many things. First of all, Your Majesty, who would not want to deprive me for two or three years of the living I owe to her, will pay the expenses of my journey, of my stay and my return, always remembering that a philosopher does not travel like a lord."

"How much do you want?"

"Fifteen hundred rubles will be enough, I think."

"I shall give you three thousand."

To this the philosopher made no objection, but continued:

"Second, Your Majesty will grant me a bagatelle which is valuable only because she has used it."

"I agree, but tell me what is that bagatelle you desire."

"Your cup and saucer."

To this unexpected demand Catherine replied that they would break, and persuaded him to withdraw his request. Instead, she surprised him, just before his departure, with a red agate ring engraved with her portrait.

"Third," continued Diderot, "let one of your officers accompany me and leave me safe and sound at The Hague."

"It will be done."

"Fourth, grant me permission to have recourse to Your Majesty in case I should be financially ruined by the operations of the government, or by any other accident."

"My friend, count on me. You will find me on any occasion, at any time."

At these words, the Philosopher shed a few tears of emotion and gratitude, and Catherine almost did, too.

"Instead of returning," she suggested, "why don't you send for your whole family?"

"Alas, madame, my wife is old and sickly, and I have a sister-in-law who is almost eighty."

The departure being inevitable, Catherine made one request of her own. "Do not say good-bye, because good-byes sadden me."

He did not, but instead sent her a letter, in which he generously begged her favor for his friends, recalling to her Galitzin's devotion and poverty, and Narishkin's debts.

Before Diderot's departure, Frederick the Great and Grimm had tried anew to get his promise to stop at Berlin. A similar attempt was made by the dowager queen Louise-Ulrica of Sweden. Politely but firmly he declined both requests, determined to return directly to The Hague. Nolcken, the Swedish ambassador, informed his government that apparently Diderot's only desire was to see his family and friends again. His letters express a highly flattering opinion of the philosopher, and praise his rare "disinterestedness." All in all, writes Nolcken, he does well to leave, for these qualities have provoked the jealousy of the courtiers; "he would have sooner or later been the victim of envy and wickedness."

Diderot set out at four in the afternoon, on March 5th, 1774, in the company of one of Catherine's officers, by name Bala, a man of culture and charm. One or two incidents marked the otherwise placid and wearisome trek. While crossing the Dvina, the thinning ice cracked under the weight of the carriage, spurting water all over. Surrounded by men armed with hooks to fish them out in case the carriage submerged, they went bravely on across the cracking ice and finally reached the other side in safety. It was a thrilling and harrowing experience, but Diderot retained his composure throughout, feeling himself, as usual, responsible for the reputation of all philosophers. A second accident occurred on a ferryboat, while they were crossing the Mittau. The philosopher slipped, fell, and nearly killed himself.

After thirty-one days, and four changes of carriage, they galloped into The Hague on the morning of April 5th. There he went immediately to the house of prince and princess Galitzin, who were awaiting him with open arms. After tender greetings, and much conversation about his life in Russia and the long journey back, he settled down to another quiet stay. Once more he spent his days working, with walks and long conversations for relaxation.

Among the things that occupied him was the project for a new edition of the *Encyclopedia,* to be done for Catherine and subsidized by her. She had encouraged him in such a scheme when he had complained of Le Breton's "crimes." Financial details were negotiated with Betzky over a long period of time, partly in Russia, partly from Holland, and Diderot grew more and more excited at the idea. "I shall not die without having worthily avenged myself of the wickedness of my enemies, and I shall not die without having raised an obelisk on which will be read: *To the honor of the Russians and of their sovereign, and to the shame of those who merit it.* I shall not die without having imprinted on the earth some traces that time will not efface." But his encyclopedic dreams were again destined to be frustrated. Betzky thought the project a costly folly, and kept postponing the matter until it was finally dropped.

This stay at The Hague was to last less than five months. Diderot had been charged by Catherine with directing the publication of her *Plans and Statutes.* As the work was slow, and left him considerable time for his own pursuits, he accomplished a good deal of writing, finishing or revising various books he had begun, and setting down the ideas inspired by his conversations with Catherine in the form of brief essays.

By the end of August, he had completed his assigned tasks. Galitzin and his wife coaxed him to prolong his stay a few weeks longer, but fifteen months had now passed since his departure, and he chafed with impatience to return to his beloved Paris, for there was all that was dear to him.

He bade his hosts farewell on September 2nd and started on a slow journey across the Low Countries, stopping off at Antwerp and at Brussels to complete his political and economic survey. As usual, he met several interesting people en route. One was an English lady who took turns at living in London and in Paris. On learning that she spoke English and French with equal facility, he asked her which language seemed purer to her.

"English to my mouth," she replied, "and French to my ears."

They spoke of manners and morals in the two countries.

"Corruption is equal in both capitals, but coarser in London. In

France, the company of women is more dangerous for women, and in England, the company of men is more dangerous for men."

All in all, she enjoyed life in Paris most.

Diderot's journeys were at an end. With Catherine, who was dearer to him than ever, he continued to maintain contact by frequent correspondence. A considerable portion of his letters consisted of that flattery, irking by its exaggeration and servility, in which it is difficult to distinguish how much is sincere and how much inspired by self-interest or notions of courtly etiquette.

Thanking Catherine again for her welcome, something he never tired of, he wrote as follows:

> How vain I should be of the welcome with which Your Majesty has honored me, if I did not attribute it entirely to that indulgence characteristic of divinity, which judges men less by what they are than by what they would like to be, and before which the virtues of the heart are as precious as the gifts of genius. All my life, I shall congratulate myself for the trip to St. Petersburg. All my life, I shall recall those moments when Your Majesty forgot the infinite distances which separated me from her, and did not disdain to lower herself to my level in order to hide my pettiness from myself.

One thing attests to his sincerity—he filled the ears of all his friends with the same compliments, up to and beyond the point of satiety. As one of them, d'Escherny, commented, "by the manner in which, since his return from Russia, I have several times heard Diderot sing like a poet the virtues of Catherine, and her great qualities, I think that he could have done an excellent translation of Homer." Catherine wrote to Grimm, in 1776, that the count de Laval was the only Frenchman who had been grateful for her favors, with the exception of Diderot, "who in all things is a man different from the others."

Of course, interest required him to stay within the good graces of his benefactress. A letter of June 1779 is a note of thanks for a "loan" of two thousand rubles. None the less, he continued in a measure the frankness that had characterized their conversations. When Russia finally won the war with Turkey that had been going on since 1768, and a treaty was signed in September 1774, he dared advise her to pay more attention to the triumphs of peace, now that her armies had won so many truly glorious victories. "I rejoice (over your victories) as a man, as a philosopher, and as a Russian, for I have become one through the ingratitude of my country and your kindness . . . I wish that Your Majesty would concern herself more with the duration of peace than with any other advantage . . . Repeated victories doubtless make brilliant reigns, but do they make happy ones?"

There is no doubt that the reception and honors Catherine had granted him were a source of satisfaction and balm for his ego. He frequently compared the recognition given him by foreign countries with the treatment he had received at the hands of his own. These declarations sound unpatriotic to modern ears. But patriotism to Diderot had a broader meaning. The age of nationalism had not yet arrived, and loyalty to a corrupt and tyrannical government could not be expected of those who looked forward to a better age. It is curious to note that Diderot seems to approve of Catherine's role in the first partition of Poland, which took place in 1772, to the discomfiture of the inept French diplomacy. The act itself he decried, declaring it is not right to dispose of peoples without consulting their wishes: "a society of men is not a herd of beasts; to treat them in the same way is to insult the human race." Again, the preoccupation with human dignity! But so far as Catherine is concerned, he rationalizes the whole matter in such a way as to exonerate his empress completely. She did not wish it, he declares, but was forced to by the wicked Frederick of Prussia!

The Russian episode was the great adventure in Diderot's life. He had undertaken it despite himself, it must be admitted, despite the warnings of the Sancho Panza that occupied half his soul. He returned richer in experience and broader in horizons. At the same time, association with royalty imparted to him an aura of respectability which he had never before enjoyed. He could now feel secure from persecution, and he loved security, like any bourgeois, although he had sometimes risked it at moments when his quixotic idealism temporarily won the upper hand. Most important of all, perhaps, he had been stimulated to setting down his ideas on government and education. The works that flowed from his pen during his two sojourns at The Hague, and immediately after, certainly enriched his "literary baggage."

2

Diderot's most interesting piece of work for Catherine was on education, of which they had talked together often and long. In the *Plan for a University,* he sketches for her his educational philosophy and outlines proposals for an entirely new school system.

His mood is determined, writes Jean Thomas, by a "revolt against Jesuit education, the purpose of which was to place the mask of the gentleman over the essential wickedness of human nature." Utilitarianism dominates Diderot's thinking. Social values, intellectual and moral progress are his declared aims. Education should not necessarily make a man profound; it should rather give him the knowledge he will need to fill his role and vocation in society. Not the savant, but the citizen is what the school must form. "I think we should give in the schools an idea of all the knowledge necessary to a citizen, from legislation to the mechanical arts which have contributed so much to the advantages and delights of civilization." Following this idea, education would be free and compulsory, with scholarships for the poor.

Diderot was the first to envisage the importance of technical studies in the civilization that the science of his time was beginning to create. He wants the emphasis in the curriculum to be on sciences and techniques, not on literature or philosophy. Things should be substituted for words. Certainly "without Greek and without Latin, one is not a man of letters." But Diderot does not wish to form the man of letters. He foresees the trend of modern education, away from schools for the elite, towards a democratic education for the entire nation. At the same time he is also concerned, as educators are today, with the problem of not sacrificing the valuable qualities of the individual. "Man must carry intact the marks that nature has imprinted on him and which distinguish him from all others."

In the program he draws up, Diderot does not follow his masters in philosophy, Montaigne and Locke. They had emphasized the development of critical and creative thought. Instead he goes back to Rabelais, and in his scheme of universal education, draws up a program of ambitious scope. Beginning with the sciences, which teach us to love the True, he would lead us through all the subjects that teach us to love the Good, and last of all, the Beautiful.

The defects of his system, which foreshadows contemporary education in so many ways, are best shown by the defects of our own. They are emphasis on purely utilitarian and technical studies, to the detriment of humanistic values, and a tendency to "survey" courses imparting an undigestible mass of facts.

On politics and allied questions, Diderot wrote a large number of essays for Catherine. Designed to continue the provocation of her thoughts long after their separation, these papers betray his mistaken confidence in her intention to carry out most of his projects and to institute a representative government in Russia. They were buried in St. Petersburg, and sharing the fate of so many of his works, some were published near the end of the last century, some only within recent years.

As usual, he flits from one subject to another, producing a *potpourri* of pure philosophy, souvenirs, politics, and technical advice. The notes on political questions are especially welcome, since elsewhere he has left only sketchy notions of his thinking in this field. In the *Encyclopedia*, it is not always easy to disentangle his own thought from the material inserted to satisfy the censors or simply compiled and copied from other authorities. What is evident there is his strong opposition to tyranny; he even proclaims the right to revolution when misery becomes unbearable. "Under any government at all," as he puts it elsewhere, "nature has placed limits to the unhappiness of peoples. Beyond those limits, it is either death, or flight, or revolt." This is pure theory, however, and what he demands, in the *Encyclopedia*, is for the most part what the upper bourgeoisie in general desired: some measure of representation, and correction of the more onerous abuses in taxation and administration. Like the physiocrats, he believes that agriculture should be favored over industry; he rejects Voltaire's argument that subsidies would destroy the farmer's incentive.

In his political thought, just as with his aesthetic ideas, Diderot had begun with general and abstract problems, as in his article, "Political Authority." Even as late as 1767, his enthusiasm for Le Mercier de la Rivière's physiocratic work *(On the Natural and Essential Order of Societies)* was due to its appealingly rationalistic character. It was coherent and systematic. Based on "human nature" and lacking empirical or historical roots, it was universally applicable to the ideal society. Diderot recognized these qualities and approved of them. But shortly after this infatuation, he became concerned with concrete problems. In the current great debate over the question of free trade in grains, he had at first followed Quesnay and Le Mercier: free trade, according to the physiocrats, was necessary to agricultural prosperity and the wealth of the nation. Then, in 1768, Diderot's friend, the Italian abbé Galiani, launched an assault on the physiocratic theory and on the edicts which, by applying it, were causing shortages, high prices, and misery

throughout the realm. Galiani argued from the real facts and prevailing conditions. He held forth, with Neapolitan eloquence and
volubility, in d'Holbach's circle, expounding arguments which he
published the following year (with Diderot's literary assistance, to
be sure) under the title of *Dialogues on the Wheat-Trade*. By this
time, Diderot was completely won over to the empirical approach,
and his enthusiasm was transferred from Le Mercier to Galiani.
Moreover, the misery he observed that summer, when he journeyed
to Langres and Bourbonne, impressed him as factual proof of
Galiani's arguments. It was then he wrote his *Defense of Galiani*,
against Morellet (published only in 1954), a letter to Sartine, also
in his support, and a published "Letter to M—— concerning the
abbé Galiani" (1771).

From then on, Diderot was to oppose the system-spinning which
was the vogue in current political thought. What the philosopher
is called upon to do is to discover the facts and, by presenting them
together with the proper conclusions, to influence the formation of
enlightened opinion. Thus Diderot now carries forward to politics
the experimental method which he had advocated for the sciences
and practised in his own ethical speculation, in his dialogues and
novels. Only thus can we explain his close questioning of Catherine
and her aides, as well as his observations on conditions in Holland,
during his stay there. Most interesting of all is the fact that Diderot's
evolution, on the question of the wheat trade, illustrates his basic
hesitation in political thought. On the one hand, he favors the pre-
capitalistic and liberal tendencies of his clan; he will not admit the
tyrannical invasion of private rights in the name of general welfare.
On the other hand, he sometimes asserts the collectivity's right and
need to use its powers over the individual, both to form good
citizens and to prevent the abuses to which human nature and its
passions give rise. In this we have a preview of the dilemma of
liberalism in the nineteenth and twentieth centuries. Moreover,
we must not forget that Marxism, equally with liberalism, is a part
of the heritage of the eighteenth century.

In other respects Diderot represents the petty bourgeoisie, rather
than the physiocrat-upper-middle-class viewpoint. He calls for a
better balance between the different sections of society, insisting on
the importance of a more equal distribution of national wealth. His
belief that the government should prevent economic injustice goes
counter to the physiocratic theory of *laissez-faire* and foreshadows
the "welfare" concept. In the great eighteenth-century controversy

over "luxury," the economic (but not moral) aspect of the question was partly a conflict between the upper and lower echelons of the economic structure. Those who believed in the benefits of excessive wealth and unequal distribution were pitted against men like Diderot and Rousseau, whose dream was of "an egalitarian nation of small property owners, virtuous like the Roman republic," in contrast to the corruption and strife of a two-class division. The effort to realize this dream, comments Charles Lipton, perished on the guillotine, in the persons of Robespierre and Saint-Just, at the hands of the upper bourgeoisie—just as the dream of a communist society was to perish a few years later, when Babeuf and his associates were put to death.

In one recently discovered piece, the *Pages against a Tyrant,* Diderot discarded the restraint required for the *Encyclopedia.* Towards the end of the 1760's, two of the most radical of all the "philosophic" works had appeared, written by his old friend baron d'Holbach. The first we have already mentioned. *The System of Nature* brought together in its pages overy known form of attack against religion, and also urged a revolt against the yoke of political tyranny. D'Holbach continued his assault in *The Essay on Prejudices,* putting special emphasis on the political aspect. These two works caused a sort of crisis in the "philosophic" movement, the more timid, or less disinterested souls becoming frightened at the extent to which iconoclastic reason was being carried.

Among the latter group was Frederick the Great. Philosophy had charmed his youth, and he had patronized the French thinkers. Now he suddenly became alarmed at the equalitarian and anarchic implications of the "philosophic" movement. He set to work and wrote *An Examination of the Essay on Prejudices,* a refutation of d'Holbach.

Diderot's counter-refutation, written in 1771, was prompted by his instinctive dislike of Frederick. The *Pages against a Tyrant* is a sharp, satirical, and eloquent reply to the man who wanted "to set a limit to the movement of enlightenment." One idea dominates Diderot's pages: the king of Prussia is a tyrant; but truth and good will eventually triumph over him. Diderot's optimism concerning the future is all the more eloquent since it is not based on any illusions concerning the present status of humanity. As he casts his eye around the world, he finds it filled with preachers of falsehood, enemies of the true and the good, bad governments, oppressors, innumerable men who find their self-interest in evil. Lies, corruption, cruelty, ingratitude, and perfidy reign supreme, because men think they can use them to satisfy their selfish interests. But as anyone can tell from their misery, they are deceived. Only when truth is discovered and spread will mankind finally realize that happiness can be founded on truth and on virtue alone.

In the papers written for Catherine, and especially the *Observations on the Drawing-up of Laws*, Diderot was able to give free expression to his political theories.

"The struggle of man against nature is the first principle of society." Society was not created, as some philosophers claimed, because all weak animals live in herds, nor because the weak united against the strong, or the strong (as Rousseau had said) exploited the weak; but rather because men banded together to provide for common needs and protect themselves against common dangers. There was no "social contract," for instinct and need had always held men in groups.

To Catherine, he minces no words. He tells her she is a despot, urges her to set up a constitutional government, and to stop pretending she has renounced her despotism. He is vigorously opposed to the theory of divine right. "There is no true sovereign, there can be no true legislator except the people . . . If the Sovereign violates the code, the people must have the right to depose and punish him." This is to be done by an elective assembly, called to pass judgment on the king every five years. Diderot is far from reality.

Boldly he proclaims the right of open opposition, and the rights of individual liberty, "without which men are reduced to the condition of animals . . ." It is liberty, he affirms, that alone can lead "the individual and society to the greatest happiness they can desire." With liberty must go equality, the sole assurance of individual dignity, and this requires that there be no exceptions or differences in the applications of the law.

We are reminded of another passage in the *Refutation of Helvétius*, in which he denounces benevolent despotism. The monarch must not be the master of the people, for either good or evil. The "general will" must be supreme, even when in error. The question is not one of utility, but of rights, and rights are what distinguish men from animals. Under a benevolent despot men are lulled into a false security; they forget their liberties, lose the habit of self-government and the sacred right of criticism, fall into a "sleep of death." So that a benevolent despotism is the most dangerous of all despotisms. But the despot will some day pay for

Diderot

his abuse. "He is bending trees that will end up by breaking his neck when they straighten up . . . The people and their leaders owe each other mutual respect." Diderot's attitude here reveals that in contrast with his more general utilitarianism, he holds the same rationally absolute conception of natural rights that inspired the American Declaration of Independence.

In similar vein, he warns against witch hunts and thought control as a sure way to check the growth of minds. "Without realizing it, people begin avoiding a certain kind of dissenting ideas, as they avoid an object that would hurt them; and when they get used to that pusillanimous and cautious gait, it is hard to get back to a frank and outspoken way."

But hatred of despotism does not mean confidence in the common people. Diderot repeatedly calls them stupid, wicked, credulous fools, vulgar in taste. "The voice of the philosopher who gainsays that of the people is the voice of reason." But then he adds: "The voice of sovereigns who gainsay that of the people is the voice of madness."

This is Diderot's program: "First of all, society must be happy, and it will be if freedom and property are assured; if commerce is unrestricted; if all classes of citizens are equally submitted to law; if taxation is distributed according to ability to pay . . . if virtue and talents are assured of reward." The good of society should be so firmly united by laws to the good of individuals, that a bad action "will punish itself." The lawmaking body must be independent of the executive, and have the power to approve or disapprove his will. It should be composed of large property owners. For legislators, he announces his fundamental principle that no law is a good one, or will be obeyed, that contradicts natural impulses or that does not satisfy the desire for happiness which is the motive of all actions. But no code of laws, however wise, can be eternal; at intervals it must be re-examined and revised. Change in the dimension of time Diderot thus allows, but not in the dimension of geography. Under the sway of abstract rationalism and the belief in a universal human nature, he turns his back—as did most of the *philosophes*—on the great work of Montesquieu. "Customs and manners are everywhere the result of legislation and government." Montesquieu had declared the opposite to be true. "They are neither African nor Asiatic nor European," continues Diderot, "they are good or bad . . . What Peter I brought into Russia, if it was good in Europe, was good everywhere." Montesquieu, far more wisely, had declared a law to be good if it met the needs and habits of a given community.

These weak generalizations Diderot topped off with some far-sighted, practical proposals. He foresees the modern civil service system, urges that all positions should be filled by competitive examination. He calls for abolition of privileges, rigid economy in the monarch's administration and private life, freedom of the press. Of particular interest is his plea for the institution of divorce laws. He suggests that the grounds should be "natural inconstancy, domestic hell," the unhappiness of the children, corrupt morals. "The ability to separate leads to mutual consideration." In case of remarriage, children should be wards of the government. Diderot defends prostitution as an institution which protects the virtue of "honest women." In the matter of judicial procedure, he makes an interesting plea against the English common law system. "The decisions of the courts should never be printed. In the long run they form a counter-authority to the law. Commentators on sacred books have committed a thousand heresies . . . No other authority before the court but the law and reason and natural justice . . . If the court has erred, to quote its judgment is to induce the same injustice a second time."

In some of his general considerations, Diderot does give evidence of realism, often in contradiction to his own favorite rationalizations. "It is evident that in a well-ordered society the wicked man cannot hurt society without hurting himself. The wicked man knows that, but what he knows even better, is that he gains more as a wicked man than he loses as a member of society." Equality before the law is a fine ideal, but how assure it when citizens are unequal in power and wealth? "That has never been, perhaps it was impossible for it to be. But it is worth thinking about." As for education, "We must teach and enlighten; but not expect too much from it." Thoughts such as these perhaps represent Catherine's influence, her share of their ardent discussions.

Diderot's political program is weak, because there is no cogently reasoned theory joined to consequent and systematic means of realization. What is praiseworthy in his loose and scattered thinking is his insistence on the sovereignty of the people and on the rights of the individual. In these two points, he was in step with the century. Liberty was ardently desired by the bourgeoisie, especially in the management of their property and their business. Diderot not only demands *laissez-faire* but declares the right of property sacred and absolute, imparting to the owner complete power to do as he wishes with his possessions. He is particularly suspicious of restrictions that may be imposed on liberty in the name of public utility, which he calls "a redoubtable and often fatal notion, limited by the rights of the individual."

He does not succeed in reconciling this belief with his theory that individual happiness is in direct proportion to community happiness. "I want society to be happy; but I want to be happy, too; and there are as many ways of being happy as there are individuals. Our own happiness is the base of all our true duties." Here we can see hovering in the background those more rebellious and radical moods when he longed for individual freedom far beyond that demanded by the bourgeois. In such a mood he will curse money and the "venal system," proclaim the right to revolution, destroy morality, destroy the right to property which he elsewhere terms sacred, destroy government itself. We recall his saying, "I am convinced that there cannot be any real happiness for mankind except in a social state in which there would be no king, no magistrate, no priest, no laws, no thine or mine, no ownership of property, no vices or virtues." We recall his open statements in the *Encyclopedia*, praising the Incas for weakening the property spirit, "source of all vices," and urging the legislator to foster community spirit instead. Obviously, these radical moments are not coordinated. Now it is anarchic individualism he longs for, now the subordination of private property to the social group. Both dreams˜ reveal an inner distrust of the bourgeois society he was helping to build.

What did Catherine think of the labors of her philosopher? Her opinion is succinctly expressed in a letter to Grimm, written after Diderot's death. "This piece is a true babble, in which there is neither knowledge of things, nor prudence, nor clairvoyance; if my instructions had been to Diderot's taste, they would have turned everything topsy-turvy."

In his papers for Catherine, and in personal letters, Diderot occasionally indulges in energetic criticism of the French political structure. The spectre of Vincennes prevented any more overt expression. Many of his most libertarian ideas, many of his most vehement criticisms of contemporary society are buried in the extensive revisions he made in Raynal's widely read *History of the Indias*, for its second edition (1774), and still more for its third edition (1780). This was an anonymous and for him a safe way of spreading ideas he had not dared to include in the *Encyclopedia* or had developed since that time as his political philosophy evolved. France appeared so decadent to him, that he judged revolution inevitable unless a great king came upon the scene, or unless the dissemination of truth suddenly enlightened the country's rulers. But such reform, he frankly admitted, was scarcely probable: "Bad customs, endlessly multiplied and incurable, have become respectable by their duration and irreformable by their number." He communicated his conclusion to Catherine: "Madame, our monarchy is very feeble . . . who knows our fate under the next reign? Personally, I think ill of it." And to his English friend, the statesman Wilkes: "Why aren't you here? The man who can arouse great emotions likes to be spectator of great revolutions . . . I was asked one day how to restore vigor to a nation that had lost it; I answered, as Medea restored youth to her father: by cutting him up and boiling him." Wilkes lived to see the revolution Diderot predicted.

Like the other *philosophes,* Diderot looked to the American colonies as the great hope of mankind, as the virgin soil where man could profit from his previous mistakes and build a society based on reason. This, of course, is what the founding fathers, impregnated with the ideas of Montesquieu, Rousseau, Voltaire and Diderot, tried to do. He predicts that the colonies will revolt against the mother country some time "before a hundred years." When the Revolution came, a great deal sooner than he expected, he offered the new country this piece of advice:

> After centuries of general oppression, may the revolution which has just taken place beyond the seas, by offering to all the inhabitants of Europe a shelter against fanaticism and tyranny, instruct those who govern men on the legitimate use of their authority!
>
> May those brave Americans, who have preferred to see their wives outraged, their children throttled, their dwellings destroyed, their fields laid waste, their cities burned, who have preferred to shed their blood and die, rather than to lose the least part of their freedom, prevent the enormous increase and unequal distribution of wealth and luxury, idleness, the corruption of morals, and provide for the preservation of their liberty and the duration of their government! . . . May the citizen either never be born, or die at once by the executioner's sword or the dagger of a Brutus, who might be powerful enough one day, and hostile enough to his own happiness, to frame the design of making himself its master!

Diderot

Let them bear in mind that it is neither by gold, nor even by the multitude of arms, that a State is upheld, but by morals.

A thousand men who fear not for their lives are more to be dreaded than ten thousand who fear for their fortunes.

These words are peculiarly interesting some one hundred and ninety years later.

CHAPTER 17

The
Triumph
of
Humanism

THROUGHOUT THE PERIOD when Diderot was working out his philosophy of materialism, extending its consequences to their extreme moral conclusions, the undercurrent of the *other* Diderot, the humanist and lover of virtue, continued to express itself, in his *Salons*, letters, plays, and tales. When the most radical conclusions were reached, explored, and set down, he found that in his heart he could not accept them as true and viable for mankind. A reaction set in that took the form of a dialectical synthesis of the two opposing currents: intuitive moral virtue and logical, materialistic amoralism.

This new phase emerges in the form of an artistic representation of reality, not as a treatise or argumentative dialogue. In this respect, the novel, *Jacques the Fatalist*, is the pendant to *Rameau's Nephew*.

A leisurely, sprawling work, particularly cherished by Diderot lovers, *Jacques the Fatalist* was written in 1773–4, published in 1796. Inspired primarily by Sterne's *Tristram Shandy*, secondarily by the *esprit gaulois* as found in the fantasy of Rabelais, Diderot takes Jacques and his master through various adventures and has them recount sundry others, with due commentary by himself. Following the teasing, digressive method of *Tristram Shandy,* the stories are interrupted and postponed by each other and by the author's or the characters' remarks. Jacques starts out to tell of his great love affair, but even at the end has not quite finished, and it is the author who has to satisfy the reader's curiosity. "Half imitating, half parodying Sterne," remarks F. C. Green, "Diderot weaves into the tissue of an imaginary conversation between two travelers, a fascinating pattern of brilliant comments on human nature, dramatic and bawdy tales, scenes and characters vibrating with life . . . Jacques is a really human character . . . He is the fatalist and the realist, destined always to experience the most romantic adventures . . . Diderot has profound sympathy for humanity beneath apparent cynicism." Of the many incidental jewels in the treasure box of *Jacques the Fatalist,* the most precious is the tale of Mme. de la Pommeraye, the powerful story of a woman's vengeance.

Jacques inevitably reminds us, however superficially, of *Don Quixote.* The master-valet antithesis, the two world-views, were doubtless suggested to Diderot by the greatest of all novels. But whereas Don Quixote and Sancho live wholly, and meaning flows from their existence, Jacques and his master are the obvious mouthpieces of the author's ideas, the incarnation of his thesis. Jacques is the fatalist, believing that all has been written in "The Great Scroll." This "fatalism" is probably only a symbolic and poetic expression of determinism, which is Jacques' true philosophy. Already in the *Thoughts on the Interpretation of Nature,* Diderot had utilized this device, and spoken of "the universal mechanism which we call Fate." The Master adheres, with temporary vacillations, to his faith in Providence and in free will. The events of the story are designed to put their doctrines to the test of action, and the consistent result is a humorous inconsistency. The Master finds that he is not free, in that the force of circumstances and Jacques' trickery determine his action. Jacques, on the other hand, discovers that his real master is chance. Still more troubling to him, he cannot help acting and feeling as if virtue and vice were genuine values. This is contrary to his professed philosophy.

> Jacques did not recognize the word vice, nor the word virtue; he claimed that we are happily or unhappily born. When he heard the words "reward" or "punishment," he shrugged his shoulders.

According to him, reward was an encouragement for the virtuous ; punishment, a warning to evildoers. What else can it be, he said, if there is no free will, and our destiny is written up there? He believed that a man wends his way to glory or ignominy as necessarily as a ball that has consciousness of itself follows the slope of a mountain ; and that if the chain of cause and effect that forms a man's life were known to us, from the first instant of his birth until his last sigh, we would be convinced that he has done nothing except what he had to do . . . The distinction between a moral and a physical world seemed meaningless to him.

In the universe there is neither good nor evil: "everything in nature thinks of itself and only of itself. What matter if it hurts others, so long as it's all right for you?"

In Diderot's dialectic, Jacques and the Master are thesis and antithesis. They cannot get along without each other, but clash at every step.

> MASTER—What are you thinking of?
>
> JACQUES—I am thinking that while you were speaking to me and I was answering you, you were speaking without wanting to, and I was answering without wanting to.
>
> MASTER—So?
>
> JACQUES—So? And that we were two genuine living and thinking machines . . .
>
> MASTER—But it seems to me that I feel within myself that I am free, as I feel that I think . . .
>
> JACQUES—My captain, alas, said that the enjoyment of a freedom that could act without any motive would be the real characteristic of a maniac.
>
> MASTER—That is too hard for me, but despite your captain and yourself, I shall believe that I want when I want.

Diderot of course is in both characters, and their opposition is the moral dilemma he has struggled with all his life. Logically, the real meaning can only be sought in the synthesis that comes out of the clash. We glimpse it in Jacques' despair at being unable to live his philosophy. "I have tried a hundred times . . . I have given up; I have decided to be as I am." For Jacques "to be as he is" means to live virtuously, to admire virtue in others, and to hate vice.

The theories of the philosophers lead only to endless intellectual war and a comic inability to explain human beings. Diderot had always been aware of this dilemma. And now, without abjuring the conclusions of his own logic, he is mocking their human validity, mocking all the *isms*. Science and scientific philosophy simply miss human values. We possess ethical desires which the most highly developed scientific knowledge cannot satisfy or explain. What *Jacques the Fatalist* demonstrates is the impossibility of living consistently according to any abstract system. The contradictions and whimsical results of the protagonists' actions are, then, a gentle spoofing of philosophical explanations of man. For man is more than any one of them, and regardless of their truth (which we can never determine anyhow), the human factor is decisive, incalculable, controlling. Certainly, *Jacques the Fatalist* is partly a satire of Spinoza—of his mysticism, his "intellectual happiness," *sub specie aeternitatis*. But that is just a case in point. The larger satire is of the human condition, of our uncertainty, inconsistency, and ignorance—a pretentious ignorance that tries to explain man and the universe with the theories of a limited mind.

The importance of this synthesis becomes apparent only when we apply it to Diderot's moral thinking, the central theme of all his work. The Master represents the formalistic aspect of his ethics. Actions are inherently good or evil, we know when they are one or the other, and in virtuous living lies the only merit. Jacques embodies both Diderot's evolutionary morality ("weak men are the dogs of strong men," he says), and his moral scepticism—no two people judge an action the same way, so there is no basis for morality. The logic of Jacques' position leads to the nihilism of Rameau's nephew.

In *Jacques the Fatalist*, we see Diderot's continuing consciousness of the reality of amoral egoism as an existential force, and his preoccupation with the difficulty of justifying moral value. *Jacques the Fatalist* is the picture of a chaotic, absurd world, reflecting no decipherable cosmic order of meaning, and with no correspondence between the supposed quality of our acts, or of our intentions, and their results. The book itself is the very image of such a world, designedly chaotic and disordered. Every so often we hear the refrain, "But in heaven's name, reader, do we know where we are going?" Nor is that all. Throughout the story, time and again, we see the dominance and power of the aggressive, egoistic drives, casting off the coat of moral restrictions, and the pervasiveness of evil and cruelty in human relations. This—together with another disastrous fact, the impossibility of judging others—constitutes the deep meaning of the two interwoven tales of Mme. de la Pommeraye and of Father Hudson. In these two characters (in contrast to other examples in the novel), the revolt against morality is seconded by a real *greatness* in evil, thus assuring its triumph. Mme. de la Pommeraye's greatness, moreover, was not called forth until she turned to evil; while she was virtuous, she was mediocre.

Jacques, however, resigns himself to living inconsistently with his theories, a resignation he expresses comically by deciding to trust only to the bottle for counsel. Diderot, in his interventions, is partly on both sides, but mostly for Jacques' deterministic amoralism. He follows his usual method, founds an arbitrary morality on social needs, and tries to justify punishment as a determining cause that will deter the evil-doer. But there are new elements which rise up against the power of nihilism. The ultimate theme of the book is the acceptance of experience despite all abstract formulas. That experience points infallibly to an intuitive feeling or power of judgment of right and wrong that is in us. Here we have the first sign of a new view. It is the first step towards the exaltation of man, whom before this Diderot had deprived of any exceptional status in nature. The reaction, though long in coming, was inevitable. "I like a philosophy," Diderot had written to Sophie Volland in 1759, "which lifts up humanity; to degrade it is to encourage men to vice." Even as he was writing *D'Alembert's Dream,* he rebelled against its conclusions in another letter we have quoted. Virtue and humanity—nothing could conquer these in his heart, not even the pitiless logic whose supreme triumph was Rameau's nephew. And the reaction will grow, grow into the thunderous denunciation of Helvetius' mechanism.

Virtue and vice are real, then, as real as the distinction between man and animal. But are not men automatons, as necessarily determined as the stone that rolls down a hill? Determined, yes, but what is the meaning of this "necessity"? Experience shows us that men do admire virtue, can modify their conduct towards an ideal. Diderot is trying hard to work out of a fallacy that has plagued all his ethical thinking. He has equated free will with freedom from cause or motivation. This is only one form of free will, an extreme form better termed "freedom of indifference," that would really make man the slave of every moment's whim. Morality is impossible without the causation of example, experience, and intention. Our freedom is our ability to evaluate motives and impulses, through our power of contemplating ourselves, and the rest of the world, in retrospect and with foresight, our ability to bring new motives to bear, and to act according to an end selected as desirable.

391

It is toward this freedom of the self that Diderot is painfully working, a freedom that tallies with our experiential knowledge of virtue. This then is the synthesis of Jacques' and his master's opposition: a belief in virtue, vice and moral freedom as human facts, as facts of life that are not affected by the proofs of abstract logic.

The author's attitude as artist, moreover, confirms the discrepancy between the theory of necessity (which is his own) and the experience of freedom. Diderot, testing and experimenting, constantly insists on his godlike power, utterly arbitrary and capricious, totally uncaused, to change the course of the story, to postpone, and to interject. Both directly, and indirectly through Jacques, he supplies the "proof" in action which cannot be given in terms of discursive reason, that life is not mechanical or predictable.

For many years *Jacques the Fatalist* was not appreciated at its true worth. Only a few unusually perceptive men pierced the veil of levity and the deceptive appearance of confusion. This select group included Goethe, Carlyle, and Stendahl, who preferred it among all of Diderot's writings. Recently *Jacques the Fatalist* has been re-evaluated. Critics admire its humor and whimsy, although these are less spontaneous than Sterne's. They extol its perceptions of human nature, and even more, its foreshadowing of the techniques of surrealism and the contemporary novel. Reality in *Jacques* is grasped not as a rational whole, but as something elusive, fragmented, and contradictory. Diderot makes a 'game of using the associative process and chains of ideas to jump ahead in Jacques' mind or to anticipate the reader's thinking—which he inevitably contradicts, either for the sport of contradiction or to show the uncertainty of the process of distinguishing reality from appearance. Reality is presented in different time levels: the present action, the story from the past and the author's own commentary. Writes one recent critic: "Past events, jumbled about in the author's time machine, become as significant and contemporaneous as present events . . . It is for the reader . . . to see such interruptions as the component part of a reality which encompasses both the external life in set molds of time and space, and the limitless interior life of the mind . . . What Diderot wants is . . . a medium whereby the processes of the mind are used for an intrinsic structure of the novel."

It is doubtful whether all this was in Diderot's mind; it is rash to find a subtle purpose in every turn and twist of his fantasy. Modern critics are reinterpreting *Jacques* in the light of what they have learned from Joyce, Proust, and Woolf—but the fact that they can find an analogy is none the less interesting. Critics have been fooled by Diderot himself. "My project is to be true," he tells us, and they have not seen the tongue in cheek, but overwork his text with a naïve zeal for "interpreting" seriously each humorous point. What is certain is that Diderot had always been interested in the problem of the imitation or creation of "reality" by the artist in any medium, and this novel may be taken as an experiment along these lines.

Jacques the Fatalist is in many respects a superb, an entertaining and a stimulating work. It is not a great novel. Both protagonists are the disembodied caricatures of an idea, of the human dilemma before reality. The episodic elements challenge the unifying force of the two characters. There is no breadth, little emotional and intellectual range, no intensity. Most of all, a great novel must embody a view of human life, in terms of concrete problems of action, not abstract problems of a philosophical nature.

2

Diderot's impulse toward the supremacy of the human is carried forward in his *Refutation of Helvétius*, written between 1773 and 1775-6, largely from notes made during his stay at The Hague, completed on his return to Paris, but published only in 1875.

He was aroused by Helvétius' attitude toward man, although that attitude was only an extreme logical consequence of materialism. In his major work, *On the Mind*, and in his subsequent treatise, *On Man*, Helvétius had developed the theory that because everything is reducible to physical sensitivity, and because we instinctively seek pleasurable sensation, selfish pleasure is the motive of all we do. We are physiologically incapable of unselfish actions. Moreover, normal men, like animals, are born essentially the same; all differences, mental and emotional, are the result of education and environment. In fact, in every respect, we resemble our fellow animals.

Such a psychology shocked and repelled Diderot, although he had himself given expression to some of these ideas. No matter how far his paradoxes might carry him, he always came back to his belief in the dignity of the individual and of the human race. In one of his paradoxical moods, he had defined love as "the voluptuous rubbing of two membranes," and this was his attitude in the *Supplement to Bougainville's Voyage* and *Rameau's Nephew*. But when Buffon declared that only the physical aspect of love was worth anything, he rose in arms. "In no circumstance," he wrote to Falconet, "can I permit that man be put on all fours, or the passion most fecund in virtuous and criminal actions be reduced to a few drops of a voluptuously spilled fluid." But did this not contradict the conclusions of his own materialism? Well, if his reason leads to such conclusions, he cannot refute them, but he can rebel against their validity. "The truths of feeling are more unshakeable than the truths of vigorous demonstration, although it is often important to satisfy our minds fully about the former. All the proofs of these, taken separately, can be disputed, but the bundle is more difficult to break."

Diderot's indignation impelled him to write a complete and decisive rebuttal. He realized more clearly than ever that there are factors in men which are beyond physics and chemistry. Certainly, he admitted the importance of education. But for Helvétius to conclude, from man's all-pervasive sensitivity, that he is born, in mind and character, a shapeless wax, ready to be molded entirely by his environment, seemed to him an absurd exaggeration. The perfection of intellectual operations depends far more on the conformation of the brain than on the senses—here is perhaps Helvétius' principal error. The defining character of man is his power of reasoning. Education can, at most, modify: "We cannot give what nature has refused; perhaps we destroy what she gives. The culture of education improves her gifts."

In a word, Diderot believes in the decisive character of the organism, of its needs, functioning, and predispositions; what we bring to experience determines behavior at least as much as experience itself. He was an adherent of the man-machine or organicist school of thought, rather than of pure sensationism. He may not have been in a position to realize that Helvétius' theory was only a prerequisite to his grand solution to the problem of making men social and "moral" beings. Helvétius' scheme was no less than the molding of behavior patterns, by conditioned reflexes (today it is called "operant conditioning") and other means of control—something that could only be brought about in totalitarian societies. But it is possible that Diderot did intuit this terminus of Helvétius' thought—so great is his revulsion.

In spite of Diderot's previous insistence that man is an integral part of nature, entirely subject to natural law and necessity, Helvétius' dehumanization of man shocked him into making concrete a feeling we can trace back to his earliest works: the feeling that man is something very special and distinct in nature. The reduction of mental and emotional life to mere physical sensitivity, and of man himself to parity with the other animals are Helvétius' inseparable errors. No longer does Diderot say, whatever the chicken is, so is man. And the difference is one of quality, not of degree. "We must make a distinction between man and animal," he argues. Helvétius' generalization passes from physical sensation to desire for happiness, to comparison, to judgment. This equivalence of sensation and judgment is too far-fetched. It may apply as a generalization to animals, but "I am a man, and I must have causes peculiar to man . . . What use is a string of conclusions that apply equally to the dog, the weasel, the oyster, the dromedary?" It would be equally logical to say, "I exist, therefore I judge." We must feel to act, and be organized to feel, but those are basic and primitive conditions, and not the immediate motives of our aversions and desires. We must not confuse condition with cause. To say that ambition, jealousy, and so forth are only physical sensitivity is "to take the condition of all animal action in general for the motive of the action of one individual of one animal species called man."

From the cosmic viewpoint, only an evolutionary morality is justifiable, and determinism makes remorse a futile masochism. From the human viewpoint, remorse is defended in the *Refutation*. Freedom is in a measure brought back, inasmuch as the individual personality is considered more important than all other influences; man is not a blind cog in the Wheel of Destiny; he is a provident collaborator, and his peculiar moral individuality is more decisive than the physical sensitivity he shares in common with all animals. In man, rational judgment is supreme over sensation and instinct.

> There is among his senses such a harmony that none predominates enough over the others to lay down the law to his judgment. It is his judgment, on the contrary, or the organ of his reason, that is the strongest. It is a judge which is neither suborned nor subjugated by any of the witnesses. It conserves all its authority, and uses it to perfect itself.

Human life differs from all other kinds of living behavior in that its consciousness and its awareness of what it strives towards make a decisive difference in the mechanical cause-effect sequence of nature.

So shocked was Diderot by Helvétius' mechanization of human

beings, so strong his reaction, that he almost renounces his theory of transformism. Evolution, as he stated it, could only account for differences in degree, not in quality; so he inquires, "Was there a time when man could not be distinguished from animals? I do not think so: he was always a man, that is to say, an animal combining ideas." No longer does he feel sure of his theory of the origin of life.

> I see clearly in the development of the egg and several other operations of nature, matter, organized but apparently inert, pass from the state of inertia to the state of sensitivity and life by purely physical agents, but the necessary link of this transition escapes me. Our notions of matter, organization, and life must still be very incomplete. We must admit it: the organization or the coordination of inert parts does not at all lead to sensitivity, and the general sensitivity of the molecules of matter is only a supposition, which derives all its strength from the difficulties it does away with, which in good philosophy is not sufficient.

After wavering so long, Diderot now recognizes the insufficiency of both theories as definitive explanations of the qualitative differences that divide brute matter from life, and mere life from rationality. He almost abandons his materialism, too, in his effort to separate man from animal by giving to him the exclusive trait of moral sensitivity. Pleasure and pain are indeed the only principles of action, but moral pleasure and moral pain (such as grief for the dead) are quite as real and intense as physical sensations. "Is not the distinction between physical and moral as solid as that between an animal that feels and an animal that reasons?" Every animal feels, but only man can judge, and it is from his judgment that his moral sensitivity derives. Men, such as philosophers and fanatics, may have completely non-sensual motives. These are, in fact, one of our distinguishing attributes. When it comes to man, we can make no sure prediction, no mechanical calculation. Double the stimulation may produce not double the pleasure, but pain. We can summarize the *Refutation* in Julian Huxley's words, by saying that Diderot has realized "the apparently contradictory but essential task of re-establishing our unity with nature while at the same time maintaining our transcendence over nature."

In reality, Diderot does not necessarily abandon his materialism here; the brain and moral sensitivity, he would have rejoined, are after all only specializations of the nervous tissue characteristic of man. Physical and moral sensitivity are distinct and different attributes of a single nervous tissue that has gone through various stages of evolution. But that this could be, he would at least admit, involves a mystery, a supposition, almost an article of faith.

Diderot has glimpsed the need of new explanations, but struggled helplessly to see over the walls that held him in. He was shackled by the thought and knowledge of his time, which conceived of material particles as the ultimate reality, leaving no room for consciousness, mind, and spirit—the things he most believed in—except in terms of the motion of particles which possessed neither consciousness, nor mind, nor spirit. Yet somehow, he felt, the organic whole was more than the sum of its parts.

3

After 1775, Diderot's productivity slowed down abruptly. In his remaining years he wrote only a few short pieces and one very long work. This was his *Essay on the Reigns of Claudius and Nero*, written in 1778. Lagrange, the tutor of d'Holbach's children, had published a translation of Lucretius and begun one of Seneca. When death cut short the latter project, Naigeon took it up and brought it to completion. Urged on by Naigeon and d'Holbach, Diderot decided to write the life of Seneca; but he soon found that he could not pass judgment on Seneca's life and character without studying his relations with the Roman emperors and reconstructing the entire background. The result was a discursive work, alternating between dryness and puffed eloquence. Here and there, however, an idea of unusual interest is encountered, more or less connected with the main subject. Most of these ideas deal with morals, religion, or politics.

As we look back over the span of Diderot's writings, a few final comments are in order. Nature and man are the two poles of his thought; science and morals the two prisms through which he views them. The search for beauty forms a third and connected phase. His conception of nature was all-embracing and integral. It was God, man, and everything else we call "nature" fused into a single dynamic concept. Diderot did not believe in an entity called "God," but his feeling for nature is suffused with the sense of divinity. "Enlarge God!" he had once cried. "Oh Nature, all that is good is enclosed in your breast! You are the fertile source of all truths!" To feel awe at the harmony of nature and ourselves, writes Hans Zinsser, "to wish to fit into the harmony of natural things, with a vision of the whole, is apparently a definite phenomenon of human psychology; it is the force that has engendered religions . . ." Diderot had rejected religions, but not the religious spirit.

Man is studied by Diderot in relation to this cosmic process and reality. At first completely integrated into cosmic law, he finally emerges in Diderot's mind with the full distinction of the human status, that of a being whose special nature is to seek and to love the True, the Good, and the Beautiful. Man, like nature, is for him an integral concept, with all phases of his behavior and activity interrelated in the total organic life. Man in the universe, in society, in his own heart—these phases of his being cannot be divorced.

Above all, man and everything else there is must be regarded from man's own viewpoint—not from that of impersonal law or a supposed supernatural Being. "Man is the single term from which we ought to set out, and to which we ought to trace all back . . . If you take away my own existence and the happiness of all my fellows, of what concern is all the rest of nature to me?" To fashion a complete science of man, such was the ambitious scope of Diderot's restless mind.

But men must live together and work out a common destiny. The self must be adjusted to other selves, its demands to those of others. Man, then, without losing his precious individuality, must become social, and moral. We have seen Diderot's constant concern with the complexities of both terms of this problem, and with their interrelations. If life showed him an amoral universe of force, a human kind propelled to evil by powerful instincts, if his naked reason could find no status for moral values, he nonetheless knew and felt their imperishable reality as human attributes, and he taught them and loved them.

In still one more sense Diderot's work was that of a synthetic intelligence. Mathematics, science, philosophy, letters, and the arts —these are not separated in his thinking. A keen sense of their interrelations runs through his writings, and his basic attitudes are carried over from one to the other.

It is the paradox of Diderot's thought that this integrating, synthesizing mind should have produced an unsystematic and disjointed body of work. He lacked not the intellect, but the temperament to fashion a rigid and persistent interpretation of reality—of the True, the Good, or the Beautiful. He followed the current of his times in scorning systematic philosophy, and his times did not have enough knowledge for more than uncertain scientific speculation. Despite this, he formulated a philosophy of materialism in its most complete and modern form. In his mental ferment, he explored various directions, covering the range from the right to the left, and from classical to romantic and naturalistic. Further, there was often no concordance between his thought and his life. After his youth, he lived as a bourgeois, with epicurean-sensual divagations. His life lacked the serenity and firm direction of a Spinoza or a Kant, just as his restless soundings contrast with their systems. To Diderot we can surely apply these words: ". . . the embrace that includes everything human, the immense zest for life of a Proteus who assumes all guises, who longs to know everything, understand everything, be everything . . . a supreme infidelity that finds pleasure in leaving disciples in the lurch, in embarrassing the partisans of any one principle by perfecting both it and its precise opposite." Thus we come to the most significant of Diderot's bifurcations. At heart an idealist, he was caught up in the tide of materialism that was to engulf Western thought. Groping and searching for a new order that would answer his needs and yet remain in accord with the new science, he could not escape the climate of ideas of his age. But his mind was always open to alternative possibilities. That is his great distinction. He was able to overflow the tight limits of materialism by admitting man's own limitations and finally refusing to allow the rigidity of a theory to submerge the distinctively human in man. He had set out far from materialism. The knowledge, preconceptions, and theories of his intellectual matrix had made that philosophy the inevitable conclusion for his logical and rebellious mind. Scarcely does his materialistic system reach its fullest formulation (largely as tentative theorizing and regarded with some doubt), when he is led to question or deny some of its essential elements, under the pressure of his humanistic ethics—which, in turn, had undergone a dialectical evolution. But while his ethics eventuated in the sketch of a true synthesis, in metaphysics the tension between his materialism and his vague and incomplete resistance to it was never resolved into a formulation on a higher level.

Montesquieu, Voltaire, Diderot, Rousseau—these are the four great names of the Age of Enlightenment. Diderot's claim to leadership in the "philosophic movement" must rest, in part, upon his esoteric works, which represented the vanguard of thought and were circulated "under the cloak" among the faithful. Still more, it rests upon his great generalship in the encyclopedic enterprise,

Diderot

which embodied a more moderate liberalism. In the field of propaganda Voltaire by far surpassed him, and was undoubtedly the "party" standard-bearer. It was the Patriarch of Ferney who led the people to the *philosophes*. But if Voltaire was the party's best popularizer, he himself lacked originality and had little direct influence on the front rank of French thinkers. The inspiration of leadership came from men with bold and original minds, from Diderot, Rousseau, and Montesquieu, from Buffon and the physiocrats, leaders of political, moral, scientific, and economic thought. Of these, Diderot is the only one who united a large group in a common endeavor. Considering the legacy of the eighteenth century, the importance of his role becomes self-evident. It was materialism, experimentalism, sensualism that were to direct the progress of science, politics, economics, and psychology. In literature, the immediate contributions of the century were sensitivity and romanticism; in politics, one aspect of its work, the destruction of feudalism and its replacement by a new social philosophy that called for representative government, for the economic individualism of capitalism, for the dignity of individual liberty. In all this, Diderot played a significant part.

Certainly he did not succeed in forging a great philosophy. He failed to produce a great and novel central idea of terrific impact, about which all the rest would turn, as did a Rousseau or a Nietzsche, a doctrine that could seize men's minds and direct them. Certainly, his thought has many weaknesses, some born of insufficient knowledge, others of lack of unity and coherence. But the first defect applies to all men, as time goes by. As for the second, consistency is not the most precious of all jewels. The soundest thinker may not be the one who develops a consistent line of reasoning, but one who is capable of changing his mind and whose thought evolves. The truest philosopher is not necessarily the builder of systems, but the seeker for truth, who is ready to see it wherever it lies, ready to lose himself in its complexity, instead of simplifying and reducing it to a pattern. We can apply to Diderot the words Voltaire said of Bayle: "wise enough, great enough to be without a system." More clearly than ever, he stands out today as a powerful and fecund genius.

CHAPTER 18

"The
Great
Voyage"

1

DIDEROT'S FAMILY and friends were shocked when he returned home. "You will find me quite aged," he had written Sophie from The Hague. He had suddenly become an old man of sixty-one—an ailing old man, thin, shaken with bronchitis. The long journey and the rigors of the northern winter had taken some vital spark out of him. Perhaps he was right, after all, about staying close to one's hearth.

There had been great changes in France, too. In May 1774, while Diderot was in Holland, died the most hated monarch in French history. Despite a surreptitious burial, in the dead of night, the jeers and curses of the populace followed Louis XV's bier. It had been one of the most disastrous reigns in French history. A succession of wars had bled the country and lost it a great colonial empire. Haughty oppression by the nobles, heavy taxation, and general misery had shaken, as Diderot himself observed, the very foundations of the monarchy, and left the country in such a weakened state that the next king was bound to face either revolution or reform. Louis, on his deathbed, is supposed to have said, *"Après moi, le déluge."* More authentically he is known to have given this message, through the Cardinal de la Roche-Aymon, to the entire court: "Gentlemen, His Majesty charges me with telling you that he asks God's forgiveness for having offended Him, and for the scandal he has given to the people; if God restores him to health, he will devote himself to making amends, to the strengthening of religion and the relief of his people." Twice before Louis had repented in illness, and twice before he had recovered and returned to a dissolute life. This time it did not work.

Little wonder that France, essentially monarchic in spirit, looked with hope reborn to the new ruler, who unfortunately was as incapable as his grandfather had been vicious. Louis XVI was a weak-kneed prince of twenty, virtuous and well-meaning, to be sure, but lacking in intelligence and will-power, awkward, shy, and lazy. At first his shortcomings were not realized, and hopes soared high when Turgot, a contributor to the *Encyclopedia*, an exponent of *laissez faire* and financial reconstruction, was named Minister of Finance. The spirit of the *Encyclopedia*, the spirit of reform was everywhere in the air. Not only Turgot, but other disgraced partisans of the new ideas, Sartine and Malesherbes, were summoned back to power. Even better, the Parlements were reconstituted, Maupeou dismissed. The entire atmosphere was changed; men seemed to breathe more easily, now that the vicious tyranny of Louis XV, the reign of his favorites, the power of the Jesuits, and the Maupeou "parlements" were only unpleasant memories.

Unfortunately, it was all too good to be true. Turgot was to fail. As had happened in Austria under Joseph II, as was to happen again in Russia under Alexander I, the forces of the Old Régime, selfish as they were, immediately united against every project for reform, and the king was too weak to resist their pressure. The Parlements, in their personal struggle against Louis XV, had pretended to represent the nation in its fight against tyranny. But now they showed that they had not really changed their stripes, and their own opposition to Turgot eventually dealt them the hardest blow they could receive. Louis XVI lost his fight. In the face of pressures and court intrigues, directed by his vivacious and irresponsible queen, Marie Antoinette, and her dear friend unto death, the princess de Lamballe, he was unable to impose reform. As Diderot had predicted, he was to face the alternative, a straw swept away by a torrent. It is one of history's ironies that France's best king after Henry IV—in his intentions, though not in his abilities—was to lose his head in payment for the sins of his fathers.

Great events were in the making, and the minds of those who were to be the new leaders were being formed by the writings of Rousseau, Voltaire, and Montesquieu, by those of Diderot and his companions. But the tired old man had lost his enthusiasm for the combat, his will to be in the thick of it. Happy to be home, he wanted to leave the fight; he had done his share. He thought only of living "a beautiful old age," a few more years devoted to rest and to writing. "The time when one counts by years is over," he wrote to Sophie; now he must count by months, and soon by days. "The less revenue one has, the more important it is to make good use of it. I have perhaps another ten years in my sack." The guess was uncannily accurate. "In these ten years, colds, rheumatism, and the rest of that uncomfortable family will take two or three; let's try to save the seven others for rest and the little joys that one can promise himself after sixty."

Even before leaving for Russia, Diderot had faced the unpleasant reality of old age. One day he chanced to look at his baptismal certificate, and the year of his birth, 1713, suddenly seemed so incredibly remote. "How old I am!" he exclaimed. "I am . . . I am . . . I don't dare to tell you: it's frightening." Within a fortnight he was to be fifty-six. But he put the matter off and reassured himself. "It doesn't show, that's sure. Nobody would ever believe it."

Now that he was really touching old age, he was perfectly serene. "As for me," he wrote to sister Denise back at Langres, "I am moving out piece by piece. I am sending the heavy baggage ahead, such as teeth, some of which are falling and others shaking, the eyes, which no longer serve me at night, the ears, which are beginning to shrivel up, the legs, which prefer rest to exercise . . . I see these preparations for the great voyage going on, without worrying about it very much. I advise the wicked to be uneasy; as for fools of good faith, like me, they will tell us that we have been fools, and that's all."

One day he hit his head against a block of marble and raised a lump on his forehead. His grand-daughter clapped her hands when she saw him. "Ha, ha, grandpa, you bump your head against doors, too." But he took the situation like a true philosopher. "I laughed, and I thought within myself that I have not done anything else since I have been in the world."

Diderot never lost this happy gift of being able to laugh at himself.

His normal tendency to sentimentality and weepiness became even more pronounced during these last years. "I used to think that the fibers of the heart hardened with age; nothing of the sort . . . Everything touches me, everything affects me. I shall be the most arrant sniveler of an old man you have ever known."

Diderot did have a happy old age. He so declared to Mme. Necker. "I enjoy a better health than usual at my age; all tormenting passions have departed, leaving me a frenzy for studying such as I felt when I was thirty . . . If there has ever been a happy father, it is I. I have just enough fortune for my needs . . . my friends have for me and I have for them a tenderness that thirty years of habit has left in all its freshness."

There was one strained note in this idyllic passage, a note that covered a melancholy resignation to faltering friendship. The two great episodes of personal emotion in Diderot's life were his love for Sophie Volland and his friendship with Grimm. Love had died first, and now friendship was growing cold.

Grimm had become more and more the courtier. Although their journey to Russia more or less coincided, they had not been able to travel together. In the Russian capital, their ways were separate, so that despite proximity in a foreign land they saw comparatively little of each other. Grimm, wrote Mme. Geoffrin, had greater success at court; she blamed Diderot for lack of grace and delicacy. "He is a very clever man, but his character and disposition make him useless for anything, and even more, would make him dangerous in any task. Grimm is quite the opposite." Shortly thereafter, Grimm gave up his *Literary Correspondence,* and devoted himself entirely to diplomatic activities. He returned to Russia for two years, traveled in Italy and elsewhere, so that he was more and more infrequently in Paris.

But there was a profounder reason for the estrangement. Their growing apart was not only the wearing away by distance and by time, the separation of paths, the dulling of habit. A chasm between their minds and hearts had been deepening over the last years. The essential rupture was in political and social thought, and the evaluation of man implied in the basic position. Here Grimm broke with what he considered the quixotism of the "philosophic" ideals.

The first trace comes as early as November 1760, in a letter to Sophie Volland. "The severity of our friend's principles is thrown away; he distinguishes two sorts of morality, one for the use of sovereigns." Evidently, the tincture of courtly Machiavelianism was staining the ideals Grimm had earlier supported, or pretended to support. Accompanying this cynicism was an interesting and typical reaction against rationalism. In February 1756, Grimm had already asserted, in the *Literary Correspondence*, that the science of society cannot be deduced from reason. Society is ruled by instinct and imagination. A people of philosophers could not exist. Consequently, we should forsake abstract principles and resort to "the charms of illusion" and the "magic of enthusiasm." Here is an abandonment of faith in man's ability to guide and mold his own destiny by his reason and understanding, an appeal to primitive irrational forces, coupled with a Machiavelian use of the lie. As has always been the case, those who would deceive and oppress mankind deny the value and validity of reason. Grimm is already in the tradition of German romantic mysticism in politics that leads from Herder to Hitler. This is precisely what Diderot had denounced in his *Pages against a Tyrant*. In 1765, Grimm wrote, also in the secret *Literary Correspondence:* "In truth there is no right in the world other than the right of the strongest; it is the only legitimate right."

But these early signs were only preliminaries which had no effect on their ardent friendship. It was only after Diderot's return from Russia that their disagreement deepened. There must have been exchanges of words between the two men, rumblings of disharmony that have been lost. Fortunately we do have the dramatic climax. Among the recently recovered manuscripts of Diderot is a lengthy "Apologetic Letter from the abbé Raynal to M. Grimm," dated March 25, 1781. The subtitle reads, "Reply to the dilemma that M. Grimm posed to the abbé Raynal, at the home of Mme. de Vermenon, and which he repeated to me, at the home of Mme. de Vandeul, my daughter."

The dilemma itself sounds innocuous: Raynal's attacks are cowardly if he believes that those he has attacked cannot avenge themselves, mad if he believes they can. Diderot denies both horns of the dilemma. Evil must be attacked and no other justification is needed. "How have we risen from barbarism?" he cries. "Only because there were men who loved truth more than they feared persecution. Certainly those men were not cowards. Shall we call them mad?"

The ultimate consequences of Grimm's position are only too clear.

> The result of your miserable, insipid dilemma . . . would be to inspire scorn for those of our fellow citizens whose enemies since the beginning of time have lived in the temples, the palaces,

the tribunals—three dens from which all the miseries of society have come out. Oh, what a useful and convenient doctrine for oppressors! As soon as I am in a good humor I shall send you a letter of thanks in the name of all the *canaille* in the world. If you are sincere, how I pity you. I pity you more if you are not. I would rather have you a bad thinker than a hypocrite . . .

The great evil of persecution is to make a nation unjust and pusillanimous for some time ; and it is not overnight that Man recovers his natural pride, that divine character which tyrants and executioners will never efface, which impels him and will ever impel him to honest and dangerous actions, amidst the infamous scoundrels that surround him and accuse him of cowardice or madness . . . The book I love and that kings and their courtiers hate is the book that gives birth to a Brutus ; give it any name you wish . . . To establish so great a distance between kings and ourselves is to think too much of a man and too little of mankind.

But Diderot is hurt in his personal feelings, as well as his beliefs.

The people say, First live, then philosophize. But he who has taken the mantle of Socrates and who loves truth and virtue more than life will say, First philosophize, and then live. If you can. You are laughing, I think? Ah, my friend, your soul has grown smaller at Petersburg, at Potsdam, in the reception rooms of the great . . .

How I pitied you when you told me, at Petersburg, 'Do you know that if you see the empress every day after dinner, I see her every evening?' My friend, I no longer recognize you. You have become, without realizing it perhaps, one of the most hidden, but one of the most (*) enemies of the *philosophes*. You live with us, but you hate us . . . The man whom nature destined to a distinguished career in letters has lowered himself to the sad rank of lackey to the great . . .

My friend, you have gangrene . . . I shall sooner cease living than stop loving you, but I should never have become your friend, if you had spoken at Jean-Jacques' where I met you for the first time as you spoke yesterday . . .

Through Raynal, Diderot was defending himself, his own contributions to Raynal's work, his own philosophy, the story of his own life. The hurt and the pain at Grimm's defection—*et tu, Brute* can be heard throughout—is dominated by the inspiring idealism of

* Break in the ms.

Diderot's faith in man, by his love for man, by his unending fight against those who would deprive man of his humanity.

As with Sophie Volland, Diderot continued his relations with Grimm until the end. But they were not the same. Grimm died in 1807, at the age of eighty-four. He lived then to see the French Revolution and the rise of Napoleon. These events only confirmed his belief that the cause of the human race was hopeless, that men could live together only under the tutelage of an absolute leader.

2

In the history of Diderot's friendships, a final interlude may be placed here. It had always been a subject of regret, on the part of all who knew them, that two of the great men of the century, Voltaire and Diderot, had never met. In December 1776, after twenty-seven years of "epistolary friendship," Voltaire wrote the philosopher about his sorrow never to have known him personally:

> I am eighty-three years old, and I repeat to you that I am inconsolable not to have seen you . . . I have not seen Paris for almost thirty years, and in all my life, which is rather long, I have never lived there two years in a row. I would gladly return and spend my last quarter of an hour there to have the pleasure of hearing you, if it were possible to spend one's last quarter of an hour in that place ; but unfortunately, it is very difficult to live and to die there as one wishes. My great misfortune is that Ferney was not exactly on your route when you returned from Catherine's country. Formerly I had a friend who was yours (Damilaville), and who did not let me lack my daily bread in my solitude ; no one has replaced him, and I die of hunger. That friend knew that we were not so far apart, and that we needed only one conversation to understand each other ; but one does not find everywhere men with whom one can talk . . . The little I have read of you makes almost all other books seem insipid to me. In a word, Monsieur, your works and your person cause me regrets. *Extremum quod te alloquor hoc est.* The old hermit wishes you a long and a happy life ; he has had only the half of what he wishes you.

Fourteen months later, Voltaire changed his mind. He journeyed for a last time to Paris on a triumphal visit, and was received by the populace, whose *état d'esprit* he had done so much to change, like a conquering monarch. In the midst of the celebrations, he took time out for a visit with the man he had waited so many years to meet.

It is even probable that he went to the suburb of Sèvres to see the ailing Diderot. Again it is to be regretted that there is no account of their memorable meeting. It is reported that Diderot took the opportunity to display his usual eloquence, and that Voltaire was forced to accept the unaccustomed role of listener. His comment, afterwards, was typical of his sharp wit: "This man is certainly intelligent, but nature has refused him one talent, and an essential talent: that of the dialogue." Diderot, on the other hand, is reported to have likened Voltaire to an old fairy castle, fallen in ruins, but still inhabited by some old sorcerer. He later described a portion of their conversation:

> I have taken the liberty to contradict M. de Voltaire by word of mouth and in writing, with the respect that I owed to that great man's years and superiority, but also with a frankness suitable to my character, and that without offending him, without receiving any disagreeable replies. I remember that he complained bitterly of the stigma put upon books and authors by the magistrates. "But," I added, "do you not know that time effaces that stigma which so grieves you and turns it back upon the unjust magistrates? The hemlock was worth a temple to the philosopher of Athens . . ." Then the old man, throwing his arms about me and pressing me to his bosom, added: "You are right, and that is what I expected of you . . ."

Voltaire was to spend his last quarter hour in Paris after all. He died of uremic poisoning on May 30, 1778, in his eighty-fourth year; the excitement of his triumph had proven more than his aged body could stand.

Just a few weeks later, on July 2nd, Rousseau died. His departure stirred no regret or sympathy in Diderot's breast. "Rousseau is no more. Although . . . he has insulted me with perfidy and cowardice, I have neither persecuted nor hated him. I esteemed the writer, but I did not esteem the man; and contempt is a cold sentiment that leads to no violent procedure." However, not long after, Diderot did resort to violence of a verbal sort.

Meanwhile Diderot's "frenzy for studying," as he called it, enabled him to complete some eight or nine works, principally before the date of Voltaire's death. Many of them had been begun during the sojourn in Holland and Russia, and required only a final revision. There were two inconsequential *Salons,* the brief *Political Principles for Sovereigns,* the *Plan for a University,* the *Refutation*

of Helvétius, the *Elements of Physiology*, and the *Essay on Claudius
and Nero*. With the exception of the last, they all appeared long
after his death. Diderot's outstanding literary feat of this period was
Is He Good, Is He Bad?, his best, and only playable play—it was
put on a few years ago at the Comédie Française. Lively, blessed
with humor and some genuine characterization, it continues his
moral exploration of limit situations and problems—in this case,
the legitimacy of means in regard to ends. It was written in 1781,
but not published until 1834. The *Conversation with the Maréchale*
(1774), a scintillating dialogue, expresses his most extreme ideas.
It makes delightful reading; the wits of both conversationalists are
sharp, and a fiery discussion is the result. He locked this manuscript
in his drawer, and it did not reach the press until 1796.

In 1781, Diderot was given the honor of membership in the
Scottish Society of Antiquaries. He was flattered, and used the
occasion to protest once more against the injustice of his own
country, and to proclaim his gratitude for the recognition he had
won abroad.

Claudius and Nero had a second edition in 1782, and that
involves a story of peculiar interest. For years Diderot had feared
the publication of Rousseau's *Confessions*. "I dread the moment,"
he had written to Hume in 1768, "when a man who loves scandal
so much, who has so little consideration, who has been so
intimately linked with innumerable people, will publish such a work,
especially with the art he has of slandering adroitly, of obscuring,
changing, of making you suspect even more by praising than by
blaming. Don't you agree, my dear philosopher, that in such circumstances it is infinitely pleasant to have made one's faithless friend
the witness only of just actions and honest speeches?"

There is no doubt that Diderot was uneasy. His quarrel with
Jean-Jacques was the weak spot in his armor, and he feared an
attack, an attack in which Rousseau would use his subtle art and
eloquence to deform everything and put him in the wrong. Then
their quarrel would become public property, the scandal would be
on every tongue, and there would be the devil to pay to make
people believe that *he* was right.

Years passed, and the threatened bomb did not explode. In the
first edition of *Claudius and Nero*, no mention was made of Rousseau. But after its publication, two things happened. First, Naigeon,
the philosopher's officious helper, had annotated the work, and
some of the notes did not spare Rousseau. To Jean-Jacques' friends,

Diderot immediately became the instigator of these criticisms. A series of attacks resulted, verbal and printed, reawakening his bitterness. Then, in 1781, three years after Rousseau's death, the first part of the *Confessions* finally appeared. Diderot hastened to devour its pages. He was relieved to find himself largely spared, but more vexed than ever to see the merciless treatment accorded his friends, Grimm and Mme. d'Epinay. The aroused philosopher, who had rarely replied to his living enemies, now proceeded to attack a dead one. He revised his *Claudius and Nero*, inserting wherever possible a systematic and vitriolic assault on Rousseau's character and ability. He tried to put the blame on Rousseau, for having himself lifted a corner of the veil, "in a posthumous work in which he has just declared himself insane, proud, hypocritical, and a liar." But this attack has not benefited Diderot's reputation, and there is no excusing it.

Diderot was old now. The task of writing the *Essay on Claudius and Nero* was too great a strain, and sapped his remaining strength. He had resolved in advance to find Seneca, who was with Montaigne and Plutarch one of his three favorites, as pure, just, and great as his philosophy. As a result, he had read nearly every work in which Seneca was mentioned. Thinking he was young again, he had worked twelve and fourteen hours at a time. Soon he began to complain in earnest about his health; he went about saying that he was always tired, that getting dressed exhausted him, that his brain was used up, and he had no more ideas.

When the work of revision was finished, the aging philosopher, his enthusiasm gone, beaten down by the feeling of the uselessness of his efforts, wrote to Naigeon: "I have done the best I could. That's all I know about it. Weariness and boredom have never done anything good; and I am weary and I am bored."

However, a dinner at his daughter's home and some games with his grandchildren were all he needed to make him feel the joy of living again. Besides, all this agitation about Rousseau, all this intensive work was not the way he had conceived his ideal of "a beautiful old age." The soul of an old man "must be seated in his body as his body is seated in his large armchair."

He was the typical "fond grandfather." After seeing his little grandson one day, he reported proudly to sister Denise: "There is no gayer or livelier child. He is happy, he laughs at anything; and already he has the bold look of a big boy." One night when his family was traveling in bad weather, the worried grandfather got up in his nightshirt and anxiously scanned the skies. Returning to the warmth of his bed, he philosophized for a while before falling asleep again. "I concluded that a good father is often a wicked man; and I bore secretly in the depths of my heart this honest, gentle, and humane feeling: perish all others, provided that my children prosper . . . There is always something that displeases us in the injustice that serves us." To Angélique he wrote humorously, "I am mad about your little children, although they think I have been badly brought up, since I wasn't able to tell them where Charlemagne died." Nor is it surprising to see the atheist philosopher writing to her, "may God keep you in His holy care."

His relations with Angélique were closer and more tender than ever. She felt the deepest admiration and love for him, and he was ever proud of her. We know that the grief his death brought her remained alive and keen for many years. Despite all of his planning and advice, her marriage was not a happy one. Caroillon did not understand her gentle, thoughtful nature, and found other women more diverting. Angélique's melancholy consolation in later years was the memory of her father.

Even life with Antoinette had become more bearable, now that age had mellowed her harshness and halted his infidelities. "I have a good wife," he wrote to Mme. Necker, whose husband was then struggling to stave off national bankruptcy, "whom I love and who cherishes me, for whom will she scold when I am no longer here?" At last, after all these years of domestic storm and strife, he had stumbled on a way to put Nanette in a good humor and to cure her of the "vapors." This great discovery he communicated to Angélique, in a letter dated July 1781.

> She bought a copy of *Gil Blas* to restore to Mlle. Goyet the one you lost. While waiting for the opportunity to return it, she began to read it, and enjoyed it ; and I saw that it was reflected in her whole day. Consequently I have become her reader ; three pinches of *Gil Blas* every day, one in the morning, one in the afternoon, one at night. When we come to the end of *Gil Blas*, we shall try the *Limping Devil*, the *Bachelor of Salamanca*, and other gay works of that kind . . . The funniest thing is that she regales all her visitors with what she remembers, and thus conversation doubles the efficaciousness of the remedy.
>
> I had always thought of novels as frivolous productions, but finally I have discovered that they are good for vapors ; I shall indicate the prescription to Dr. Tronchin the next time I see him.

Recipe eight to ten pages of the *Comic Novel ;* four chapters of *Don Quixote ;* a carefully chosen paragraph of Rabelais ; make an infusion of the whole business in a reasonable quantity of *Jacques the Fatalist* or *Manon Lescaut ;* and vary these drugs as you vary plants, substituting others having approximately the same virtue.

The situation at Langres was unchanged. Relations with Denise were as cordial as ever, and the abbé maintained his uncompromising hatred. In fact, his spite had been further irritated by the philosopher's ever-spreading fame, which had come uncomfortably close. When a former member of the king's guard presented Langres with a complete copy of the *Encyclopedia,* in August 1780, the city accepted it officially and celebrated the gift by unveiling a bust of its greatest son at the Hôtel de Ville. The town council had asked him for a portrait, but instead he sent them the bust which Houdon had done for the Salon of 1773. The abbé, requested naturally to take part in the celebration in his brother's honor, brusquely turned down the invitation. But he was no longer a source of vexation for the philosopher, who scarcely thought of him now, resigned at last to his hatred, and to the loss of his inheritance.

The abbé was to be heard from just once more. A short time after Diderot's death he wrote to Angélique, requesting that any remaining manuscripts be sent to him so that he could "take care" of them. Mme. de Vandeul replied politely that they had all been sent to Russia together with her father's books. This was true, but she neglected to mention the fact that she possessed a complete set of her own.

The "philosophic sect" was growing old. Helvétius had died in 1771, Voltaire and Rousseau in 1778. Two years before, Diderot had urged Grimm, traveling as usual, to hasten to return to Paris if he wanted to see all his friends again. Their ranks were thinning at a fearful pace. Those who remained awoke each day with a new pain and a new ache. D'Holbach was suffering the tortures of nephritis and Mme. de Meaux dragged about with a purulent ear. "Hello, my friend, my old friend; we have lost Roux; we almost lost the baron; Mlle. de Lespinasse is no more; Mme. Geoffrin may be gone tomorrow . . . We are all ailing. When we meet each morning at lunch, one has slept badly, the other was more tired when he got up than when he went to bed; it's the stomach, it's the back, it's the chest, the teeth, or the eyes. We are dragging a miserable carriage in which there is always something getting loose, and those loosenings will only increase, until the happy or unhappy moment when the carriage and its driver will go to the devil."

Diderot and d'Alembert, despite the latter's ignominious retreat from the encyclopedic battle, remained friends until the end. For years the great mathematician had lived with the brilliant and passionate Julie de Lespinasse. Yet it appears that their relations had always been platonic, and Julie, to d'Alembert's grief, had given herself passionately to other men. Her letters to them, and d'Alembert's words after her death, form one of the most fascinating "intimate" episodes in literary history. Malicious gossip had for years affirmed d'Alembert's lack of virility, a rumor which his high pitched voice did not discourage. Consequently, it is amusing to read of his peturbation when he learned that he was suspected of being the father of several illegitimate children. It was in September 1781, and d'Alembert had dropped into his friend's study.

Noticing his worried look, the philosopher inquired, "What's the matter, old friend?"

"Trouble, and it always comes from those whom I cherish most. I had a servant for many years; finally I discovered he was a thief and I was obliged to put him out. But since he has a wife and three children, I took upon myself to look after the needs of the children."

"Well?"

"Well, they are saying, and it is my best friends who are saying it, that I am only doing it because the children are mine."

Hearing this, the philosopher did his best to console the unhappy mathematician. Too delicate, for once, to refer to an obvious reason for consolation, he searched for more appealing grounds.

"And that worries you? Why, one of two things. Either you are the father of the children, or you are not. In the first case, you are a just man; in the second case, a charitable man. There you are placed between two virtues, and it is in such a position that you are unhappy, you, my philosopher?"

"You are right," replied d'Alembert, and thereafter felt reassured.

In 1783 both Diderot and d'Alembert became gravely ill, one with an attack of pleurisy, the other with bladder trouble and general debility. Diderot pulled through, but d'Alembert succumbed. "He died," comments André Billy, "as he had lived, without courage." That same year died Mme. d'Epinay, the most important woman in the encyclopedic group, and one of Diderot's closest friends. It was a hard blow. Gone now were the delightful days spent at La Chevrette and La Briche, where a select company practiced the fine art of living.

Slowly, Diderot retired into the shell of his own personal and family life. His intellectual vitality and enthusiasm were gone, his thought had slowed down. He did nothing important after 1778; only one tale and some miscellaneous pages mark the remaining six years. Once he had become excited during the Quarrel of the Bouffons, between Rameau's supporters and those of Pergolesi; now he took no notice of the new musical quarrel, between adherents of Piccini and Glück. Perhaps he did not relish seeing Italian music, for which he had fought, condemned in favor of the German. There had also been important political developments during thesε last years, and more were on the horizon—American independence, Franklin's visit, the successful war with England, Louis XVI's serious attempts to abolish privileges, Necker's financial reforms, followed by his dismissal. Diderot rejoiced over the American Revolution; we do not know how he was impressed by the other events.

More and more he lost interest in society and took pleasure in living by himself, either in Paris, or in the country, at Sèvres, with his friend Belle, a jeweler. More and more now, he found that he was bored in the company of his old comrades, that they no longer had anything to say to each other. Doubtless the feeling was reciprocal. These were now old men, intent on the struggle to cling to existence, and not the happy companions of old, primed for battle and for the high joys of life. "I see with a certain satisfaction," Diderot wrote to Angélique, "all my friendships gradually dissolving . . . I no longer frequent Mme. Duclos' salon. The baron has gone to Contréxéville without saying good-bye to me. Grimm has done the same; and I should have believed him in Paris, if I hadn't learned by chance that he was roaming Germany."

Diderot declares he is glad things are ending that way, but the note of sadness is obvious, especially when he writes of Grimm. Deep in his heart, he felt that friendship had failed him. There is a beautiful passage in the *Essay on Claudius and Nero* where he speaks of friendship as the passion of youth that becomes dulled by interest and by habit. "I am old, and I admit, not without bitterness and without regret, that in our later years we have relationships of habit, that there exists in us, and beside us, only the vain semblance of friendship." Some time before, he had written to Grimm giving up forever the dream he had cherished so many years—ever since they had met—of a beautiful journey through the ancient and modern splendors of Italy. That trip would never be made, he knew it now: "I no longer think of it. I have said *adieu* to Venus, Apollo, and the Pantheon."

One spark, though, could never entirely die: his interest in pretty women. Curiously, he repeated in January of 1781 the same "mistake" he had made about forty-five years earlier, of going into the wrong apartment. "I had mistaken the floor. It was in the afternoon. I go into the anteroom, into the dining room, into the bedroom, where I find a woman stretched out and asleep on a sofa, her face turned to the wall. I approach, take her by the hand; I am about to kiss her, and taking her for you, ask her by what chance you are still in Paris, when I find myself in the arms of a strange woman whom I do not know, and who doesn't know me, both of us equally surprised." With remarkable distraction, he had not recognized the strangeness of the rooms he was traversing! Confused and apologetic, the erring philosopher gallantly begged the lady to continue her sleep, which he had "so ridiculously interrupted, assuring her that after sixty-eight years of silly blunders, this one, the second of its kind, would not be the last."

He still enjoyed flirting with young girls, when he had the chance. Among the dinner guests at Sèvres, one day, was a particularly charming maiden. "Meanwhile, I eat and say pretty nothings to Mlle. Pauline. It is a pleasure how girls are naïve with old men. They turn quite freely about the decrepit cat who no longer has claws or teeth. They attach no more importance to what they think and say than they will at sixty to what they have done."

The thought of death had never frightened him. He had meditated upon it at length before leaving on the dangerous journey to Russia, and come to the conclusion "that the earth is as light in St. Petersburg as in Paris; that the worms there have as good an appetite, and that it is quite indifferent in what spot of the earth we fatten them." All in all, life is not worth so very much. And when you have had a full and active life, it is much easier to resign yourself to the inevitable end. "You desire the end of life, just as after working hard you desire the end of day. After all, life for many people is only a long day of fatigue, and death a long sleep, and the coffin a bed of worms, and the earth a pillow on which it is sweet to lay your head finally, never to lift it up again. I admit to you that death, considered from that viewpoint, after all the troubles

I have been through, is exceedingly agreeable to me. I want to accustom myself more and more to seeing it that way."

Diderot did have a full life; and he also had a happy one, judging by his own standards. Not in ambition, riches, or glory did he ever place the seeds of happiness, but rather in the pleasures of the mind and the heart. "A delightful rest, a good book, a walk in a fresh and lonely spot, a conversation in which you open your heart, in which you abandon yourself to all your sensibilities, a strong emotion that brings tears to your eyelids, that fills you with ecstasy, whether it comes from the tale of a generous deed or a feeling of tenderness . . . there is true happiness; I shall never know any other." If his life was not so quiet and peaceful as his wish, it was at least more in harmony with the enthusiasm and energy of his character, with his devotion to the true, the good and the beautiful.

In February 1784, it seemed to all that the end was near. He was suffering simultaneously from his kidneys, from swollen legs, gastritis, and pituitary trouble, in addition to losing his last teeth. Then he had a slight hemorrhage; he suddenly coughed and spit forth blood. Inflammation of the lungs, declared the doctors. "It's all over," the philosopher said to Angélique. "We shall have to be separated. I am strong, perhaps it won't be in two days, but in two weeks, two months, a year."

As he predicted, Diderot recovered from this first attack. But three days after it occurred, on February 22, the woman who had once meant more to him than any other being, Sophie Volland, passed away. Quite possibly, it was the news of this death that took the last bit of resistance out of him. Some have maintained, following Mme. de Vandeul's words, that he had never stopped loving her. "My father could only console himself for Mlle. Volland's loss by the certainty that he would not long survive her." But was this not only the inevitable and grievous nostalgia for the golden past? As he thought of her once again, and dreamed of the years gone by, it must have seemed to him that his last tie with the earth had been cut. His body was weakened by three bleedings in twenty-four hours, his heart by the memories of a tender and passionate friendship, and he felt more strongly than ever that all was at an end, and properly so.

In her will, Sophie left him a ring and her copy of Montaigne's essays, in seven volumes.

But he was not destined to follow her so quickly. There was one more false alarm. It happened while he was talking, one week after his first attack. Suddenly he felt his mind confused, twisted a sentence he was in the middle of. Realizing it, he tried again, and again could not say it correctly. Then he stood up.

"Apoplexy," he said to Angélique, pointing to a limp arm and his slightly twisted mouth.

Then he went into his room and lay down. Thinking he was about to die, he kissed Antoinette and said good-bye to her. After all, he had lived his life with her, for better or for worse. Then he kissed Angélique. Everyone had lost his head, except himself. He explained where they would find certain books that did not belong to him, and then stopped talking. It was eleven at night when the doctors and surgeons arrived. They wanted to change his position, and frightened everybody by saying they had seen a lot of people die in the position he was in. But Diderot, who understood them perfectly, indicated that he wished to be left alone. They did succeed in applying vesicatories to his back and legs, and in getting him to drink some milk.

At one o'clock he felt so much better that he got up and sat in his armchair. From time to time he took a grain of emetic, and as this remedy tormented him, he said gently, "You are prolonging my life with very unpleasant things."

For three days he suffered a kind of delirium, discoursing on the tragedy, on Greek and Latin epitaphs, reciting verses of Horace and Vergil. He would talk all night long, ask what time it was, decide it was time to go to bed, lie down completely dressed, and get up five minutes later.

On the fourth day his delirium vanished together with any recollection of it. He took a decided turn for the better, talked as gaily as ever, and as usual, ate more than was good for him. After the sores from the vesicatories were healed, he even went out and took short walks. But he was weak and languishing, and the doctors warned the family that this new lease on life was the last one.

Meanwhile, his good wife was having worries of her own. If the philosopher refused the last sacraments, the Church would be unwilling to grant him a religious burial, and she was most anxious to avert such a disgrace. And so, a few days later, M. de Tersac, the curate of Saint-Sulpice, made a brief call on him, and then returned several times. He was too intelligent to try to do the thing abruptly. At first they chatted about charity work, an interest they had in common. Then they discussed religion and theology for a while, in an off-hand way. Finally, one day when they found themselves in agreement on several points of moral theory, the curate thought the right moment had come and insinuated that a little retraction on Diderot's part would certainly have a most salutary effect in the world. At this word the philosopher cut him short.

"I believe it, but admit, monsieur le curé, that I would be saying an impudent lie. "

The curate insisted. He reminded Diderot that sacred burial had been refused Voltaire, even though Voltaire, more preoccupied than Diderot with his *post mortem* disposal, had signed a retraction.

"I understand you, monsieur le curé. You refused to bury Voltaire because he did not believe in the divinity of the Son. Well, when I am dead, they can bury me wherever they want, but I declare that I believe neither in the Father, nor in the Holy Ghost, nor in any of the Family."

When the warm days of late Spring came, Diderot was taken from his beloved home in the Rue Taranne, which he was destined never to see again, and transported to M. Belle's house at Sèvres. Meanwhile, Grimm, immediately after Diderot's first attack in February, had written to Catherine about the condition of her philosopher. He pointed out to her the dangers of having to climb four flights of stairs, and the inconvenience of a dwelling divided on two floors, which deprived him of the use of "her books." Catherine immediately instructed Grimm to find a lodging more worthy of "a great man who had performed so many services for her and for humanity." Grimm promptly set about apartment hunting, and his search ended at a house in the Rue de Richelieu. (This house is still standing, hard by the Comédie Française.) It was planned that Diderot should spend the hot summer in the country, while everything was moved and the new apartment put in order. However, for a year now the small but interesting company that used to visit the Belle home had deserted it. Diderot was soon overwhelmed by boredom and insisted on being brought back to Paris. On the seventeenth or eighteenth of July, he moved into "the superb apartment," quite certain that he would soon die there. He was feeling weaker all the time, but out of concern for his family said nothing about it. Instead, he supervised the installation of his books and prints, in the very midst of which was the bust of Catherine to which he had always devoted a sort of cult.

On July 29, a new and more comfortable bed was delivered. "My friends," he said to the men who were carrying it up, "you are taking a lot of trouble there for a piece of furniture that I won't use four days."

The next evening he had his last philosophical discussion with some visitors who came to see him. "The first step towards philosophy," he affirmed, "is doubt." The phrase was a distant echo of his youth, of the *Philosophic Thoughts*. This was the last word his daughter heard him speak.

The following morning, Saturday, July 31, 1784, he arose as usual. His son-in-law, Caroillon de Vandeul, and the doctor came to pay him a routine visit. Later he sat down at the dinner table, took soup, boiled mutton, and chicory. For dessert he took an apricot. His wife tried to stop him, but he would pay no attention to her, as intemperate at table as ever.

"How in the devil can it hurt me?" he replied, and downed the apricot. Then he leaned his elbow on the table to take some stewed cherries. At that moment, he coughed slightly. Antoinette asked him a question to which he made no answer. She looked at him. He was dead.

Caroillon immediately ran for the priest of their new parish. He told him that his father-in-law was dying. They rushed back, but when the priest saw that Diderot was quite dead, he refused to perform the last sacrament. Besides, he contended, it was a notorious fact that the defunct was an atheist. But Vandeul set to work on the vicar, pointed out that the funeral would be performed in a most lavish way, that a pompous church burial would make everyone believe that the most hardened atheist and enemy of the Church had finally begged its forgiveness and indulgence. Neither of these profits, material or religious, was to be scorned. Reluctantly, the priest agreed.

According to Diderot's own wishes, an autopsy was performed. He had often declared that a dead man might still be useful to the living. His brain was found to be perfect, as well preserved as that of a man of twenty. One of his lungs contained a pint and a half of fluid; his heart was enlarged one third beyond the normal size. The liver was enlarged and hard. Worse still, the bile sac was completely dry; it contained, instead of bile, twenty-one stones of which the least was as large as a small nut. No wonder he had complained of frequent "indigestion"! However, his attacks may have been been caused by colic systitis. The kidneys were also considerably enlarged, and their tubes extremely dilated—a consequence of prostate trouble. According to modern diagnosis, Diderot was arteriosclerotic, and the immediate cause of death was coronary thrombosis; it is possible that uremia precipitated heart failure.

All night long a priest watched over the bier, while the house was sumptuously draped in black. Diderot would certainly not have relished this last touch of irony. The rumor ran that he had died in the country, for his recent removal to the Rue de Richelieu was as yet known only to a few. The funeral, on August first, was in keeping with Caroillon's promise, a splendid tribute to his more simple father-in-law. The body was carried to the parish church of Saint-Roch, and, the words of absolution pronounced, was lowered beneath the slabs in the Chapel of the Virgin.

When it was next looked for, it had disappeared. And, strangely enough, it is not known, nor in all probability will it ever be known, where the remains of Diderot have found their last resting place.

In this same year of 1784, Mirabeau published an open attack on that instrument of tyranny, the *lettre de cachet*. Ten years earlier, such a book would have sent him to the dungeon. Now it had a different result. Now, bowing to the new winds of doctrine, Louis XVI ordered the emptying of the Vincennes prison, its opening to public view as a relic of barbarism. Could there have been a more symbolic victory for Diderot, a surer harbinger of the new world he had fought for?

But the Bastille was yet to come.